Walking with Asafo in Ghana

An Ethnographic Account of Kormantse Bentsir Warrior Music

Ama Oforiwaa Aduonum
With Kormantse Bentsir Scholars

UNIVERSITY OF ROCHESTER PRESS

Copyright © 2022 Ama Oforiwaa Aduonum
CC-BY-ND-NC

All rights reserved. Except as permitted under current legislation, no part of this work may be photocopied, stored in a retrieval system, published, performed in public, adapted, broadcast, transmitted, recorded, or reproduced in any form or by any means, without the prior permission of the copyright owner.

First published 2022

University of Rochester Press
668 Mt. Hope Avenue, Rochester, NY 14620, USA
www.urpress.com
and Boydell & Brewer Limited
PO Box 9, Woodbridge, Suffolk IP12 3DF, UK
www.boydellandbrewer.com

ISBN: 978-1-64825-044-6 (paperback)
ISBN: 978-1-80010-589-8 (ePub)
ISBN: 978-1-80010-588-1 (ePDF)
ISSN: 2161-0290

Library of Congress Cataloging-in-Publication Data
A catalogue record for this title is available from the British Library.

WALKING WITH ASAFO

EASTMAN/ROCHESTER STUDIES IN ETHNOMUSICOLOGY
Ellen Koskoff, Series Editor
Eastman School of Music
(ISSN: 2161–0290)

*Burma's Pop Music Industry:
Creators, Distributors, Censors*
Heather MacLachlan

*Yorùbá Music in the Twentieth Century:
Identity, Agency and Performance Practice*
Bode Omojola

Javanese Gamelan and the West
Sumarsam

Gender in Chinese Music
Edited by Rachel Harris, Rowan Pease, and Shzr Ee Tan

*Performing Gender, Place, and Emotion in Music:
Global Perspectives*
Edited by Fiona Magowan and Louise Wrazen

Music, Indigeneity, Digital Media
Edited by Thomas R. Hilder, Henry Stobart, and Shzr Ee Tan

*Listen with the Ear of the Heart:
Music and Monastery Life at Weston Priory*
Maria S. Guarino

*Tuning the Kingdom:
Kawuugulu Musical Performance, Politics, and Storytelling in Buganda*
Damascus Kafumbe

*New York Klezmer in the Twentieth Century:
The Music of Naftule Brandwein and Dave Tarras*
Joel E. Rubin

*Songs for Cabo Verde:
Norberto Tavares's Musical Visions for a New Republic*
Susan Hurley-Glowa

The Kecak and Cultural Tourism on Bali
Kendra Stepputat

For the children, grandchildren, and great-grandchildren of Kormantse
and families of Asafo

I write this book

For all the beautiful and high-spirited scholars along the Ghana littoral

I write

Akokɔ nom nsuo a, ɔde kyerɛ Onyankopɔn

Scholars

Mentors

Theorists

You are the experts

Asafommba

For your time, effort, and support

I write

For the descendants and the grand descendants

I write

Engaging, applicable, and useful

Centering our Akan intellectual traditions and voice

Storytelling and proverbs

Onipa yɛ adeɛ a, ɔyɛ gye ayeyie

When a person performs good deeds, she deserves praise. Aaa.
Precious beads

Esie ne kagya nni aseda

I Dedicate this nwoma book to You

ɔkɔtɔ nwo anoma . . . (The crab does not give birth to a bird)
ɔhemaa Akosua Pokua Agyei, Maame
Aaa . . .
ɔkɔtɔ nwo anoma
ɛnam wo so
ɔbenfoɔ Dr Kwasi Aduonum, Agya
ɔkyerɛma, ɔkyerɛkyerɛfo, anansesɛm wura, nwoma wura, nwomtofoɔ
asa wura, nimdeɛ nhwehwɛmu wura ee
ɛnam wo so ooo
Aburoo bɛtem a me yɛ apata mma má ɛkɔm guo
ɔbaa kokoɔdurufoɔ
Esie ne kagya nni aseda
Da mo ase a, ɛnsa
Daasebrɛ

S|H The Sustainable History Monograph Pilot
M|P Opening Up the Past, Publishing for the Future

This book is published as part of the Sustainable History Monograph Pilot. With the generous support of the Andrew W. Mellon Foundation, the Pilot uses cutting-edge publishing technology to produce open access digital editions of high-quality, peer-reviewed monographs from leading university presses. Free digital editions can be downloaded from: Books at JSTOR, EBSCO, Internet Archive, OAPEN, Project MUSE, ScienceOpen, and many other open repositories.

While the digital edition is free to download, read, and share, the book is under copyright and covered by the following Creative Commons License: CC BY-NC-ND 4.0. Please consult www.creativecommons.org if you have questions about your rights to reuse the material in this book.

When you cite the book, please include the following URL for its Digital Object Identifier (DOI): https://doi.org/10.38051/9781800105898

> We are eager to learn more about how you discovered this title and how you are using it. We hope you will spend a few minutes answering a couple of questions at this URL:
> **https://www.longleafservices.org/shmp-survey/**

More information about the Sustainable History Monograph Pilot can be found at https://www.longleafservices.org.

CONTENTS

Nnianim / Prologue xi

Aseda / Acknowledgements xvii

Note to the Reader xxi

Nkankyeɛ / Summoning Asafo xxiii

Introduction 1

PART I.
Walking into the Past 37

CHAPTER 1
Walking for Asafo: Entangled Meanings, Abakɔsɛm, Awakenings 38

CHAPTER 2
Knocking: History Walking 61

CHAPTER 3
Memory Walking: A Haptic Way of Knowing 80

PART II.
Walking with Women 107

CHAPTER 4
Walking with Women at Kokoado Hill and Kormantse Seaside 108

CHAPTER 5
"It Was Too Sweet!" Walking with Two Kormantse Women 144

PART III.
Walking with Asafo Music 193

CHAPTER 6
The Listening and Musicking Walk 194

CHAPTER 7
"*Kenkan* Makes it Sweet": Walking with Asafo *Ndwom* 250

CHAPTER 8
Anammɔn: Shadows in the Field, Leaving Footprints 321

Nkekaho / Re-Invocation 339

Notes 347

References 359

Index 373

NNIANIM / PROLOGUE

"Don't Ask about Slavery!" Where and How I Walked with Asafo Ndwom

ɔnantefoɔ na odi adɔdɔdeɛ
(It is the walker who eats sweet things)

—Ghanaian Akan Proverb

Aboa kɔkɔsɛkyi se ɔde ne kwasea pɛ nyinkyɛ
(The vulture says it uses its stupidity to seek long life)

As our Ford bus sped by several Fante fishing towns along the coast of Ghana one early morning, I peered through the window to view one of the many former forts, lodges, warehouses, "castles," and dungeons that dot the coast of Ghana. During Ghana's identity as the Gold Coast, many of these held enslaved Africans for months before their forced shipment across *ɛpopɔn Nana Bosompo* Atlantic Ocean to plantations in the Americas. The fort I saw at Abandze mattered more this time than it did when we passed it eight years earlier. I was on a different mission with a different project in mind.

I had already completed my first performance art piece, *Walking with My Ancestors: Elmina Castle* (2014), based on ethnographic research at another fort at Elmina, also located on the coast of Ghana.[1] That piece uses dance, drama, songs, and live drumming to examine the interiority of the enslaved Africans, their songs, and how they survived in those dungeons. As a Ghanaian African woman living in the United States, I wanted to see, hear, smell, feel, and experience those spaces for myself. By focusing on the experiences of the enslaved Africans who languished in the dark dungeons for months, I wanted to bring fresh and important perspectives to the experiences of the forgotten and nameless enslaved Africans who once suffered in the dungeons.

On this second trip, I wanted to travel and walk along the nine routes that crossed Ghana and follow the footsteps of my Ancestors, from the interior to the coast, and visit as many of the European forts along the coast as I could, to experience through my senses their transition from free to enslaved Africans.[2] I could not travel and walk around the nine routes that crossed Ghana because my two children were in school. Importantly, I wanted to investigate the performances the enslaved Africans enacted to protest their capture and enslavement. If they sang during their odyssey, how do the songs serve as archives for that period? My tentative title, "Music from the Dungeons of Enslaved Africans to #BlackLivesMatter," aimed to compare the musical experiences of enslaved Africans in the sixteenth century with those of contemporary Blacks and the Black Lives Matter Movement. I wanted to find connections between performances by enslaved Africans on the Long March and in the dungeons and those by contemporary Black Americans. I went looking for a genealogy of a performance tradition that resisted and challenged the assault and systemic brutality on beautiful Black bodies. I also wanted to offer an Africanist and womanist analysis of those spaces. What songs did the women sing? How would consideration of the spaces inform theories about Black feminism and Africana womanism? How would they contribute to our understanding of the origins of Black music?

Fort Amsterdam stood on the highest point on a hill at Abandze, towering over the town and overlooking *εpopɔn Nana Bosompo* Atlantic Ocean. Parts of its outer walls were covered in dark and green algae, while other parts showed signs of deterioration. I reflected on its contribution to the displacement of millions of Africans as the bus sped away:

> Fort Amsterdam (Kormantine)
> You look lonely
> An overused rug
> Worn out
> Discarded
> Days of glory
> Gone
> Forgotten

ɛpopɔn *Nana Bosompo* Great Atlantic
Washes your feet
Kisses you with her great waves
Yet you smell
Ntoma suane deɛ ɛyɛ herɛ
The cloth tears along its weakest point
Useless you!

You hold my Ancestors' memories, dreams, songs
In your belly
Womb
The axe forgets
The tree remembers
What can you tell me
Us
About the nameless and forgotten
The Souls of those Black folk
Who languished in your belly
Their menstrual disorders
Dripping breasts
Milk
Swollen prostrates
Diseased gums
Death

I
Want to know them
Understand
Sing
Talk
Rock them
Ask questions
Who, what, when, why
How
Massage their tied backs
Achy bones
Numbed buttocks

> Caress their hearts
> Feet
> Moa......n with them

The fort was built in the 1630s by the British with permission from the King of Kormantse, who loaned the land.³ Fort Kormantine became the headquarters for the British trading business in enslaved Africans and other goods in West Africa until the Dutch captured it in 1685 and renamed it Fort Amsterdam. In the nineteenth century, when the Asante stormed the coast on their mission to trade directly with the Europeans, they seized the fort and strategized from the site. Before this journey, I knew that the name Kromanti is associated with several groups and cultural traditions of Africans in Jamaica, Suriname, and other diasporic groups, many of whom trace their ancestry to this small town. I would later learn from the few published references on Kormantse that they are ferocious, proud, arrogant, and hard-working people whose Ancestors were among those sent to the Americas because of their strength and endurance. I was excited to learn more about the *ndwom* (songs) they performed in those dungeons for enslaved Africans.

I found out quickly that slavery is a taboo topic among Ghanaians in general. Ghanaians keep the topic of slavery at a distance.⁴ Whether out of shame, denial, or guilt, the Ghanaian government does not provide any meaningful platform to discuss slavery and its effects on the country from the revenue generated by former dungeons to tourism, which contributes immensely to Ghana's GDP.⁵ This amounts to double commodification. Instead, state officials revel in the country's "independence" from the British on March 6, 1957. Each year on this date, school children dressed in starched uniforms, along with the president of the state, other government officials, and the masses, assemble at Independence Square to commemorate our "defeat" of colonialism with parades, long speeches, and cultural displays.⁶

As a Ghanaian Akan female who once lived and was educated in the Central Region and spoke the Fante language quite well, I was confident my "insider identities" would be beneficial. When I arrived, one of my mentors advised, "Don't ask about slavery." A colleague cautioned, "Don't speak English. Speak the Fante language; go native; do not ask about slavery; rather, ask them what *ndwom* the Asafo warriors sang about *nnɔnkɔfo* (the enslaved)." Asafo companies are a good starting point for the songs that protest slavery. This point is affirmed by Rebecca Shumway when she stated, "The history of Asafo companies [has] been treated as separate from the history of the slave trade, in spite of the obvious impact of the slave trade on the development [of] the institution." Shumway further explained that "the role of Asafo companies as a core institution throughout southern Ghana's communities indisputably began during the era of the slave trade."[7]

How does a native go native? Each day, I wore a traditional cloth around my waist, a blouse, and a silk headcover to conceal my locks. It was a performance. I even wore beads around my ankle, something I started wearing just for the fun of it, but I also thought they connected me more deeply to our culture since our female priests wear them. Because most Ghanaian women around my age wore T-shirts and a skirt or pants and almost everyone wore braids, wigs, or weave-on hairstyles, my look confused people. Some people thought I was a Black American who happened to speak Fante fluently. Before I spoke, others thought I was a South African. One gentleman retorted, "Ghanaians do not dress like that!" The alienation I experienced and the homelessness I felt, at times, could only be remedied with ambiguous and ever-changing labels that rejected dichotomies: unbelonging; dangling with multiple identities; rootless. Like Ama Ata Aidoo's Ato in her play, *The Dilemma of a Ghost*, who returned to Ghana with an African-American wife, after spending years in America I felt strange in my own home. And like Jacqueline in Mariama Ba's *So Long a Letter*, who believed she "should have been able to fit into Senegal" because she was a native, black African (1981, 42), I did not fit in. People said I looked different, talked different, walked different, and asked too many questions. I had become an ɔhɔhoɔ stranger in the land of my birth, my motherland. My sense of unbelonging came to define how I proceeded with my study, underscoring the notion that "fieldwork at home never simply equates to insider research."[8] I must admit, I was relieved no one called me *Oburonyi*, "a white person," a term that some Ghanaians call African Americans.

At Elmina, where I started because of my initial work at the former dungeons, people did not want to discuss slavery—whether the town engaged in the business or warriors sang about the enslaved. Many insisted that citizens of Elmina were never enslaved or participated in the transactions. A typical response was that the enslaved were brought to the coast from the north. One elderly lady vehemently denied that Elmina Castle, built by the Portuguese in 1482 to store traded items including enslaved Africans, once held enslaved Africans. She insisted that the site was used for training the police in Ghana. "Slaves and slavery were not practiced here. There are no slaves in the world. They sold them by stealing them. If you call someone a slave, you would be called to the *ahenfie* King's palace to answer where you bought the slave, how you know. You came all the way for this? You have nothing better to do? I would not waste my time on this!" A few days later, another gentleman from an adjacent town, Bantuma, assured me, "In this land today, you cannot say whose Ancestor is a slave . . . *yɛ mbisa obi n'aase.* You cannot ask about someone's roots or someone is a slave. Today, you can't say that; I swear Yakubu and my mother, wherever you got me from, you will take me back!" Ghanaian Akan Elders say, *Akokɔ di ahwete-ahwete a, ohu gyansakyi bopaa,* "When the chicken scratches ceaselessly, it sees a mystical object"; or *Afeefee de akaakayee ba,* "Too much probing brings unpleasant memories"; and *Aboa kɔkɔsɛkyi se ɔde ne kwasea pɛ nyinkyɛ,* "The vulture says it uses its stupidity for long life." I changed my topic from "Music from the Dungeons of Enslaved Africans to #BlackLivesMatter." I pursued another idea whose seeds had "dropped" during this initial inquiry: *Ndwom* song of Asafo warriors! *Biribi ansɛe a, biribi nyɛ yie,* "If something does not rot, something does not succeed." I started to walk, alone.

ASEDA / ACKNOWLEDGMENTS

Tón-tón-tón-tón-tón-tón-tón
Kormantse Bentsir *abenfo* scholars
Egya Kwesi Mprah ("Teacher Hammond," Safohen Nana Odum III)
Egya Kwesi Amissah, Egya Kwesi Kom, Egya Kobena Bedu, Egya Kwesi Bedu, Egya Ekow Ninsin, Egya Kwesi Nako, Egya Yiiyi, Maame Ama Aprokuwa, Maame Ama Owusuma, Maame Ekua Atta, Maame Ama Esuon, Maame Ama Poli, Maame Ekua Tekyiwa, Maame Aba Sackey, Egya Jojo, Me Na Ekua, Egya Kwesi Annan, Asafo Supi Wobir, Okyeame Anointing and Kweku Suapim, Egya Afɛdzi, Egya Me Nyame, Sɔfo Pastor David, Paapa, Uncle John, Kormantse Methodist Elementary students Desmond and Ophelia, Egya Kwesi Bronya, Nana Kweku Ntsiwa, Kofi Nkrumah, Kwame Alaataki, Kofi Fakyem
Ngyedum
Ngyedum gye do
ɛnam dua so na ahumu ɛduru ɛsoro
ɛnam mo so-oooo

ɔdomankoma Kyerɛma Kwamena Pra, Cape Coast
ɔdomankoma Kyerɛma Paul Ankomah, Gomoa-Obokrom
ɛnam mo so
Esie ne kagya nni aseda

Cape Coast Anaafo Asafo #2
Tweramponn Traditionals
Anomabo scholar Ekow Safo
Akyemfo scholar Nana Budu III
Kormantse Nkum scholars Egya Dwenadwenpa, Aunty Gifty
ɛnam mo so

Edna scholars
Egya Kwasi Badu, Uncle Ebo, Ato Eshun, Aunty Suzie

Egya Kwamena Amissah
Yɛyɛ Edenafo
Your *posuban* identifies you
ɛnam dua so na ahumu ɛduru ɛsoro
ɛnam mo so-oooo

ɔsɔfo Semanhyia Boateng-Mensah
You encouraged me
Emmanuel Saboro and Sister Kɔkɔ
You walked with me

University of Cape Coast Music and Dance Department
Florian Carl, Eric Otchere, students, faculty, staff
You sheltered me in your womb during my 2016–2017 residency
Recorded our Kormantse warrior *ndwom*
German Academic Exchange Service (DAAD) grant
Francis Kofi Essel, research assistant
Walked with me
Aseda-ooo

University of Cape Coast
Department of Africana Studies
Dr. Yayoh, Dr. Nnuroh, Dr. Wilson
You, allowed me into classes
Initiated my first walk at Kormantse
Onipa yɛ adeɛ a, ɔyɛ gye ayeyie

Illinois State University Cartographer Jill Freund Thomas
You charted my walking trails
With earnest and diligence
Illinois State University Outstanding Creativity Award fund
Supported my trails
Catherine Kukua Mensah, James Aidoo
Fante translators
Mankessim scholar Egya J. B. Crayner
Yɛkɔɔ Amankooo
ɛnam mo so-oooo

Mr. Awotwi Thompson
Mfantseman High School music teacher
You named me Komfo Lady
Akokɔ nom nsuo a, ɔde kyerɛ Onyankopɔn

Aaaa
Jamillah Gilbert
Adwoa Abbiam Aduonum
ɛyyɛ-Adom Kofi Danso Aduonum
Dr. Kwasi Aduonum
Maame Akosua Pokua Aduonum
5os
Abusua Family yɛ dɛ sweet
My children Kwadwo Kisseh Nyamekye Aduonum, MaAdwoa Pokua Aduonum
Your patience, beautiful bothering
Your screams, fights, endless arguments, and laughs
Fed my creative impulses
Abotare tutu mmopɔ
Patience moves mountains
You moved the joys of motherhood to a different level
No cap
Kwadwo, Dark Chocolate Mix
You redesigned and adapted the Adinkra symbol
Ma te masie
Beautifully
You epitomize African excellence

ɛnam mo nyinara so
Esie ne kagya nni aseda

Julia Cook, editor
Ellen Koskoff, series editor
University of Rochester Press
Outside reviewers
Copyeditors, indexer, SMP
For your encouragement

Work
Wisdom is not in one person's head
Sustainable History Monograph Pilot
Andrew W. Mellon Foundation
Aseda

ɔdomankoma Kyerɛma Ekow Abakah Ebusua
Frankaahuntanyi Ekow Sekyi Ebusua Ebusua
Maame Aba Aframba Egya Akodee Afful, Auntie Monica
Menua Panin Sister Abenaa Dedaa
Aaaa
Owuo begya hwan
Who will death leave behind
Dammirifua Due
Due ne amanehunu
Go mu brɛbrɛ, brɛbrɛ, brɛbrɛ
Sleep well

Because *ɔnantefoɔ sene oni ne ɔse asɛm nti*
The walker knows more than her mother and father
Because *nsateaa baako ntumi mpopa animu*
One finger cannot effectively clean the face
Each of you
Allowed me to walk with you
Eat sweet things
Me ma mo nyinara mooo mo
Daasebrɛ

I am grateful to all of you
Your brilliance, passion, diligence, beauty
The walk was too sweet
Onipa yɛ adeɛ a, ɔyɛ gye ayeyie-oooo
Lo-lo-lo-lo-lo-lo-lo
Tón-tón
Tón

NOTE TO THE READER

Orthography

Below is a guide for the Akan syllables employed in the book.

Vowels

a	as in f**a**ther
e	as in l**a**ke
ɛ	as in r**e**d
i	as in **ea**t
o	as in thr**o**ne
ɔ	as in b**ough**t/c**augh**t
u	as in fl**u**

Consonants and Their Combinations

Consonants are pronounced just they are in English when they stand alone. However, when they are combined with other consonants they are pronounced as one syllable.

ky	as in **ch**ange or **ch**arm
gy	as in **ju**ice
hy	as in **sh**irt
ny	palatalized n
nk	as in si**nk**
kw	as in **qu**antity
tw	**chw** pronounced together
hw	as in **wh**istle

Capitalization

I have capitalized the following terms for political reasons, also because of their status and important roles they play in Fante societies.

King
God
Deity

Companion Website

This book is accompanied by a companion website (http://hdl.handle.net/1802/36848) containing song texts and spoken word pieces. These are identified in text by the Ghanaian Adinkra symbol ⁂ (*mate masie*), which means, "I have heard it and kept it." It signifies wisdom and prudence. The sound/audio files are identified in text by this symbol: 🔊.

Previously Published Material

Portions of the book contain material originally published elsewhere. In the acknowledgments and introduction, I use brief excerpts from my poem "Ethnomusicology, Ayɛ Kradow," published in *Ethnomusicology* 65 (2): 203–220 (Summer 2021). In the introduction, my section on "Walking as Fieldwork Method" was adapted from my recently published article, "Walking as Fieldwork Method in Ethnomusicology," *Ethnomusicology* 65 (2): 221–258 (Summer 2021). Both are reprinted here with permission of the publisher.

NKANKYEE | SUMMONING ASAFO

ɔnantefoɔ sene oni ne ɔse asɛm
(The walker knows more than her mother and father)

—Ghanaian Akan Proverb

    Asafo!
    Elders dying
    The youth disown you
    The church has silenced you
    Outdrummed your *kyen* drums
    They say your essence is fading
    You are now ceremonial
    Rise up

    Asafo ééi
    Ebueii
    Your ɔkyerɛma master drummer
    Silenced
    Where is your *ndwom*
    That asserted that your lives matter
    Your drums are quiet
    Wake up, wake up, wake up
    Sɔr, Sɔr, Sɔr

    Ah!
    Oguaa Asafo Bentsir!
    Kormantse Bentsir!
    Edna Ankɔbeafo!
    You hold the keys to the town
    Animguase mfata Akan nii
    Disgrace does not befit the Akan

The cock crows
Ko-kuro-kooo
You continue to sleep
Wake up

Asafo!
Oguaa Anaafo
Obo Noma Etsiwa Asafo
Wombir
Anyampafo
Wo tu ahen, si ahen
You who enstool Kings
The King is waiting
To be bathed at Nana Atrɛdɛ
Wake up

ɔkwan tware asuo
Asuo tware kwan
The path crosses the water
Water crosses path
Who is the Elder?
When ɔdomankoma Nana Nyakropɔng Kwame
Ototroponso, Ahuntanhunu, ɔbɔɔ adea Nyakropɔng
Bɔɔ wo
She created you
Show them you are an Elder

You were once the bedrock of society
I am calling you
ɛbɔɔ pae a yɛ mpam
When a rock cracks, we don't sew it
I, *Aburoo bɛtem a me yɛ apata ma má ɛkɔm guo*
Will try to sew you

ɔnantefoɔ sene oni ne ɔse asɛm
The walker knows more than her mother and father
I am walking

Walking to talk with you
A good conversation never ends
Do you see me
Walking?

ɔnantefoɔ na odi adɔdɔdeɛ
I am the walker who wants to eat sweet things
Summoning you
Massaging you
Consoling you
Wokɔɔ baabi a bra
Merefrɛ mo; me se mommra
Akokɔ bɔn anɔpa[1]
Akokɔ tua bɔn nhemanhema
I am studying; let me know
Meresua; momma menhu
Meresua ooo
Momma menhu

Introduction

ɔnantefoɔ sene oni ne ɔse asɛm
(The walker knows more than her mother and father)

Asafo ko eyi hɔn! 🔊
Yeyi hɔn!
Yeyi hɔn a wɔnfrɛ sika ɛ!
Sika mbra!
Ana ɔman bi botum hɛn?
Oo-ho!
Ebiasa a?
Yɛ tse hɔn do!

(Warriors you have triumphed over your enemies!
They are conquered!
If so, bring money!
Let money come!
Can any nation face us?
No!
What about threesome?
We conquer them!)

—Asafo rousing call[1]

This book is a story. It is a story about my walk with the *ndwom* (songs) of Asafo, warrior organizations of the Akan, Ewe, and Ga in Ghana, who protected their lands against inside and outside aggressors. Especially among the Akan Fante warriors of the coast, Asafo *ndwom* called people together to rescue a drowning victim; they called people together for a search when someone got lost. Their drums embodied the whole spirit of Asafo and the *ɔkyerɛma* master drummer, whose position was so important that in the olden days, sometimes a person was bought to hold the position, was regarded as the "wife" of the Asafo. Furthermore, upon appointment, the Asafo gave the drummer a silk loincloth and a sum of 25s.[2] Asafo drumming "put fear in people's hearts" and was not played recklessly; so, whenever the drummer sounded the drum (*si kyen do*), people expected that something serious had happened. Today, the menacing songs, drum patterns, and bodily reenactments by Asafo and its other performative acts are labeled "fetish" by modern people and have fallen into disuse.³

What is Asafo *ndwom*? How do they differ from other Ghanaian *ndwom*? How are they used, when are they performed, by whom, for whom? What is the state of this tradition that once served as the bedrock of the societies? What instruments are used in their performance? How do these instruments accompany dances that enact the past and serve as archives for the people?

One day, I was walking down the street with the director of Elmina Castle, where I had walked with slavery eight years earlier. On our walk over the Elmina bridge, I asked him about protest songs. He responded that Asafo warriors, whose tradition is now "ceremonial," performed such songs. Then he sang a short phrase of a song that he cited as Asafo. *Hɛn ara yɛyɛ Edenafo, yɛyɛ Edenafo* . . . ("We are Elmina people"). It was declamatory, raw, and unlike many Ghanaian songs I grew up singing and dancing. He acted and sounded as if he was drunk because, according to him, the warriors drink a lot when they perform the songs. He also said he could get me in touch with some members of Asafo. Before I could ask him about the context for the song, he hopped into a taxi and rode away.⁴ Very quickly, I sang a meager version of the song into my phone. I continued to walk.

I learned that the Asafo tradition is considered fetish by some, especially modern people, who frown on it and even chastise those who practice it. One of the teachers remarked that young men who practiced Asafo had a difficult time finding wives. There were other factors for its demise: colonial rule, unemployment, an aging community, education system, and government institutions. I wanted to learn more. Would people talk to me? Where could I find descendants of these fierce warriors who resisted and insisted that their lives matter? Though Our Elders say, *ɔhɔhoɔ ani akɛseakɛse nso ɔnfa nhunu kuro mu*, "The stranger has big eyes, but she does not see the town," I started to walk.⁵

During the early stages of the study, few people were willing to talk to me. However, because *ɔnantefoɔ sene oni ne ɔse asɛm*, "the walker knows more than her mother and father," the more I walked and learned to ask the right questions, the more I learned about the pasts of Asafo *ndwom* from shoemakers (cobblers), store owners, Asafo drummers, Asafo captains, Asafo military post caretakers, lineage elders, fisherfolk, Kings, and even pastors. As the project progressed and I focused on Kormantse, more beautiful and high-spirited mentors were eager to talk with me. In fact, one lady, who later became my friend, said to me, "Right now, if our Asafo would survive, it stands on you!" As I walked and became immersed in lived experiences, from everyday work to joyful celebrations to sorrowful funerals, residents began to trust and connect with me. I was there every day and showed genuine interest. My journeys with Nana (Teacher Hammond), the respected Asafo captain at Kormantse, also added credibility to my work.

Walking as Fieldwork Method

Ethnomusicologists walk a lot (Aduonum 2019, 2021).[6] A lot of our knowledge about people making music is acquired through walking. Walking "offers an opportunity for serendipitous discovery of unexpected contexts for social and spatial conjunctions" (Pierce and Lawhon 2015, 661). Walking is one approach without which we would not be laughing, dancing, singing, sharing, or eating with people through music; taking us to our teachers' houses for lessons and interviews; or going to archives, rituals, and performances. Yet, discussions and presentations about methodology in the many publications that address fieldwork in ethnomusicology overlook this crucial part of our research process.[7] Except for Angela Impey's recent publication in which she elaborates on walking as a method that helped to produce a "different kind of remembering" for her female collaborators (2018, 37), the practice of walking is minimally reported in our published work.[8] When mentioned in books, it is left without any analysis of how it improved or impeded the learning process.[9] What embodied knowledge did Beaudry (2008) acquire about Inuit society and music as she trudged through the snow? What did walking contribute to Nettl's (1992) understanding of Iranian *radif* systems and Kidula's (2014) understanding of the music of Kenya? How did walking aid in the studies by Seeger (1982) and Kisliuk (1998)? If ɔnantefoɔ sene oni ne ɔse asɛm, "the walker knows more than her mother and father," how did walking with Mujuru expand Berliner's (1978) knowledge and thinking about Shona *mbira* culture? How did walking inform Maria Abé's understanding of Shindoya performance as she traversed the streets of Osaka, Japan, with Shindoya musicians (2015)?[10]

I walked. My physical and figurative walks and other peripatetic practices helped me acquire knowledge about the depth of Asafo *ndwom* and culture. Walking brought me closer to my teachers, who gave me knowledge about people making *ndwom*. Walking took me places and revealed essential insights into how the locale is laid out, helping me, like geographers, develop local literacy and an embodied understanding of the scales and rhythms of the society. Walking offered an "opportunity for serendipitous discovery of unexpected contexts for social and spatial conjunctions" (Pierce and Lawhon 2015, 661). Walking is one approach without which I would not have laughed, danced, sung, shared, or eaten with people making *ndwom*. Neither going to my teachers' houses for lessons and interviews nor going to archives, rituals, and performances would have been possible without walking.[11] My ways of feeling, seeing, listening, hearing, and even smelling in local ways were heightened through walking. "Being aware while walking and thinking with stories provided context for the acquisition of new knowledge" (See Legat 2008, 39).

I took long history walks, memory walks, listening, and musicking walks at Kormantse. I walked through the dusty main street, the sandy seaside, tarred roads, the rocky and slippery hill, through the burial site, and the muddy paths to listen to and to talk with different people about the warrior tradition and its *ndwom*. When people felt uncomfortable talking to me for fear of being chastised by members, we walked and talked. These walking interviews helped situate my body in interaction with locales imbued with significance by research participants. Site-based questions elicit stories more difficult to access through structured protocols and created a sense of intimacy between me and my mentors as we engaged in a shared experience. (See Wiederhold 2015, 613). The walking interview has its shortcomings however, such as not being able to record what one learns,[12] or forgetting some of the details of what is shared, but its benefits outweigh its limitations because one could always bring back the topic in a seated interview to recall the details that were lost during the walk.

When my mentors were too busy for a sit-down talk, I walked with them on their errands to the farm to collect monies owed to them or to go to the seaside. I walked to funerals, where I heard the sole Asafo drummer invoke the spirit of the dead from a distance. I took "memory walks"[13] to reconcile and experience the memories and songs my mentors shared about specific spaces. Sometimes I walked alone, reflecting on ideas and conversations, standing alone in spaces where specific memories and songs had been shared, heightening my vision and hearing, breathing the air and the various elements around me, and wrapping myself in my mentors' memories of

Asafo songs. I walked and walked and walked, thinking as I walked. The structure of my walk guided and enabled me to experience the surroundings imaginatively, via my unconsciousness, and through my "sensory and cultural history connections to the particular environment.[14] Other times, I walked with my mentors whose walking rhythms merged with mine into a flow that enabled us to talk. My walks earned me the title *Ewuraba no a, ɔnam rokɔ no a ahwondze gu ne nan no,* "the walking Lady with the beads around her ankle," or *Ewuraba no a ɔnam kyerɛkyerɛ Asafo ho abakɔsɛm na ne ndwom no,* "the Lady who walks and learns about Asafo 'matters that have come and gone' (*abakɔsɛm*) and songs." My former secondary school (high school) music teacher, Mr. Thompson, nicknamed me *Kɔmfo Lady*, "Lady Priest." Over the months, I expanded my walking trails across the town (figs. I.1–I.4).[15]

Toward the end of my eighteen months' *nhwɛhwɛmu* search, I was walking into my teachers' compound with Kormantse Asafo *ndwom* and dance "*Ya Ya araa Nkyɛ*" (example 1a 🔊) and its response (example 1b 🔊). Walking was crucial to my process and connected me to the land and community so that when I did not walk, like the one day I rode to my mentor's house in a friend's car, people did not recognize me when I got out of the car. The other time I rode in a motorized vehicle at Kormantse, I almost got injured or killed.

August 1, 2017, *Akɔfena* Walk

Nana has asked his brother, Kwesi Annan, to come with us to Kokoado to show Nana's Asafo *Akɔfena* sword. Annan is the mouthpiece for Ancestral spirits; he speaks with them, for them. He tells me, "If it were not for you, I would not have come." I thank him. We purchase a bottle of schnapps. Annan does not want to climb the hill and insists that we take a taxi and go on the tarred road on the Nkum side (see fig. I.5). Nana chooses to climb the Kokoado hill on the Kormantse side. While we wait on the Accra-Takoradi Highway for a taxi, a truck stops by and offers us a ride. The driver is Annan's brother-in-law. He will drive us to Kokoado by going on Gyegyentwi hill, a steep tarred hill that is believed to be the dwelling of the Deity Gyegyentwi and her children. According to my scholars, any vehicle that goes up and down the hill must honk its horn because the children of Gyegyentwi play on the street. Honking the horn allows her to rescue or call her children from the street. One week before our ride up, a car had rolled

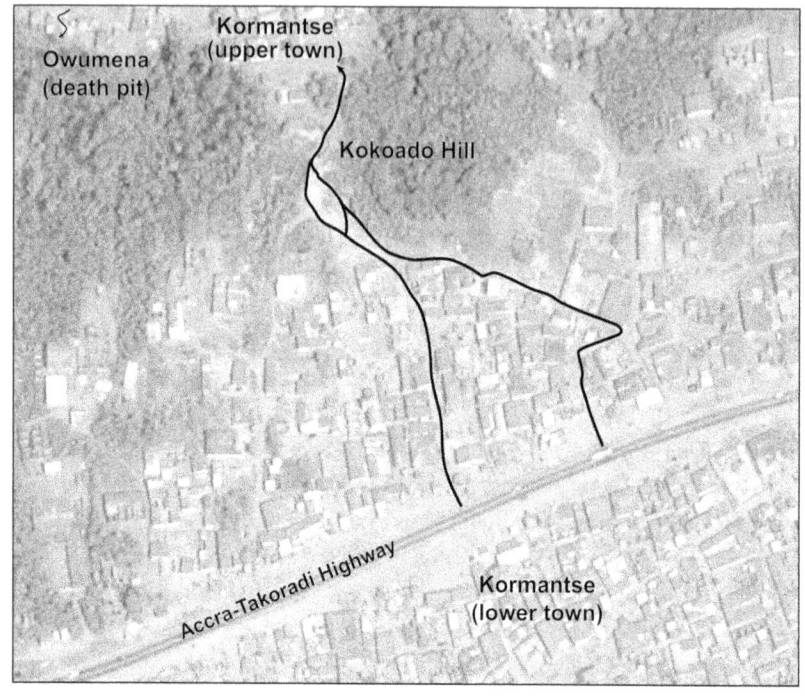

FIGURE. I.I. Aduonum Walking Trail 1. Map by Jill Freund Thomas.

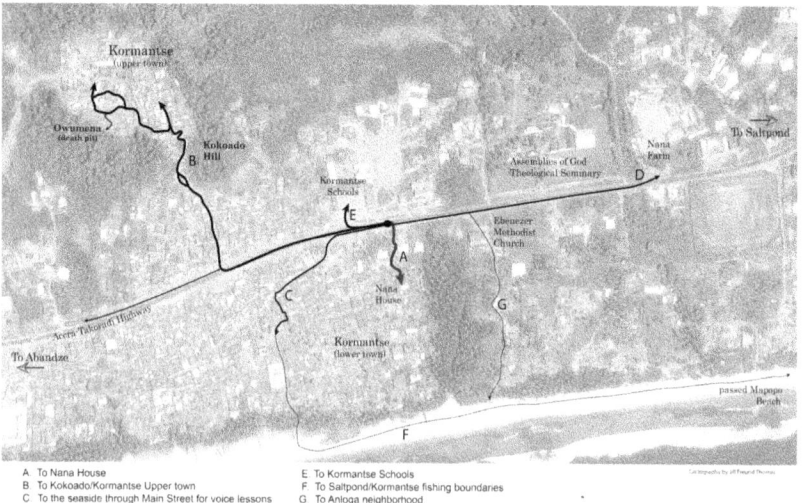

FIGURE I.2. Aduonum Walking Trail 2. Map by Jill Freund Thomas.

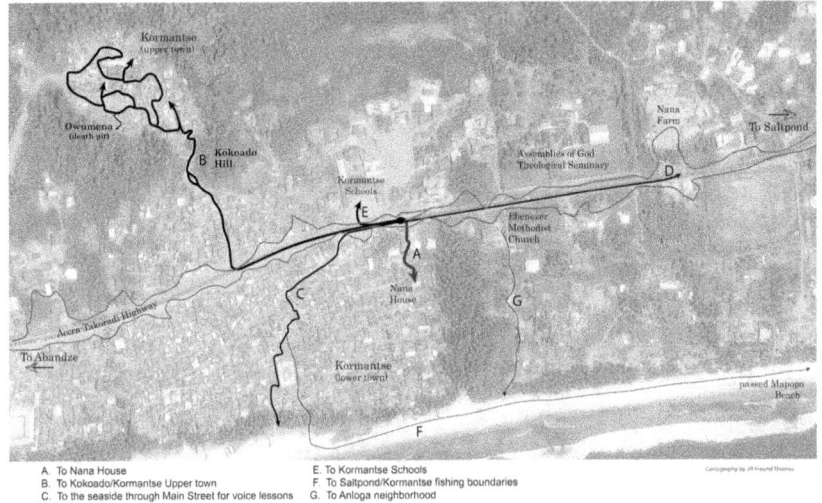

FIGURE I.3. Aduonum Walking Trail 3. Map by Jill Freund Thomas.

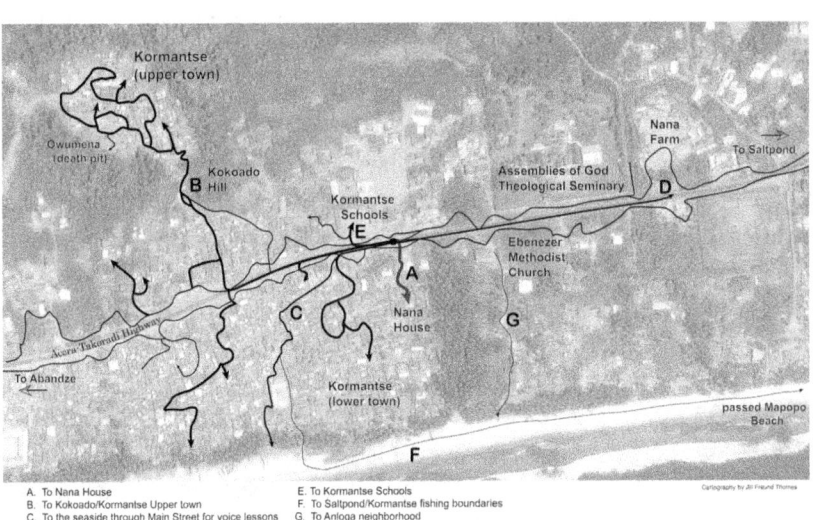

FIGURE I.4. Aduonum Walking Trail 4. Map by Jill Freund Thomas.

back and crashed, injuring all its occupants, some seriously. Gyegyentwi's children were playing, but the driver forgot or failed to honk his horn. I had heard about this incident; everyone talked about it. So, I was a little concerned when we started the drive up Gyegyentwi. As we climbed, the driver pressed on his horn twice with both hands, but there was no sound. He pressed the horn again—no sound. He was nervous. I was nervous. None of us was wearing a seat belt. I watched him closely. Then he feverishly started to press and push on his light signals.

"Are you going to sound the horn?" I asked.

"I know what I am doing for them," he replied nervously.

"Is this where the vehicle went backwards and crashed?" He did not answer. I watched him closely as he continued to fidget with the lights and horns.

"I pressed the horn, but it has no air," he answered.

He was frantically pressing on both the lights and the soundless horn as he drove up slowly. He continued to press and flick the buttons up and down. Atop the hill, he stopped the car, the engine, and gave out a sigh of relief. I was relieved. I opened the door and hopped out quickly. I wished him well on his descent. Later, when I told Nana about the drive up Gyegyentwi hill, he laughed and replied, "He (driver) would have seen (what would have happened)!" Due to this incident with the motorized vehicle at Kormantse and for many other practical reasons, I continued to walk. *Nea ɔwɔ aka no suro sonsono*, "She who has been bitten by a snake is afraid of a worm." I walked and wore out my shoes so much that I developed a relationship with cobblers who mended my shoes along the way. Some taught me Asafo songs. Sometimes, in my efforts to make it on time to appointments, I left my broken shoes with cobblers and walked barefoot. *Sɛ wo mpaboa te a, na wo nanteɛ asesa*, "When your sandals tear, your style of walking changes."[16] Walking barefoot slowed my walk.

The long walks also led to developing an "ethnographic voice," a narrative and writing style that allowed me to convey specific experiences and information poetically. The ethnographic voice is performative, evocative, and reflective. It draws on our Ancestors' wisdom, narrative, and rhetorical style through proverbs, symbolism, direct talk, metaphors, simile, and other oratorical skills. They are meant to be performed. With this creative writing style, I can capture the essence of the information without overshadowing them with unnecessary words. For example, while I walked from a session about the Kormantse Asafo drummer, I reflected on what I had learned:

Asafo ɔkyerɛma!
Master drummer
You playing the *gyina hɔ hwɛ* talking drum
You
Son of Kormantse Ngyedum
You who put out enemies' fires
Descendant of Nana Kɔmer
Brawny one
You make the silenced
ɔdabɔ antelope speak
Sing
Sling strap on your left shoulder
Tilt drum in front of you
Drum face must look out
Vigilant
Disgrace does not fit the Akan child
Use *kɔtɔkorba*
L-shaped stick in one hand
Together with the other hand
Talk to your warriors
Bu bɛ
Proverbs
To *ndwom*
Caution
Galvanize
Taunt your enemies
Intimidate

The path crosses the river
The river crosses the path
Who is the Elder
ɛpopɔn Great Atlantic
Came and met the rock
Who is the Elder?
Tweaa!
Show them
You are the Elder

Ko-ku-roo-koooooo
Ken-ken-ke ken
Pe-tem pa pa
Pe-tem pe-tem
Ko-ku-roo-koooooo
Ngyedum
Ngyedum gye do!

Walking as method helped me solidify bonds with my mentors; it gave me places of memory and memory of places.[17] The constant validation from people we passed along the way helped validate my mentors' knowledge base. Walking allowed me to learn about cultural ideas while connecting with the land and people sensorially. It promoted thinking, encouraged creativity, and allowed me to experience a place in ways that offered a "potentially rich medium of sensory ethnographic representation."[18] I was able to wrap myself in the memories and patterns of Kormantse culture and *ndwom*, creating ritual paths that would later become my cultural map of the society. As I walked, the songs I learned about specific places and the land became one; the various footpaths I trod became my "song lines"[19] or "song maps," a trail of historical facts and songs I recalled and sang as I walked through the town. "The walker knows more than her mother and father." Also, ɔnantefoɔ na odi adɔdɔdeɛ, "It is the walker who eats sweet things." I ate sweet things.

Akan Woman Walking

I am a Kwahu-Akan of the Aduana lineage, who grew up in postcolonial Ghana in the late 1970s. In elementary school, I was taught that Africa is the Dark Continent and that our Ancestors were monkeys. I was beaten for speaking Twi at school and learned about the music of dead white male composers. We sang "Let It Snow" at Christmas, though in tropical Ghana it never snowed! We learned Euro-American rhymes, including "London Bridge Is Falling Down" and "Ring around the Roses," though I did not know the London Bridge or what a rose was. I remember wishing I was Heidi, a white girl who got all the attention because of her hair and pale skin. She had many toys and white dolls and lived across the street from the Institute of African Studies at Legon. Whenever I saw her, my wish to be white intensified. Heidi symbolized what had been indoctrinated into us through our education as valuable, beautiful, and powerful: whiteness. Luckily, my parents taught us, their three daughters and one boy, how to drum. They taught us at a very young age that girls and boys could do anything they chose.[20] Our sex did not define or box us into a particular spot because everyone occupies a "multiplicity of overlapping and intersecting positions, with various relationships to privilege and disadvantage" (Oyěwúmi 2003, 2). They cautioned us about stereotypes and advised us to question and challenge norms, to "push the envelope," speak honestly, be confident, be proud of who we are, be passionate about everything we do, and celebrate differences; love ourselves. We were proud. We played drums with my brother and parents at home and at school with my father, Dr. Kwasi Aduonum, a musicologist who studied at the Institute of African Studies (IAS), a Scholar on Ghanaian drumming and *Akosua Tuntum* women's ensemble, and an archivist of folktales and proverbs.[21] We also played for a program at the Ghana Broadcasting Corporation (GBC).[22] Because we wanted our friends to like us and wanted so much to be like them, at the time we did not understand what our parents were instilling in us. "Be yourself; you will never be happy if you live by other people's definitions. Be You!" Neither did we realize that our parents were preparing us—three girls—for a world in which men like to dominate. The drumming ensemble, with its different rhythms and tones and performances, became an important medium for raising our consciousness about diversity, community, pushing boundaries, and questioning norms and has made me who I am today.

>Dr. Ama Oforiwaa Aduonum
>Child of Akan Ghana
>Daughter of Professor Kwasi Aduonum
>Daughter of Ohemaa Akosua Pokua Agyei
>Foriwaa Amanfo, Aburoo Du-é
>A grain of corn that feeds a multitude
>A woman of indomitable and fiery spirit
>Audacious, energetic, and steadfast woman from the Aduana lineage
>Phenomenal woman
>Pioneering scholar
>Got shackled and sat in former dungeons for enslaved Africans
>To learn about the suffering of her Ancestors

Ahwene pa!
Professor Aduonum
African Music instructor and Ethnomusicologist
Dynamic, innovative, and passionate

Eiii!
ɔbenfoɔ Aduonum, eeee
She directs African Music Ensemble
Drummer, singer, composer, storyteller, dancer
Combines live drumming and dancing to explore
Truths of our painful pasts
Obokrom Queen Mother and founder of a school
Author of children's books
Ama Oforiwaa Aduonum
ɔnantefoɔ sene oni ne ɔse asɛm nti
She walks with Asafo!

ɔbenfoɔ Ama Oforiwaa Aduonum
ɔkani ba a ofi ɔman Ghana
Okunii Akwasi Aduonum ne
ɔhemaa Akosua Pokua Adjei ba
Foriwaa Amanfo, Aburoo Du-é
Aburoo bɛtem a ɛyɛ apata ma ma ɛkɔm guo
ɔboɔba
ɔbaa kokoɔdurofoɔ a, ofiri Aduana Abusua mu
ɔbaa a osi pi si tá
ɔbenfoɔ nimdifoɔ a otwa ɛsa pa to hɔ ma nkyiremma
*ɔno ɛna otiatia ne nananom a tetebi aborɔfo ɛfaa wɔn
nnɔmum no anammɔn mu*
*Saa kyerɛ sɛ yɛbɛhunu amanehunu a yɛ nananom ɛfa
mu wo nkoasom mu*
Ahwene pa
Nimdifoɔ Aduonum
*ɔbenfoɔ a ne nimdeɛ wɔ ndwom mu ɛbunkam ewiase
afanan nnwom ahodoɔ nyinaa so*
ɔno na ɔma dada ɛdane mono
ɔno na ɔnna kɔpem sɛ obedi nkunim

ɔbaa sima prɛko pɛ
ɔde ɔseɛ ɛyɛ ɔyɔ

Eiii!
ɔbenfoɔ Aduonum, eeee
ɔno ne panin a ɔda abibinwom ɛne asa ekuo a ɛwo Illinois Sukuupɔn no mu ano
Twenekafoɔ, nwomtofoɔ, nwomsaifoɔ, asa wura, anansesɛm wura
Te-te wɔ bi ka, te-te wɔ bi kyerɛ
Foriwaa tweneka, ne nwomtoɔ, ne nwomsai, ne asa, ne anansesɛm nyina soɔ ɛne no

ɔbokrom Hemaa, nimdefoɔ a w'asi adesua bia a mmɔfra mmɔfra ɛnya nimdeɛ ahyɛase ho nteteɛ
ɔtwerɛfoɔ a otwerɛ mmɔfra mmɔfra nwoma
Ama Oforiwaa Aduonum
ɛnam se ɔnantefoɔ sene oni ne ɔse asɛm nti
ɔne Asafo na ɛbɔ anante

I started to play the *dawuro* bell around age three, the *torowa* rattle at about four years old, mastering the patterns for *adowa, fɔntɔmfrɔm, sikyi, gahu,* and *agbadza* patterns before playing *apentemma, ɔperenten, donno, sogo,* and other drums. We learned proverbs, storytelling, sang mostly responsorial songs, and performed short dances that my father choreographed. Some of the choreographies involved reenactments of *Ananse* stories, which helped to instill the essence of community, morality, pride, and love for ourselves. I also observed dance rehearsals at the Institute of African Studies, where my father, Kwasi Aduonum, was a student and research fellow for the late Professor Nketia. These early teachings have profound implications in my adult life and inform my anticolonial stance, how I teach, create, and use art. Currently, I am an *ɔkwantufoɔ* expatriate who has lived in the United States of America for over two decades, but I travel back to Ghana to visit family and strengthen my ties to my homeland. When I walked into Kormantse and other fishing towns along the coast of Ghana to learn about the menacing songs of Asafo in 2016–2017, I was "a sample."[23] According to my teachers, I was the first Ghanaian

Akan female to express an interest in their Asafo *ndwom*.[24] I believed I was still connected to the culture and considered myself a "full insider" when I decided to research "home." My walks and encounters, engaging and challenging—and frustrating—provided opportunities for questioning, destabilizing, and reimagining insider/outsider labels and opened these ever-changing statuses to new significations. The alienation I experienced while learning about Asafo, a warrior tradition, and the homelessness I felt at times could only be remedied with ambiguous and ever-changing labels that rejected dichotomies. Several of the encounters earlier in my search challenged my sense of belonging and defined how I proceeded with my study, underscoring the notion that "fieldwork at home never simply equates to insider research."[25]

How do women's walks differ from men's walks? Do women easily engage in walking expeditions as men do? Are women limited by feelings of vulnerability, unwanted attention they might encounter, or perceived dangers they might face? Is it considered unfeminine to walk? Despite the assertion made by several Anglo-American researchers that women in non-Anglo-American spaces fear urban violence, female victimization, and male dominance, I walked alone many times to my mentors' houses, to the seaside, at different times throughout the day.[26] Not once did I consider that I might be assaulted during my walks just because I was a woman, and I did not conceive of my "walking body" as problematic or as a site of struggle, danger, vulnerability, or shame. If I did consider myself a target of attack, I did so because of the audiovisual equipment I carried in my bag, which I believe could happen to a man or woman. Still, I should be clear that I practiced specific "ways of walking" that contributed to my comfort on foot. I took "possession of the space" by using it repeatedly, expressing courage by the way I dressed, and conveying boldness by the way I walked. I made eye contact and talked to people I met on the way.

One evening, I slipped and fell into a gutter and hurt my leg and elbow. *Agya ee*! As I hobbled along, *ko-ko-gya, ko-ko-gya, ko-ko-gya, ko-ko-gya,* an older man approached me and asked for some money to take a taxi to his house. I was in pain and tempted to ignore him, but I stopped, spoke with him, and gave him some money. He thanked me and walked away. The following day, I saw him again, at the adjacent town, walking. Had he been walking all night? Did he not use the money? I went up to him and asked if he had made it home safely. He recognized me and replied, "Yes," and thanked me again. He told me he was a fisherman, Egya Bedu, and told me where to find him. He happened to be a respected member of the fisherfolk community, an honorable man. During a discussion, he told me that he was once a member of an Asafo company but left because membership became too costly. Many members left as the Asafo company did not help defray the expensive cost of their funerary rites. According to him, this has also contributed to Asafo's slow "passing." He gave me this reason for why Asafo is fading in the community, one that I had not heard about.[27]

I also felt safe walking alone because of the beads around my ankle. People thought I was a priest and left me alone. One day, a lady called out to me while I was walking down the Kormantse main street, "Lady, are you selling medicine?" Another from across the street replied, "Ebueii, don't you know her? She has been here with us working on Asafo. She is always here with us." Furthermore, some of the mentors, including the fisherfolk' assured me, "We will never allow anyone to bother or hurt you." Since Asafo is primarily a male tradition, I walked into it and asserted myself. I was able to delve deeper into the *ndwom* by entering specific spaces that vulnerability could have prevented. I also relied on the many Gods and the people to protect me.

One night I traveled alone to Edena, another town, to experience the first of three celebrations (*dombo*) that marked the onset of a festival (*bakatue*). One of my mentors told me it was one of the few times that their fading Asafo company would perform. When I arrived, the Asafo drummers and percussionists had assembled. They played their four drums and bells; they sang and danced. The chief priestess danced and prophesied the state of their town. Other priestesses danced while the Asafo players continued to perform the multisensory-evoking *ndwom*. Around 11:00 p.m., at the height of the event, I got worried about getting stranded, so I left. All taxis and other public transportation had stopped working; all the hotels were full, and I had no other place to go. Without a second thought about the sixteen-kilometer distance, I took off my shoes and started to walk briskly. I jogged. I skipped. I ran—barefoot. Never stopping, I called out the names of the protector guardian, path-openers, and warrior Gods of Kormantse—*Nana Eminsa* (Principal Goddess), *Nana Bohimahi* (Warrior Goddess), *Nana Sésa* (Guardian God), *Nana Dzɛrma* (Path-opener), and *ɛpopɔn Nana Bosompo* (Great Atlantic Ocean)—beseeching them to walk with me. I sang their songs, such as Kormantse Nana Dzerma *ndwom* "*Kweku Anankor ei*" (example 2 🔊) and a song that Kormantse Asafo warriors performed when returning from a victorious fight, "*Ye him Abo*" (example 3 🔊). The Atlantic

Ocean roared and tumbled beside me as if warning anyone or anything from interfering with my walk. This night was the first time I evoked the Kormantse Deities through song. I made it to my apartment safely. To this day, I still marvel at how I walked and took control of those dark and deserted streets alone.

To be clear, I am not discounting the real fear and vulnerability experienced by some women walkers. I am not belittling or blaming victims of assault. Nor am I ignoring the intersection of gender, ethnicity, and power in field research.[28] While walking transcends racial, class, economic, and other boundaries and is a practice of everyday life,[29] I recognize that walking is not for everyone. It can be a privilege for some, while dangerous and life threatening and fatal for others.[30] I am merely pointing out that fear and vulnerability are just as culturally constructed as they are socially engineered, that different societies conceive of fear differently; some instill ways to deal with and address these head-on. Walking alone can be empowering or disempowering depending on the cultural lens through which we practice and perceive it.[31] Since I was not socialized to be afraid because of my body but taught to claim the space, public or private, in which I found myself, and because I was taught that my body is an independent and powerful entity, walking alone in my search for the pasts of Kormantse Asafo *ndwom* was an empowering experience. The walker eats sweet things.

I am also a single parent who balanced research on foot with raising my two beautiful children, KoJo, then eleven years old in class six, now a six-foot-three sixteen-year-old Black boy, and MaAdwoa, then five years old in kindergarten, now ten.[32] When we arrived at Ghana in August 2016, I enrolled them at a school about eight kilometers from our residence. Each morning, I cooked breakfast, checked their homework, walked to a taxi rank, got in a taxi, and dropped them off at school. Then, I went about my business at Kormantse or the other towns along the coast. I picked them up from school in the evening, cooked dinner, helped with homework, prepared them for bed, then typed my field notes. Some days were more exhausting than others. Once, on my way from Kormantse to pick up KoJo and MaAdwoa from school, our taxi crashed into another taxi in front of us. None of the passengers, including me, had on seatbelts. My head got smashed into the windshield, aggravating the scars from the two brain surgeries I had had earlier while a graduate student at Florida State University (September and December 1992), causing severe headaches and panic. I was taken to Cape Coast Interbeton Teaching Hospital at Abura, where I had an MRI and CT scans. There was no internal bleeding, but my body shut down for days.

KoJo and MaAdwoa talked about missing their friends and some of the many conveniences in America—no power outages, no long traffic, reliable Internet, phone, and so on. They were very challenging times. I seriously thought about ending my walk with Asafo, but we decided to stay for the duration of our stay. KoJo had been traumatized by the numerous killings of unarmed Black men and had once asked me, "Will they kill me too when I grow up, Mama?" Then he said to me one day in Ghana, "We love the food here. All the children look like us. They are very open, friendly, and free. I am not afraid here." *What is walking in America doing to my children? My dear children, I will wrap you up with love, keep you close to me, very close. Your life will be happy till eternity. Wai*! OK? I found joy, inspiration, and love in their screams, disagreements, minor quibbles, and smiles. Aaaa. The joys of a single-parent walk. The joys of motherhood![33]

I used the act of walking as a discursive framework broadly to examine how walking, literally and metaphorically, informed my search for Asafo *ndwom* and examined how our practices can be incorporated as a crucial part of our fieldwork. My aim is not to elevate or privilege the method of walking over other forms of investigation (e.g., formal interviews, participatory observation, musical and textual analysis). Instead, it is to draw attention to how this practice can be better incorporated into our research method and explicitly recognize and report those learning methods as crucial aspects of our method. If walking is employed as part of our investigative process, we should clearly state the type of walking and how it informed our understanding of the music culture, society, or history. When we embark on a listening walk, we should report and publish how that approach helped us appreciate and understand the music. It is our scholarly responsibility to do so in sufficient detail for our colleagues who may attempt it.[34] Explicitly including and reporting walking in our scholarly and published work also adds rigor to our process and findings, distinguishing it from those that do not apply the practice. Based on their research and citing Guba's work, Joseph Pierce and Mary Lawhon advise urban geographers, "Reporting observational walking can thus be conceptualized as improving rigor both internally and externally. Internally, rigor is enhanced by making explicit the relationships among data, analysis, and findings.[35] They suggest further that credibility depends on our unfailing documentation of these internal relationships, and to the degree that researchers walk as a method, the knowledge we acquire should be made available to readers. Additionally, while it communicates our positionality and adds credence to our reflexive analysis, understanding how we gather information is crucial to how our readers appreciate and have faith in the reliability of our findings. When I went to Kormantse to learn about their Asafo *ndwom*, I did not know that it was a fading tradition; neither did I expect to rely on walking as a method. Yet over the days, weeks, and months, that practice became necessary to how I learned about Asafo *ndwom* culture. Ah! The walker knows more than her mother and father, indeed! *Ɔkwantunyi no nyim nsɛm pii kyɛn ne na na n'egya. Ampa!*

Kormantse Bentsir Asafo: The Ethnographic Setting

Kormantse No. 1, also known as Kormantse Bentsir, Kormantse Benstil, Kormantine, and Cormantin (henceforth Kormantse), is a small fishing town situated on a hill about 121 kilometers west of Accra, along the coast of Ghana in the Central Region on the Accra-Takoradi Highway.[36] It is one of many Fante-speaking towns—Saltpond, Abandze, Anomabo, Biriwa, Akatakyiwa, Nyamoransa, and Moree—between Mankessim and Cape Coast. Upper Kormantse, the location of the first fort that the British tried to build in the 1630s in the Gold Coast for the shipment of enslaved Africans to the New World, is protected on three of the four sides by deep trenches, a feature that according to residents protects them from invaders. Kormantse (Kormanti, Koromante) has been associated with several groups and cultural traditions of Africans in Jamaica, Suriname, and other diasporic groups, many of whom trace their ancestry to this small town.[37] There is some published work on Kormantse.[38]

Archaeologists Agorsah and Butler (2008) investigated the cultural formation and transformation of the historic Kormantse settlement on the Gold Coast in response to adaptation occurring through colonial times. They "sought to explain, by use of ethnographic and archaeological material, the processes and cultural manifestations by which the settlement's population, including those who passed through Kormantse during the trans-Atlantic slave trade between the 16th and 20th centuries, negotiated their survival and identities" (7). They also attempted to identify material indicative of internal and external trade contacts and exchanges, migration routes and patterns of market traffic, and, ultimately, the different groups represented in the colonial encounter with Kormantse and surrounding areas as the

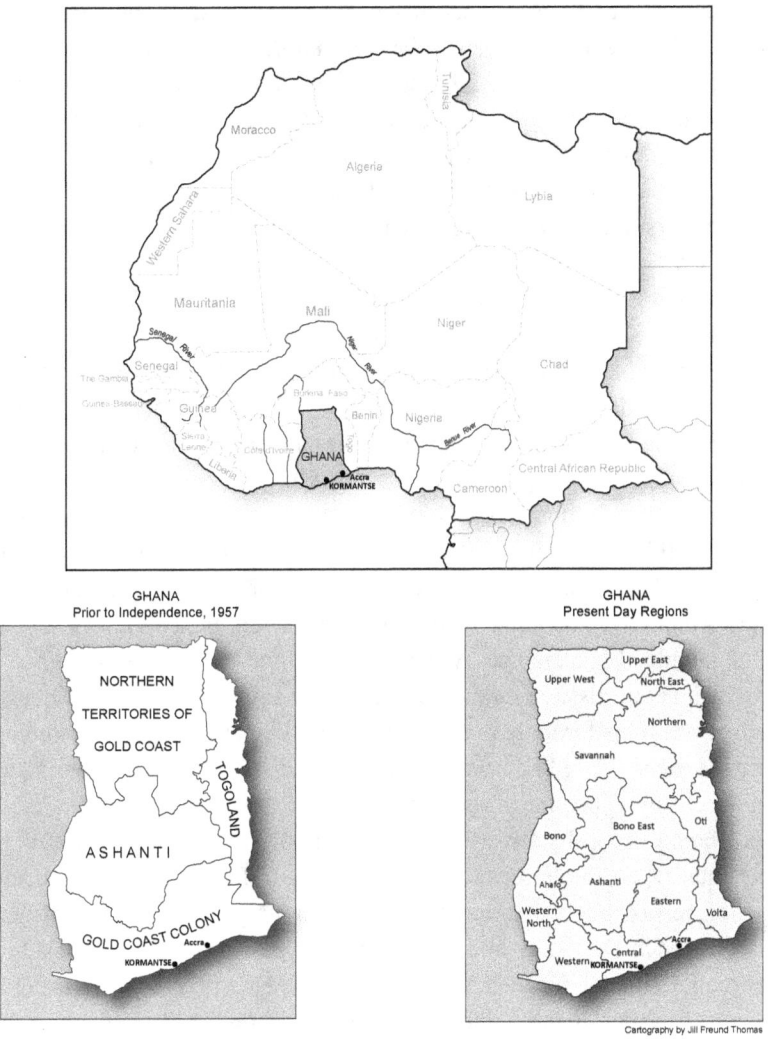

FIGURE I.5. Map of West Africa, showing Ghana, Kormantse. Map by Jill Freund Thomas.

connecting links. It was expected that "evidence of changing burial and other social practices as indices of the community's shifting identity, would help determine how the communities in and around Kormantse adjusted to changing conditions of the colonial encounter" (Agorsah and Schaffer 2010, 2). They divided the site into three areas, surveyed the site and its surroundings, commenced mapping of the main physical features of the site, and identified activity areas such as shrines, burial grounds, house structures, abandoned grinding stones, and other community areas as well delineation of the site boundaries.[39] Initial results of this crucial undertaking, which also sought to investigate the connections between residents there and those in the diaspora, indicated the richness of the site and suggested several appropriate directions for further investigations and their implications for an understanding of the identities of those who played a crucial role in the colonial encounter along the Gold Coast (now Ghana). The findings are published in Schaffer and Agorsah (2010). Nothing, however, has been published on Kormantse *ndwom* or its Asafo association.

Kormantse has a population of about ten thousand people.[40] They live in Kokoado/Kormantse Upper Town (on a hill), with six divisions, and Lower Town Kormantse, with eight sections. Today they speak Fante, a western-Kwa language along the west coast of West Africa, though according to Safohen Nana Odum III, my primary mentor, their original language was quite different from the Fante language. They are ferocious, proud, arrogant, and hard-working people whose Ancestors were among those sent to the Americas. There are several accounts about the migratory history of the people at Kormantse. According to a June 1925 correspondence to the district commissioner, marked (signed) by several Kings and Elders of Kormantse, their forefathers emigrated from Upper Dahomey. In another correspondence dated February 23, 1932, the district commissioner stated that "their own account of their origin is that they came from the region of Krobo on the Volta River" and were found in their present position by the Fante, when the latter migrated south from Takyimang." A June 20, 1932, correspondence that they "migrated from Ngyedum in the Northern part of French Dahomey and trekked to this part probably as a result of the frequent inter-Tribal Wars in all parts of West Africa those days, until they reached their locality and halted and settled on the hill now known as Upper Kormantine," supports the reference to Dahomey.[41]

Asa-fo, or war people, a warrior association mainly comprising adult males and women, was once the bedrock of society, preexisting European arrival to the continent in the fifteenth century. Asafo members combined dance, bodily enactments, poetry, song, and drum talk to deride their aggressors and protect their lands and people against outside and internal aggression. They walked. They cleared the paths to the various shrines and were responsible for keeping the neighborhoods clean. They were the modern-day equivalent of army, navy, police, and fire service combined. Asafo members were also responsible for enstooling and destooling a King.

These days, Asafo is coded as "fetish," a word modern people use to denigrate traditional practices. Christians who sing Asafo songs or perform in the Asafo group are criticized by their fellow Christians and sometimes reprimanded at church for engaging in such "ungodly acts." One mentor explained, "The church people will come to your house at night, stand behind your window, and preach against you!" (Egya Ekow Nunsin, personal communication, June 20, 2017, Kormantse, Ghana). Asafo is a tradition in crisis. So, I walked the various paths alone and with others to feel, learn about, and understand the *ndwom* of this vanishing but important tradition.

On the very first day of my walk, three men at the King's palace pronounced that Kormantse Asafo "has disintegrated" (*egu*). Several people in the community confirmed the statement with remarks like, "Asafo is no longer here." More people join churches, and the locality "no longer has the power to wage wars having lost it with the advent of the *Pax Britannica*."[42] Many Asafo Elders are dying. The indifferent youth do not want to get involved, and many others have moved away to the cities for employment. Kormantse Asafo has collapsed.

One elderly woman explained, "Their (Asafo) mistake is, they did not form it as a group like they do in Asante where they have different *adowa* groups in the various towns, so when the Elders started dying, they fell apart. They should have brought in young ones to replace them. At first, it was what they did; now they don't have anyone who pay them or give them other incentives, especially now that the sea business is bad" (personal communication, Auntie Gifty Nkum, July 12, 2017, Kormantse, Ghana).

As a result, the drums that embodied the whole spirit of Asafo were silent.[43] The ɔkyerɛma master drummer, who spoke to his warriors, regarded as the "wife" of the Asafo and upon whose appointment the Asafo gave him a silk loincloth and 25 shillings,[44] has been rendered invisible. The symbolic Asafo flags are no longer displayed to tell of past victories, taunt enemies, and instill pride in the citizens.[45] The significant functions of the Asafo, such as cleaning the roads leading to the shrines and feeding the Gods have ceased, leaving the various Gods hungry and angry.[46] I did not experience Datta and Porter's claim that Asafo still operated "a police force in certain circumstances."[47] In 1972 Kormantse celebrated its last *Afahyɛ* (festival), the annual ceremony that commemorated their alleged defeat of the Asante army in the early 1800s.[48] I walked to experience the pasts of what was left of this tradition and *ndwom*.[49]

> Asafo-ééé!
> Aså-fo
> You said you knocked down the powerful Asante army
> Those who said
> *Wo kum apem a, apem bɛba!*
> Hm!
>
> Asafo ééiii
> Kormantse *Ngyedum* Asafo
> You combined dance, bodily enactments, poetry, song
> Drum talk to deride your aggressors
> Today
> Silent
> Some say you have fallen
> Elders dying
> Is it true
> *Wontumi wo nnɔɔma a, wose wo kahyire nyɛ*
> When you cannot carry your load, you say the carrying pad is not good
>
> Where are those menacing songs, drumming, and dances
> Led you to victory
> What happened to the *gyina hɔ hwɛ, ampaa*
> *Dɛnkyerɛma,* and *ɔtoapentsen* drums
> *Pu-tu pu-tu puuuuú*
> *Pe-tem pa*
> *Dawur* bell
> *Ken-ke-ren ken-ke-ren*
> Your *ɔkyerɛma* drummer
> Cautioned and consoled
> Summoned Gods to rise
> Protect you

Ah! Asafo
Where is the *ndwom* that once saved your lives
Asserted that your lives matter
Kormantse Lives Matter
Is it because Our Elders say
ɛdɛ nka anomu
Sweetness does not remain permanently in the mouth

Ebueii!
Asa-fo!
You
Warriors who walked the walk
Tɔn-tɔn-te ne Tɔn-te: Yɛrenom nsa no na yɛrefa Adwene
The blind and the cripple: While we are drinking, we
are considering our strategy[50]
Wake up
Dance
Sing-ɛ

Undoing Heidi's Ghost: Toward an Anticolonial and Decolonialist African Musicology

The process of colonization erased, suppressed, and demonized most, if not all, indigenous African knowledge systems. In particular, "knowledges of women . . . or peasants and working classes and of the earth-centered religion worshippers were all subjugated and criminalized" (Tamale 2020, 29), though, as Joseph Ki-Zerbo reflects, "Our oral traditions constitute 'a real museum, conserver and transmitter of the social and cultural creations stored up by peoples said to have no written records.'" Decolonization, thus, "speaks to the dismantling of several layers of complex and entrenched colonial structures, ideologies, narratives, identities, and practices that pervade and (invade) every aspect of our lives" (Tamale 2020, 20). We must become true to ourselves, souls, spirits, bodies, and minds as indigenous scholars. We must become a distinctive voice—an indigenous/anticolonial voice that embraces politics of embodiment and questions how we work and what we work within. Anticolonial is a "discursive framework that seeks to work with alternative oppositional paradigms based on the use of indigenous concepts and analytical systems and cultural frames of reference" (Dei 2015).

In his TED Talk, Ghanaian-Canadian social scientist George Sefa Dei (2015) describes decolonization as a framework concerned with the "politics of knowledge production," one that "subverts the colonial and challenges the dominance of particular bodies of knowledge to resist the persistence of dominant knowledge." He is very critical of how we seek "legitimation and validation in the eyes of the dominant culture and "proximity to whiteness" in our presentations and representations. We present knowledge so that it is understood and accepted by the dominant, so we mimic. The "indigenous scholar," a phrase he proposes, is "a holistic, embodied learner working with myriad identities, including spiritual identities." The scholar has a deeper appreciation of her society's rich intellectual heritage and knowledge and puts them on equal footing with another knowledge. According to Dei, indigenous allows us to seek decolonization; it speaks about resistance to colonial imposition; it speaks about coloniality and colonial oppression. We cannot talk about decolonization without talking about indigenous knowledge, Dei insists. Decolonization "must begin by asking new questions informed by non-Western, Indigenous epistemes, epistemologies, and philosophies" (Dei 2021).

If *Akokɔ ne aburoo nna*, "the chicken and maize cannot sleep together," since the ax forgets but the tree remembers, can colonizers, the descendants, or direct benefactors decolonize? Can descendants of the enslaved and enslavers, descendants of the colonized and colonizers, agree on humanistic and empowering stories about the colonized or enslaved? Can they decide how to use anticolonial and antiracist frameworks as intersecting paradigms to challenge dehumanizing dominant and exoticizing narratives? Those unhealed and hidden wounds from slavery and colonialism run deep. Whether we can move beyond Eurocentric knowledge hegemonies depends on our genuine and concerted efforts to claim ourselves, humanize Africans, and recenter our voices, our indigenous knowledge, how we write, how we challenge dominant narratives, how we re-present ourselves, insist on our humanity, and how often we celebrate our language, our Ancestors/Elders, and their ways of knowing.

In response to Dei's question, "What are our commitments to the land on which we do our scholarship?" and the work of past and present African anticolonialists and decolonials, I frame my discussion to engage the following:[51]

1. What is anticolonial African musicology?
2. What is decolonialist African musicology?
3. How could anticolonial and decolonialist discursive frameworks shape how we
   (1) mentor
   (2) conduct ethnographic *nhwehwɛmu* fieldwork
   (3) present knowledge acquired from scholars in the field?
4. How does an anticolonial/decolonialist paradigm shape our writing?
5. Who is our audience?
   Whose knowledge are we curating, rescuing, and discovering
   What are our commitments to the land on which we do our *nhwehwɛmu*?
   When our ways of telling their stories, musicking are framed in whiteness
   Burying their scholarship in theoretical jargons borrowed from other people's lived
   experiences
   Obi nkɔ obi kurom nkɔkyerɛ ne ho sɛ: Meye dehyeɛ"
   How about using the culture's rich intellectual traditions as frameworks
   Reflective of the societies whose musicking we surgically analyze?
   The societies from whom we learn are creative, poetic
   Using indigenous ways of knowing and framing
   Away from whiteness
   Not *Under* Dr. Chandra Talpade Mohanty's *Western Eyes*
   Creative strategies and outlets for academic writers

This book is my attempt at an anticolonial and decolonialist African musicology, one that subverts, disrupts, and decenters white racial framing of research, analysis, and presentation, disrupting how Euro-American concepts frame our ways of telling, being, and experiencing *ndwom*.[52] Our colonial histories must not stop us, so we must recognize and dismantle coloniality for our humanity and healing. Therefore, I have not provided a literature review. References and nods to the work of other scholars are incorporated into the storytelling. In my attempt to privilege the voices of my Kormantse scholars, sometimes, only work titles, names of authors, or passing references are made. I have also refrained from using Western music notation, a primary tool of colonialization that has silenced and "buried" many brilliant indigenous scholars who do not partake in that mode of framing and discourse, sending them to their emotional underground. ɔdomankoma Kyerɛma Ankoma, ɔdomankoma Kyerɛma Kwamena Pra. *Du-é*! In my mind, Western notation reduces our *ndwom* to objects. It mutes their drive and vitality and reduces them to things, thingifying them. Furthermore, the standard Western notation does not adequately capture the nuances and subtleties that define the richness, wavering, colors, and complexities of the *ndwom*. It is an art form transmitted through oral tradition, an art form that thrives on free-flowing declamatory passages and interlocking and embodied call and response phrases, an art form that bends, curls, and throws itself like sea waves, and an impermanent art form that evolves, shifts, and shapes with each rendition. Western notation presents it as a fixed, static idea. It is not an object. It is a *spirit*. It lives, breathes, and grows with each performance. Like a walk, *ndwom* performance traverses different textures and terrains, sounds, memories, proverbs, moods, feelings, rhythms, and histories. Instead, I will make the audio and video recordings available for readers to sing along while they read through the text. Performance is the soul of Asafo *ndwom* scholarship. Performance encodes and decodes the epistemology of *ndwom*. Still, I will add a disclaimer clause that every performance we hear is one of many possibilities. *Woforo dua a, foro tenten na wote hwe a, atumpan ama wo dammirifua*, "When you climb a tree, climb a tall one so that if you fall down, the talking drums will play condolences for you."

In the following narratives, I share the different walks through which I learned about Asafo *ndwom*. As an observer, a knower, and a learner, I pay particular attention to the ethical equation and position my writing and analysis accordingly. *Obi nkɔ obi kurom nkɔkyrɛ ne ho sɛ: 'Meyɛ ɔdehyeɛ,'* "One should not go to another person's town and declare: 'I am a royal,'" or *Obi nkɔ obi kurom nkɔfrɛ ne ho Agyeman,* "One should not go to another person's town and call herself a Liberator." Therefore, I am intentional about centering the voices of my mentors on the various issues, including multiple and divergent voices, in my telling and analysis to provide an active performative discourse. I problematize the colonial gaze and our practice of "speaking for others." I problematize and destabilize our practice of burying our mentors' experiences and performance arts in theoretical jargon based on other people's lived experiences, as if my mentors' ways of knowing, ways of being, and worldviews are not theoretical in and of themselves. My mentors are "living and breathing libraries"—the experts: scholars, theorists. They theorize through their words, performances, songs, proverbs, lived experiences, expressions, their walk, and their bodies. It is their unique experiences with Kormantse *ndwom* that I set out to understand. My interpretations of that understanding are filtered through my location as a Ghanaian Akan female, an expatriate living and teaching in the United States of America, a knower, an observer, a learner, and a walker whose peripatetic practices, headscarves, and beads around my ankle and waist informed how I learned and understood.

This book is a story. It is my story as a member of the Aduana lineage. Our totemic symbols of fire and dog inform my honesty, candor, and sincerity. *Ogyaba*! Child of fire. Child of rock. *Asaase Aban, Yɛnte Gyae* (appellations). This is my walk with many scholars at Kormantse and along the coast of Ghana in search of Asafo *ndwom*. It is a document of my understanding of Kormantse Asafo *ndwom* and ways of doing and being. It is my distinctive voice and experience as an indigenous scholar. I join African authors who felt the need and saw the importance of telling our own stories, the story and rhetoric of the many scholars who shared their *nyimdze* knowledge, theories, and memories about Asafo. As Chinua Achebe noted, it is important to pursue a "balance of stories where every people will be able to contribute to a definition of themselves, where we are not victims of other people's accounts. This is not to say that nobody should write about anybody else—I think they should, but those that have been written about should also participate in the making of these stories" (Achebe in Fretter, 2013). Chimamanda Ngozi Adichie has warned us about "The Danger of a Single Story" (2009).

For the same reason of "doing it for our grandchildren and great-grandchildren," and as part of my anticolonial approach, I have refrained from devoting chapters to specific issues (e.g., religion, gender, history). There were many overlapping and recurring themes during my different encounters, which caused much jumping around from date, time, and session. *Wode w'ani mienu hwɛ toa mu a, baako bɔ*, "If you look into a bottle with two eyes, one gets blinded." Instead, the multiple layers and themes that I present—memory, documented and otherwise, history, issues of gender, splits within the community, effects, and conflicts with Christianity—*ndwom*, present-day attitudes toward Asafo, are incorporated throughout the various chapters and presented as mini-stories or episodes within the larger story. The multiple layers and textures are woven into a thick tapestry like the Ghanaian *kente* cloth. Each chapter captures the structure of a typical conversation with my teachers. It meanders through a discursive framework using direct answers, songs, rhetorical questions, journal entries, sounds, emotions, silences, indigenous knowledge, and many rich intellectual traditions—folktales, appellations, and proverbs. The structure of each chapter epitomizes the character of the walk, traversing different terrains, memories, songs, boundaries, histories, and their entanglements. I end most of the chapters with my *ethnographic voice*, a poetic, performative, distinctively African, and evocative style that privileges my voice as a knower and learner in the field, blending my knowledge with my mentors, proverbs, drum patterns, appellations, and other rhetorical forms. The ethnographic voice allows me to summarize and collapse otherwise long material into short, evocative, poetic, and performative phrases.

By emphasizing the discursive rather than the theoretical, I hope to avoid, like social scientists George Dei and Alireza Asgharzadeh, the rigidity and inflexibility with which theory has come to be identified. Instead, I aim to work within a more flexible, transparent, and fluid language that the discourse and discursive frameworks provide (2001). *Adwene nsa da*, "Wisdom never ends," and *Tikorɔ mu nni nyansa,* "One head does not store all wisdom."[53] Therefore, the book is not exhaustive. It is the story of one walker. Me. It is written with Kormantse citizens in mind. In a readable fashion, this book strives to present the critical elements of Asafo *ndwom*, instruments, performance style, its history, and its role in society. It is a document that I hope the grandchildren and great-grandchildren of my mentors and other readers will read, critique, and add to.

In chapter 2, I share my initial encounters with the Asafo tradition, my search, especially at Elmina, Anomabo, and Cape Coast. These early encounters and narratives about Asafo became crucial for my search. They were fragments that would later help me patch the different strands of Asafo history and significance in society, their *posuban* military posts, and the war between the Fante and Elmina, a topic that came up again and again in my work at Kormantse. Every step I took helped peel off another layer that encased Asafo, bringing me closer to its *ndwom*.

In chapter 3, I use *Ani a ɛhunuu tetehɔ na ɛnni hɔ, na aso a ɛtee tetehɔ asɛm deɛ ɛwɔ hɔ*, "The eyes that witnessed the past were not there, but the ears that heard the past are there" as a discursive framework to examine my history walk through Kormantse town with local scholars. We walked and walked. It was an *abakɔsɛm* walk that allowed me to see the town's layout from their perspective. I learned that the land holds people's dreams, *ndwom*, and memories, affording me local ways of seeing and reading their textured landscapes. It was a walk filled with entangled memories about matters that have come and gone and *ndwom*, opportunities to experience the texture of memories and the Asafo tradition, the soul of the people.

Chapter 4 is about my walk alone and with others through Kormantse town to engage with the memories shared with me. I employ Yarimar Bonilla's (2011) "memory walk" and the work of soundwalk artists to explore a particular walking practice. I tease out the benefits of my memory walks. Over the course of my search, I took many such walks to recall my mentors' memories. What does it mean to walk with others' memories? What does it mean to walk through spaces about which memories, *abakɔsɛm*, and *ndwom* have been shared? This type of walking allows the walker to walk into and experience the past. I discuss how those types of walks allowed me to "work out" the inconsistencies in how matters that have come and gone are remembered and shared, while I share my experience of how "the past in part becomes the present," and how "one can become in direct contact with it and touch it." The "memory walk" provided contexts for the performance and experience of songs that I would not have experienced otherwise. Could others' memories be invoked for more profound meaning and connection to that space? What are the implications of such a recall? What do such engagements do to our senses? To the songs?

In the spirit of filmmaker Safi Faye, chapters 5 and 6 are praise songs for Kormantse women, specifically, and for Ghanaian and all African women. Through my sharing of conversations with Kormantse women and using several proverbs, including *Mmarimma nyɛ sumyɛ na yɛ de yɛ ti ato so*, "Men are not pillows for us to put our heads" and *ɔbaa na ɔwo barima*, "It is woman who gives birth to man," I shift the narrative away from what Oyěwumí contests as the "image of a weak and helpless African woman who needs to be saved from barbaric customs and a brutal, all-powerful, misogynistic group of men" (Oyěwumí 2003, 34) that prevail in some feminist writings. I present this personal perspective as a counternarrative to the portrayal of African women as barbaric, "servile, childlike people who need to be rescued and protected by one Western group or another in some foreground" (ibid., 35). The Kormantse women, and indeed the African women I have interacted with, including my mother, whom I observed as a child and as an adult, were not servile or childlike persons who needed to be rescued by some Western groups. They carried themselves with confidence, self-determination, dignity, and pride. Since Asafo is often presented as a male tradition, I also discovered and uncovered the following: What do women know about Asafo? What are their thoughts and memories? What songs do women sing about Asafo, Kormantse history, culture, society, and men? How do women relate with each other? How much do women know? I focus on their doings, goings, ways of beings, memories, and stories about Asafo *ndwom*. Chapter 5 examines my walk with women at Kokoado, Kormantse Upper Town. Chapter 6 explores my walk with two women at Kormantse Lower town. Are women reliant on men, defined by the relationships with men, or *Mmarimma nyɛ sumyɛ na yɛ de yɛ ti ato so*?

In chapter 6, I reflect on my experience of live Asafo drumming, most of which occurred at funerals and at live performances that I helped organize. Sometimes, people invited me to funerals, or I went on my own; I ran into them a few times while walking through the city or town. I joined mourners who paraded gifts for the deceased, viewed and fanned corpses, ate and danced to live Asafo drumming, ran alongside a hearse to the lineage house, or watched the Asafo flag dancer. Sometimes, I walked up to the performers, listened for a while, and then walked away, paying attention to the different sounds that filled the air. The Listening Walk has been explored and analyzed by several walking artists through their awareness of the rhythmicity in the environment (Wunderlich 2008). Through my experience of walking to death rituals, I explored the Listening Walk as an essential approach for ethnomusicologists and I promote its potential for helping to tease out the layers of a piece of music against the backdrop of its composite sound. How does walking contribute to our listening, learning, and musicking?

In chapter 7, I explore the performance, structure, and politics of Asafo *ndwom*. What is Asafo *ndwom*? How is it organized? Who performs Asafo *ndwom*? Who creates Asafo *ndwom*? What processes are involved in learning Asafo songs? Learning how to sing Asafo *ndwom* offered additional insights into Asafo aesthetic preferences' valuation and structure. Some of these challenged and expanded my training in African music. *Tete ka aso mu*, "Repetitive listening leaves an indelible mark in the ear."

In response to Sefa Dei's question, "What are our commitments to the lands on which we do our scholarship?" I attempted to give back to the community. I visited schools and shared what I learned with the students. I also went "on-air" and played and discussed Asafo songs, *abakɔsɛm*, and politics. In chapter 8, I examine my minor effort to help sustain Asafo *ndwom* at Kormantse. After interviewing teachers, recording, transcribing, and translating songs and lyrics, taking long walks, attending funerals, and visiting historical sites with my mentors to contextualize the songs that they and their Ancestors once performed, I sought ways to share that knowledge with citizens of Kormantse. The Asafo tradition and *ndwom*, as noted, are labeled "fetish" by modern people and seem to be losing their significance at Kormantse and, indeed, at most coastal towns in Ghana. Therefore, I went to the schools to share what I had learned; I also initiated a radio program, *Sankɔfa wɔ nkyir* ("It is not a taboo to go back and fetch what has been left behind") at the Kormantse Communication Centre. I shared what I had learned and played examples of Kormantse Asafo songs and drumming I had recorded, Asafo history, instrumentation, and its significance to society. The program became a favorite among both old and young. With more people joining churches, no imminent wars, condescension and chastisement from the church, an indifferent youth loath to take over, Asafo Elders dying, and the existence of government institutions, the *ndwom* of Asafo companies along the coast of Ghana are fading slowly from people's memory. I also examine attempts by Elders of Kormantse and other Fante communities to sustain Asafo. Cogitating UNESCO Sustainability Development Initiatives, Article 5 specifically, and UNESCO's Convention on Cultural Diversity (2005), the Ghana Cultural Policy (1975, 2004), and models by Schippers (2015) and Titon (2009), I reflect on other attempts to help curate and encourage creativity that will help to sustain the Asafo tradition.

Finally, in *Nkekaho*—Re-Invocation—I reflect on my long walk toward Asafo *ndwom*.

Reclaiming My Voice, My Center: Towards a Performative Scholarly Discourse

> Are we ready to center the performative, the creative modes of our scholars in the field?
> Privilege and value creative strategies as outlets for writers?
> Celebrate the spoken word, appellations, poetry, proverbs as discursive frameworks?
> Some music and field experiences are best articulated poetically
> Are we ready to expand our ways of *nhwehwemu* research and framing

Mentoring
Decolonize methodologies?

My parents tell me I loved to dance, sing, put dramatic scenes together for my friends to perform, and sing. My mother, Akosua Pokua Adjei, tells me that people nicknamed me *Twene wura ba*, "the daughter of the scholar-artist" because my father ɔ*benfoɔ* Professor Kwasi Aduonum, is a *Twenekafoɔ*, or a scholar-artist. ɔ*kɔtɔ nwo anoma*, "The crab does not give birth to a bird." According to my mother, one of her sisters used to say, *Ei, Ama Oforiwaa, daakye ɔbɛtɔn efieha foɔ nyinaa*, "Eh, Ama Oforiwaa, one day she will sell everyone in this household," to which another sister would respond, Kwasi Aduonum *na ɔbɛtɔn no kane*! "It is Kwasi Aduonum that she will sell first!" *Na w'ani yɛ den ankása, hwɛ*! "You were really brave," Maame Pokua added. Writing and speaking were performative acts, blending proverbs, storytelling, gesturing, movement, poetry, spoken word, and appellations—multiple forms of scholarship. Western-style education, especially my training in ethnomusicology, with its rigid emphasis on "scholarly" writing, white racial framing, and a "publish or perish" culture, buried, silenced, and restricted my creative voice. However, as Audre Lorde writes, when "we become more in touch with our own ancient, non-European consciousness of living as a situation to be more experienced and interacted with, we learn more and more to cherish our feelings and respect those hidden sources of our power from where true knowledge and therefore, lasting action comes" (2). *Duʃɔkyeɛ da nsuo mu, da da a, ɛrennane ɔdɛnkyɛm*, "If a piece of log lies in water every day, it would not turn into a crocodile!" Hm!

This is the first full-length study on the *ndwom* musical pasts of Asafo warrior associations, based on my "ways of walking" with local scholars along the Ghanaian littoral.

I use narratives and the performative extensively to convey the complex sociohistorical events that inform the depth and complexity of Asafo, its *abakɔsɛm* matters that have come and gone, and identity within society.[54] I illustrate how integral Asafo is to all sectors of society, even when it is not physically present or functional. Though dubbed "ceremonial" and shunned by some in the society, Asafo is present spiritually and lives in the hearts of people even in its absence. My mentors spoke fondly about its past glories, its effectiveness, its *ndwom*, and how it brought their societies together. How does a "fading" tradition evoke such powerful memories and sentiments?

My goal on this trajectory is to tell my truth, invite someone in, create something new, and chart a new path. *Tete ka aso mu,* "Repetitive hearing (reading) leaves an indelible mark in the ear," so I repeat some phrases, ideas, songs, proverbs. And repeat. And repeat. And repeat. Some of the sections are meant to be repeated, read, reread, and performed. Through this fluid and complex manuscript, I reposition African Elders' knowledge as "Epistemologies of Decolonization and de-coloniality." I center the stories shared by African Scholars as "metaphors of resistance" (Dei 2021) and present a text that challenges the colonialist definitions of knowledge.

Nsateaa baako ntumi mpopa animu, "One finger cannot effectively clean the face." Therefore, it is polyvocal, multimodal, multiperspective, multicentric, performative, reflexive, and dialogic. It is informed by the structure of Asafo *ndwom,* using appellations, poetry, narratives, repetitions, proverbs, *abakɔsɛm,* calling and responding, and amid a strong pulse. It is a performative scholarly discourse, a dance of joy, storytelling, a performance that ensues from an anticolonial and decolonialist stance. As a celebration of Asafo, and those warriors who insisted their lives matter, it is meant to be read, performed, read, and performed again. Tete ka aso mu.

    Tón, Tón, Tón, Tón, Tón ton-ton-ton-ton-ton-ton,
    Tón
    Asafo
    Asafo montie, Asafo montie, ASAFO MONTIE
    Asafo listen, Asafo listen, ASAFO LISTEN
    Yɛnkɔ Yɛnkɔ ooo
    Let's go
    *Ndwom-*o *ndwom*
    Ken-ke-ren
    Ken-ken-ke-ren-ke
    Pu-tum pu-tum pa
    Yɛɛ yɛɛɛɛ
    N'ɛɛkɔ N'ɛɛba
    Ogya! Ogya! Ogya!

    Asafo
    Ayɛ kradow
    Didn't bell hooks say moving from silence to speech is for the oppressed

The colonized, the exploited, and those who stand and struggle
Side by side a gesture of defiance that heals, that makes
New life
New growth possible
Our movement from object to subject
The liberated voice
Talking Back
Twene ani da hɔ a yɛn nyan nkyɛn
When the drumhead is there, we don't play the side
Are you ready
To dance again
Talk back
De-center white racial framing
Center your ways and rich intellectual traditions
Are you ready?

Asafo
You asserted and insisted that your people's lives matter
African, Kormantse, Black Lives
Disgrace does not befit the Akan child
ɔkyerɛma is talking on his drums
Let's walk
Walk, walk slow
With all due respect
Woforo dua a, foro tenten na wote hwe a, atumpan ama wo dammirifua
When you climb a tree, climb the tall one, so that when you fall
The talking drum will play condolences for you
I am climbing your big tree
Walking
Help me
Search for you
Find you
Walk with me
For your *ndwom*
Asafo *abakɔsɛm*

Wofeefee asɛm mu a, wohunu mu yie
It is the ɔ*nantefoɔ* who eats sweet things
Let's make this walk sweet
Sweet
Too sweet-ooooooo
Daasebrɛ
Tón!

PART I

Walking into the Past

CHAPTER ONE

Walking for Asafo

Entangled Meanings, Abakɔsɛm, Awakenings

ɔnantefoɔ na odi adɔdɔdeɛ
(It is the walker who eats sweet things)

Wofeefee asɛm mu a, wohunu mu yie
(When you look into a problem closely, you can see it clearly)

—Ghanaian Akan Proverbs

Yɛyɛ Edenafo oo!
Yɛyɛ Edenafo oo!
Nana Borɔntɔ Kwesi e!
Yɛyɛ Edenafo oo
(We are Elmina people oo!
We are Elmina people oo!
Nana Borɔntɔ Kwesi ee!
We are Elmina people oo)

—Elmina Asafo *ndwom* (Excerpt)

My search for Asafo *abakɔsɛm*, "matters that have come and gone'" and the *ndwom* that members sang to celebrate their victories, to taunt other members, to secure lands, and to assert the value of their lives took me to different localities and different people. I learned many versions of Asafo *abakɔsɛm*. One gentleman said Asafo was brought to Elmina from Asebu by one Obarima Osam. Another asserted that Asafo came when the Akan people migrated from the north to their current settlements; another noted that Asafo came when people sought land with water. The varied versions point to Anna Hoefnagel's "microhistories," which subvert cultural analyses that take imagined homogenous cultural groups as their point of reference. It also points to Michael Herzfeld's observation that much of the "anthropological engagement is with the multiple histories that one finds in a single social context, often articulated by the same people as they respond to the conflicting exigencies of their social, political, and cultural predicaments."[1]

Importantly, the versions point to a philosophy of Akan Elders, *Ani a ɛhunuu tetehɔ na ɛnni hɔ, na aso a ɛtee tetehɔ asɛm deɛ ɛwɔ hɔ*, "The eyes that witnessed the past were not there, but the ears that heard the past are there."

These sometimes divergent versions helped frame the tradition, so that before I read De Graft Johnson (1932)—who observed, "The Asafu organization arose out of a national crisis when it became necessary for all able-bodied males in the community to combine and organize themselves into a fighting body (Asafu) with a view of protecting their women, the young, and the infirm against outside aggression"—Datta (1972), Labi (2002), and all the other scholars who have written about Asafo companies, I had been able to tease out and piece together several multilayered and intersecting themes that would later inform my work at Kormantse. These included memory about Asafo, splits within the community, *ndwom*, conflicts with Christian practices, present-day attitudes toward Asafo, colonialism, Kingship disputes, history and function of Asafo, and inter-Asafo structural differentiation illustrated in their use of drums, flags, and their emblems.

When I arrived on the coast, I expected to experience what Datta and Porter (1971) had observed and expressed almost five decades earlier. "Anyone visiting a coastal town in central or western Ghana on an appropriate occasion cannot fail to be impressed by the pace of the organized military bands (*asafo*) in indigenous society. He is likely to see men, and even women, marching out in animated processions, singing, and dancing, beating drums, and dressed in colorful uniforms. Some of the marchers will be carrying a variety of flags embroidered with different motifs" (279).

I did not witness an appropriate occasion or see "men, and even women, marching out on animated processions, singing, and dancing, beating drums, and dressed in colorful uniforms" or "marchers . . . carrying a variety of flags embroidered with different motifs."

One gentleman, Mr. Ato Eshun, who helped with my work on dungeons for enslaved Africans mentioned that "Asafo is not as strong as it used to be.

These days they are just ceremonial. They mystified the tradition and surrounded it with so much mystery (*hu-huu-hu*) that it scared people and put some off." He offered to introduce me to some prominent people in town. He also indicated that the town is dotted with several Asafo *posuban*, military posts that house their symbols and serve as an archive for their glorious days. Our Nigerian Ibo Elders say, *Otu nzo ukwu biri ogologo njem*, "A step taken marks the end of a long journey." So, I started to walk. These "purposive walks" (Wunderlich 2008) were at times the only means by which I could locate these posts because most were nestled between houses. I learned local ways of seeing and interpreting symbols and Asafo's role in society.

What the *Posuban* Said: I am *The* Heart of Asafo

My initial direct encounter with Asafo began with their *posuban*. *Posuban* are structures that house war accouterments, instruments, items seized at war, and the "soul" of the specific company. Ato Eshun told me these were located throughout most Fante towns that had Asafo companies. Elmina was no exception. So, I walked. I usually started my walk from the taxi rank by the cathedral at downtown Elmina and walked down Dutch Cemetery Street, one of the major streets in the town, interacting with people, some of whom shared their knowledge about Asafo. From Dutch Cemetery Street, I made a left turn, walked down Benya street, made a right turn onto the Elmina bridge, made a right turn, walked through the market, and moved toward a neighboring town, Bantuma. Sometimes I stopped and bought *nkate* cake (groundnut cake), *toogbɛɛ* (goat balls or doughnuts), roasted fish or corn, or *waakye* (rice and beans), developing relationships with the women who controlled the markets. Some shared their memories of Asafo with me. Repeating these routes over a few weeks became my version of "place-ballets" (Seamon 1980) and allowed me to know the paths in intimate ways that other mobility methods could not afford. I walked down the streets, by houses, businesses, a church, the Dutch cemetery, the Benya shrine—Elmina's main shrine—makeshift shops, entrepreneurs, and fishermen trading their catch of the day or mending their nets.

The first *posuban* I saw was the military post for Elmina No. 2 Akyemfo Asafo. It was a vast two-storied building with different symbols, including cement replicas of a man and a woman on the front porch carrying two items, a man on a platform in the middle, and metal replicas of what looked like airline jets on either side. According to a plaque by it, the proverb,

"*Mbogya pata ase*" referred to the blood the company has shed throughout its history, the eagle represented the company's courage, the statues represented the Asafo Supi and two tutelary spirits, and the airplanes were the company's symbol.

At a "T" junction of the street, I ran into another military post belonging to No. 4 Wombir. This post was elaborately designed with a bell and other symbols on top. It also had images of a man and woman, symbolically titled Adam and Eve. I could not get any closer because two taxis were parked in front of it, while a big poster about a funeral draped its front. Down the street to my left, I walked by another post—Asafo No. 1 Ankobea. An entrepreneur who managed a shop nearby, Auntie Suzie, had placed big bowls of rice, beans, and groundnuts on a table in front of the post for sale. According to her, the cockerel on the roof symbolized the cock crowing to signal the approach of dawn. The bells symbolized the fact that Ankobea Asafo were the ones who mustered the courage to galvanize the people to go to war. So, the town leaders took the No. 1 title from Wombir, together with the keys to the town, and gave them to No. 1 Ankobea. She added that the custodian of the *posuban* had a stroke and could not be reached. I continued to walk. On my way back down the street and not too far from the No. 2 *posuban*, I saw the No. 5 Abese post wedged between houses. It had a replica of a boat with two European men looking out and another guarding the ship. I could not get any closer or ask questions about it because funeral tents and preparations for a funeral were underway. Within a twenty-minute timeframe, I saw four of the ten Elmina *posuban*. My walk for Asafo continued.

I walked to Bantuma, a neighboring town that I had been told had Asafo companies. It was about a two-kilometer walk, but it felt long and was exhausting. I strove through the busy street, maneuvering my way through the market, dodging speeding and impatient taxi drivers who blew their horns at people, covering my nose from exhaust fumes, and trying to tune out overlapping embodied calls from entrepreneurs peddling their wares. I was not oblivious to the stares, most of which were directed at my feet and my ankle. I had heeded my colleagues' advice: "Go native, otherwise, they would think you are a Black American and will not be ready to help you. They will also charge you big bucks because they think you have secured some grant money. That is the legacy those who came before us have left behind, though we don't usually get the grants because even receiving grant money is determined by the color of your skin and where you come from. Also, speak the local language. Don't wear jeans!" How does a native "go native?" Perform the native to the nth degree—an overkill. So, uncommon for a young woman my age, I wore a *kaba* traditional top or a plain "T" shirt, a wrap around my waist to below my knees, a traditional necklace with a talisman around my neck, a scarf covering my head, and, especially, my Bob Marley–style locks. I did not want people to think I was Jamaican, which I believe could limit my access to mentors or prolong my search. I also wore beads around my ankle to be as "native" as possible. I hoped to avoid being called *oburonyi* (white person), a term that Black Americans "disdain." Yet, people stared at me. People whispered to others about me as I passed them. Though I was not the only one moving fast, I slowed down because I thought I could be walking too fast. It seemed as if I was the only one walking alone, the only one not trading, carrying a load, hawking, or walking with someone. I tried to walk close to and among people. That slowed my pace, looked strange, suspicious. I continued to walk.

After about two kilometers walking, I came upon an older man fixing his fishing nets. I asked him about Asafo *posuban*. He pointed to a building across the street from his house. "Go between those buildings. The Anyampa *posuban* is there." I thanked him and crossed the street, walked through several houses, and came upon a square-shaped structure painted red, black, and white vertical stripes. A lady who lived near the post asked a young boy to take me to the now-late Egya Akɔdɛɛ Afful. He was the custodian of the post and a dignified-looking gentleman. I told Egya Afful (Akɔdɛɛ) about my mission. We scheduled our first formal talk. Over several meetings, I received a brief history of the town, the significance of Asafo in Fante society generally, and about Elmina No. 7 Anyampa Asafo.

What the Late Egya Akɔdɛɛ Afful, the Asafo Custodian, Said: "Asafo Is People Who Dance, Your *Posuban* Identifies You"

Ama: "What is Asafo?"

Egya Akɔdɛɛ: "We are playing to dance. We are playing the drums to dance. That is why it is called Asao fo—people who dance. All the drums that you hear, don't they dance when it is played?"

Ama: "Do the Asafo sing, play drums?

Egya Akɔdeɛ: "They sing and dance. The songs they sing are nsaa. They sing, drum, and dance."

Ama: "What is nsaa?"

Egya Akɔdeɛ: "Nsaa, they destroy or spoil or attack one Asafo, you that I don't like. Asafo songs are serious matter. When they sing the songs, then there is serious matter."

Ama: "They say the Asafo used to fight? Is that all they did?"

Egya Akɔdeɛ: "Yes. They fought. I am here sitting here. Then you come to me and say, 'Your stupid things that you said, I am looking for you in the Nser mu (bush/woods).' Me too, I have not said anything. Then you go and take your drum, the Asafo drum, and you play it and call your crowd. You play for a while and have a meeting. Sometimes you won't know about it. You are there, and one day, they will call you. They will call you that 'Today, we are looking for you in the Nser mu.' The bush is over there. It is like women walking and one throws a rock to offend the other. I will also offend that person. That is what brings war."

Ama: "So, the war is between two Asafo?"

Egya Akɔdeɛ: "Yes, between two Asafo. Maybe between Abese and Akyemfo. Anyampa and Ankobea."

Ama: "Was there a fight between the whites and Asafo?"

Egya Akɔdeɛ: "As for that, it is not there. The European wars were between themselves."

Ama: "So, all the Asafo associations do is fight?"

Egya Akɔdeɛ: "Fighting is all they do. When the Ancestors created them, fighting. Unless you don't talk about another, they will sing you nsaa, to say, 'What you said the other day, let's go and see who is a man (tougher/stronger)!'"

Ama: "Where did the numbers come from?"

Egya Akɔdeɛ: "We are No. 7. We have No. 1 Ankobea; No. 5 Abese, No. 6. It is called Asao fo. It is the name that they put on their sign board. They have horns; each has a different horn. Some are animal tusks; some are bugles; some are hollowed out wood. We (No. 7 Anyampa) use a hollowed-out wood. Brofommba, they use a European bell."

Ama: "Where are they?"

Egya Akɔdeɛ: "They have all perished."

Ama: "Why have they perished?"

Egya Akɔdεε: "They have fought aaaa . . . their 'under is burned.' Nobody came after them." [During one of our sessions, Egya Akɔdεε provided some background to the different Asafo companies, their colors, and significance.]

Egya Akɔdεε: "People organized drums; each organized its own drum. Each time a drum sounds, it means there is war. They organized themselves into names: Wombir, Ankobea, Anyampa. They each have their dresses. Wombir is bright red; Ankobea wears white. Us Anyampa we wear, we say, Ahaba tetee akuamoa, edze wadwen ma odasani a, yε dze wo tsir na yε dze bu gya. Edze wo nyansa ma wo nyanko a, wo tsir bu gya. 'Don't give your wisdom to someone; keep it. If you give your wisdom to a human being, your head catches fire.' Us Anyampafo, all we say is, you saw the colors, black, white, and red. All they say is that 'whatever you are telling us, we will say it hu-huu-hu, let's say it in the dark. If we say it in the dark and you don't hear it, we will bring in the plain, in light for everybody to hear it. If you don't hear it, fire/blood will come, bogya bε ba (there will be bloodshed). They call us (No. 7 Anyampa) tu ahen, si ahen. Bantuma—King town—Ahenkro because of Anyampafo. They (We) enstool and destool a King. If they are looking for a King and Anyampafo is not involved, they will never enstool the chief. They call them (us) Anomansafo. If we call a King to an event and he does not come, we will destool him. Benya Deity is in the water; it is located up there. This is where all the birds assemble. They call them Anomansafo, tu ahen, si ahen. The sea used to be very far away. We walked through dark dirt before we got to the white sand. Today, the water has come home. All the Deities have gone away. The sea is coming. Most of the Deities have ended up in the sea. Every place has its tradition. So those who say, we don't have tradition don't know it or have not bothered to ask."

Ama: "Why don't they come and join Asafo?"

Egya Akɔdεε: "It is the church! There was no church in the world then. Today, church has destroyed everything! I am a Roman Catholic; every Sunday, I go to church for communion. However, if something happens and they say they are going to enstool a chief, or someone is coming, going to take over the land, can I say because of church, I can't go? Is that right? Do I want them to take the land? At first our Ancestors, did both; they made offerings to the Roman deities, St. Anthony. Today, it is all gone. They are not here in the land. The things that our Ancestors did, today it is not there. They will not come. Their mothers will not let them (their children) come. There was no church then. The Elders put me in charge of a Deity. All the Elders in the town, they have placed me in charge. Our Deity, Nana Atrede, he is the one who when we carry (enstool) a King, we take him there to bathe him in it."

Ama: "Where did the name Anyampa come from?"

Egya Akɔdɛɛ: "It came from nowhere. All of us, it is from Edna Butwe eku asankoma. Kɛtɛkrɛnkɛ. Abokyir kakra. I have seen you somewhere, I have married you and had children. All the children do not take your blood. So, if I come and there is a drum, Asafo there, my children, is it not for them? It is the ebusua that they belong. My children will be Anomansafo or Abesefo or Ankobeafo, like that. Your posuban identifies you. Nobody will ask you to remove it. Unless war when it could be burnt. We have lots of names and appellations. We are Anyampafo; we are Anomansafo, when you drink us (kill us), we will never finish; Butwe eku, Kɛtɛkrɛnkɛ. These are our appellations. If we are going somewhere and you don't mention them, I will not go. I will not allow you to pass, until you have given me the names. Then there is singing, dancing, rivalry songs, all to destroy you."

[Egya Akɔdɛɛ gave me an awakening one day after he explained his role]:

Egya Akɔdɛɛ: "The food that they bring, the things that they bring; I am in the room (posuban); I don't come out; and I watch the Elders. The drums that they have played, we go to the bush to get parts to fix them. When they buy new ones, we must go to the bush and bathe them and sacrifice chicken, sheep for them. Then the Asafo is here in the open. We have different responsibilities, like Asafo hen. I am Asafoafua—custodian. When the crowd sets out . . . my father was in the front, where the flag is. My father nominated me to replace him. When the crowd is going with their songs and all their noise, when they are going, they are going to come back again. They are going to perform amandze (customs) there. Like at first, they would fire the gun, pi-po, pi-po, pi-po pooo!!! When they finish, they will come back. When they finish, the food that they prepare, the leftover trash, we clean up after them. Every garbage that is left behind in the land, we clean up till the next year."

[Since Egya Akɔdɛɛ was the custodian of the posuban and cared for all the items in them, including the drums, I asked if he would take me to their posuban and show me their drums.]

Egya Akɔdɛɛ: "Women are not allowed in there."

Ama: "Why?" I did not show my surprise and disappointment.

Egya Akɔdɛɛ: "Wo bu hɔn nsa" ("They break their hands" [they menstruate]).

I got quiet. I had read works by scholars who remarked that women were not allowed to play drums in certain parts of Africa. Francis Bebey proclaims that

> Because the drum is, in certain circumstances, equated with a man (and a rather exceptional man, at that, whose powerful voice can send messages far and wide), women must consequently treat it with the same respect that they show towards their menfolk. No woman would dream of beating her husband in public (even though she may occasionally do so in private!), nor may she beat the drum in the village square. In some African societies, women are not even permitted to touch a drum under any circumstances. (1975, 14)

I remembered that some people scorned my father for teaching his three daughters how to drum. However, this was the first time in my life someone told me I could not see drums, let alone touch them because I am a woman!

I respected Egya Akɔdɛɛ's contention and chose not to push it any further or challenge him. I did not tell him that I was premenopausal—too much information. What difference would that have made, anyway? Neither did I tell him that I am a drummer, that I have been playing drums most of my life, and have been teaching drumming to students for many years. *Akokɔ de awhete-ahwetee a, ohu gyansakyi boapea*, "When the chicken scratches ceaselessly, it sees mystical objects." I respected his decision also because *Wofeefee afunu ani a, wohunu saman*, "If you play with the eyelids of a dead person, you will see a ghost." Egya Akɔdɛɛ's response rattled me. I was not happy. However, I behaved like *Aboa kɔkɔsɛkyi*, the vulture that acts stupid in order to live longer. I consider myself an empowered and enlightened woman who does not allow the words of others to define or bother me. So, I thought such a pronouncement would not bother me. But it did. It challenged my sense of self. It hurt my pride. His claim and assertion that somehow, I might be "unclean" because I am a woman and thus not allowed or worthy of seeing their drums, threw me into entangled emotions. This was our fifteenth meeting over eight months, and I assumed I had earned his trust to the point where such "restrictions" and concerns would not apply. But this was not about trust. Who I am, my gender, my womanness was the problem! My womanness defined what information I could access and the knowledge I would produce—what I would be allowed to see. How does our gender limit our access to information. What information is left out during our research? Do we even know what is left out? Of course, we cannot possibly know everything in the field, but how could we determine whether the information we receive is accurate, skewed, or partial? With that in mind, should we even define ourselves as experts? *Tweaa*! Capable of carrying a child because I am a woman, nurturing a life in my womb for nine long, painful months—tender breasts, sore nipples, cramping, sickness, raging hormones, carrying around additional weight, and delivering a child successfully, but not allowed to see drums because I am a woman! *Tweaa*! Isn't it ɔ*baa na ɔwo barima*, "a woman gives birth to a man"? *Tweaaaa*! Is this why the Akan say, *Akokɔbedeɛ nim adekyeɛ nso otie no wɔ onini ano*, "The hen knows when dawn breaks but she waits for the announcement from the rooster"? Again, *Akokɔ de awhete-ahwetee a, ohu gyansakyi boapea*, "When the chicken scratches ceaselessly, it sees mystical objects," so I left it alone. I expressed my frustration and discontent in my journal later that day:

> Gender ééé iiiii i
> Female
> Woman
> Whatever you call yourself
> ɔ*baa basia*
> You are a pain
> An obstruction
> An abstraction
> You
> Narrower of experience! (October 17, 2016).

I did not ask to see the drums again. I learned a lot from Egya Akɔdeɛ Afful. He was the first to tell me about the conflict between the "church and state"—one of the main causes of Asafo's demise. He was the first to tell me about why children do not join Asafo. He was the very first to share that one's posuban identifies her/him.

When I returned to the United States, I often asked a friend, Mr. Fiifi Essel, to visit Egya Afful with food items, medication for his eyes, ears, rheumatoid arthritis, and some money. I spoke with him on the phone whenever Essel arrived at his house. This past year, in January 2021, when Essel got there, he called in a solemn voice to say Egya Akɔdεε Afful had "walked on" to join our Ancestors. He explained, "When the people in the area saw me, because they knew I had come to see Egya Akɔdεε Afful and that I had come on your behalf, they started wailing and followed me to his house. His daughter greeted me, led me to a room and gave me the *amandzeε* news that Egya Akɔdεε Afful had 'gone to the village' a month earlier." I cried and cried. I felt guilty I had not asked Fiifi to reach out to him in months. I asked Fiifi to give the items to his daughter, an entrepreneur in the fishing industry. Buooo. . . . Bueeeeiiiiiii! *Agya-é! Ena-é! ɔbenten-é! Eno-é! ɔdeyeε-é! Asomasi-é! yéé*! Hmm. . . . Ah! Egya Akɔdεε Afful. Anyampa Asafo ba. Ah. Dammirifua Du-é! *Owuo begya hwan*? "Who will death spare?" *Owuo ne yεn reko, ɔpatafoɔ ne hwan*? "Death is fighting with us, who will mediate?" Du-é! *Owuo nim adeε kyε*. Death does not know how to share fairly." Hyiee! Du-é-oooooo. . . . Ah. Anyampa Asafo. You who enstool and destool a King. Our *ɔdehyeε* royal has slipped through our fingers. Death has robbed us-ooooo! Egya Akɔdεε Afful, you were my first Asafo scholar. Bu-ééé! Mmm. . . .

What Uncle Ebo, the Radio Host, Said: "The Dutch Organized Them into Battalions"

I had my third experience with "Asafo" song on October 6, 2016, while on a visit with Uncle Ebo,[2] the host of *Asafo FM*, a radio program about Elmina *abakɔsεm* and Asafo.[3] He also worked at the Municipal Assembly at Elmina. I walked to Uncle Ebo's house, and his wife directed me to his office. On my walk over, I thought about how best to relay my *amandzeε* mission to him. What if my purpose was not interesting enough? What if my interest in Asafo sounded ridiculous? I had heard that Elmina Asafo was on the brink of collapsing. Would he admit that? The three-kilometer walking and thinking allowed me to work through all these concerns. By the time I arrived at Uncle Ebo's office, I had practiced what to say and how to present it.

I met two men and one woman at the office who asked why I was looking for Uncle Ebo. At the end of my speech, one of the gentlemen left and entered another office. He came back out almost immediately. "This is Uncle Ebo," the other gentleman pointed to him. Uncle Ebo had a grin on his face. I was confused. "I had to be sure nobody was after me," he mused. He sat next to me. I told him I studied *abakɔsɛm* and that I was interested in studying Asafo songs that protested slavery. He thought about my inquiry for a moment, and asked, *Ayɛ kradow*, "Are you ready?" He proceeded to tell me about the people and history of Elmina. He asserted that the Anomansafo, people of Elmina, are not Fante; they are Asante who migrated from Tachiman and settled there. This information was contrary to what I had learned thus far about the history of Elmina; however, he supported his claim by citing the role of Kwaa Amankwah, the founder of Anomansa (now Elmina).[4]

After a short discussion, Uncle Ebo started a song and stopped as abruptly as he started. He explained that the song was an Asafo song that members performed at a river, Nana Bonta, before crossing it. I asked if he could sing it again. He replied that he would sing it at our meeting the following day. As I walked back to town, I tried to recall the words and movement of the song (example 4, Elmina Asafo *ndwom* "*Yɛyɛ ɛdenafo*" 🎵).

Uncle Ebo and I met the next day. We sat on a wooden deck across the Gramsdell Spot, a bar and an eatery overlooking the Atlantic Ocean. It was a hot day. The ocean roared, rolled, tumbled, crashed, and threw its waves at the mercy of the sand. Against this backdrop, Uncle Ebo spoke:

Asafo was organized because of intertribal wars. It is from Asebu. Obarima Osam brought it to Elmina. It was there before the Dutch arrived, but the Dutch helped them to organize into groups because they became large, uncontrollable, and were creating problems.[5]

Each group had about 1,500 members. The Dutch organized them into battalions with a leader. We had ten Asafo groups. They were given numbers by Dutch government to identify them. Initially, Asafo Wombir was No. 1 (personal communication with author, Elmina, October 7, 2016).

According to Uncle Ebo, Wombir became No. 4 because they were late to the meeting organized by the Dutch. The Dutch assigned the groups according to the time they arrived. After the meeting the numbers were assigned: No. 1 Ankobea, No. 2 Akyemfo, No. 3 Akyem-Nkodwo, No. 4 Wombir, No. 5 Abese (also Abesi), No. 6 Alatamanfo (also Allade, Adjadie), No. 7 Anyampa, No. 8 Brofommba, No. 9 Maa Wore, and No. 10 Akrampafo.[6]

According to Uncle Ebo, these warriors existed before the Dutch seized Elmina Castle from the Portuguese in 1637; however, the group became large and uncontrollable, so the Dutch helped organize them into smaller units. Uncle Ebo did not repeat the song.

What Agya Kwasi Badu, the Savvy Cobbler, Said: "Asafo is Dying"

I walked and wore out my shoes so often that I developed relationships with shoemakers (cobblers) along the way. The first shoemaker who mended my sandals, Agya Kwasi Badu, had a small table on Kwamena Ansah Street. I stopped by his table one day after hobbling on one bare foot for an hour. Probably by how I walked, spoke, or was dressed, he figured I was a stranger to Elmina; so, while I waited, he asked about my mission at Elmina. I told him about my search for Asafo *ndwom* and asked if he knew any Asafo members in town who would speak with me. He responded with a popular Ghanaian Fante hymn (example 5, "*Hɛn Nananom*" ♫).[7]

Badu began, "The Asafo is dying because of church, too much church. All our traditions are labeled 'fetish' (*abosomsɛm*). Nobody patronizes. The people are discouraged. We have lost all our traditions to European ways that we can't even emulate properly." I immediately thought about Homi Bhabha's "mimicry" (1994) and Charles Grant's analysis of the effects of "partial reform" (1792). Badu continued, "Some Asafo members have joined churches and can't seem to distinguish between the two, though the Bible says, 'Do what is due God, and do what is due Asafo." He was referring to Jesus' teachings to his disciples, "Give back to Caesar what is Caesar's and to God what is God's" (Mark 12:17). He pointed out an older gentleman across the street. The gentleman was the flagbearer for the No. 4 Wombir Asafo. According to Badu, flagbearers are responsible for displaying and dancing the company flag. "They can enter the spiritual realm and communicate with Ancestors. While they dance, a group of about six men guard and prevent them from falling on the ground or being seized by an enemy." I walked over to the gentleman and presented my mission. He spoke nonchalantly.

The Wombir Asafo man explained: "Dispute between the chieftaincy and Asafo companies for over fifteen years has brought our Asafo to its knees. Also, too much church. We defended and fought for Elmina. Without us, Elmina won't be Elmina. But today, they have forgotten. All our traditions are labeled fetish. Every Asafo has a specific responsibility. Ankobea No. 1 played the drums to signal the beginning and end to Bakatue." At this brief meeting, I learned that No. 4 Wombir has more flags than any other company at Elmina; they have flags for every occasion. I learned from Badu that the gentleman never fought in any wars, though his Ancestors did during the town's wars with Cape Coast and other enemies in the early 1900s. Agya Badu was the first person to tell me about the role of the Asafo flagbearer.

What the Late Auntie Monica Said: "They Put Him on the Coffin . . . Esiwdo Is Where They Meet"

Auntie Monica started her reflections on Asafo with a version of the Elmina Asafo *ndwom* that I heard. She was the first woman to give me extensive information about Asafo, especially as it pertains to their funerals. The two women I interacted with earlier directed me to men because they claimed that the men knew more than they did, as if to validate the saying, *Akokɔbedeɛ nim adekyeɛ nso otie no wɔ onini ano*, "The hen knows when dawn breaks, but she waits for the announcement from the rooster"; not Auntie Monica. She was visually impaired and lived in a house behind the No. 5 Abese *posuban* and *esiwdo*, the meeting place for the Abese Asafo company. The house was adjacent to the Elmina Shrine. She was feisty and confident. Her responses were interspersed with songs.

Auntie Monica began, "This is a song that Ahomka FM plays before they give the 6:00 p.m. news. They play with drums." She sang an extended version of "*Yɛyɛ ɛdenafo*" (example 6 🔊). She was the fourth person so far to sing this song, but she was the only woman, and she was the first to reference the accompanied drumming. I could not imagine how the drums would align with the pulse of the song, because it was declamatory and nonmetered.

> Auntie Monica: "Borɔntɔ is a river. It is a river. Before you get to Elmina Beach Resort Hotel, it is there.
> Ama: "Why did they sing the song?"
> Auntie Monica: "Well, they sang the song to the river. It is for us. So, we can use it."
> Ama: "Is it a God or a Deity?"
> Auntie Monica: "You know in our African belief, stones and rivers are believed to have powers. So, we believe it is a God."

Ama: "Why did they sing that song? Where does it come from? Where are its roots? What are its 'matters that have come and gone?'"

Auntie Monica: "Oh, it is like any other song. That is what it is."

Ama: "Do you know who wrote it and made it?"

Auntie Monica: "No."

Ama: "I have heard people sing it, but I have not really listened to it well."

Auntie Monica: "They sing it, especially when they launch Bakatue. They usually play it on FM very much."

Ama: "When they play it, it means what? What does it do?"

Auntie Monica: "It means it is reminding us. I remember when I was a schoolgirl, I used to go to minstrel choir; it is a choral musical group. While we were in the group, they said they were going to open a Tema branch. So, we came from here to Tema (a suburb of Accra). Dunkwa people and others from all over came. Our mother choir is Sekondi (a city to the west of Elmina); they all came. We met at Tema. Anyway, it is a type of song that identifies us. You see?"

Ama: "As what?"

Auntie Monica: "As Edena people. So, when we went, this one is singing; this one is singing; this one is singing. Every choir sang its song. When it got to us, we started. When they were teaching us, we used to play around. But we sang it well; we started slowly and then as it went, then as it was going, the momentum was rising, was rising. We sang aaaa . . . the moment we finished, 'Encore, encore, encore, encore!' We did not know all those there were Edena people. 'Encore, encore!' We even cried. Because of happiness, we cried. So, it is an identification thing. Anyone who is serious and sings it, is from Edena. They call here Abese Esiwdo."

Ama: "What is esiwdo?"

Auntie Monica: "Where they meet at their posuban. Where the Abese Asafo meet."

Ama: "Where are the Abese people?"

Auntie Monica: "They are there. They wear green. When something happens, this is where they meet. Like when they have a meeting or there is an issue."

Ama: "They don't meet if there is no issue?"

Auntie Monica: "No. The time that they really meet is when one of their members dies. When they come, they play Asafo aaaa. . . . When they finish, then the dead person's son, they put powder on him and put him on the coffin with the dead body in it. They pick him up together with the coffin. The music they play is very interesting. This place is busy, no time at all. You will even dance. One happened about a year ago. They played for a long time. Their main thing is when they are going to bury their dead member. As for that day there is no time; if it is in the morning, they would pick him up, roam the town with him in the coffin, while the son was still sitting on it. Then they would take it to Tarkwa house. When you get there, you will see a marble stone. A Portuguese who died was buried there, by the road by the Tarkwa house. If you go and ask for the marble stone, they will show you. So, they would go there and put the casket on it. Then they would go and drink. They would leave the coffin and the boy sitting on it. When they finished, they would come and pick it up; sometimes it would be around evening before they got to the burying place."

Ama: "So, if I am looking for someone who can teach me about Asafo, their songs, and their 'matters that have come and gone,' could I get someone to teach me?"

Auntie Monica: "At first, when Asafo used to play. But today, our everything has become chapel, chapel, and all our everything is lost. A schoolboy could even teach you then. When we were children, they taught us. I remember they taught us akɔm dancing. I have been an ɔkɔmfo priest before. We danced for a long time. They have left everything, even wedding arrangements, they say it is fetishism. Everything is lost. But the Asante are not like that. So, when the Pope came, he bypassed us and went to Asante. This is the first place that Roman Catholic Church came in Ghana, but he passed and went to Kumase. Yes. There is nothing for us to show. He passed us to Kumase."

That the Pope passed their town and went straight to Kumase disturbed Auntie Monica. She blamed it on the fact that Elmina had lost "its traditions to European ways" and, especially, to Christianity. She was not the first to connect the slow demise of Asafo to Christianity. Christianity and its effects would come up again and again in the many discussions I had with others. Many stated in Fante, *Asɔr asɛɛ hɛn amandze nyinara*, "Church has destroyed all our traditions." Auntie Monica was the first person to tell me about how Asafo members buried their dead. Her vivid description of those events fascinated me so much that funerals, especially those for Asafo members, became one of the many spaces I walked; often, experiencing live Asafo drumming. The more I learned about these Asafo traditions, the more excited I got about them.

When I left Auntie Monica's house that day, I walked to the Tarkwa house that she spoke about. It was a huge brick house located on the main Elmina street in the Mount Plaisant District. The house was built by the Dutch and used Dutch architecture. In front of the house was a cement slab, as she indicated. I asked the neighbors across the street if they knew the significance of the cement slab. They did not. I shared what I had learned with them. I stood at the spot and recalled Auntie Monica's words: "As for that day there was no time; if it was in the morning, they would pick him up, roam the town with him in the coffin, while the son was sitting on it. Then they would take it to Tarkwa house. . . . So, they would go there and put the casket on it. Then they would go and drink. They would leave the coffin and the boy sitting on it. When they finished, they would come and pick it up; sometimes it would be around evening before they got to the burying place." One thing that Auntie Monica did not mention in her description was the singing of songs and drumming that accompanied such ceremonies. So, as I stood in that space, I imagined them singing the only Asafo song I had heard thus far: *Yɛyɛ Edenafo oo . . . Eburbur eburbur . . . Yɛyɛ Edenafo oo.* Throughout my walk at Elmina, I heard different versions of this Asafo song at political rallies, on the radio, and in other contexts. One of my favorite versions was a choral arrangement by a school choir.

Months later, I stopped by Auntie Monica to update her on my search. She was not at her usual place on the porch outside her house, nor was she on the cement porch in the corner wedged between hers and the adjoining house. I waited around a bit until a young girl came out of the house. She had a blank stare on her face when I asked for Auntie Monica. "Auntie Monica passed away," she replied. Bué! Goosebumps. Tingly toes. I stared back at her, then mumbled, "My condolences." After what seemed like thirty minutes of standing in one place, I walked away in silence. Buéé iiii! I cried. As I walked away, I hummed a Fante lullaby Auntie Monica sang for me.

> *Woana ne baa nye 'yi*
> *Egya Kwesi ne ba*
> *Wɔnye nn' nkɔ abɛ ase*
> *Abɛ ase wɔ nsɔɛ*
> *Wɔnye no nkɔ onyina ase*
> *Onyina bobu abɔ me ba*
> *Abɔ me ba*

Abɔ me ba
Abɔ me ba

(Whose child is this
Mr. Kwesi's child
Take him to the palm tree
There are thorns under the palm tree
Take him to the silk-cotton tree
The silk-cotton tree will fall on him
Fall on my child
Fall on my child
Fall on my child)

Tears ran down my face. Auntie Monica *Damirifua Due*! *Due ne amanehunu*, Auntie Monica, my condolences. Condolences for your suffering. *Ewuradze mfa wo kra nsie.* "May the Spirit of Life keep your soul." *Owuo begya hwan?* "Who will death spare?" Ah! *Owuo ama yɛn ahotɔ abɔ yɛn.* Mean death, you have stripped us of peace! Bué. Cry . . . y. This walk is becoming too difficult. *Nanso obi mfa ne nsa nto ɔyarefoɔ aduane mu nyi ne nsa.* "One does not put her hand in the food of a sick person and withdraw the hand." Crying has not killed anyone. I kept walking.

What Egya Kwamena Amissah, the King's Attendant, Said: "Asafo, They Go to *Asa*"

I learned about a gentleman of the No. 4 Wombir Asafo from Auntie Monica. He knew a lot about Kingship matters, the politics, history, and policies of Elmina because he was an attendant at the *ahenfie* palace and worked closely with the Elmina King. The first time I met Egya Kwamena Amissah, he asked for an offering to perform a prayer, which he offered at the front steps of his liquor store. He gave me detailed information about the various rituals associated with their annual festival, Bakatue. At our next meeting, he talked about Kingship, Asafo, and sang several Asafo songs, including "*Yɛyɛ ɛdenafo.*"

Ama: "What is Asafo?"
Egya Amissah: "Asafo, in the olden days, they said they were soldiers. Those who go to asa."
Ama: "What is asa?"

Egya Amissah: "Fight, war. If anybody tells you that this person is going to asa, then the person is going to fight/war. So Asafo are those who go to war. They protect the society. If a fight is coming, it is these people who they place around at different points. We have ten groups. The Asafo protect this land, so if war is coming, whatever is coming, it is the Asafo. The chief directs them. 'You go here; you go there.' There was a lot of fighting earlier on. When the Europeans came, there was a lot of fighting. The Asafo fought with the Europeans." [That the Asafo fought with the Europeans was contrary to what Akɔdeɛ had shared with me.]

Ama: "Why did they fight with the Europeans?"

Egya Amissah: "Because of land poll issue. The Europeans thought they should take money from the Edena people; the people said they would not agree. So, it brought war. Asides from that if another town wants to come and war with us, the spirits here showed us. Remember the shrine that I said, if there is no one there, it shakes? There is a priest there. It is not the priest inside. There is one outside, it does not dance. The Edena people and the Fante fought."

Ama: "Are Edena people not Fante?"

Egya Amissah: "Well, there are Fante and there are Fante. You see that the way we talk is different . . . so the Fante and Edena fought."

Ama: "Why did they fight?"

Egya Amissah: "What our Elders said was that they were there and then the spirit came to the shrine and shook the structure. Those passing by saw that aaaa . . . a God has come into the shrine. Then they called the ɔmanhene King and the spirit told the ɔmanhene that the Fante have decided that they are coming to take this land because where they were, they couldn't find a good place to put their boats. Here at Edena, we have lots of places where we can keep our boats. So, they would come and fight us and take the land. The Fante know that we do not play drums on Tuesdays; we don't fire guns on Tuesdays, so they had decided to come on Tuesday and fight the Edena people. So, the Spirit told them, 'Go! If they come on Tuesday, fire that gun! If they come on Tuesday, play the drum. I, the God, will knock them down, destroy them.'" [Egya Amissah described in detail how Elmina Asafo fought and defeated the Fante.] "When the Edenafo defeated them and the fighting cooled down, the Spirit entered someone and told them, 'When I said it, someone did not believe me, what I said, I did not turn it, change it. What I said that when they come, I will knock them over, I did not go back on my word.'"

Other teachers corroborated what I had learned thus far about Elmina Asafo companies, their roots in Asebu, how they acquired their numbers, the role of Asafo in defending the town against the Fante, and details about the fight that brought the Asante to the coast. Other authors have documented this latter fact (Baah 2001; Duah 1953; Shumway 2011). I learned from members of Elmina Ankobea, Wombir, Abese, and Anyampa Asafo.

What ɔdomankoma Kwamena Kyerɛma Pra, the Divine Lead Drummer, Sang and Said: "Asafo Is a Spirit"

Journal Entries
I started dance lessons today. Learned about the spiritual nature of Asafo dance—the different spirits. Asafo comes from dwarfs. Need to explore this further. Talked excessively about religion and how it has corrupted most "matters that have come and gone." My teacher worked as a public-school teacher, then resigned after his study request was denied. He knows my father and has been involved with cultural programming since the 1980s. Did a warmup that really, really stretched me. Rushed to Yayoh's African history class. Learned about the class' fieldwork preparation to Kormantse. I will seek permission to join them; however, I will depart from Kormantse daily (Tuesday, 1st November 2016).

I went to dance today. Did few warm-ups. Togbe or Tokoe. Warm up included movements from kpanlogo and tokoe. Asked to illustrate Adowa dance. I felt awkward. Later, learned about this Cape Coast No. 2 Asafo's first song call to performance, "Nyew Nana Nyame" (example 7 ♫).

Very powerful song. I had a difficult time articulating the declamatory style. I learned that a major drummer for Asafo had died (Wednesday, 2nd November 2016).

In November 2016, I started dance lessons at Cape Coast with Divine Master Drummer ɔdomankoma Kyerɛma Kwamena Pra. He is a member of Cape Coast No. 2 Anaafo Asafo, who can communicate with the spiritual world through drumming. Weeks into our lessons, I told him I wanted to devote a few of the sessions to Asafo *ndwom* and dance. On the first day of my Asafo lesson, he pulled out a blackboard and asked, "What comes to mind when I say Asafo?" By this time, I had learned a lot from my teachers at Elmina, so I replied, "Costumes, dancers, warriors, drumming, singers."

ɔdomankoma Pra replied, "Asafo formed because of nomadic life, migration, people in search of fertile land, rivers. There was no pipe-borne water at the time. Every river has fertile land for water and food. You have life. People wanted to become powerful. Migration led to fighting. Why not organize a group to defend the community? Organize the people to fight—how to fight with rocks, whoever is the strongest survives." I learned about the different training tactics warriors used to prepare for war, including a dance performed in a circle by the sea during the full moon to see who is the strongest, and *atetar*, a challenge between two boys. Whoever threw the other down was the leader. "Also, to prepare for war, warriors ate herbs, some of which was mixed with menstrual blood from a girl's first menses and bathed in special herbs to withstand gunshots. They provide many services for the society: community developers and builders, protect the state, some have spiritual powers."

He elaborated on the spiritual aspect of Asafo. According to him there are about six spiritual entities: *suman* (protective spirits), *bosom* (Gods of trees, rivers, rocks), *mmotia* (dwarfs who teach about herbs), *samanta* (elves), *nsu-mba* (water spirits), *ewu-akɔ* (ancestral spirits). Drumming is very important. Each Asafo company has a drum call that can be played to mount a specific priestess. He also told me about the different offices in Asafo: the priest, captain, drummer, flagbearers, and others. He would not teach me Asafo dance because it enters the spiritual realm and could be dangerous. Again, I did not challenge him because *Onifrani mfa abufuo wa kwaeɛ ase*, "A blind person should not become angry whilst in the forest." Furthermore, *aboa kɔkɔsɛkyi se ɔde ne kwasea pɛ nyinkyɛ*. ɔdomankoma Pra was the first to teach me the patterns of the various drums and bells that accompany *ndwom* and dance; he was the first to invite me to an Asafo funeral (see chapter 6). By the time I witnessed my first live performance of Asafo *ndwom*, I knew the songs were declamatory and responsorial and that the ensemble used four drums.

Adwene ni ɔkro tirim, "Wisdom in not in one person's head." I continued to walk and was able to patch together a narrative about Asafo's history and significance in society. Every step I took helped peel off a different layer that encased Asafo, taking me closer to its *ndwom*.

Asafo
I started my walk
Scholars
Yɛyɛ Edenafo

Hɛn Nananom
Who will carry you
You are spirit
Go to *asa*
Posuban identifies you
Asafo
They say you are dying

I saw your *Posuban*
Shrines, posts
Hidden behind funeral tents
Taxi, tables, groundnut basins
Bowls of *bambara* beans outstage you
They say your essence is fading
Christianity has silenced you
Outdrummed your drums
Ankobeafo
The cock crows
Ko-kro-kooo
You continue to sleep
Anyampafo
Wo tu ahen, si ahen
You enstool and destool a King
A King is waiting
To be enstooled
Bathed at Nana Atrede
You lost a royalty
Death has robbed us-ooooo

Asafo
Aboa kɔkɔsɛkyi se ɔde ne kwasea pɛ nyinkyɛ
Can you hear me calling

I
A Woman!

Asafo
Owuo begya hwan?
Who will death spare
My first Asafo scholars
My first Asafo scholars
Brilliant
Du-é-oooooo . . . Mmm . . .

Woana ne ba baa nyi

Still stepping

CHAPTER TWO

Knocking

History Walking

Ani a ɛhunuu tetehɔ na ɛnni hɔ,
na aso a ɛtee tetehɔ asɛm deɛ ɛwɔ hɔ
(The eyes that witnessed the past were not there,
but ears that heard the past are there)

—Akan proverb

The past is made by walking

—Yarimar Bonilla

Wɔmfa nyɛ hɔn nanom 🔊
Wɔmfa nyɛ hɔn egyanom
Adze a wɔdze yɛ Kyirem e
Wɔmfa nyɛ hɔn nanom
Wɔnnyɛ mbanyin bi a!
(May it be done to your mothers
May it be done to your fathers
What you've done to Kyirem
May it be done to your mothers
You are not men at all!)

—Kormantse Asafo *ndwom*, "*Wɔmfa nyɛ hɔn Nanom*"

Kɔ-kɔɔ-kɔ (Knock, Knock): When and How I Entered Kormantse

I traveled to Kormantse for the first time on December 9, 2016, with the Africana Studies class from the University of Cape Coast (UCC). The students went there to conduct ethnographic research on the town's history, shrine, Gods, family lineages, and politics.[1] I was interested in learning about the history and *ndwom* of their Asafo warrior organization.[2] Though the professor of the class had finalized protocols with the King and the Elders of the town, I decided to walk to the *ahenfie* palace and introduce myself. *Obisafoɔ nto kwan*, "She who asks for directions never misses her way," so I asked for directions from an older gentleman who escorted me through a network of paths to the *ahenfie*. From the main highway, we walked through a small market, made a left turn onto a lane that ran (runs?) through the center of the town (their main street) by many buildings, including the meeting place for the lineage Elders and King, houses displaying colorful images, several kiosks, tabletop shops, a church, women, men, and children playing.

We arrived at a big unfinished two-storied cement building and met three gentlemen. The building was considered *mmrantse dan*, "young men's building." I greeted the men and told them I was part of the group from the "varsity." I indicated the purpose of my visit and my interest in Asafo *ndwom*. They told me the King was not available and that their Asafo was dying and no longer functioning as it had in the past. They shared a brief history of the town, their wars with their neighbor, Nkum, the Asante war, their mother Goddess Eminsa, and a brief history of a nearby fort.[3] The three men stated that their town was Kormantse No. 1, Bentsir ("head of the building"), and their color is red.[4] After discussing other topics, one of the gentlemen started *"Kormantse na Abandze,"* an Asafo song that had been popularized by the Ghanaian Hi-Life singer, C. K. Mann (example 8 ♫).[5]

They said the song served as an archive for a bloody conflict between two neighboring towns, Kormantse Nkum and Abandze. The song, as they performed it, did not resemble the pulse-driven Hi-Life style version of C. K. Mann. It was declamatory, with no specific pulse, and performed in a responsorial style. After sitting with the men for a while, I left for a meeting with the Elders of the town and the students.

Here on the ground for the first time, I was nervous about this work on Asafo *ndwom* and Kormantse as a site because it had not been my original plan of study. *ɛmmrɛ dani a, wo so dane wo ho bi*, "When time changes, you too change yourself," the Akan say. So, I improvised along the way. Fortunately, I did not have to relinquish my housing, which was now about a sixteen-kilometer ride on public transportation. On my first walk along the busy Accra-Takoradi Highway to find accommodation for the weekend, one of the three gentlemen at the *ahenfie* offered to perform several Asafo songs for me. *Obi se ɔbɛsoa wo a, wonse sɛ: 'mɛ nante,'* "If someone says she would carry you, you don't say, 'I will walk.'" I accepted his offer. He said he would have to come to the hotel because he did not want to draw the attention of other residents. At the time, I did not know about the politics of and repercussions for performing Asafo songs, especially by Christians. We agreed on a time and date and negotiated a fee, which I paid. He did not show up.

After settling in a hotel with my children, we visited a section of the town on a steep hill overlooking lower Kormantse township, the Accra-Takoradi Highway, and the Atlantic Ocean. From this vantage point, I saw the town's layout, the sea, and the different fishing boats on the sea. I learned that this is Kokoado, their first settlement. Over the days, weeks, and months, I walked up this hill, and through different parts of the town, embarking on memory walks, history walks, walking interviews, and listening walks observing, eating, singing, sharing stories, mourning, running alongside a hearse, walking through a burial site, broadcasting the songs I had learned at their communication center, and teaching Kormantse schoolchildren what I had learned about Asafo *ndwom* and *abakɔsɛm*.

December 12, 2016—History Walk I

Because "history is folded into landscape and into soundscape" (Ogborn 2012) and the "past is made by walking" (Bonilla 2011), I joined the group of twenty students on an "*abakɔsɛm* walk" through Kormantse town to learn about the various shrines and other landmarks in the town. The trek was a qualitative one.[6] In this type of walk, one is in complete awareness of the surroundings and consciously explores the landscape while sensorially experiencing it. In this type of participatory walk, familiarity with the environment is deepened, which allows one to envision and experience the landscape differently, evoking senses, heightening sense of place, and connecting deeply to the landscape.

I arrived late because the public transport that drove me from Cape Coast to Kormantse was delayed at a security checkpoint, so unlike the students who walked up the clayey hill, I ran to the meeting site through the neighboring town via a tarred road.[7] I later learned from a lady, who would become my friend and one of my mentors, that the neighboring town was Nkum, their rival town, and I should avoid passing through it. Our

Elders say, *Wo nsa hyɛ obi anum a, yɛ mpae na pampam*, "If your hand is in someone's mouth, you don't strike the person's head" (the person would bite off your hand). Out of courtesy, and most importantly because I did not intend to offend citizens of the town, jeopardize my connections with Kormantse No. 1 town, and my study, I took her advice seriously.

Prior to this *abakɔsɛm* walk, the students, their professors, and I had met with the Kings of the town. They shared the town's migratory history, its Gods and family lineages, and conflicts with their neighbors. In a discussion about the significance of the three bottles (*amodaka*) that were presented before approaching the Kings, and before I was introduced as a professor with an interest in Asafo *abakɔsɛm* and *ndwom*, we were told, "When the Elders were coming from Ngyedum, they traveled with three Asafo groups. They were holding a lot of items, so here at Kormantse, we have three Asafo groups—*amfɛrfo*, *kyiremfo*, and *adzewafo*; the three bottles represent the three groups" (Supi Kobena Wombir, Focus group discussion, December 12, 2016, Kormantse, Ghana).[8] We also learned from the Queen Mother's spokesman, Anointing, that Asafo fought and defended the land.

"It is the government that has made our traditions go down, not the church people. They like to blame the church people. But it is because, at first, when someone's house was on fire or when someone's child was missing, they would sound the drum and the Asafo members would go to the rescue. Today when someone's child is missing, she goes to the police station. Today, there is zoomlion, so Asafo members do not have to clean up the town. So, let's not blame the church folk. Let's blame the government itself."[9]

One of the Elders, Safohen Nana Odum III, who would later become my primary mentor, shared another interesting perspective about Asafo. "The English took our Asafo traditions and made it the army and police. The three Asafo companies have their own colors—*amfɛrfo*, they wear danger, red; it is they who led when the fight comes; then there is *adzewafo*, they are second, so when the fight comes, they step in and help the *amfɛrfo*; there is *kyiremfo*, they wear *duawusu*, black cloth; they are Elders who are behind. It is from us that the British took the tradition away." I asked the group whether Kormantse had fought before, how many wars, with whom, and if they won the fight:

Respondent 1: "Yes, we have fought wars."
Respondent 2: "A lot."
Respondent 3: "We fought with Nkum in 1873 at Tsetse Nkwanta."

Respondent 4: "Never defeated."
Respondent 5: "We are warriors!"

This was my first encounter with Kormantse Asafo, and I was already getting important information. *Edwa bɛba a, efiri anɔpa,* "If a good market would come, it starts in the morning," the Akan say. This gathering and meeting with Kings added momentum to my research. I became more excited about my topic and looked forward to disentangling the different strands of Asafo.

The Kokoado landscape was dry, hard, rough, and rocky. The rocks were sharp, so sharp that though I had shoes on, they still poked me. I noticed that the children had developed ways of walking these sharp and rocky landscape with much ease. They glided and ran laughing and playing different games with their friends. I envied them. We walked through several pathways and stopped at different points where our guides provided information. At each stop, the leaders shared a short narrative or reflection and instructed us on how to look and read the site. We learned about the history of the town, the various landmarks, the buildings, and shrines and took in the stories and memories of the people. The land held people's memories, we were told. It was a sensory-filled walk.[10]

I met the group at the *posuban* (military post).[11] In front of the post was a cement platform on which stood a statue of one of their Asafo female captains, their founder, Komer, his gun, and a replica of an elephant. While we stood at the *posuban,* the guides directed our attention to its colors and symbols. The icon of a cock on top of the military post, we were told as we stared at it, symbolized the rooster's character as one that wakes up the world in the morning—*ko-ku-roo-koooooo!* They recited a proverb that epitomized why the cock, rather than the hen, crows in the morning, *Akokɔberɛ nim adekyeɛ, nanso otie no wɔ onini ano,* "The hen knows when the day breaks, but it listens to it from the cockerel." Therefore, their Asafo company reigned supreme among other companies. That also explained their pride and valor as a people.

Students asked many questions.

Student 1: "Why is the founder's statue and his gun on the floor?"
Student 2: "Why has the town not reinstated it?"
Student 1: "Why is the posuban in ruins?"
Guide: "It is the children who play here. They knocked them down."
Student 3: "So why don't they build a fence around it?"

FIGURE 2.1. Kormantse No. 1 *posuban* (military post). Photo by author.

Behind the *posuban* stood the Shrine of Nana Eminsa, the mother of their seventy-seven Kormantse Bentsir Gods. We were told she is summoned before every war expedition; her taboos include a woman who is menstruating and a widow who is still grieving. Her favorite drink is lemonade; her favorite oil is palm oil, and she likes fowls and sheep. After additional discussion about her significance to Kormantse Bentsir society, the male guides sang Mother Goddess Eminsa *ndwom*, "Eminsa Osuom" (example 9 ⁝ 🔊).

This walk taught me local ways of seeing, feeling, and what is valued. The land held people's memories, histories, spiritual beliefs, and songs. It pointed to the idea that historical knowledge is acquired not through textual or discursive engagement but through material and sensorial experience (Bonilla 2011, 327). Just as Angela Impey discovered that by walking with the women, she began to appreciate "how routes and mobilities are refracted sonically, both present in and resounding from their pasts" (2018, 74),[12] I began to connect the land with people's histories, appreciate their beliefs and worldviews, and to respect the land, as it held their memories.

We continued to walk through the town, sometimes walking behind windows looking into people's bedrooms and by their kitchens. We stopped at a site where the guides told us their great Ancestor hunter and founder, Nana Komer, who led them to the current settlement, killed an elephant and declared the place safe for habitation. According to them, Komer and his younger brother trekked through the forest and arrived at Kormantse. The older brother came upon an elephant that he shot and killed. He and his followers decided to settle in the vicinity of that place. Our guides pointed to a muddy pond with debris as the site where the Ancestor shot the elephant. The students asked them to point to the exact location where Komer killed the elephant. One gentleman moved to a spot; the others asked him to move to the right, then to the left, then closer to the center of the pond. These back-and-forth instructions went on for some time, till the gentleman stopped. He had become an *actor* and a *subject* to history as social process (Trouillot 1997). There was some discrepancy and disagreement among the guides about the exact location, an impossible feat since no one was around when this happened except Komer himself. *ɔbaako akɔhunu, ɔdasani wɔ hene*? "When only one person sees an act, who will corroborate the evidence?" There were no physical markers or traces in this instance. "Facts are not created equal; the production of traces is always also the creation of silences. Some occurrences are noted from the start; others are not. Some are engraved in individual or collective bodies; others are not. Some leave physical markers; others do not. What happened leaves traces, some of which are quite concrete—buildings, dead bodies, censuses, monuments, diaries, political boundaries—that limit the range and significance of any historical narrative" (ibid., 29).

My mind went back to the meeting with the Elders and Kings earlier. To the question, "Who founded Bentsir land?" the Queen Mother's spokesman replied,

> History, Nana Abosee, makes us understand, that our background, that we have gone into books to discover, is from Sudan; from Sudan we came to Ngyedum, northwest part of French Dahomey before we came to Dahomey. From Dahomey we got to Nkonya Ekyir, which means, 'You will not see our back," and it became Nkonya Ekyir. From there we came to what is now Nkoransa. Nkoransa before we came to Techiman. Everywhere they got to, they stayed there for a while

before they continued. From Techiman, they met with the Asante who started harassing them on the way. Because of that they did not have any useful settlement, until they arrived at what is Akyease before they got a little settlement there. From there, they set off and came to what is Mankessim. When they came to Mankessim, they did not climb and come here straight; they veered to Nkokodo (some of the Elders were mumbling here); it is at Nkokodo where he settled. He and all the people with him. Then Egya Komer cleared path and wandered alone to what has become this Kokoado. He stayed there for a while; he went back to the siblings there and told them, "I have found a place that is good where if we all went and stayed, it would be peaceful. They said that they were convinced that where they were was good, so they did not respond. "Let's stay here; this place is also good." He came back here, stayed here, and hunted for a while and then went back again. He stayed here for about three months, before going back. At one point, Egya Komer came here and saw a big elephant drinking water at what is now Kokoado. And because he was a hunter, he killed the elephant. When he killed the elephant, because he was alone, he could not work on it, so he went back to his siblings with blood on his body and told them, "Come and see the animal that I have killed at the place where I said we should go and settle." When he got there and he had blood on his body, they said, "Ah Komer, you don't listen to advice. When we tell you something, you don't listen. Stay here. When we tell you something, look at the blood on your body. Had you died, you would have died for nothing!" He said, "Come and see." They chose a few from the crowd to go back with him to bear witness. Truthfully, he had killed an elephant that everyone could get some to eat and be at peace. So, they said, "Komer, as for you, you don't listen to advice." So, when he got back, they said, "Komer, you don't listen to advice (*Komer ntse fo*)," and it became Kormantsefo. So, his name came to stand for this town, and we became *Kormantsefo*, Kormantse people. (King's spokesman Anointing, December 12, 2016, Kormantse, Ghana)

This was, by far, the most comprehensive narrative I had heard about the migratory history of Kormantse.

I remembered a building on the main street at Lower Kormantse. Like many houses in Kormantse, this house displayed a colorful image of a woman breast-feeding a baby by a stream. On either side of her stood a young boy. The woman's hair was braided in the *nyansapɔ* wisdom 3-knot hairstyle that was worn by dignified and respectable women.[13] In the foreground, down the stream, a young man stood with a gun pointed at an elephant, which though still standing, had blood trickling down its ear. I later learned that this was the *Anona fie* lineage house and that the woman was the first Ancestress of the Anona lineage. The words on it stated, *Kɔmer kuum ɔson*, "Komer killed an elephant." The leader Komer belonged to the Anona, and the image served as a document for the Anona and the founding of Kormantse township. I merged this information with what had been shared on this walk.

While we stood around the muddy pond and watched the gentleman try to determine the exact site, one of the students asked, "This is important to Kormantse history. Why has the town not marked this place with a signpost commemorating its importance and Komer's achievement?" There was mumbling among the guides, but nobody answered. All our guides were men. What information would women share about this history? I wondered. The men did not sing a song about this place. We continued our walk through other parts, such as the local parliament, which is the area around an old tree; they performed several chants that are sung when new laws for the town are legislated. Finally, we arrived at the famous Owumena death pit, where every adult member claims the Kormantse chased the Asante to their deaths.

I first learned about the Kormantse death pit from my dance teacher and mentor, ɔdomankoma Kyerɛma Kwamena Pra, during a lesson on Asafo history and role in Fante society. According to him, "The Kormantse Asafo chased the Asante into a big pit. They died. Today, that pit is full of plantains and bananas. They are the spirits of the Asante who died in there. The plantains do not bear any fruit. They are just plants" (personal communication, November 11, 2016, Cape Coast, Ghana). I heard about the death pit for the second time from the three men at the King's palace, and I visited it for the first time with my children. I had walked around it and had an idea of what to expect before our group got there.

The tour guides repeated the narrative about the Asante coming through the town. They did not offer much detail about why the Asante were there. They reiterated the assertion that the plantains and bananas in the pit were the incarnation of the Asante army. Some mentioned that the plantains do not bear fruit, though we stared at plantains with fruit. Students asked questions.

Student 1: "When did the war happen?"
Student 2: "Why did the Asante come through Kormantse?"
Student 3: "Why has the town not erected a monument to commemorate this defeat of the Asante?"
Student 2: "Why has this place not been developed into a big tourist destination?"

We did not get a response to any of the questions. I asked one gentleman why they insisted the plants were the spirits of the Asante and that the plants did not bear fruits, though we saw fruits on them. He replied flatly, "The coconuts were planted, but the plantain and bananas were gifts that the Asante gave us" (Egya Kojo Amissah, personal communication, December 15, 2016, Kormantse, Ghana). *Kurotwiamansa mfemfem yɛ nson pɛ, nanso hwan na ɔbɛtumi akɔgyina n'anim akan*? "The leopard has only seven whiskers, but who can stand in front of it and count?"

Many people I spoke with along the coast, including market women and men, Kings, a painter, and fishermen, knew about the death pit. A painter from Anomabo, about five miles from Kormantse, asserted that the "Asante met around Kormantse. At that time, Kormantse had also knocked them over. When they were coming, they were groups, and they divided themselves. The first went to Kormantse and they fell into the Kormantse pit, they fell in" (Ekow Safo, personal communication, February 14, 2017, Anomabo, Ghana). Obaatan Nana Budo III, a King and Asafo Elder for the neighboring town, noted the significance of the Owumena to Gold Coast history and to Kormantse: "As for the Owumena, if anyone tells you that it is not true, she is telling a lie. *Tsir, tsir, tsir,* then they [Asante] fell in. *Tsir, tsir, tsir,* then they fell in. *Tsir, tsir, tsir,* then they fell in. Kormantse is one of Asante great oaths" (personal communication, July 15, 2018, Saltpond, Ghana). He was the first to acknowledge that the Kormantse never fought the Asante. "When they heard the Asante were coming, they were afraid and ran away. Some went to Otsir. Those who are down the hill are descendants of those who ran from the Asante and settled down there" (ibid.).[14]

I looked down at the pit again. It was deep. If it was indeed true that the plantains represented the spirits of Asante army, then we were standing in their midst, on Asante Ancestral grounds and a sacred site. If it is true that the Asante were defeated in this pit, then this walk brought us closer to this past, one that could be touched and smelled and experienced sensorially. Then the walk helped validate the notion that "physical landscape can provide a unique testimony to history. Animate materiality of nature generates a particular aura of truth and credibility" and creates a "feeling of historical intimacy" (Bonilla 2011, 328). The gentlemen did not sing a song about this site. I was told there were no songs about the hole. Why would a town that sang about most events, a town whose identity and pride, from what I had gathered, rested on their defeat of the powerful Asante army, not have a song to commemorate that event? We lingered around the pit and then started our slow descent down the hill to the lower part of the town.

The descent was slow. I skipped around to avoid the potholed, clayey, and slippery landscape. Students and I discussed and analyzed what we had learned. The plantains in the death pit were a popular topic.

"How could dead people be reincarnated as plantains?" someone remarked.

"These people believe anything!" another retorted. Some discussed how ridiculous it was that the residents believed such a myth. Our ways of walking and discussions changed as the landscape transformed from the rocky undulating path, the clayey slippery hill, the potholed muddy basin, to the tarred highway. When we got to the bottom of the hill, we crossed the tarred Accra-Takoradi Highway and walked through the sandy town to the seaside. The guides led us to a lagoon by a grove of coconut trees. This, we were told, was God Nana Dzerma; people come to him for good luck. Our teachers sang a short-phrased and repetitive song celebrating Nana Dzerma's qualities and achievements. By this time, the sun was at its hottest and the students were tired, so no one asked questions. The guides dismissed us.

On our walk away, I reflected on what I had learned from the history walk. I wondered how much of this knowledge had developed over the years and how much of that was accurate. If it was indeed true that the plantains represented the spirits of the Asante army and that Komer shot the elephant at the muddy pond, then I had stood on *tsetse* ancient grounds, engaging with people's *abakɔsɛm* and memories of place. Though Asafo history and songs did not come up as often as I had hoped, the walk was crucial to my understanding of Kormantse history, their shrines, and deities, which could only be experienced on foot; it also gave me a sense of what my research would entail. I recognized the importance of walking as an integral part of my method. ɔnantefoɔ sene oni ne ɔse asɛm, "The walker knows more than her mother and father," *ampa*! Or as the Fante Akan say, Ɔnantsewfo no nyim nsɛm pii kyɛn ne na na n'egya, *ampa!* Some of the students walked back to their residences to rest or to transcribe their recordings; some continued to explore the town; others went on to their appointments with residents. I walked to the uncompleted two-storied palace for a performance of Asafo songs. It would be my first live experience of Kormantse Asafo *ndwom* (see chapter 7).

Abakɔsɛm: Agents and Makers

Ghanaian Akan Elders say, *Ani a ɛhunuu tetehɔ na ɛnni hɔ, na aso a ɛtee tetehɔ asɛm deɛ ɛwɔ hɔ,* "The eyes that saw ancient events were not there, but as for the ears that heard ancient events, they are there." There are no eyewitnesses to *abakɔsɛm*, but there are commentators, such as our walking guides, my mentors, and the few documenters who interpret *abakɔsɛm* and points of origin. For example, a June 1925 correspondence to the district commissioner signed (marked "x") by several Kormantse Kings and Elders indicated that their forefathers emigrated from the Upper Dahomey. In another correspondence dated February 23, 1932, the European district commissioner states, "Their own account of their origin is that they came from the region of Krobo on the Volta River and were found in their present position by the Fante when the latter migrated south from Takyimang." A third correspondence dated June 20, 1932, supports the earlier reference to Dahomey. It states, "[They] migrated from Ngyedum in the Northern part of French Dahomey and trekked to this part probably as a result of the frequent inter-Tribal Wars in all parts of West Africa those days, until they reached their locality and halted and settled on the hill now known as UPPER KORMANTINE."[15] Meyerowitz supports the Ngyedum version of their migratory history, stating, "The fighting and confusion in the Benin caused the Njedum people to leave their homes in the palm forest west of the Niger Delta and follow the beach, the men carrying the children and women moaning under heavy burdens, particularly firewood. They discovered the Etsi again and settled not far from them founding Koromantse, a few miles from Onyinatsiadze and on the beach. Being still unskilled in fishing and farming they started worrying the Etsi again, many of whom left the coast and went inland" (1952, 60–61).

The 2016 account by the Elders at Kormantse asserting that they migrated from Sudan and settled at Tekyiman before making it to their final settlement with not one but with two leaders, who were also hunters—Nana Komer Panyin and his younger brother, Komer Kakra— points further to how "agents of history" are themselves "makers of that history." Here is an excerpt from Nana, my primary mentor:

> As for Kormantse, they are from Sudan and came here. They wandered through an Anwona town called Anglo. They wandered till they came to Akra. The Elders with whom they walked were hunter Nana Kormer, The Elder, and Nana Kormer Junior, and Nana Egyir Mamon. From Akra they settled at the hill at Akyenfo Ankaful. The hill is called Kokoowdo, it is behind Kuntu and Ankaful. The meat they ate was snails. One day, he left his people and cleared path and came to Kormantse pit and climbed the hill. He came upon an elephant by a tree and killed it. He went and brought his people to Kormantse. He came with two hundred and fifty people. They constructed a shed and smoked the meat on it. The meat that they ate is elephant. (Safohen Nana Odum III, Notes, December 19, 2016)

It goes on to talk about how the town acquired its name—the younger brother, Kakra, called out to his older brother who did not respond. The younger said, *Kormer, mefrɛ wo yi entsie?* "Kormer, when I called you didn't you hear?" *Kormer entsie.*

Accounts about how the town acquired its name are just as diverse. Recall the version that the King's spokesman shared at the gathering of Kings. According to his account with only one Komer, the town is named after their Ancestors' chastised Komer, *Ah Komer, an tsefo. Yɛ ka biribi kyerɛ wo a entsie*, "Ah Komer, you don't listen to advice. When we tell you something, you don't listen." In another account, it is rather a young Kakra, who, in complaining that his older brother did not heed to his advice, said "Komer did not hear/listen," *Komer antse*, leading to the name, Kormantse. In an online version, it is the older Komer who accuses the younger for not listening:

> After settling here for some period of time, Nana Kome and his followers decided to move on. But his junior brother, Kome Kuma refused to accompany the main party and chose to stay behind. Soon the Denkyira armed bandits invaded the area and Kome Kuma was captured. Both Crayner and folkloric Guan historian, Kwame Ampene contend that the capture of Kome Kuma caused his aggrieved senior brother, Nana Kome Panyin to exclaim: "Sɛ Kome Kuma tsie me a,

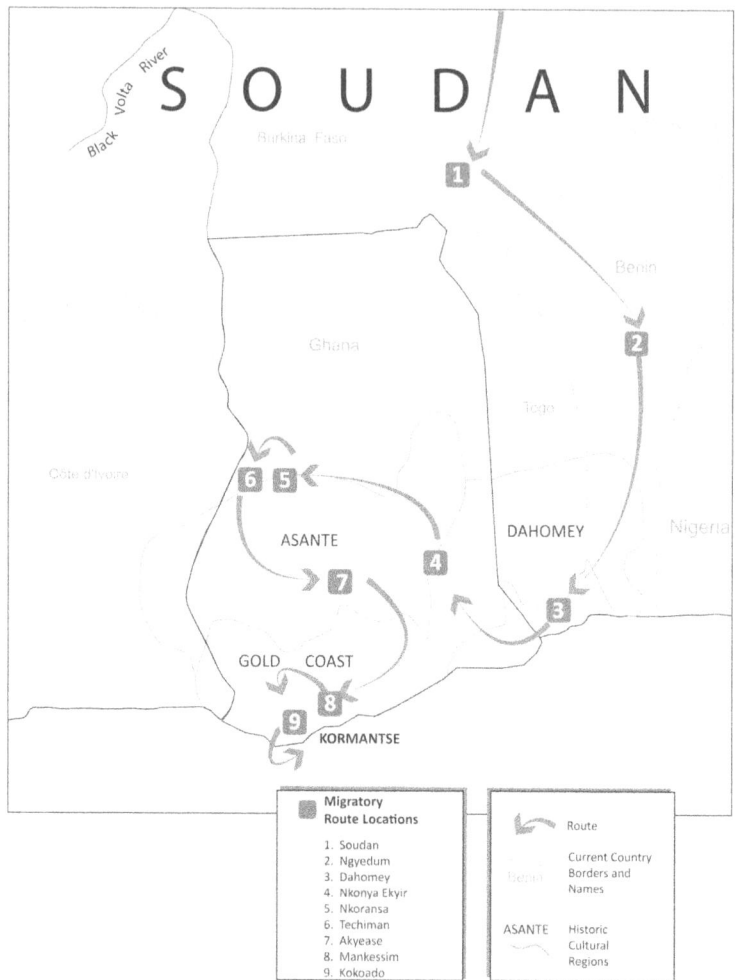

FIGURE 2.2. Approximate Trajectory of Kormantse Migration to Current Location. Map by Jill Freund Thomas.

nkyɛ wo ankyɛr no" (If Kome Kuma had listened to me, he wouldn't have been captured). Thus, he said, "Kome antse" (Kome did not listen). Out of the expression Komeantse, emerged the town's name Kormantse or Komeantse. (Dokosi 2017)

That some accounts have one brother and others have two brothers is interesting, but also it is useful in illustrating how history is constructed and results from the "intersection of incommensurable memories" (Connerton

1989, 3). Connerton's observation is instructive: "It is an implicit rule that participants in any social order must presuppose a shared memory. To the extent that their memories of a society's past diverge, to that extent its members can share neither experience nor assumptions. The effect is seen perhaps most obviously when communication across generations is impeded by different sets of memories. Across generations, different sets of memories, frequently in the shape of implicit background narratives, will encounter each other" (ibid.).

The interpretation of narratives of the past that have been passed down orally over generations are often merged with information from published materials. Consider the King's spokesman's retelling of their migratory history. "Nana Abosee, history makes us understand, our background *that we have gone into books to discover* [my emphasis], is from Sudan." The reference to books came up often. Though it seemed odd to me, it appeared that this practice of incorporating information from published European materials into oral accounts is quite common among the Fante along the littoral because many of the people of coastal Ghana are literate, had been for centuries, and have had access to published materials (see Decorse 2001). This "feedback" process of garnering information (Henige 1973, 1974) allowed Kormantse Kings and Elders to fill in the gaps in their recollection. When discussing the nineteenth-century Kormantse-Asante war, my mentor indicated he learned about it at school and referred me to *The History of the Gold Coast of West Africa*, an 1893 book by A. B. Ellis (chapter 3).

If *Ani a ɛhunuu teteho na ɛnni ho na aso a ɛtee teteho asɛm deɛ ɛwo ho*, then *abakɔsɛm* could be shifted and shaped in the hands of whoever is telling it, by the needs of the society, as a moral obligation, and by the cultural context in which it unfolds. *Abakɔsɛm* is as much an event of the past as it is of the present. The past does not exist separately from the present. *Tete wo bi ka, tete wo bi kyerɛ*, "The past has something to say, and the past has something to teach us." Trouillot reminds us, "Thus, between the mechanically 'realist' and naively 'constructivist' extremes, there is the more serious task of determining not what history is—a hopeless goal if phrased in essentialist terms—but how history works. For what history is changes with time and place or, better said, history reveals itself only through the production of specific narratives. What matters most are the processes and conditions of production of such narratives" (1997, 25). I reminded myself that the Kings and my other mentors were talking about a narrative history of more than a thousand years ago; they could not remember the details of all that had been passed down to them over time; they were recollecting what they could in their recent memory.

Despite these varied accounts about their *abakɔsɛm*, many observers and Kormantse residents, including our guides, agree on one thing: the people of Kormantse are proud, fierce, and hard working. They consider themselves to be ferocious warriors and claim that their Asafo has never been defeated. In her account, Meyerowitz remarks that "The Njadum people . . . were warriors and had once been herdsmen in the north. They knew nothing of farming in the forest and, faced with starvation, they started to capture Etsi women to do the farming" (1952, 64).[16] Colonial district commissioners described them as "rowdy," "indisciplined," "ill-behaved," "defiant," "truculent," and so on. One colonial district commissioner, E. C. Elliot, who represented Kormantse township, reported in an 1891 correspondence to the regional commissioner, "I am much in sympathy with the Kormantines as they repair the loss of their fishing trade and believe that strong measures to enforce the present orders are inadvisable, at the same time, you are well aware that the Kormantines are a truculent people and the withdrawal of troupes without the orders of the government having been enforced, will probably be construed by them as an act of weakness on our part" (PRAAD ADM 11/1/748). In a 1907 correspondence from the Provincial Commissioner's Office at Cape Coast, another colonial officer wrote, "The CORMANTYNE people have frequently given trouble over their use of drums and native customs and are by no means amenable to discipline. When I was at Saltpond in 1904-5, I had to take police and forcibly prevent a custom which they were holding in defiance of my orders" (PRAAD ADM 11/1/748).

In fact, because of their strength and valor, Africans obtained from Kormantse market, referred to as Cormantees, were believed by the British and American planters to be physically the strongest to be bought in Africa, the most suited to withstand the harsh working conditions in the plantations, and the preferred ones (see St. Clair 2006 and Ward 1948). These observations and the texts of their many Asafo songs support the claim that they are valiant warriors. Their appellation

> *Ngyedum!*
> *Okusu Bentsir a*
> *Wɔdze kɛntɛn kɔ nsu a*
> *Wɔdze nkatsefuw bɔ kar*
> *Ekua Yaaba mba!*

(Dowsers of fire
The valiant ones
They fetch water with basket
They use thorny plant as a pad for carrying (loads)
Ekua Yaaba's children)

sums up their combative temperament. Though our Elders say, *Akatakyisɛm bebrebe ne owuo na ɛnam*, "Bravado walks hand in hand with death," they claimed they had never been defeated. Asked why their Ancestors did not mark and claim the different lands they conquered, one Elder remarked, "Because we were busy fighting, just fighting!" At the session with the Kings and Elders, when I asked if Kormantse people liked to fight, several of them replied as follows:

Respondent 1: "Yes!"
Respondent 2: "We like to fight."
Respondent 3: "One of our Kings relinquished the throne after only one year because he said we fight too much."

As I walked away from our final stop to meet with the group that would perform my first experience of Kormantse Asafo songs, I reflected on what I had learned about the town's *abakɔsɛm*.

Kormantse Ngyedum!
You proud people
From Sudan
Ngyedum
Long walk
One hunter
Komer
Anona precious bead
Two brother hunters
Komer Panyin and Kome Kakra
Three *Asafommba* groups
Amfɛrfo, Kyiremfo, Adzewafo
Led you
Settling at Kokoado
Komer *kuum ɔson* elephant
At the pond
Tsetsepɔn long, long time ago

Before the Fante arrived from Techiman
Komer did not listen to advice
Kormantse
Okusu Bentsir a
Wɔdze kɛntɛn kɔ nsu a
Did you fight the Asante or not
Plantains in Owumena bear fruit
Intersecting *abakɔsɛm*
Entangled entanglements
Our Elders say
Ani a ɛhunuu tetehɔ na ɛnni hɔ
na aso a ɛtee tetehɔ asɛm deɛ ɛwɔ hɔ
The eyes that saw ancient events were not there,
but as for the ears that heard them, they are there
ɔnantefoɔ see oni asɛm
A walker told her mother a tale
Where there are no witnesses, tall stories can be told with impunity[17]

Kormantse Ngyedum
Okusu Bentsir a
Wɔdze kɛntɛn kɔ nsu a
Wɔdze nkatsefuw bɔ kar
Ekua Yaaba mba!
Proud truculent warriors
Wa-la!
You who support your water pot with thorny bush
Hwɛ!
Brave people
Wa-la hwɛ-a!
Your Ancestors caused havoc in the Caribbean
Put fear in the hearts of New World slave owners
You like to fight
Fought aaaa . . .
Your King relinquished his throne
Ebueii!
Kormantse Ngyedum!

Knocking

Nana Eminsa and her entourage protect you
Nana Bohimahi, warrior Goddess
Nana Sesa guards you
The cockerel crows
Ko-kuro-kooooo
Signaling your bravado
Nana Dzerma brings luck

Your *abakɔsɛm* says
You knocked Asante into Owumena
Death pit
Plantains are reincarnations
Gifts from the Asante
wo kum apem a, apem bɛba
They spread without boundaries
Fighters
Doused by you
Hm

Eii!
Kormantse Ngyedum
As for the ears that heard them, they are there
Good conversations never end
The walker knows more than her mother and father
It is because of the tree that the rope reached the sky
Wɔdze nkatsefuw bɔ kar
Till our walk next time
Ngyedum
Gyedo-ooo!

CHAPTER THREE

Memory Walking

A Haptic Way of Knowing

We are stepping in the footprints of our Ancestors.
We must step in their paths to continue what they left behind

—Safohen Nana Odum III (a.k.a. Teacher Hammond)

When we walk, we're not walking alone.
Our parents and ancestors are walking with us.
They're present in every cell of our bodies

—Thich Nhat Hanh 2016, 166

Wadweoo waadwe waadwe (2x)
Hɛn nananom Bentsir Tuafo ee
Wenyi ayɛw wenyi ayɛw anokwafo
Wenyi ayɛw bi
(It is calm, it is calm, it is calm
It is calm, it is calm, it is calm
Our Ancestors of Bentsir Tuafo ee
They were ungrateful faithfuls
They were not any grateful)

—Kormantse Asafo *ndwom*, "Waadweoo waadwe"

Memory Walking 1

It was Friday, November 11, 2016, when I first learned about the Kormantse death pit (Owumena) from my dance teacher during the lesson on Asafo history and role in Fante society. I learned about it again when I traveled to Kormantse for the first time. I met three men at the King's palace who

FIGURE 3.1. Kormantse Kokoado Hill. Photo by author.

gave me a brief history about Kormantse, the Asante and Kormantse war, and the death pit where, according to them, the Asante were defeated. Later that day, I walked up the Kormantse Kokoado hill with my children to visit the death pit to take all those memories on my walk.

We made a steady climb on the rocky, undulating, and meandering footpath that looked like it had been traversed for centuries. We started by walking between a row of houses, most of which were occupied by female residents who sat at their front entrances and watched us walk by. Some smoked, dried, or fried fish. As expected, I greeted each one of them. "I give you afternoon ooo." At the time, I had not learned that here, at Kormantse and, in Fanteland, I also had to include my father's lineage response to the greeting. This would allow my respondents to give an appropriate answer to my salutation. I should have said, "I give you afternoon ooo, they respond Yaa Amu to me" (salutation of my father's lineage). Then they would say, "Yaa Amu." Since I did not provide that crucial information, most gave the incomplete, "Yaaa . . ." ("We respond . . ."). Others gave the generic, "Yaaa nua" (We respond to you our sibling").

The hill was steep, with a winding and aged cement staircase on one side and a bare, rocky, and clayey surface on the other side. There were bushes and pits on either side of the hill. We took off our shoes and went on the cement staircase. With caution, and on our hands and knees, we crawled onto the first step, second step, third step; we straightened up and stepped on the next and the next till we got to the top of the staircase. We hopped onto the dry, clayey and slippery land and continued the climb to the top. It was a slow, steady, and scary climb on a clayey, slippery, and steep hill. I felt being watched from above, so I looked up and saw a row of young men seated along the top edge of the hill watching us intently. We trudged and dodged the potholed and bumpy landscape to avoid any slips, slides, and falls. *Animguase mfata Akan nii ba*, "Disgrace does not befit the Akan child." I would later learn that residents on the hill keep up with the happenings in the Lower Town from this vantage point. They watch funeral proceedings, getting a birds-eye view of the goings and comings of their family members down the hill. From this vantage point, they could also spot any enemy coming into their town and alert other residents. From this point, overlooking the sea, they could also see the vast Atlantic Ocean *Nana Bosompo* and predict her character that day.

This is the original Kormantse settlement whose population has since spread down the hill across the Accra-Takoradi Highway and toward the sea. The land is rocky, hard, and full of stones. The stony and undulating terrain (*atwerbo*) is very sharp and pierced the soles of our shoes. My children trekked carefully. I would later learn that in the past, women sharpened these *atwerbo* stones for their Asafo warriors to hurl at their enemies. A network of footpaths ran between and behind the houses. Some, I would find out later, led to the town's cemetery, the Asafo military post, the many shrines, the famous death pit, and the neighboring town. On this part of town, no motorized vehicles existed, so everyone walked. Most of the residents work as farmers, fisherfolk, and fish processors. Here in this new space, the succession of our steps effectively rewrote the spaces that opened before us, even when done in the slightest of action modes (Auyogard 2007). Sometimes, rather than following an existing path, sometimes rather than hewing a new one, we moved within a space that never tolerated the absolute exclusion of the one or the other (ibid.).

I noticed the plantains and banana trees at the top of the hill. Eager to see them, I tripped. The few plantain plants I saw had no fruit or flowers on them. It *is* true! My dance teacher and the Kormantse Elders were right! Then I saw other trees blossoming with flowers; some had budding fruit; others had matured plantains hanging on their branches. I stared at the plants. It is *not* true! I took pictures. *Had they seen these plants? How did they come to these conclusions? Should I tell them, challenge their claims?* I continued to walk through the town, looking for anybody who could help me figure this out.

I walked to a house, introduced myself, and told a lady about my search for Asafo songs and the death pit. She said the death pit was a security measure for the town. Any thieves or unwanted strangers who wanted to harm residents fell into it. She directed me to her mother, Maame Ama Poli. Maame Poli confirmed the story about the Asante-Kormantse battle but rejected the claim that the banana trees do not bear fruit. "*Wɔ boa, wɔ boa, wɔ boa!*" "They are lying; they are lying; they are lying!" I asked her if she knew any Asafo songs, especially any that recounted the historic event. She could not recall any; however, she directed me to an eighty-five-year-old woman, who was reluctant to share anything at first because she said she may have memory lapses. Maame Ekua Tekyiwa and her sister, Ama Esuon, gave a brief history of the town and shared important information and song about their great-great-grandmother, a rich Asafo warrior, who led the war between the Asante and Elmina. According to their narrative, their great-great-grandmother purchased cloth for the Asafo warriors to shield their rifles and gun powder from the rain. They too rejected the claims by my dance teacher and male teachers that the plantains did not bear any fruit. In fact, they said that their great-great-grandmother planted some bananas in the death pit. What stories do women tell? What stories do men tell?

The next day, I climbed up Kokoado hill again and headed straight to the death pit and walked slowly along the edge, down into the pit, and thought about what had been shared with me about this space: the Asante army running in here to their death; the gunshots and the ensuing chaos.

I took pictures of the banana and plantain fruits but did not show them to my dance teacher; neither did I tell him about my discovery. I focused, rather, on the memories I conjured and the footprints I left in those spaces and memories of this space, for "without oneself walking and leaving footprints, one can only listen to and repeat the narrative of others who have walked the story" (Legat 2008).

FIGURE 3.2. Plantains growing down in the Kormantse death pit. Photo by KoJo Kisseh Aduonum.

Memory Walk . . . toward Shadow Walking

On Thursday, May 12, 2017, I trudged up the steep Kokoado hill with Egya Kwesi Mprah (a.k.a. Safohen Nana Odum III, Teacher Hammond, or "T," henceforth "Nana"), a man who almost every Kormantse adult advised me to consult about Asafo *abakɔsɛm* and its *ndwom*. We went on a type of walk that British composer, vocalist, and sound artist Vi Corringham calls "shadow walks." Shadow walks "involve three main elements: walking with others, listening to environmental sounds, and improvised singing" (2013, 156). She asks to be taken on a special walk, one that has been repeated many times and has meaning or significance for that person. While walking together, she records environmental sounds and conversations. A solo walk follows in which she attempts to sense her previous companion's traces on the walk and to make the memory audible through improvised singing. Recordings are later combined and edited to become the final composition (ibid.). At this level, mine was not quite a shadow walk, for I did not record environmental sounds while I walked with Nana; neither did I improvise songs on the way. Also, mine was a "reverse" shadow walk since I had walked the paths with my children before this walk with Nana.

Nana, eighty-nine, was a petite eighty-three-year-old man at the time and made frequent stops to rest. According to him, his Ancestors settled here when they migrated from present-day Sudan. First, we stopped at his Kɔna lineage house. He informed his sisters that we had come to walk through the town and to visit the death pit. After catching his breath, we made our way to the famous death pit. As we traversed through the streets, between and behind houses, we walked the landscape of the town in a way that I had not. For while I had walked the town many times before, walking alongside him allowed me to see the landscape through his eyes. His pace, the paths he took, the frequent stops to greet and chat with people, explanations, and discussions about the land and the historical significance of specific spaces made the walking more impactful. He pointed out places that had meaning for him and for the residents, telling stories about those landmarks, connecting stories and places. Sometimes, he sang. Like Impey, who walked through the town with her mentors, walking with Nana and others through Kormantse town made me aware of how "their lives and those of their families are so implicated with their land and natural resources" (82).

After we had walked through the network of paths, Nana stood cautiously at the edge of the pit and recounted the events leading to the Asante's defeat. This is where—according to Kormantse Elders and my other mentors and friends, as noted earlier—the Kormantse defeated the Asante army in the early nineteenth century. Almost every Kormantse adult resident I talked with shared this story. For Kormantse residents, this historic event was a source of pride because the Asante are known for their pride and bravery for having fought and defeated the British in the War of the Golden Stool. I asked Nana about Asafo songs that were associated with this place. He projected his voice and sang *"Wadweoo waadwe waadwe"* (example 10). The song was typical of some Asafo songs that I had heard. It was short phrased, in free meter, and repetitive. He sang again, *Wadweoo waadwe waadwe . . . Wenyi ayɛw bi*. He sang it a third time.

This is it? For a song that commemorates their victory of the Asante and defies Asante intention to take all their gold and enslave them, it was rather dull. I expected something jubilant and exciting, performed with pride and defiance. But the tune did not match the mood of their triumph. It was calm, pensive, almost mournful. Its flow was anything but jagged; it was smooth and soft, like a lullaby, and quite unlike some of the other Asafo songs that I had heard about victory, defiance, and pride. The melody was rather "simple" and did not reflect or mirror the complexities of the battle; nor did it conjure the sounds of the gunshots and pandemonium that led the Asante into the pit. *Where was that imaginative investment, projection, and creation (*Hirsch 2017*) with which he narrated the defeat? Where was the gusto? Could it be that he was tired, old? Perhaps it was the absence of the dawur bell's heart-throbbing ken-ken-ke-ken, ken-ken-ke-ken, the interlocking patterns of the four drums whose incisive rhythms could wake up the dead, the complex handclapping, and the dancing that "lifts up" everyone. Why did he not sing the Kormantse-Asante ndwom he had sung months earlier, "Akyem Esuantse?"* that teased the Asante to come for more? (See chapter 7)

Sɛ ano patrɛ a ɛkyen namɔn, "A slipped tongue damages more than a slipped foot," so I did not voice my disappointment. Furthermore, I thought, who am I, a student, an outsider, to dictate how an Asafo song should be performed? *Obi nkɔ obi kuro mu nkɔfrɛ ne ho Agyeman*, "One should not go to another person's town and call herself a Liberator."[1]

A woman came out of her house and started a conversation. "'T,' we have not seen much of you since you moved downhill." While they conversed, I tried to hum the song with the *dawur* pattern in my mind.

> ken-ken-ke-ken
> *Wadweoo waadwe waadwe* (2x)
> ken-ken-ke-ken
> *Hɛn nananom Bentsir Tuafo ee*
> ken-ken-ke-ken
> *Wenyi ayɛw wenyi ayɛw anokwafo*
> ken-ken-ke-ken
> *Wenyi ayɛw bi*

We continued to walk through the town. Since "walking and talking with participants allows them to recall embodied experiences that are difficult in a seated, more analytical environment" (Pierce and Lawhon 2015, 260), every step we took, slow or fast, depending on the topography, every turn we made, evoked memories for Nana. Like Seeger, for whom every trip up the river with the Suya was a lesson in history (1982, 11), every turn conjured up memories for Nana. "This is where the Asafo drummers gathered and sounded the drum." "This is where Nana Komer killed the elephant." "This is the tree that took the priest, ɔkɔmfo Sisi, to drink palm-wine." Sometimes he asked, "I have told you about the significance of this place, right?" If I answered "No," he would tell me. If I answered, "Yes," he would ask me to share that memory. The Fante Akan say, *Tsetse kaasoa fir ɔkakyerɛ a wɔ kaakyerɛ asowa ma asowa ɔtsee*, "Ancient knowledge is from what was told to the ear that the ear heard." My ears heard. My eyes saw; my body walked and felt his memories.

As we moved through the various paths, I experienced why many Kormantse residents, young and old, revered this sage who brought the first school and church to Kormantse. They shouted out, "T," "Teacher," "Teacher Hammond, long time!" It is through this and other walks that my confidence in Safohen Nana Odum III as my mentor and collaborator swelled. One gentleman said to me one day, "I saw you walking with Teacher. You have found him; he is the only one you need. Your search is over. He knows more about Asafo matters that have come and gone than anybody in this town!" Another told me, "I saw you walking with 'T.' He is Safohen." Walking with Nana helped me verify his claims and credentials. I understood through this particular walk that "When we walk, we're not walking alone. Our parents and Ancestors are walking with us. They're present in every cell of our bodies" (Thich Nhat Hanh 2016, 166). We walked in the footsteps of the Ancestors and his memories. The act of walking, although it does not constitute a physical construction of a space, implies a transformation of a place and its meaning. The mere physical presence of humans in an unmapped space, as well as the variations of perceptions they register while crossing it, already constitute forms of transformation of the landscape that—without leaving tangible signs—culturally modify the meaning of space and therefore the space itself (Careri 2017, back cover).

I took more walks to the death pit, alone, after my walk with Nana. Each time, I recalled the song Nana taught me about Kormantse taunting the Asante to come back. I worked out the versions of the *abakɔsɛm* I had learned. While standing in that space, staring at the plantains with fruits, I scanned my memory for another version of this narrative in which Maame Ama Poli rejected the idea that the plantains are spirits of the conquered

Asante and thus do not have fruit: "They are lying! The bananas and plantains have fruit on them" (personal communication, December 12, 2016). I scanned also for the version by the lady who insisted that her grandmother brought the bananas and plantains and planted them in the pit and that the plants do "give birth."

That the bananas and plantains I was staring at had fruits on them, contrary to the narratives of some Kormantse Elders and my dance teacher, did not in any way diminish the importance of this place in Kormantse matters that have come and gone, the rituals that memorialize the important event, the many songs that are performed to commemorate it, or the pride that it brings to the people. I decided not to challenge my teachers who insisted the plantains did not bear fruit. Neither did I show them the pictures. *Aboa kɔkɔsɛkyi se ɔde ne kwasea pɛ nyinkyɛ*!

The versions of the narrative were derived from many factors, of which I was ignorant. Furthermore, the overlapping interpretations of what happened also point to Herzfeld's suggestion that the "anthropological engagement with the multiple histories that one finds in a single social context, are often articulated by the same people as they respond to the conflicting exigencies of their social, political, and cultural predicaments" (Herzfeld 2001, 55). One person's assertion that "the coconuts were planted, but the plantains and bananas were gifts that the Asante gave us" could be worked out and made sense of in this space through my memory walk. It was quite interesting, though, to observe that it was mostly the men who insisted that "the Asante bones turned into plantains," a version that supports their claim that they had never been conquered. The women said, "It's a lie." These conflicting versions call for a careful consideration of how matters that have come and gone are remembered and constructed along gender lines.

A Balancing Walk: between Oral and Written Accounts

Though oral[2] and written accounts acknowledge that the Asante army came through the coastal region in search of two Assin Kings (Ward 1948; Fynn 1971; Perbi 2004; etc.), what occurred at Kormantse or the Kormantse Upper Town in the 1800s with the Asante is mired in mystery and *abakɔsɛm*. As I paced along the edge of the death pit, alone, during my most recent walk (2018) with others' memories in my head, I reflected on what authors had documented about the battle between the Asante and the Akyem at a town variously named "Akromanti," "Kormanti," and

"Koromante" and how that could have been interpreted by my mentors as their war and victory over the Asante. It was a "balancing walk," the kind that anthropologists, historians, and ethnomusicologists grapple with concerning oral and written narratives. How do we respond to *abakɔsɛm* crafted according to criteria of relevance that do not fit? How do I reconcile the discrepancies between oral and written accounts to settle on an answer that coincides with my teachers' narrative about the Asante? This is the root of Kormantse pride. Trying to balance the accounts was walking a tightrope, a risky walk that could potentially discredit my teachers sense of history, question their moral compass, and unsettle their sense of pride. It was a walk that could impose my—and other's—"notions of truth" over those of my mentors. Who chooses to remember? Who records *abakɔsɛm*, why, and whose tellings matter, underscored this probe.

None of the written accounts directly document an actual battle between Asante and Kormantse during which the latter defeated or chased the Asante into a death pit.[3] The name "Kromanti" is mentioned in relation to the death of Asante King Osei Tutu, who was shot and killed by the Akim in 1731 when he fell flat upon the River Prah. In fact, whenever the variously spelled Koromante, Akromanti, or Kormantse name is mentioned by authors, it is always in the context of the wars between Asante and Akyem (Akim), during which the Asante King Nana Osei Tutu was shot and killed. Carl Reindorf observes that "In about 1730 Akyem again rebelled. Osei Tutu immediately marched an army into the disloyal province and fought a bloody battle at Koromante, in which the Akems, being defeated, were obliged to cross the Pra and placed an ambuscade there. The victorious sovereign fell into it one Monday and was slain whilst crossing the river—some say, while ascending the hill which got the name Koromante, in memory of the battle."[4] This observation is important because by citing the battle of Koromante, the author seems to validate Kormantse residents' claims that they fought and defeated the Asante. Even A. B. Ellis, whose text Nana advised me to consult about their battle with Asante, notes where the battle occurred and with whom it happened. However, he does not corroborate the oral narratives that Kormantse defeated the Asante.

According to Ellis, the Akyem army that killed the Asante King had halted overnight: "A terrible example was made of Acromanti, the town in which the party of Akims who had slain Osai Tutu had halted on the night previous to the attack, every living creature found in it being put to death, and every house razed to the ground. To commemorate the death of the King, the oath of *Akromanti Memereda* (Akromanti Saturday) was established by law as one of the most sacred oaths of Ashanti."[5] Ellis further recorded, "The Ashanti force under Appia Dunkwa, after defeating Akum, moved leisurely down the coast, destroying Mankessim and several other towns, and first gained sight of the sea about Coromantine. They destroyed the town, and Appia Dunkwa, after sending several calabashes full of salt water to the King, in proof of his victories, took up his quarters in Coromantine Fort, which the Dutch commandant surrendered without firing a shot" (111). Freeman (1898) also cites Akromanti as the town where the Asante King was slain, though he credits the Assins, not the Akromanti, for killing him.[6] He recorded, "The King was traveling with quite a small escort when he was attacked by a body of Assins who had been encamped at Akromanti, and he and most of his followers were put to death. The tragic event still lives in the memory of Ashantis, whose solemn oath to this day is that sworn by the head of Osai Tutu and Akromanti Saturday [*Akromanti Memeneda*]" (440).

Ward (1948) connects the Ashanti war with a "Koromante" town, when he reinforces Reindorf's assessment that the King was killed at Koromante. He even makes a connection between the Koromante town and present-day Kormantse. "The disaster of Osei Tutu's death was commemorated in the establishment of the great oath Memeneda. The name of the place where he was killed' Koromante, also became an oath; this village was named after the better known Koromante (Kormantine) on the coast, by an Akim chief who had visited the coast and was struck with the similarity of the physical situation on a long ridge hill" (125–26).

This latter observation is also significant, for while it does not confirm the claim that the Kormantse fought and defeated the Asante, it makes a connection between "Koromante," where the Asante King was killed, and "the better known Koromante (Kormantine)." Could this be the key to the mystery surrounding what happened? Could it be a case of mistaken identity of a town? The only other discussion and connection between the Asante and Kormantse is made by John K. Fynn, who notes, "The Asante army attacked the Adjumako and set Adjumako town on fire and then prepared to march to Cape Coast, Kormantse, and Elmina."[7] He does not, however, give any reasons for why the Asante prepared to march to Kormantse.

Finally, Kofi Afrifah states, "The Akyem organized an ambuscade. They stationed excellent marksmen at the village Akromanti on the banks of the river Pra. There they succeeded in assassinating Osei Tutu and killing his retinue almost to a man" (2000, 37).

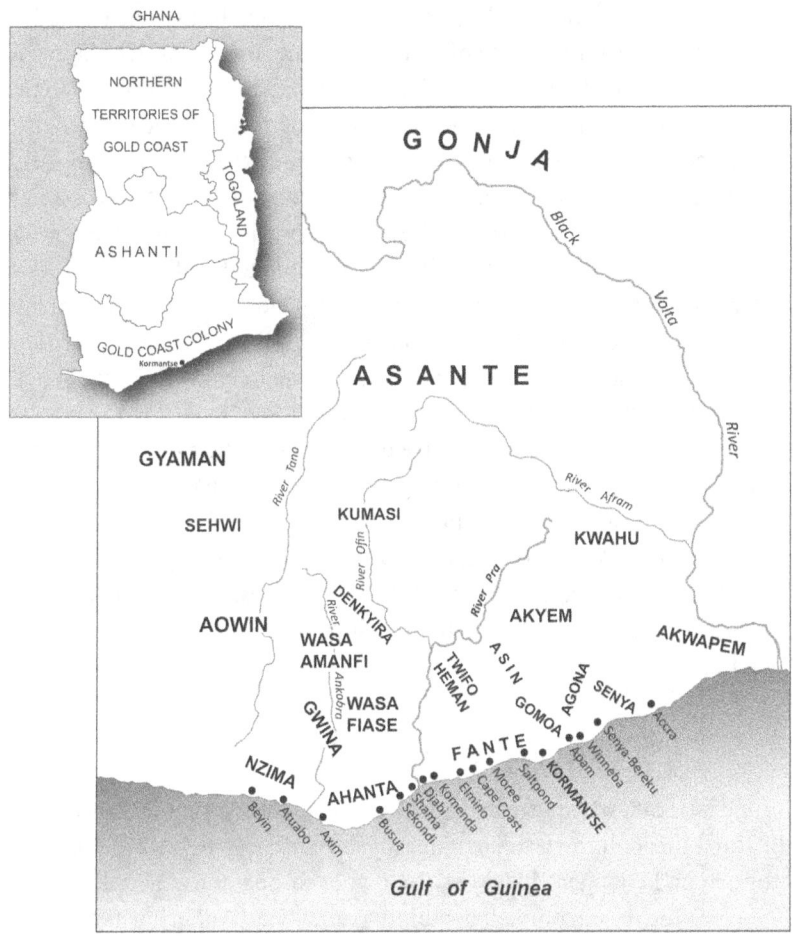

FIGURE 3.3. Map showing the location of the Asante, Akyem, Pra River, and Kormantse.

Did the documenters who wrote things down get it wrong? Did Kormantse residents get it wrong? How did they acquire their information? Would the hunter and lion tell the same story? What do all these versions mean? Whose stories matter? Was there a different town called Acromanti, Koromantse, or Akromanti near or on the banks of the Asubɔntene River Pra? Did they just misspell the name of the town or gloss over some other details—the death pit? Present-day Kormantse is not that close to Asubɔntene Pra (See Figure 3.3).

There is no indication of Akromanti on the maps I have seen thus far. Was a "terrible example made of Acromanti, the town in which the party of Akims who had slain Osai Tutu had halted on the night previous to the attack, every living creature found in it being put to death, and every house razed to the ground," (Ellis above), so it does not exist? What about Ellis' other assertion that the Asante army first gained sight of the sea about Coromantine and they destroyed the town? *ɔbra te sɛ ntentan yɛtete no nyansafoɔ*, "Life is like a cobweb, it takes wisdom to handle it."

There at the death pit, as I paced through my memory walk and shadow walks, and I reflected on the variations between the oral and the written, the meaning of the songs I had learned and come to enjoy did not change. They did not alter or diminish the respect and love I felt for Kormantse residents. I had traveled to Kormantse to learn about their Asafo songs, not to dispute their historical accounts, validate their matters that have come and gone, or question their memories. *Wo nsa hyɛ obi anomu a yɛ mpae n'apampam mu*, "When your hand is in someone's mouth you don't strike the person on the head." Furthermore, Elders also say, *Yɛde brɛbrɛ na ɛdwa tɛtea hunu ne yam adeɛ*, "It is with utmost patience that we dissect the ant to reach its entrails."

Memory Walk 3 . . . Ego Anan

On June 29, 2018, when I traveled back to Kormantse a year later, I walked with Nana through town to acquaint myself with any new developments. Not much had changed; however, the owner of one house had added another level to his uncompleted building, drastically altering the spatial awareness and sensing of main street. Main street felt crowded and empty at the same time. The building stood opposite the King's palace, where the group of men had performed Asafo songs the year before. How would this development affect the acoustics of another performance? How would it contribute to my walk and interactions through main street?

It was *Ego anan Fida*, fourth ego Friday at Kormantse, the day when Kormantse citizens were supposed to go "in front of the government" or "to the parliament" (Aban Enyim) to set the laws of the town. As we walked, Nana told me they usually would put up three mud mounds at Kokoado Upper Town as part of the day's activities. But nothing happened that day, not even the Asafo drumming that accompanied the event. Nana complained about the town's inaction and nonchalant attitude toward the tradition. *Hɛnn kɛse butuw a ɔnka biako*, "If a big ship capsizes, it would not be left with one," he warned. He greeted everyone, young and old, on the way. Asked why he greeted even the young ones, he answered, "So that they can learn the practice of greeting properly. There is a specific greeting for the morning, one for the afternoon, and one for the evening." He added, "Imagine how awkward it would be if you had to come back and ask a question of the same people you passed without greeting." Walking with Nana continued to be a learning experience; his interactions with people on our walk afforded additional opportunities to learn about Asafo. When we passed an older gentleman, we stopped and exchanged greetings. The gentleman reminisced about Asafo's pasts. "When we used to play Asafo, Nana used to lead and control the crowd and the song makers with his commanding stick."

I walked Nana back to his house and decided to go up the hill to Kokoado, Kormantse Upper Town, and visit my female mentors. Several people had told me that because Kokoado was the original settlement, many of the customs are still performed there; most of the shrines are there; furthermore, residents on the hill are knowledgeable about Kormantse's *abakɔsɛm*. Before I started my ascent, I saw one of my mentors, Maame Ekua Atta, sitting outside a house. She did not recognize me due to her poor vision. By this time, I had begun to associate people and places with songs I learned. I started to sing "*ɔawar Eminsa*," the Mother Goddess Eminsa song that she and another lady had taught me months earlier. Maame Atta recognized my voice immediately, sat up, and sang with me (example 11 🔊).

"You and your songs!" She laughed and laughed. I sat by her and shared what Nana had told me about *ego anan*. She reflected:

> They used to go up there to discuss matters and set the laws of the land. Asafo drums were sounding; the Kokoado path was cleared; *Akwambo* drumming was sounded. It was no play! People climbed Kokoado, young and old; drummers drummed. Hah! By this time, around 3:00 in the afternoon, Asafo drummers would be up there, calling those down there. Old and young ran and climbed the hill. Men and women dressed in danger, red scarves. The town was a sea of red! They assembled at Safohen Panyin Amissah's house before going to deliberate the rules about divorce, marriage, funeral fees, adultery, theft, and other issues. The three Asafo companies drummed, sang, and praised the Mother Goddess: 'Nana Eminsa! Ama Amine! ɔkɔtɔ

Kurase, ɔno nyi o o, ɔno nyi!' Today we don't do that anymore, no Asafo, excerpt for this *ke-ke-ren, ke-ke-ren* (hiplife popular music). All the Elders are gone.[8]

I sat with her for a while, thanked her, and walked up the hill, greeting residents along the way.

Honoring Ahɔr

According to Fante oral traditions, scholars, and Elders, during their migration from Techiman due to unstable and oppressive conditions, the Fante people were afflicted with an epidemic that killed many. When they consulted their Gods, they were advised to pacify the Deities in the form of a sacrifice. ɔsɔfo Ahɔr, a priest who was also a royal man, offered himself as a martyr for the community. "They cut off his head and put his blood into a pot because blood is the soul of the body" (J. B. Crayner, personal communication, January 21, 2017, Mankessim, Ghana). Soon after Ahɔr's sacrifice, the epidemic ceased, and the population continued to thrive. Christensen also recounted, "A great plague swept through Fanti country which could not be controlled, and they were told by Nananom that a member of the group would have to be sacrificed. No one was willing to offer himself except Ahɔr, and because of this, he was praised by the people, many gold ornaments were placed on his shoulders, and there was much mourning at his death. Today Ahoba Kuma is in memory of his burial, and Ahoba Kese to commemorate his funeral" (1954, 31). Therefore, each year, the Fante in the Central Region honor Ahɔr with many festivities to commemorate his life, sacrifice, and death.

The first of these festivals, small Ahoba (*Ahuba Kuma, Ahooba Kuma, Ahoba Ketsewa*), is celebrated at the end of May. It marks the end of the old year and begins the new year. According to Mensah Sarbah, an author and observer, "Ahuba Kuma is a religious festival in the Fanti districts, from the conclusion of which, time is computed. The Monday succeeding the Ahuba Kuma is called Gopon" (1968, 13–14);[9] or week one is the "First Great Monday" or *Eguapon*. Week two is *Ego Ebien*; week three is *Ego Ebiasa*; week four is *Ego Anan*; week five is *Ego Enum*, and so on, up to *Egua Duebien*, the twelfth Monday. The Friday following is *Ahoba Kese*, when additional festivities occur along the coast. *Ego Anan Fida*, the day I walked with Nana, was the Friday of the fourth week.

As I climbed the hill on that *Ego Anan Fida*, I noticed that the hill had been carved into steps and stacked with sacks of clay, so the ground was not as slippery as the other times I climbed it. I learned later that the project was commissioned by the chief's nephew, who, because of the latter's illness, was acting as regent for the town. As usual, a group of young men that often sits atop the hill observed me climb up. I stopped at the shrine for Nana Sésa, the guardian God of the town, and reflected on his song.

> *Nana Sésa Kwesi pom' andwe a bisa Kwesi ɛ*
> (Nana Sésa Kwesi, if the sea is calm ask Kwesi ɛ)
> . . .

I walked up the hill and veered right to the house of another mentor, Maame Ama Esuon, who taught me many songs, including several about her lineage and her great-grandmother, an Asafo warrior who fought in the war at Elmina. When I entered the house, I raised "*Yɛyɛ Kɔnafo,*" one of the Kona lineage songs that she taught me (example 12 ♫). She sang with me.

On our way out of her house, I asked about an offering they made to the Mother Goddess Nana Eminsa. She told me she supplied all the items: two hens and a sheep. However, she did not participate in the preparation because, as she explained, "They used widows to help, but widows are not supposed to be there. When I inquired, they told me the curse will go to those women's families."

She walked me to the house of another woman, Maame Aba Sackey, the death of whose father, a Kormantse Asafo bell player, caused a riot between the two rival towns, Kormantse No. 1 and Kormantse No. 2. We stopped at the house of another mentor, Maame Ama Aprokuwa, who taught me many Asafo *ndwom*, including one that warriors performed at night to ward off evil spirits during the town's drumming ban. According to her, community members stamped wooden pestles on the ground and walked around the town, singing:

> *Yie osenkyire ɔreba o*
> *Abofra Kakraba ɔakɛfa manso aba*
> *Yie osenkyire ɔreba o*
> . . .
> A small child has brought dispute

I asked her about *Ego Anan Fida*. She corroborated what I had learned and expressed her disappointment, adding that the Elders had to teach the young ones about their traditions, otherwise "Our town would fall!"

I started to sing two of the songs that had been taught to me by another teacher. Both songs are about loss—appropriate, I thought, since we were talking about lost traditions:

> *Daano dua kakraka no a osi hɔ no a onnyi hɔ!*
> (Last time, the big tree that was standing there is not there).
> *ɔrokó e waanyɛ yie*
> (S/He was fighting, but s/he did not succeed)

She sang with me and corrected my projection and pronunciation. On my way back down the hill, she and her son elaborated on the importance of *Ego Anan Fida*.

When I got to the bottom of the hill, I thought to myself: *I must go back up and visit the local parliament to think through what I have learned about this day and that place. I want to take those memories I have learned about this event for a "walk." This would be my way of memorializing and envisioning the event.* Since "Walking produces a different set of mnemonics, offering other ways of reimagining places, of unearthing connections and inventing them with meanings" (Impey 2018, 74), returning to the hill would be my way of imagining and reimagining the place. Such a repeated walk, with new intentions, I thought, would allow me to view the paths differently. One sees again what had been missed or taken for granted the first time. Furthermore, if it is true that places and paths remember events and everything that happens leaves a trace, then I might be able to sense those events. *Etua wo yɔnko ho a, etua dua mu*, "When it's pierced into someone, it's pierced into a tree," the Akan say. I wanted to experience memories of this event myself, in my body: a haptic way of knowing.

As I headed back up, a woman who saw me go up earlier asked, "You are going up again?" I replied that I left something up there. I made the slow, steady climb up the steps. I was panting. I tried to hurry as the Asafo performers had done in the past; however, I was very tired, so I stopped to catch my breath. How did they run up this hill while drumming and singing? This time, I was critically aware of the overgrown bushes on either side of the hill that I had not paid attention to the first time. According to my mentor, had the event occurred, the men of the town would have cleared these bushes. I walked to the Asafo *posuban* military post and stood in front of the female statue; I had been told she was a warrior and the sister of the town's founder, Nana Komer. She was holding a sword with her hair parted and fashioned into three *nyansapɔ* wisdom knots, a sign of her high social standing. One of the wisdom knots had fallen off. I reflected on her honorable mention in one Asafo song:

> Call: *Oye! Oye! Oye! Oye! Oye! Kofi Dedu mba ya ara ee . . .*
> (It's good/It's good/It's good/It's good/It's good/ We are Kofi Dedu's children/It is us . . .)
> Answer: *Oye ooo! Oye ooo! Oye ooo!*
> (It's good/It's good/It's good)
> . . .
>
> Call: *Sɔ wo itur ano/sɔ wo itur ano/Ekua Yaaba aa*
> (Hold your gun/Hold your gun/ Ekua Yaaba)
>
> Answer: *Sɔ wo itur ano!*
> (Hold your gun!)

The statue of Nana Komer, the town's founder, was still on the floor, his gun by his side (see chapter 2). I walked behind the *posuban*, stopped by the shrine of Nana Eminsa, and reflected on her appellations, "Ama Amine e!" "Osuom Ampong!" "ɔkɔtɔ Kurase!" "Obaa basia a ne tɔma akron!" and her song, "*Eminsa Osuom e, Nana Eminsa Osuom (e), Obi mfra hɛn (o). . .* (see example 9 ♫).[10] This time, as I walked away, I noticed a sheepskin, from the offering they made, nailed onto a wall next to the shrine.

I continued to walk between and behind houses and arrived at the Aban Enyim. This was the local parliament where local laws were deliberated. It was an old tree (*adɔma dua*), with its roots exposed. Its branches and leaves provided a nice shade from the hot sun. Empty green schnapps bottles laid at the foot of the tree—evidence of the many libations that had been offered over the years to ensure the success of the occasion. According to Kormantse oral tradition, the tree was here when the first settlers arrived. No shoes are allowed here; only the King is exempt. I took off my shoes and recalled what had been shared about the law deliberation day (*mmra hyɛ da*):

By this time, around 3:00 p.m., the Kings and townspeople had gathered; the three Asafo companies had also congregated, drumming and singing many of their songs:
1. *"Kofi Dedu"*
   Oye! Oye! Oye! Oye! Oye! Kofi Dedu mba ya ara e

(It's good/It's good/It's good/It's good/ It's good/Kofi Dedu's children/It is us . . .)

2. *"Adende"*
Adende, Tuafo mba, waa-ka bosom nsu a ya ara . . .
(Alas, Tuafo's children, if it is left with water from the gods, it is ourselves . . .)

3. *"Nkum na Abandze"*
Ya ara nkyɛ, ya ara nkyɛ, ya ara nkyɛ, ya ara nkyɛ, ya ara nkyɛ . . .
(If it were us; if it were us; if it were us; if it were us; if it were us . . .)

4. *"Itur tein!"*
Itur tein ɔnye hɛn ara/Abanyinsɛm ɔnye hɛn ara/Wɔ ma hɛn kakraba a/Yɛnnkɛgye!
(Gun fires/We are the gun fires/We are the courageous men/ If you give us small, we would not accept it..!)

. . . .

Since "memories and recollections won't give . . . total access to the unwritten interior life of . . . people. Only the act of the imagination can help" (Morrison 1995), I walked around the tree, imagining myself among the people, witnessing the important event. I stopped at various points around the tree. Sometimes I stooped or sat on the floor. I reflected on what my mentor and friend, Maame Ama Aprokuwa, shared about the proceedings:

> The other day I was telling you that when we set the laws, there are three Asafo battalions/groups. We have Amfɛrfo battalion; we have Kyiremfo; we have Adzewafo. Each one has where it is located, playing Asafo. Everyone and his Asafo. So, when they bring the laws, they would give it to the Amfɛrfo and they take out what they want and add some; then they would give it to Kyiremfo battalion. "This one if we add if to it, it would not work." Then they would take it out and add some to it. Then they will take it to Adzewafo battalion, aaaa . . . before they come to an end and seal it. So about 6:00 p.m. before we go to the Aban Enyim; there is a God there. We call the place Aban Enyim. They used bamboo to construct a fence for the place and they constructed three mounds and placed it in front of the God. That is where they stand with schnapps. When they recite each law, the Asafo would drum in response; if they read one, then they would play Asafo and pour alcohol aaa . . . until they read all the laws till about 7:00 in the evening before they finish. Today, they have stopped all of this.

I continued to imagine myself among the crowd as an observer. *The crowd of Kings, lineage Elders, children, men, women, old, and young are here. During the legislating, no electric lights are used. They use the torchlight, so it is not very bright. A dawur bell is played before each law is read. Sometimes Nkum people, the neighbors, also come and listen to the laws. After the laws have been read out loud, deliberated, and approved, the ɔkyeame King's spokesman calls out, "Oye ooo, O ye o!" the crowd answers, "Oye o!" "Oye ooo, O ye o!" "Oye o!" "Oye ooo, O ye o!" "Oye o!" Three times because ɔbosom anim yɛko no mprɛnsa, "Appearance before the fetish is made three times." The three Asafo battalions—amfɛrfo, adzewafo, kyiremfo—play their battery of four drums and bell enthusiastically after each law is read to seal it. The townsmen burst out loud with approval, clapping, singing, cheering, and dancing. After all the laws have been read and approved, the Kings leave first, then the crowd disperses with an understanding of the laws; they walk through the town with their chattering, excitement, and disappointment down the hill to their homes. Nana makes copies and gives them to all the Elders. Each ebusuapanyin lineage Elder meets with her/his members to ensure that they understand the laws of the land. In addition, the King's spokesperson visits various sections of the town, plays the dawur bell to get people's attention, Tón-Tón-Tón-Tón-Tón-Tón-Tón-Tón-Tón-Tón-Tón-Tón-Tón! reads out each law, and ends the announcement with another Tón!*

After about twenty minutes at the parliament, I walked away. On my way, I asked a lady who had been watching me the entire time if she knew *Ego Enan Fida*. "You are the lady who studies Kormantse *abakɔsɛm* and Asafo songs?" she asked. She did not know that the day was *ego anan*. I asked if she knew the name of the tree; she did not, but she advised me to ask Teacher Hammond (Nana Odum III), my mentor. As I walked back, I ran into one of the guides who led our first history walk through Kokoado town eighteen months earlier. I asked him about the event that was supposed to have happened at the parliament. "I don't know why they do not do that anymore." He seemed concerned and walked away. I continued to stride through the town, then down Kokoado hill thinking . . . *by this time, the laws had been accepted; people would have descended the hill. Everyone understood the consequences for certain activities, rules about divorce, marriages, theft, adultery, funerals, weddings, and so on. These laws apply to all Kormantse residents. Everyone is clear on how to conduct themselves.*[11] What happens now that this event did not take place *today? Would the townspeople use the old laws instead? Does everyone know those laws? What about a visitor like me?* Our Elders say, *ɔhohoɔ nto mmra,* "The visitor does not break the law."

ɔkwan wɔ aso (The Path Has Ears)

Anthropologists Tim Ingold and Jo Lee Vergunst's study on the phenomenology of walking (2008) offers important perspectives on the extent to which walking allows us to engage with the land, our environment, other people, and ourselves.[12] Ethnomusicologist Angela Impey's discussion about how crucial walking was to her method in her study of the music of women in western Maputaland is instructive.[13] Walking allowed her to experience and connect with the women's music and songs as they strode the different paths the women had traversed in their youth. She notes, "By walking with the women, I begin to appreciate how routes and mobilities are refracted sonically, both present in and resounding from their pasts" (2018, 74); like me, she also emphasizes the importance of playing instruments or singing on these walks. "We walked as an entire group and occasionally in pairs, tracing some of the routes and pathways that the women had taken as young girls while playing their instruments. Walking and playing produced a different kind of remembering" (37).

As I traversed the various pathways and around the local parliament, my body recalled and "worked out" memories my mentors had shared with me. It helped me connect with the events that occurred along those spaces, the land, and stories. "The walking body can be in the places it has made. Walking shares with making and working that crucial element of engagement of the body and the mind with the world, of knowing the world through the body and the body through the world" (Solnit 2000, 29). By engaging the mind, body, and soul, I connected with what had been shared by others about those spaces and landscapes. Furthermore, walking the path from which oral narratives grow and thinking with the multitude of stories I had heard as I walked those paths provided an important opportunity to experience and re-present those stories and memories in new ways. On this walk, I was no longer the student or searcher listening to stories and memories people shared with me. The stories were no longer in my mentors' heads. They were in my body and they took over my body as I relived and reimagined them. No longer the passive listener, I became an active agent who embodied those stories, walked them, and reexperienced them, becoming more knowledgeable and aware of the paths I traversed, allowing for the acquisition of new knowledge. ɔnantefoɔ sene oni ne ɔse asɛm.

But what are the implications of "walking and thinking with" others' memories? I tried to climb the hill like the Asafo drummers had done in the past; I walked to the adɔma dua tree as Kormantse Ancestors had done; I stood by it and reflected on the proceedings that happened in the past. I re-created and lived a historical moment. Those "acquired memories" are forever warped onto my body and brain and now my "prosthetic memory" (Landsberg 2004). However, could I take them off as I would a prosthetic device? If Joseph Ki-Zerbo is right that "one cannot live a memory that belongs to someone else," then what good are these memories? I reflected on these and the implications of my walk with others' memories as I stepped away. I recalled Bonilla's "memory walk" (2011) with labor activists in Guadeloupe.[14] My walk with the memories of Kormantse teachers and Asafo pasts was no different from hers, though I did not stop for refreshments or eat from the trees on my path as she did; neither was my walk with a group. I developed a personal relationship with the surrounding area, which had since become my asɛnkyerɛdze (symbol/witness) to this event, a site of memory for the Kormantse legislative process. As I walked back through the alleys, behind people's bedrooms and kitchens, I thought about the footprints I left behind with others before me.

I was happy I made that walk—quiet and alone, but important for contextualizing an event that I would not have experienced otherwise. Memory walks helped bring the past into the present. The presence of the tree, my reflections on others' memories, the imagination I crafted, and the Asafo songs I performed along the way made it a unique experience. Far from Papua New Guinea, whose Kaluli "song paths," according to Feld, served as "waterfalls of song, a sense of place resounding,"[15] or from Australia, whose Aborigines use "songlines"[16] to memorialize, connect, and recreate the land, these walks linked walking, singing, memory, and the sense of that place. When I got to the bottom of the Kokoado hill, I told the woman, "I have finished!" I was exhausted. Still, ɔtotɔn mfɔn, "The purchaser (of food) never grows lean." A walker knows more than her mother and father.

ɔnantefoo Hunu Amane, "The Walker Also Suffers": Are We Going or Coming?

Ten days later, on Monday, July 9, as Nana and I stood by a fruit stall at their night market, an announcement, reminding the Kings and lineage

Elders (*ebusuapanyin*) to attend a gathering at the King's palace (*ahenfie*) to set the laws of the land, blared from a loudspeaker from the communication center. The announcer gave the day, date, and time of the meeting. Normally, the King's spokesman would have sounded the *dawur* Tón-Tón-Tón-Tón-Tón-Tón-Tón-Tón-Tón-Tón-Tón-Tón! to get people's attention, deliver the message, then end with Tón! He would walk to the various vicinities, and Tón-Tón-Tón-Tón-Tón-Tón-Tón-Tón-Tón-Tón-Tón-Tón-Tón!, repeat the announcement, and Tón! Nana was livid. "Laws of the land too is it the palace that we do that? *Ego anan* came and went; they did not deliberate laws at the right place. It is sixth Monday after Ahobaa kuma (*Ego Esia Dwowda*); they are now making announcement to set laws!" (July 9, 2018). I asked Nana if he would attend the meeting. "I would go if they invited me." He advised me to attend and report back to him. They did not invite him.

The next day, on Tuesday, I walked to the King's palace to attend the meeting, but it had been postponed till the following Friday. Nana was not happy the meeting had been cancelled. To show that I did not walk for nothing, he took that opportunity to tell me about one Asafo warrior (*Asafoakyerɛ*) from Abandze who marched her people through Kormantse No. 2 (Nkum) town, after Nkum residents refused to allow her group to pass through to play their drums at a neighboring town. According to Nana, with a sword in hand and her Asafo drummers behind her, she stormed through the town. The Nkum residents, fearing her wrath, stepped on either side of the path as the performers processed through with drumming. Nana sang a song that commemorated that occasion called "*Ekua Oguanyi na ɔreba n*" (example 13 ♪).

On Friday, July 13 (*Ego Esia Fida*), I walked to the palace again to attend the gathering with the Elders. As I walked down the street to the palace, people asked if I was going to the lawmaking meeting. Beautiful women leaders and lineage Elders adorned in multicolored and patterned long skirts with slits on one side, *kaba* (blouses), and carefully wrapped headscarves strolled majestically down the street. How a woman wore her scarf designated their status: proud, distinguished royals, daughters of Mama Africa. Beautiful men, draped in colorful cloths from their shoulders down to the feet, promenaded the main street. How a man draped his cloth indicated his status: proud and dignified royals, sons of Mama Africa. I walked up the stairs and waited. I mused with pride. This is Kormantse. Africa. The womb of humankind. As I stood outside on the porch waiting for the program to begin, I reflected on what was supposed to have happened two weeks earlier but did not occur. The King's spokesman was frustrated. "As for lawmaking, is it not the Aban Enyim where we do it? I have been in office for eight years. I have only seen it done once at Aban Enyim at Kokoado Upper Town! They should have played the *dawur* to remind people" (Kyeame Kweku Suapim, July 9, 2018, Kormantse, Ghana).

There was no Asafo drumming or ɔkyerema drummer to usher in the event. After all the lineage Elders and Kings settled, I stood by the entrance and observed the proceedings. It began with a moment of prayer by the Okyeame and Asafo Supi Wobir to the Supreme Being, *Nananom* Ancestors, and the various Kormantse Deities.

> Asafo Supi Wobir
> Okyeame King's Orator
> Show respect
> Slide your feet from sandals
> Lower your cloth from your left shoulders to your elbow
> Lift up bottle of schnapps
> Summon Supreme Being
> Nananom Ancestors
> Deities
> Guidance
> Blessing
>
> Queen Mother
> Lineage Elders
> Kings
> Deliberate
> Wayward youth
> Teen pregnancy
> Galamsey illegal gold mining
> Tomb robbing
> Marriage fees
> Funerary customs
> Infidelity
> Deliberation
> Disagreements
> More deliberations
> Adjourn

> No Asafo drumming
> No *ɔkyerɛma* master drummer
> No *dawur*
> *Diinn . . .*
> Silent
> Ah, Kormantse
> Land of warriors
> Granddaughters and sons of Komer
> Dousers of Asante fire
> Proud descendants of Ekua Yaaba
> Proud daughters and sons of Mama Africa
> Wearing colorful and beautifully designed cloth
> Walking in beauty
> Kormantse Ngyedum
> *Rehuru anaa rehra*
> Are we going or coming?

Before I left the palace, the King's spokesman assured me that once the laws had been reviewed, they would climb Kokoado hill and finalize them at the Aban Enyim local parliament. They would invite me. That did not happen the following three weeks I was in town.

> Tón-Tón-Tón-Tón-Tón-Tón-Tón-Tón-Tón-Tón-Tón-Tón-Tón!
> Ebueii
> Kormantse Ngyedum
> Ngyedum gyedo
> *Egua anan Fida*
> Came and went
> Memory walking in beauty
> Balancing shadows
> Shadowing

> "Oye ooo, O ye o!" "Oye o!"
> Amfɛrfo, kyiremfo, adzewafo
> Adɔma dua
> Owumena death pit holds your matters that have come and gone
> Your memories

I climbed and climbed
Slipping

Yɛde brɛbrɛ na ɛdwa tɛtea hunu ne yam adeɛ
It is with utmost patience that we dissect the ant to reach its entrails
Wo nsa hyɛ obi anomu a yɛ mpae n'apampam mu
When your hand is in someone's mouth you don't strike the person on the head

Ah Kormantse
When we walk, we're not walking alone
It is the walker who eats sweet things
Who knows more than her mother and father
Ken-ke-ren ken-ke-ren
Wadweoo, waadwe
You don't go to someone's town and proclaim yourself a royal

ɔtotɔn mfɔn
The purchaser (of food) never grows lean
The path has ears
So
Yɛde brɛbrɛ na ɛdwa tɛtea hunu ne yam adeɛ

Memory walk
Yes, you
Etua wo nyɔnko ho a, etua dua mu
When it's inserted into someone's skin, it's in a tree
Enter into the lives of others
Their memories
The haptic way
I climbed and climbed
Memory walking
The path has ears, eyes
Memories
Tón-Tón
Tón!

PART 2

Walking with Women

CHAPTER FOUR

Walking with Women at Kokoado Hill and Kormantse Seaside

Mmarimma nyɛ sumyɛ na yɛ de yɛ ti ato so
(Men are not pillows for us to put our heads)

—Ghanaian Akan Proverb

ɔbaa na ɔwo barima
(It is the woman who gives birth to a man)

I more or less experienced that with my childhood girlfriends in Senegal, and I wanted to tell it as such. This film that I have made, is for me, is a song to women. The things I find so beautiful, the things that I have lived, that I have experienced or that I have been told.

—Safi Faye in Beti Ellerson,
"Africa Through a Woman's Eyes," 196

Nyew o sogya ɔreba o
Nyew o sogya ɔreba o
Nyew sogya
Abofra kakraba akɔtwe manso aba fie
Nyew o sogya
Abofra kakraba akɔtwe manso aba fie
Nyew o sogya, nyew o sogya, nyew o sogya
(Yes o; Soldier is coming o
Yes o; Soldier is coming o
Yes o Soldier
A small child has brought dispute into the family
Yes o Soldier)

—Kormantse Asafo song, *"Nyew o Sogya"*

"Precious Beads of Africa: Through Indigenous Eyes"

I grew up around educated, strong, independent, proud, and beautiful women. For these women, female agency and self-determination defined their core values. They worked at home and/or outside the home because they had been told *mmarimma nyɛ sumyɛ na yɛ de yɛ ti ato so*, "men are not pillows for us to put our heads." They had power over their bodies, wombs. I was shocked to learn in my adult life that white women in some European and American countries had to "fight" to work outside the home and made a big movement about it. *Abrewa hwe ase a, ɔde hyɛ ne poma*, "When an old woman falls down, she blames her walking stick." Hm! Who is hapless, weak, and servile? Carried unto carriages? Finances, properties controlled, bodies objectified and wombs policed. Projecting. *Kwatereka se ɔbɛ ma wo ntoma a, tie ne din*. "If a naked person promises to give you a cloth, listen to her name." Sojourner Truth who had worked outside the home all her life since childhood asked, "Ain't I a Woman?"

Like Oduyoye who writes that all the women she "knew worked: farming, trading, or processing and selling food and other daily necessities," the women I grew up with worked as farmers, office workers, teachers, entrepreneurs, homeworkers, cooks, headmistresses, politicians, activists, warrior women, artists, doctors, priests, and so on. They did not have to fight to work. Marriage did not change women's economic involvement or status either, and for the "Akan family, meetings included both women and men. Women's concerns in the larger community were taken care of by a chain of decision-making that culminated in the ɔ*hemaa* (Queen Mother), who is in fact senior to the ɔ*hene* (King) in the ruling hierarchy" (1997, 7). I do not remember any woman who stayed home and just took care of the children, what people call a "homemaker" or "housewife." When they stayed home, they still worked outside the home. They had stalls, tables, or stores in front of the houses from which they traded. Those who did not have kiosks stored the merchandize in their rooms; if you needed something, you went to them, and they got the stocks for you. Women owned farmlands, houses, and other properties. Controlling their finances, their inheritance, and their livelihood made them independent because *mmarimma nyɛ sumyɛ na yɛ de yɛ ti ato so*. My mother traded many items at home and in town. Sometimes she put trays of goods—oranges, bananas, scarves, iced water —on our heads to peddle in the neighborhood. All these entrepreneurs, though savvy, fine, controlled a lot of wealth, had their own *súsú* banking system, and controlled the stock markets, were called "petty traders." Hm!

The African women I interacted with as a child and as an adult, including my mother, were not servile or childlike persons who needed to be rescued by some Western groups (Oyéwumi 2003); they were women who carried themselves with confidence, self-determination, dignity, and pride. My sisters and I, and the girls in our community, aspired to become independent like the women. We wanted to control our own finances. Learning that *mmarimma nyɛ sumyɛ na yɛ de yɛ ti ato so* and *ɔbaa na ɔwo barima* made us girls feel powerful and proud. Such positive and empowering images and the fact that I belonged to a matrilineal lineage informed how I carried myself.

Because Asafo is often presented as a male institution and one in which men dominate (Chukwukere, Christensen, Datta, De Graft Johnson, Nketia, Okeke, Shumway), I made it a priority to walk with women and to learn from their knowledge of Kormantse *abakɔsɛm* and Asafo.[1] What do women know about Kormantse *abakɔsɛm*, politics, and Asafo *ndwom*? The women I interacted with at Kormantse were hardworking, caring, loving, and independent women who did not wait for others to define their lives or conditions. They defined themselves through their words, actions, the way they walked and swung their arms and hips. They were not afraid to walk alone, and they allowed their buttocks to jiggle side to side when they walked, with permission from nobody. She-ke-re, she-ke-re, ke-re-ke-ke. They were not afraid to speak their minds, either. At times, they remained silent because *Fɛfɛ na ɛyɛ fɛ, nti na ɔdɛɛmaani/ababaawa tu mmirika a, osɔ ni nufu mu, ɛnyɛ sɛ ɛbɛte atɔ ntira.* "It is because of her beauty/fashion, that is why the beautiful Black woman holds her breasts when she runs, not that they will drop off" or *Aboa kɔkɔsɛkyi se ɔde ne kwasea pɛ nyin kyɛ.* When they were angry, you knew it; you felt it. They would not smile if they were unhappy with you. They were also very vocal, because *Sɛ woankasa wo tiri hoa, yɛyi wo ayi bɔne,* "If you don't talk about your head, you get a bad haircut." When they did speak, you felt their anger. They did not hide the anger to appease anyone. Claiming the angry Black woman definition, with pride. Anger has not killed anyone. They were also passionate, loving, and candid. *Twene ti da hɔ a yɛnyan nkyɛn,* "When the vellum of the drum is there, we don't play on its side." They were loud and proud. Oh, and they talked about men! "*Mmarimma nyɛ sumyɛ na yɛ de yɛ ti ato so!*" "The trouble with men." "As for men. Hm!" "Leave them to their own issues. They have many." "Ah! When a man leaves you, don't cry-o. You will not eat rocks! Ebueii." "*ɔbaa na ɔwo barima!*" "*ɔbaa na ɔwo barima*! They know not to cross us."

Most Kormantse women lived in houses of their lineage or lived in the company of other family members and women. They led independent lives of honor, respect, dignity, pride, and were major players in many activities. They continue to serve as custodians of a deceased family member; they sing *ebusua* lineage songs for the deceased during funeral ceremonies; they control the fishing trade; they are the guardians of the family history and songs, keepers of tradition in Kormantse society, and they have a lot of knowledge about Asafo matters that have come and gone and *ndwom*. Contrary to Ba's pronouncement that some women have to emerge from shadows (speaking about her experience in Senegal, an Islamic society), Akan Kormantse women I interacted with did not "emerge from the shadows." They were always visible through their strategic positioning as citizens of Kormantse, culture bearers, savvy politicians, and entrepreneurs, and they were definitely not the women who have been portrayed as "hapless victims of a totalizing patriarchal-capitalist oppression" (Tamale 2020, 58; see also Chandra Mohanty 1984).

These graceful Kormantse entrepreneurs traded goods by the road, in stores, or from their rooms. Sometimes, they conducted business from door to door or walked from one town to another. They controlled their finances. Like the women I grew up with, walking alone and with others was something that Kormantse women did. They walked to their friends' houses; they walked to the farm alone; they walked to church alone; they crossed the street alone; they peddled their stocks alone. They walked through the countryside and through the town and did not perceive walking as a dangerous and disorderly zone from which women must be largely excluded for their own protection. The women, who would later become my mentors—Maame Ama Poli, Maame Ekua Tekyiwa, Maame Ama Esuon, Maame Ama Aprokuwa, Maame Aba Sackey, Maame Ama Owusuma, Maame Ekua Atta, and others—walked with pride and dignity.

Thus, contrary to Careri's observation in South America, their walking did not mean "coming to terms with many fears: fear of the city, fear of the public space, fear of breaking rules, fear of usurping space, fear of crossing often non-existent barriers, fear of other inhabitants, nearly always perceived as potential enemies" (2017, 13). Still, I should be clear that Kormantse women practiced certain ways of walking that I believe contributed to their comfort on foot. They interacted with people. They knew the environment and their awareness was enhanced by the many trails that they had carved over time. They walked with confidence and took possession of the space by using it repeatedly and feeling at home in the new space, taking note of every detail and expressing courage by the way they dressed, and conveying boldness by how they walked and swung their hips. They made eye contact and talked to people they met on the way.

Like African women, Kormantse women are intelligent. Brilliant. I learned important lessons about Asafo *abakɔsɛm*, *ndwom*, aesthetics, and performance, how to ask questions, how to sit, how to sing, how to present myself, and how to speak with Elders. The walks conjured memories of my walk with women during my childhood. They evoked the wisdom that *mmarimma nyɛ sumyɛ na yɛ de yɛ ti ato so*. Their stories were engaging, playful, funny, personal, critical of the state of Kormantse affairs, rich, and full of songs with details that only they shared. When we went on physical walks, they pointed out specific landmarks and shared memories and songs those sites evoked. What became clear to me was the extent to which women's landscape memories differed from those of men—how age, interests, lineage affiliation, and "gender affects the way landscape is seen" and that "gaz[ing] upon the landscape means something quite different for a woman than it does for a man" (Wenner 2006, 4). Besides knowing the land and Asafo songs, the women I walked with were especially knowledgeable about the seventy-seven Gods, and they were the first to share a list of their names, early on in my search. I celebrate Kormantse women's beauty and wisdom, their vulnerability and resilience, their agency and pride, their voice, their songs and dreams, their memories, their generosity and humanity, and their audacity to define themselves for themselves with permission from nobody. Here is my walk with beautiful women at Kormantse seaside and Kokoado hill. Proud daughters of Africa.

Kormantse Women: The Seaside Is Home

I interacted with Kormantse women for the first time at the seaside during my second day at Kormantse. The seaside was sandy, with aged coconut trees whose large and overgrown roots protruded through the sand. Children climbed them, while ropes tied around others kept fishing boats in place. The Atlantic Ocean rolled, bellowed, and thundered, while crashing waves threw themselves at the mercy of the land and against the moored fishing boats. Boats on the sea or by the sea danced with the waves. This is a fishing town; fishing is the primary economic enterprise. Men go out to sea to fish and the women smoke, dry, fry, and package them for sale and storage. Entrepreneurs. Here at the seaside, children ran freely, while adults walked easily and confidently. They had mastered how to balance the sand on their bare feet and shoes over the years and were oblivious to whether it got into their eyes, whipped their heels or soiled their clothes. They planted their feet firmly into the sand and danced with it, while I trudged lightly and slowly, stepping from side to side, trying without success to avoid the sand's splash on my body and clothes. Sometimes, it got into my eyes; I blinked frantically and wiped them. At times, I stopped in my tracks to regain my vision. People stared at me, some with suspicion. Who is she? Why is she walking like that? The beads around my ankle drew more attention to me. My calculated steps and inability to move about without care gave me away as an ɔhɔhoɔ stranger, new to the landscape, new to town. New woman at the seaside. My ways of walking defined me.

The place was packed with beautiful women walking, conversing, and trading their prized merchandise; children walking, laughing out loud, running, and playing; beautiful men walking, chatting, mending their fishing nets, or playing board games. With particular attention to the beautiful women, I stood in one corner by a coconut tree and took it all to mean that

> The seaside is home
> A gathering place
> Stock market
> Playground
> Political rally
> No white policing here
> Black African women, men
> Walk freely
> With permission from nobody
> Children run, jog
> Freely
> Dive into sand like it's the sea
> Play football
> No care for sand
> Screaming, shouting
> Being children
> Rambunctious. Free to be themselves.
> No school to prison pipe-line here
> The seaside is home

CHAPTER FOUR

If sand had ears and eyes
What would it say
The seaside is home
Women
Precious Kormantse beads
Spread cloth on the sand
Commune with other women
Chatting, laughing, singing
Solidifying bonds
Swinging arms and hips
Buttocks shaking with each step
Jiggle-step, jiggle-step
Jiggling
She-ke-re, she-ke-re
Hm!
Loud and clear
Relaxing
Entrepreneurs
Trading
Fried cassava and sweet stew aroma fill the air[2]
Men are not pillows
ɔbaa na ɔwo barima
Abrewatsia
No care for sand
Not under western eyes

Men gather and chat
Play cards
Board games
Talk politics
Mend nets
Free to breathe and walk
They are not pillows

As for women
Converse, politicking
Oblivious to men
Men are not pillows

> ɔbaa na ɔwo barima
> These Kormantse Bentsir women
> It is because of the beauty of the African woman
> That is why she runs she holds her breats
> Not because they would fall down
> Ei!
> Independent and determined
> Witty
> Pa-paa-pa
> *Hwɛ!*
> The seaside is home

After a while, I walked back to the main town and joined a political rally and street parade celebrating the results of the presidential elections.³ Later I walked up Kokoado hill to Kokoado Upper Town.

What Maame Ama Poli Said: *Wɔ boa.* "They Are Lying!"

The first woman I encountered at Kokoado Upper Town and walked with, though briefly, Maame Ama Poli, had a warm smile. She had a short haircut with a mix of black and gray hair. Beautiful. She reminded me of my third-grade teacher. Like many of the women, she lived in a family house with a huge indoor patio for socializing. I knocked and entered the house. I greeted her and told her about my search for Kormantse and Asafo *abakɔsɛm*. She confirmed the stories I had heard about the Kormantse-Asante war, but as previously noted, she vehemently denied the claim that the bananas and plantains did not bear any fruit. *"Wɔ boa! Wɔ boa! Wɔ boa!"* she insisted.⁴ She did not remember any Asafo songs, so she asked a young boy to take me to another woman, Maame Ekua Tekyiwa, an elderly woman of about eighty-five years.

What Maame Ekua Tekyiwa, the Farmer, Said: "Ki-kim! Ki-kim! Hri-di-di-di-di-di, sru!"

Maame Tekyiwa belonged to the Kɔna *ebusua* lineage and lived in an older house built by her great-great-grandmother. In my haste to hear the story, I did not notice the artwork on the house. Built into the wall, a small trough, a family altar (*ebusua akor*), was filled with water. I learned that members pour water or alcohol into it and pray to their Deity every Friday. I introduced myself and told her about my interest in learning about Kormantse Asafo *abakɔsɛm*, songs, and especially about the war between Kormantse and Asante and the death pit. She was hesitant because, she said, "I may have some memory lapses." However, I assured her that her story is part of many stories that would help craft a larger picture of this *abakɔsɛm*.

Maame Ekua Tekyiwa began, "The hole was already there; *tse-tse kaa-so-mu te-teeba* [ancient narratives that have been shared repeatedly in the ear], when they came, the hole was there. Plantains were in it; bananas were in it. The Asante, they set out tsim, tsim, tsim, tsim; they set out to come and fight them. They said they were going to burn the sea."

Ama: "Why?"
Maame Tekyiwa: "They were going to burn the sea. And the Elders said they will not allow them to burn the sea."
Ama: "But why did they want to burn the sea?"
Maame Tekyiwa: "The early settlers thought that since the sea makes lather, they thought if they go and burn it, it will burn. They said they would not allow. If they would not allow, then they must put something in place (a collateral). And they would give them [the Asante] gold; they would take the gold and they would go with it. Then they realized that all the town's gold was finished. So, the next time they came, they did not give them the gold. So, they said, 'if they come, they would take someone away.'"
Ama: "They will take who away?"
Maame Tekyiwa: "They would burn the sea. Then, one day, when our men were going to sea, one man had his pipe; so, when the fire was on it, it fell in the sea. And the fire went out. And they said, 'Aaaa ... so this thing, this sea, it boils but it does not burn! (Ohur na ɔnhyew).' Aaa ... so, if they [the Asante] burn it, it won't burn. And because of this they have taken all our gold away. As for this year, if the Asante come, we will let them burn the sea.' When they came, they told them that the road is there; they should go and burn the sea. And they went. They [the Asante] put fire in the sea; it went out. They put it in; it went out. They put it in; it went out. They came back and they said, 'If that is the case, then we are going to take an Elder from here and take him to become a slave at Kumase.' And they [Kormantse Elders] said they would not allow that. And one person, Egyir, offered himself. He told

our Elders, 'I will go. When we get on the road, I will shoot myself.' He arranged with the townspeople here that when he goes, when he gets on the way, he will kill himself . . . so when that happened, he went; he told the Asante he was going to toilet. When he went into the bush, he took the gun and shot himself. And the gun fired. By that time, the Asante had come aaa . . . they had come aaaa . . . . and when they heard the gun, it created confusion and chaos. Kim! Kim! Kim! Kim! Kim! Kim! Kim! Kim! Ki-Kim! They said, 'We were going to burn the sea, we couldn't; we were taking you; you have killed yourself. Even if you kill yourself, we will take you. Even if you are dead, we will take you.' When the gun fired, they came running Hri-di-di-di-di-di, hri-di-di-di-di-di; they came and fell in the hole. Hri-di-di-di-di-di, hri-di-di-di-di-di; they came and fell in the hole. Hri-di-di-di-di-di, hri-di-di-di-di-di; they came and fell in the hole."

Ama: "They did not know that a hole was there?"

Maame Tekyiwa: "The plantains had made a bush; they had filled the hole, covered it up. Bushes had filled the hole, so they did not know that it was a hole. So, when they went, they went, they went and entered (fell in)."

Ama: "Where were the townspeople?"

Maame Tekyiwa: "The townspeople were in the bushes; it is their town, so they knew the landscape and where to hide . . ."

Ama: "Did they know the Asante were coming?"

Maame Tekyiwa: "They knew. They said they were coming to burn the sea; they couldn't; then they said they would take an Elder to Kumase to enslave him, but he killed himself. When that happened, the guns 'talked.' These people fired; those people fired. These people fired; those people fired. And the Asante, they said, 'Kwasi e, outside is here!' When they went, they fell into the hole, 'Sru.' They fell into the hole 'Kim! kim! kim! kim! kim! kim! kim! kim! kim! Ki-kim. Sru. Hri-di-di-di-di-di, sru! Hri-di-di-di-di-di, sru! Hri-di-di-di-di-di, sru! Sru! Sru! Sru!' All of them did not come back. [They died]. And they said, *Wo kum apem a, apem bɛba,* "If you kill a thousand, a thousand would come." They said, they [the Elders] should meet them at Edena. That one too, they went to fight with them. These people [Kormantse warriors] were victorious at Edna. Hri-di-di-di-di-di, sru! Hri-di-di-di-di-di, sru! Hri-di-di-di-di-di, sru! Sru! Sru! Sru!"

Ama: "So, this is where they started and then went to Edena?"

Maame Tekyiwa: "Yes. They said, Wo kum apem a, apem bɛba! If you kill a thousand, a thousand would come. So, they should meet them at Edna. And they met them at Edna."

Ama: "Do they have a song that memorializes that fight?"

Maame Tekyiwa: "The Asafo song? "Kormantse and Abandze," as for that one, it is recent. As for the Asafo songs, there are plenty. Right now, they have all left my head."

[At this early stage in the search, I had not learned about the Asafo song that commemorated the Edena war "Oye, Oye, Oye, Oye, Kofi Dedu mbaa e ya ara e . . . yɛ wɔ itur, yɛ wɔ aboo, yɛ ma tanfo dzi hyirew. Yɛ kɔ Edena sa. Sɔ wo itur ano" (It's good; It's good; it's good, Kofi Dedu's children, it is us. We have guns; we have rocks; we made the enemy eat white clay. We went to Edena war. Hold the mouth of your gun). (See chapter 7)

Ama: "You don't remember the one with the Asante and the one with reference to the hole?"

Maame Tekyiwa: "No, as for that one, even if my grandparents sang it, I have forgotten."

Ama: "Would you like to see what it looks like?" [I showed her the recording I made.]

From this brief interaction, I learned about a cause of the Kormantse-Asante war and the subsequent one at Elmina. What Maame Takyiwa shared sounded credible since this was my first lesson about the cause of the war. I loved and enjoyed how she sang and evoked the chaos and battle with sounds—her repetitions: "Kim! kim! kim! kim! kim! kim! kim! kim! Ki-kim. Sru. Hri-di-di-di-di-di, sru! Hri-di-di-di-di-di, sru! Hri-di-di-di-di-di, sru! Sru! Sru! Sru!" A few days later, the town's Kings repeated a similar story, though not as colorful, at a townhall meeting about how the Asante threatened to burn the sea, took their gold, and how they defeated the Asante army by "knocking them" into the death pit.

At this time of my initial search, I had not read the various reports about the Asante presence on the coast in the early nineteenth century or the reasons why they came to the coast, two of which were (1) to search for two Assin Kings who affronted the Asante and (2) to have direct access to the European trading establishments on the coast. Neither did I know about Koromante/Akromanti, where the Akyem staged their defensive attack on the

Asante and killed King Osei Tutu—a town whose name and history, I now believe, could provide another possible piece to this narrative (see chapter 3).

A year and a half later, I read in Ellis that "The Asante force under Appia Dunkwa, after defeating Akum, moved leisurely down to the coast, destroying Mankassim and several other towns, and first gained sight of the sea in the neighborhood of Cormantine. They destroyed the town" (1893, 111). This complicated the narrative, especially since Kofi Affrifah wrote that the "Akyem organized an ambushcade.... They stationed excellent marksmen at the village of Akromanti on the banks of river Pra. There they succeeded in assassinating Osei Tutu and killing his retinue almost to a man" (2000, 37). After reading these accounts about the Asante and Akyem at a village named Akromanti, I started to ask more informed questions and continued to inquire about what happened at the Owumena. Some of my sources outside Kormantse contributed to the puzzle. One source said the Asante never fought the Kormantse and that when Kormantse residents heard the Asante were coming, they were afraid and ran away. He said that some went to Otsir, a neighboring town, and that those who live at Kormantse Lower Town currently are descendants of those who ran from the Asante and settled down there. He added, however, "Owumena is significant in Gold Coast history. If anyone tells you that it is not true, they are telling a lie. *Tsir, tsir, tsir*, then they fell in. They came to find Tsibu and Apotei" (Obaatan Nana Budo III, personal communication, July 25, 2018, Saltpond, Ghana).

Though Maame Tekyiwa did not recall a song about the Asante-Kormantse war or any Asafo songs, she started to sing *"Wɔma yɛnkɔ ne fie"* about her great-great-grandmother, Nana Yaa Gyaahyewaa, a rich unmarried Asafo captain who built the lineage house and led the war at Edena (example 14 ※).

While she sang, two women staggered into the house, wailing.[5] They were taunting former president John Mahama for losing the presidential elections.

Woman 1: What are they taking away oo? What are they taking away oo? (wailing)
Woman 2: Mahama-éé! Mahama-éé! Bu-é (wailing)
Woman 1: Paapa-é! Paapa-é!
Woman 2: John-é! John-é!

Woman 1: What did you leave for us? What will your children eat? ɔbaatan na onim nea ne ba bedie. A mother knows what her children will eat.
Woman 2: John é! John é!

One of the women joined Maame Tekyiwa, punctuating the singing with her wails. They went back and forth until Maame Tekyiwa raised "*Santrofi Anoma*," an *adzewa* song (example 15 ♫). One of the two ladies translated the song: "It says, 'Santrofi bird, santrofi bird, if you take it, you've taken calamity; If you leave it, you've left oil behind—prosperity. What does the servant say?'" They accompanied the song with clapping Pa! Pa! Pa! Pa! Pa! and calls, *"Ebuei, ebuei, ebuei, ebuei!"* (My goodness, my goodness, my goodness, etc.). After this impromptu performance, one of the women, Maame Ama Esuon, escorted me out of the house. We walked down a path that led to a structure behind their house. As we walked, she told me she was taking me to the Asafo military post. "Asafo is still here, but church has destroyed some traditions. However, when offerings are made, everyone shows up for the betterment of the society. Christianity is put aside," she added.

What Maame Ama Aprokuwa, the Entrepreneur, Said: "Asafo is Our *Fapem, Aaba!*"

On my way down the hill that day, I walked by a woman dressed in all black—a sign that she was mourning. She had seen me come out of Maame Tekyiwa's house and walk with Ama Esuon to the Asafo *posuban*. She moved quickly, sidestepping holes and undulating clayey ground with ease and confidence, while I trod with care to prevent any slips and falls. *Animguase mfata Akan nii ba*. Furthermore, any misstep and fall would stall my progress. She proved that she had traveled this path many, many times and knew the land. As we descended, she told me about Kormantse Bentsir and Nkum communities in an impromptu walking interview. According to her, Bentsir (Kormantse No. 1), their town, is the original town. Their Elders brought drummers from outside to perform for a ritual during which the roof of their principal Deity's shrine was replaced. "After some time," she continued, "our Elders recommended that the drummers be asked to stay. The mistake we made was allowing them to have a King." I asked her about the Kormantse-Asante war. She did not respond. I asked for her name, but she did not tell me.

Four days later, I was walking along the busy Accra-Takoradi Highway and ran into the same woman still dressed in all black. She was walking alone and heading toward the Ebenezer Methodist Church on the highway (see introduction). I greeted her. She stopped and asked if we, the searchers from the University of Cape Coast, had arrived. Upon learning that I was with the search group and that I was conducting a search on Kormantse *abakosɛm* and Asafo, she repeated the history of the tensions between their town and their neighbor about whom she had shared information earlier. She gave me permission to record on my phone.

Lady-in-all-black: "The other day I said that our principal God called Eminsa, every year they have to renew her roof. When the time comes, they remove the roof and replace it with a new one. They used to play a drum when they removed the roof."

Ama: "Do you know the type of drum?"

Lady-in-all-black: "The drum was called Tén-té. So, when the time came, they would go to a place and bring Akwaafo, people from the bush, to come and play the drum. They brought them and when it was time, they played the drum. They would return and then they would go and bring them again. The Elders sat down and said, 'No, what we are doing is causing trouble, so we should give them a place to stay so that when the time comes, they would not be walking,' meaning they would be here. And we gave that place to them."

Ama: "Where?"

Lady-in-all-black: "At the top. So, we gave them a small place to sleep so that when our God's time comes, they would play the drum for us to replace the roof."

Ama: "Didn't you have a drum?"

Lady-in-all-black: "Okay, there is always something that some people do better. Those who knew how to play the drums were in the bush and they went and brought them. That is why that happened."

Ama: "You gave them a place to stay and what happened?"

Lady-in-all-black: "Those people, since we gave them a place to stay, it meant they were under us. We shouldn't have given them way. It came a time when they installed a King. We shouldn't have given them the permission to install a King because they are under us, since we went and brought them here. Our people did not think like that. So, after they installed a King then they started to create issues with us."

Ama: "So, you are still not fine?"
Lady-in-all-black: "We are not fine."
Ama: "Do they know that?"
Lady-in-all-black: "The Nkum people?"
Ama: "Yes."
Lady-in-all-black: "They know. As for us, there is nothing in our heads. They must know that we are one people. Their mind is that they are half the town."
Ama: "Do you have songs that are about these matters?"
Lady-in-all-black: "As for Asafo songs, we have plenty. If we were at the top, I would have found people who would sing some of the songs for you. Asafo songs are not scarce. They have songs that they sing against us, and we have songs that we sing to chastise them."
Ama: "With the tension, was there a time when you fought?"
Lady-in-all-black: "Yes, we have fought before."
Ama: "When you fought, who won?"
Lady-in-all-black: "Whatever happens, we are the Elders. So, for everything, we are victorious over them."
Ama: "You don't remember any of the songs at all?"
Lady-in-all-black: "The songs . . . hmm. . . . The songs, I don't remember right now. When you come up [to Kokoado Upper Town], I will see you."
Ama: "I will come. If I come, how would you see me?"
Lady-in-all-black: "I will see you. Pass this side [she points to the side closer to where we stood]; don't go on the other side, the tarred road. We had the government put the tar on the road. But they say, it belongs to them. We have big problems, so there is tension. When you come up, you will hear all about matters that have come and gone. How they play Asafo, how other things are done. Have all of you arrived or not yet?"
Ama: "We have all arrived. One even passed us right now."
Lady-in-all-black: "As for matters that have come and gone, there are so many. So later."
Ama: "You said I should pass this side?"
Lady-in-all-black: "Yes. Do not pass the side with the coal tar."
Ama: "Ok, I have heard. Thank you."

The lady-in-all-black was the first person to tell me about the replacement of Goddess Eminsa shrine and the tensions between the towns. She helped me contextualize and appreciate many Kormantse Asafo songs.

I asked for her name again, but she did not tell me. I took her advice, "Pass on this side," seriously and stayed on "their side." ɔba nyansafoɔ yebu no bɛ na yɛnka no asɛm, "The wise individual is spoken to in proverbs, not in plain language." Though she did not tell me why directly, I knew exactly what she meant by "pass on the other side." I did not want to exacerbate the tensions between the two towns, something that could also impede my search. As I walked away, I thought about how, according to her, a drum and a ceremony to renew the roof of the principal Deity's shrine led to the creation of the Nkum township and the subsequent friction and clashes between them.

I later learned from an Elder at Nkum that, in fact, both Nkum and Bentsir migrated to Kokoado together. They came with the same leader, Komer. Asked why the town is split, he said it was because of tension over land and burial grounds. Asked why there is a No.1 (Bentsir) and No. 2 (Nkum), he said when the district came to register them, they stopped at the Bentsir side first.

As to who was the Great Kormantine, a title that Nana asserted the British conferred onto them after they defeated the Asante, a letter from the Provisional Governor's Office dated April 8, 1910, referred to Nkum company as "Great Kormantyne." Entanglements. On my way back to town, I taught,

> Tén-té
> Is it true that you birthed Nkum
> That it is through your beautiful tones and pulsating rhythms
> That Nkum came
>
> Tén-té
> Is it true
> That you came from bush
> Helped renew Eminsa roof
> Replenish the Great God of Kormantse
> Ah!
> Tén-té
> They gave you land
> You elected a King
> *Wotena dufɔkyeɛ di bɔfrɛ a, wo to fɔ, w'ano nso fɔ*
> When you sit on rotten wood to eat pawpaw (papaya), your buttocks gets wet, your mouth gets wet

> Tension
> Clashes
> You are not fine
>
> *Akokɔ didi a, ɔde na na no pepa*
> When the chicken eats, it wipes its mouth on the ground
> It forgets
> Are you the chicken
> That forgot
> The axe forgets
> The tree remembers
>
> Tén-té
> Did No. 1 and No. 2 migrate together
> Settle together
> With Egya Komer
> Who is Great Kormantine
> #1 or #2
> *Okwan tware asuo, asuo tware okwan*
> Who is the Elder
>
> Tén-té
> Is it true?

Five days later, I climbed the hill to Kokoado Upper Town. I ran into the lady-in-all-black again. She was sitting atop the hill overlooking the Lower Town and the Atlantic Ocean. I stood by her. This is what she meant by "I will see you coming up" in our earlier conversation. From this vantage point, people up here caught up on all events happening down at the Lower Town, and one could spot anyone approaching the town or walking through the street. This is why Nana Sésa, the guardian Deity whom I would later learn about, was situated at the edge of the town. Sésa could spot anyone who was coming into town with evil intentions and intervene on the town's behalf. From this vantage point, I listened to the lady-in-all-black. "*Wɔ frɛ me Ama Aprokuwa* (They call me Ama Aprokuwa)." She told me her name: Ama—girl born on Saturday! My namesake. At last! I had won her trust. She wore all black every day because her husband, the *Ebusua panyin* Elder of the Kona lineage, had died months earlier.[6] Among the Fante, she explained, widows and widowers must wear black till their spouse's funeral, and many traditions must be performed and observed by the surviving spouse.[7]

Writing in the 1950s, Christensen recorded why widows are not allowed to touch sacred objects:

> The spirit of the deceased is believed to remain close to the wife for some time following death, and the widow isolates herself in the room where the body of her husband has been. She remains in seclusion for three months, being attended by an old woman, and during this time, she is considered to be unclean. At midnight before the final day of the funeral she carries a clay vessel of embers to the edge of town, or if it is a coastal village, to the sea. She is accompanied by an elderly person who keeps calling out that no one should meet them, for it is believed that the spirit of the husband is following. She throws the vessel into the sea, or on the ground, which is supposed to induce the spirit to leave her, and if she is at the sea, she is shoved into the water three times by her attendant to cleanse her further . . . as no other water is believed to possess the cleansing power of the sea, for it is the residence of Bosompo, god of the sea, and a powerful deity. At the end of her period of isolation, all hair is shaved from her body, all utensils and clothing she has been using are discarded as contaminated. After a year, she dresses in white clothing and goes through the town greeting people to announce her return to society, and she is again eligible for marriage. (73–74)

What Christensen described had not changed much, although some practices have stopped, others have been added. The mother of the widow of an Asafo flag bearer at Cape Coast shared what happens to a woman when her husband passes on:

> At first the woman is placed in a room for three months. Though she can come out of the house, she cannot touch money or sell anything. After the body is taken for burial, the woman is taken to the sea to wash in the sea. She scratches money in her palm three times and then throws it away for children to scramble. She wears white after that, then she pounds into an empty wooden mortar three times and grinds on an empty grinding stone three times to remove dirt from her. During this period, she wakes up early in the morning and

does not talk to anyone till after she bathes. The next day, she buys three boiled corn meal (*kenkey*) and sells them to her sister-in-law for money. She also buys and sells firewood to her sister-in-law. (Personal communication, March 24, 2017, Cape Coast, Ghana)

The period of seclusion has been reduced considerably. However, the surviving spouse is still taken to the sea on Saturday when the deceased is taken to the burial site because the widow or widower is not supposed to see or witness the burial. *ɔdɔfɔ wu a, ɔdɔfɔ nkɔ ayie*. "When a loved one dies, the surviving lover does not attend the funeral." Furthermore, the bath symbolizes the final break between the deceased and widow or widower. She carries fresh water in a bucket and walks to the sea in her black clothing. At the sea, she is bathed and cleansed of all the elements that connected her to the late spouse. Someone pushes her into the sea three times. After the third push, she removes the dark clothes and tosses them into the sea. Then she bathes in the fresh water and changes into her white clothes, symbolizing renewal, a new status. She continues to wear white for six months or more.[8] That widows are not allowed to touch anything related to sacred objects or pass by shrines explains why Aprokuwa would not walk with me to the shrine of the principal Deity when I asked her to help me identify the statue at the *posuban*.

It had been over a year since her husband's funeral when she agreed to sit and chat with me. Aprokuwa still had on white jewelry, a white scarf, and a white patterned top and wrap around her waist. When I asked her why, especially since her son advised her to change from the white attire, she smiled and did not respond. That day, she told me about the *tue nkyen ano* banning of drumming ceremony during which evil spirits are chased out of the town. She had a guest with her who chimed in occasionally.

> Aprokuwa: "Kormantse when it got to some time, we had a bosom thing; we don't play the bell; we don't sing a song; they don't make noise and they place bells under a shed. They call them nkodwoa; they put them on the shed; so, when the time comes, they go and take them. So, when they go and take them, and they sing . . .
> Ama: "How many bells?"
> Aprokuwa: "Three. They are nkodwoa; they call them nkodwoa (clapper bells); they put them on the shed; so, when the time comes, they

go and take them. So, when they go and take them, then they sing a song, Nyew o sogya oreba o . . . Nyew o sogya, Nyew o sogya, nyew o sogya [see epigraph].

Ama: "What does Nyew o sogya mean?"

Aprokuwa: "Teacher (Nana) will teach you. When they do that aaa. . . . The town, led by Asafo, goes around the town, three times, stomping pestles on the ground. After the third round, they assemble at the edge of Kokoado hill by the Nkodwobo and ring the bells, sing songs. Then they fire a shot. They go and throw the pestles into the pit. That concludes it. In the morning, they can play drums or Asafo or can sing any song that you like. After that, you can make any noise you like. Because we stopped doing this, the town is in disarray. Nothing is going well. The ritual ends the ban on drumming. It signifies the driving away of evil and brings health to the town."

Ama: "What is that ceremony called?"

Aprokuwa: *Wo siw kyen ano.* They block the mouth of the drum. When they block the mouth of the drum, they don't make noise. They don't sing songs."

Guest: "Like how the Ga people celebrate their *homowo*."

Aprokuwa: "So, when the time comes, they go and get the bells from shed and then sing the songs and go around the town before you can make a noise." [She sang the song again, with a slightly different text, Nyew o sogya oreba o . . .]

Aprokuwa: "They sing it aaa . . ., and go around the town three times at night stomping ndwoma pestles on the ground to stomp out evil spirits; it is about 12 midnight that they do that thing. So, when they finish, then they take the ndwoma wooden pestles that they used and throw them away into a pit."

Ama: "What are ndwoma?"

Aprokuwa: "What they make fufu with. When they finish, they go and throw them away. That morning after if you have a song, you can play."

Ama: "What about funeral? Can you have a funeral?"

Aprokuwa: "You can have a funeral, but you cannot play a song."

Guest: "You cannot cry. You cannot do anything; the town is quiet. Even if you strike a bowl, they will arrest you. If you strike a bowl, tón-tón-tón-tón-ton-tón, they will arrest you immediately."

Ama: "Can a child cry?"

Aprokuwa: "A child can cry. However, if someone dies, you cannot cry."
Ama: "Can you bury it?"
Aprokuwa: "You can bury it, but you cannot cry. They will arrest you."
Ama: "Do they still perform these traditions?"
Guest: "Right now, they have left it somewhere."
Aprokuwa: "Right now, they have stopped all of them."

During my twelve-month stay, I visited Ama Aprokuwa almost every other day, sat, and chatted with her. She liked to begin, insert, or end phrases with "*Aaba!*" "My goodness." It has become an appellation she and I exchange each time we see each other or talk on the phone. *Aaba*! Aprokuwa is an entrepreneur specializing in groundnut (peanut) oil. She did not have a store at the time, so people came to her to purchase the oil; at times, she would deliver the items at her clients' house. The business was not reliable because many of the clients purchased on credit basis, forcing her to go after them for payment often. *Aaba*!

Aprokuwa lived in a neighborhood with other women and their children. The women knew all the town's gossip and gave me updates on what had happened—the town's thieves, people who stole from egwuaradze items at funerals, those who did not make offerings at funerals, and those who had breached a tradition. I even heard gossips about neighboring towns. I learned very quickly that Aprokuwa was more comfortable sharing information off-the-cuff than sitting for a formal interview. So sometimes, I just went up there, sat, then without any warning she would start to talk about Asafo. *Aso ha ano*, "the ear puts the mouth in trouble," so I learned to control my mouth and did not interrupt.

During one of these impromptu walks up the hill, Aprokuwa shared more light on the renewal of the principal Deity's roof. This was still very early on in my research when most of my teachers who taught me about Asafo, Kormantse *abakɔsɛm*, the various Deities, and songs were women.

Aprokuwa: "That God called Eminsa, when the time comes to remove and renew the roof, our Elders here go to a town, they called Enyineyin; it is by the Ankaful side. That is where they go and cut the God's wood and the men place it on their shoulders and they walk along the mouth of the sea aaaa . . ., someone's foot does not touch the back of the other."
Ama: "The foot touches or does not touch?"

Aprokuwa: "The foot does not touch; if the foot touches here [she pointed at the heel], one year will not reach you; you will die. That is how it is. We have people who carry the roof itself and during the walk along the mouth of the sea. And they use *nyenya* to put on their heads to balance the wood."

Ama: "What is nyenya?"

Aprokuwa: "It is a bush; they use it as a pad to support the loads on their heads and they walk along the beach and then climb the hill. When they bring it, they remove the old roofing and throw it away; if it falls facing up then this year fish will come; if it faces down, then it means dirt has come into the town. During the time when we used to perform those things, our Kormantse here was fine; today, they have stopped all of it; they don't do anything. *Woama ɔman no mu ayɛ hyew,* 'It has made the inside of town to become hot.' Our Gods have gone away because we have ignored them."

Ama: "So, if you look at it, what can the Asafo do for the town?"

Aprokuwa: "The Asafo?"

Ama: "Yes."

Aprokuwa: "One thing is that if you go to any town and there is a posuban, there has to be an Asafo in it. Because the Asafo is our *fapem*."

Ama" "What is fapem?"

Aprokuwa: "Fapem is something that is standing. Our 'standing on,' *nyinado*. Fapem is foundation. So, any town that does not play Asafo, it means it is not a good town because the Asafo is the foundation. It means every town must play Asafo . . . if you play Asafo, it also means foundation. At first, in our town Kormantse, the Elders were there; so those things were also there. Right now, it seems the young men do not involve themselves. So, with the Elders dying, it has made the matter diminish a bit. Unless those like you people who have come and the few who have accepted themselves, help out. Otherwise, the Asafo was our duty; it was our real duty. We did it very well. But these days, the young men have thrown it away.

Ama: "So, when they removed Eminsa's roofing, did they play Asafo when they went for the wood and were coming?"

Aprokuwa: "Eminsa has her song. She has her own song. It is not part of Asafo. Eminsa has her song. Eminsa has her song. Eminsa is not part of Asafo at all. She has her separate song."

Ama: "Do you know it?"

Aprokuwa: "This God here has its song."
Ama: "Which one?"
Aprokuwa: "The ones there." [She motioned her head towards the sea.]
Ama: "It is a God?"
Aprokuwa: "Yes. It is Sésa. It is called Sésa no enyim (Sesa's face). Every God has its song."
Ama: "Sésa is which one?"
Aprokuwa: "These . . ." [She pointed at two rocks in front of us overlooking the town, located right at the entrance of the hill.]
Ama: "These two?" [I pointed.]
Aprokuwa: "These two."
Ama: "What do they do?"
Aprokuwa: "Sésa too, what our Elders say was that let's say, the town, when heat comes into it, illness, hardship, or when a different God is coming from somewhere, if you come, you would come and meet it (Sésa); he would turn into a dog, white like that, a big one. It would not give you way. It would not allow you to bring those things into the town. So, during the time when all these things were there, when they performed rituals for our Gods, death did not deliberately come into our town. When they used to perform those traditions, people did not die so much."
Ama: "People did not die?"
Aprokuwa: "Death did not deliberately come. It is not like today, when they have stopped; it has made heat come into the town. As for the Gods, each one with its song; each with its song."
Ama: "So why do some people say Asafo is fetish?"
Aprokuwa: "Some people say that, but really, if you go to the Bible, the children of Israel, they were in Asafo (groups). Is it not how it is? Asafo groups are there. When they say that, we would say it is culture. That is how it is. Then you see it is culture."

By the time Aprokuwa agreed to an interview, I had concluded as a Ghanaian Akan woman studying with other Ghanaian Akan women that my gender and cultural background did not necessarily guarantee a full insider status or easy access. After all, *Abusua te sɛ kwaeɛ, wobɛn ho a, na wohunu dua biara siberɛ*, "Family is like a forest, on approaching it, you discover that each tree has its own location." I concurred with feminist ethnographers (Kisliuk 1998; Abu-Lughod 1993; Visweswaran 1994; etc.) who address and deconstruct dichotomies between "self" and "other" or insider/outsider labels. The "complexity and fluidity of the boundaries around community 'insiders' and 'outsiders' mean that they can be contested" and even dissolved, because "positionality is malleable and as such it is up to us, researchers, to make the most of it" (Zhao 2017, 189). I was reminded daily that one was never simply "at home," that there are many shades of "at homeness" (Collins and Gallinat 2016, 10), not fully in, and not fully out.[9] I concluded, through my walks with the women as a Ghanaian female at Kormantse, that "insider"/"out-sider" categories are layered, complex, and multifaceted.

By the time Aprokuwa agreed to a formal interview, I had participated in her husband's funeral, made *nsawa* gift offering toward her funeral expenses, spent many times with her family, walked with her to purchase raffia to fence her kitchen and to collect money owed her. I had eaten with her and shared many, many laughs. Before this formal interview, I had sat with her and her family while they awaited her husband's body from the morgue. I cried with her. Before this formal interview, I had visited her husband's Kona house and spent some time with their Queen Mother and other women of the lineage, when they awaited the body of the deceased husband. The women in the house showed me the burial items that the widow and her children had presented for the deceased's final bath and burial. They were like the ones I had seen at Cape Coast (see chapter 6), though on a smaller scale—bags of clothes, a pillow, towel, a mat, chewing sponge, bucket, drinks, coffin, and so forth. Most of the items were wrapped except for the mat, which would be used to receive the body from the hearse. They stood around the burial items, staring blankly at them. They sang a series of dirges and songs of their lineage, such as "*Yɛyɛ Kɔnafo*" (see example 12 ♫).

I had heard another one of these songs before, so I hummed the last line, "*ɔko e ɔko ne ba.*" They accompanied the singing with *insisido* interlocking handclapping patterns. Pa! Pa! Pa! Pa! Pa! Pa! Pa-paa! Pa-paa! Pa-paa! Pa-pa-pa! Pa-pa-pa! Pa-pa-pa! Pa-pa-pa! Pa-pa-pa.... Sometimes they stopped singing and just clapped different patterns, Pa! Pa! Pa! Pa! Pa! Pa! Pa-paa! Pa-paa! Pa-paa! Pa-pa-pa! Pa-pa-pa! Pa-pa-pa! Pa-pa-pa! Pa-pa-pa ... mixed with their lineage appellation, *ɔko wɔya, wɔya, wɔya, wɔya!* They wailed and moaned. Grief. With the burial items in their midst, reality hit home. The great Asafo *kɔtɔkorbanyi Kobena*, their Elder, was really gone and the time had come to send him off to his final resting place. In the absence of his body, the burial items embodied, symbolized him. They talked to him, sang to him, asked him questions, "Why? Why? wailed the Queen Mother, staring, pointing, and shaking her index finger at the burial items, speaking through her tears: "Kobena, you have troubled me o; you have troubled me too much!" *Kɔbena ahaw m' o! Ahaw m' papa! "Buei, buei, buei, buei mmmmmm. . . .* Her sobs, her facial expression, her tone, and gestures expressed profound grief and loss. She could not contain herself, so she left the room. This very small, impromptu, yet intense group performance mirrored the dirges that Nketia describes. Some of the women had their "arms clasped across the breast or down . . . or held at the sides or at the back or supported on the head—all to convey the anguish of the singer" (1955, 9), bouncing, bouncing on their feet, up and down, bouncing up and down. Some just stood and stared. Silent. Disbelief. However, they did not "pace about or rock the body" (10) as the body was absent. Music heightened the mood; it soothed; enacted lineage values, created self, and offered autonomy. Later, the women walked me through a dark passage to where the deceased would be given his final bath and laid in state. Cry . . . y.

Also, before this formal interview with Aprokuwa, I had run with her children, family, and community members alongside the hearse that carried her husband's body, paraded on the main highway and through the town under a scorching sun. A brass band and Hi-Life group played for mourners to mourn. Asafo members gathered and sang to bells and other drums. At one point, I stopped, watched, and listened to the lone Asafo drummer announce the body's arrival with his incisive *gyina hɔ hwɛ kyen* drum language on the talking drum. I did not understand what he was saying, but I imagined him sounding the deceased's appellation.

> Here he comes
> Asafo *kɔtɔkorbanyi*
> He who paves the way
> *Owuo atwedeɛ, baakofoɔ mforo*
> Death's ladder, one person does not climb
> *Dammirifua due*
> Condolences!
> Lineage Elder
> For Kona

FIGURE 4.1. Kormantse drummer Ekow Nunsin playing *gyina hɔ hwɛ*. Photo by author.

Those who come from precious beads
Ahwene pa
The mighty duiker
Who allows the bird to nest in its antlers
Symbol of patience
Dua kɔntɔnkyi na ɛma yehunu odwumfoɔ
It is the crooked sticks that reveals a skilled sculptor
Here he comes
He who speaks articulately
ɛko parrot
Today
Diinn . . .
Silent
Bué

On my way out, after the body had been received into the crowded house, female Elders of the Domna, Aprokuwa's lineage, brought her in to see her deceased husband. She wailed, "Kobena, is this your resting place? Is this your resting place?" Aprokuwa. Dué! Aaba! I walked away in silence and grief. Cry . . . y.

One of the recurring themes that emerged from most of my conversations with Aprokuwa and the other beautiful women concerned the effect of churches on the town and its Asafo traditions. During my stay, the town of barely 10,000 residents had about twenty-five churches—Methodist, Baptist, Assemblies of God, Presbyterian, Twelve Apostles, Catholic, and a host of evangelical churches. On Sundays, all the classrooms at the Methodist elementary, junior-high, and other private schools served as meeting halls for the various churches; other buildings housed additional worship services. Loudspeakers blasted the sermons and hymns across the town. My mentors were distraught by the state of their town. Asafo, especially, had suffered because according to them, churchgoers who sing Asafo *ndwom* or play Asafo were chastised by the pastor in front of the entire congregation.

Ama Aprokuwa knew a lot about Asafo matters and song, but she underestimated herself, and, like many of the other women, she sent me to someone else when I asked. The depth of her knowledge was incredible. Our Elders say, *Wohunu kɔtɔ ani a, wose abaa, nanso n'ani ara ne no,* "When you see the eyes of a crab, you say they are sticks, but those are its eyes." That is Aprokuwa. She is intelligent and unassuming; modest. She spoke passionately about the effects of the fading traditions on Kormantse, blaming not only the leadership but also the younger generation. She was the one who, in her discussions with me, tied Asafo to the other traditions and spoke of how integral Asafo was to the larger Kormantse society. Aprokuwa would not accept any remuneration from me, so whenever possible I purchased groundnut oil to support her business. My experience with her and the other women prepared me for my physical and purposive walk with Aba Sackey, a prominent singer in *Adzewa*, a female type of the Asafo ensemble.[10]

Maame Aba Sackey, Samantaadze: Sensing Place, Placing Senses

Aba Sackey lived at *Owumena kɔn do*, "neck of the death pit," or very close to the death pit. Her house, on the border with Nkum township, was once inhabited by a famous priest, *Kɔmfo* Sisi, who according to Nana would hop on a tree in his yard and ask it to take him to drink *nsa* wine. A wooden bench was placed so close to the death pit that anyone who sat on it had to be extremely cautious. Maame Aba Sackey, I would learn later, was named after her deceased father, Egya Sackey. According to several accounts, before his death Egya Sackey, an Asafo captain, predicted that his death will cause a fight between the neighboring towns.[11] He was right. His burial occurred while an Nkum resident was being buried. Tensions over the right to the land and the right to bury him at a particular spot led to the conflict and a fight during which rocks were hurled back and forth. Aba Sackey's mother was pregnant with her when this happened. According to custom, in ancient times, if a child was in the stomach when the father died, they named it after its father. When, Sackey, the father died and the mother gave birth, they named the child after him. The Elders said, *Samantaadze*, "Even if you have died, your name lives." They named her Aba Sackey.

I had many opportunities to walk with Maame Aba Sackey. The first was an informal talk in which she articulated the circumstances surrounding her name and birth. She also shared a version of the circumstances leading to the conflict between Kormantse and Asante, though hers was markedly differently from what I had heard thus far. According to her, the war occurred at a time when Komer, their Ancestor who led them to their settlement, was still alive. She also indicated that the Asante never got to the sea, countering the many oral narratives I had heard and read later about the Asante presence on the coast. I also attended a funeral with her later during my search.

Maame Sackey agreed to walk with me to the bottom of the Owumena death pit. She was ready and waiting when I arrived at her house at 9:00 a.m. She was holding a six-foot-long walking staff. *Ayɛ kradow*, "Are you ready?" she asked. *ɔbosom anim yɛkɔ no mprɛnsa*, "Appearance before a fetish is made three times." Maame Sackey stomped the stick three times and led our descent into the pit. I stepped behind her; my son, KoJo, followed with a video camera. According to Maame Sackey, this was the safest and shortest route down the pit. I stopped and held onto the tree branches for support as we made our initial descent. Within a few seconds of starting the walk down, she turned around and gave me the stick and instructed me to take off my slippers and took them from me. I asked KoJo to take off his sandals. The wooden staff allowed me to have a firm footing on the ground. As we walked down, Sackey held onto plantain branches for support; even with the guiding stick in my left hand, I too reached out to hold anything that would support me. I turned around to see if KoJo was okay; he trudged behind, trying to balance the video camera.

The footpath appeared to have been traversed for many years; it was worn, pitted and smooth, and seemed to have taken on a "different character according to the patterns of use and social networks that encompass it" (Vergunst 2008, 114). I focused on stepping carefully and in the right spots. Some places had grooves that allowed a firmer support. Other places were less steady and stable. Sometimes my steps were slow and short; other times, because of the slope, I could not help but hurry down the path, once bumping into Maame Sackey. I came to appreciate Edensor's observation while walking through ruins: "The temporal experience of walking is usually far from a successive, episodic events. . . . Walking through ruins characteristically involves circularity and a choreographic repetition through which the same ground is approached and traversed from different perspectives" (2008, 136). "The improvisational performances of the walking body in response to the ad hoc structure . . . can trigger unfamiliar or half remembered maneuvers that jolt the body of the complacent, fixed composure and habitually inexpressive and self-conscious performances played out in the city's streets" (132). My steps were disorganized, a disorganization that was constantly informed by my self-consciousness and awareness of the landscape and space.

I watched how Maame Sackey stepped and tried to replicate it. I could not. I was clumsy.

She knew the path and had control over it. This was home. She meandered and maneuvered it with ease and comfort. We hardly spoke as all three of us focused on the path. This was not the place and time for small talk or walking interview. Since I was barefoot, I was careful to not step on the many splinters, twigs, and sharp objects that covered the textured landscape. We trudged pass plantain and banana trees with fruit, coconut palms, thick shrubs, big trees, and a lot of garbage—broken bottles, cutlery, pots and pans, food remains, and lots of plastic bags—that people had hurled into the pit over time. Some parts of the path were soft, mushy, and wet with leaves; other parts were dry and hard. Some areas were covered with dried leaves or mushy soil, while others were bare, bumpy, and slippery. Are these the grounds onto which the Asante warriors fell to their deaths? My body was "enlivened and challenged by a wealth of multisensual effects—smells, sounds, and "tactilities" (ibid.) from the freshness of the early morning breeze, the dense undergrowth, the moving nonhuman forms, the morning dew on my skin, sounds of birds chirping, scurrying lizards and rodents, to the early morning sun piercing through the leaves. It reminded me of the early morning visits to the farm with my mother and grandmother at our village. This walk presented us with a defamiliarized space in which modes of passage were improvisatory, uninformed by conventions, continually disrupted and expressive" (129; see Kisliuk and Seeger).

I slipped many times. One time, I staggered, slipped, and landed on my buttocks. My bag slipped off my left shoulder and fell to the ground. Most of the items in it fell out. My son bumped into me while I was on ground, dropping the camera. "Be careful," Maame Sackey advised. She stopped and waited for us to get back on our feet. Frustrated at my clumsiness, I asked KoJo to stop recording and took the camera from him. I applauded him for hanging in there. It was a difficult trek. I also asked him to walk ahead of me. We continued to descend deeper and lower into the depths of the earth. So many thoughts flooded my mind; Solnit contends that walking generates "rhythms of thinking" (2000, 2). More than that, the multiple memories—those of my childhood walks to our farm in our village, those from my Kormantse mentors about this place, and those by scholars of walking—meshed into a "tapestry of walking memories." Suffused with this "kaleidoscope of intermingling thoughts, experiences, and sensations," I followed.

Maame Sackey had told me earlier, before the walk, that she comes down this path daily to work on her farm, so she knew the path very well and walked fast, leaving us behind. At some distance ahead of us, she called out, "Are you coming?" "Yes, we are!" I replied. She stopped and waited for us. We continued to walk further into the pit. She staggered and made a sudden turn through and under some thick bushes and disappeared into them. "Maame Aba Sackey-éééée!" I called out. She called back, "*Yééée!*" ("Yes!") "*εwɔ he?*" ("Where are you?"), I asked. "*Me wɔ aha-ooooo!*" ("I am here ooo"), she replied. *This is not how to lead a walk*, I thought to myself in frustration. We finally caught up with her. Because *Onifirani mfa abufuo kwaeε ase,* "The blind does not get angry in the jungle," I did not show my irritation. "Where are we going now?" "We are going there," she said and pointed into the distance. "What is there?" "There is a hole there," she told me. She hopped onto a big mound. I tried to hop onto it three times but could not. "A! How did you get up there?" "Climb and come," she instructed. She helped KoJo up onto the mound. I tried to get onto it on my own. Maame Sackey saw my futile attempts and helped me.

We descended further onto more clayey and rocky landscape. She took off her shoes and continued to walk. We came upon a big mound of garbage. I gave KoJo the walking staff. I was exhausted when we finally got to what seemed like the bottom of the seemingly bottomless pit, though it was not. It had eroded over the years, creating more deep trenches and gutters. Here also, we saw the signs of "Galamsey," the illegal small-scale gold mining that had caused the pollution and drying up of many rivers and other water bodies in Ghana. Deep holes had been dug into the ground by men and women looking for gold deposits. I had been told that at one point, this pit had a lot of gold deposits, much of which was given to the Asante when they threatened to burn the sea. Thinking we were journalists with a camera to confront them about the illegal activity, a group of "galamseyers" disappeared into the bushes.[12]

I looked around. Garbage, plantains with and without fruit, coconut trees, shrubs, other plants, and more garbage characterized the landscape; it looked like a garbage assembly, a site in ruins. Standing and walking around felt like walking through industrial ruin as Tim Edensor describes it. There was disorder, filth, danger, and a sense of loss in this space; at the same time, the trees, fresh shrubs, insects, nonhuman living things that scurried away from us, the hooting sounds of owls, singing birds, the sunlight, and colorful flowers brought beauty and life to it. The plantain and coconut palms and other farmed portions that contributed to the subsistence living of the inhabitants contrasted with the chaotic and disorganized layout of the landscape. *Abɛ bi rebewu a, na esɔ.* "When some palm trees are about to die, they give good wine." *What wine will these palm trees give?* I wondered. The pit was deep, though according to residents it had filled up considerably over time from earthquakes, falling rocks, and illegal mining. As I looked up at the coconut and plantain trees, I thought, *Am I standing in the midst of Asante spirits? If they indeed ran into the pit, they would not have survived.* I thought about the Asafo song, "Akyem Esuantse wom bra o."

Maame Sackey pointed at the largest tree before us that grew close to a huge rock. "This tree is called *bientehur.*" It was enormous! Its big roots spread and penetrated deep into the earth and massive red rock. I asked if we could get closer. She shook her head. I looked up at the tree and pointed at it from a distance. This is the tree, the top of whose enormous branches one sees up at the edge of the pit. This is the tree that, according to Nana, served as the highlight for the *afahyɛ*, their annual ceremony that commemorated their defeat of the Asante. According to Nana, every year in July, they must wake them up and *ka go hɔn do* "put them down again."[13] I recalled what Nana and others told me about *afahyɛ* at what turned out to be another memory walk:

> Afahyɛ!
> Thursday in July
> Go to Owumena
> Wake them up
> Throw them in
> 3 Kormantse Asafo battalions
> Amferfo in red
> Adzewafo in yellow
> Kyiremfo in blue
> Drum
> Dance
> Vigorously
> Chief flag bearer
> Climb tree
> Throw raw egg to him
> In mouth
> Dance the flag
> Drum, dance, sing
> Keep them down!
> Fire!
> Poo! Poo! Poo!
> Po-poo, po-poo, po-poo
> Fire!

According to Nana, during this celebration Kormantse women wore pawpaw necklaces to taunt residents of the neighboring town for the time they chased the latter into the pit and Nkum people had to eat raw budding pawpaw for four days. I asked Maame Sackey about the significance of the tree. She did not know. *Obi nnim a, obi kyerɛ.* "If someone does not know, someone teaches." So, I shared what I had learned with her. After a few minutes of standing, studying *beintehur,* and walking around, she suggested we go back. We started the climb on a different route because according to her, to repeat the same route would be hectic. She helped me

FIGURE 4.2. Aduonum and Maame Aba Sackey in Owumena pit by *beintehur* tree. Photo by KoJo Kisseh Aduonum.

hop onto higher ground and made our ascent through many more undulating paths. Though different, it was difficult nonetheless.

As we walked back up, many thoughts filled my mind, conjuring up other times and places. Since we can "always travel elsewhere, not just along the immediate path but outwards to distant sights and scenes, back to the past and to places in the imagination, and to remembered smells, noises, and non-visual sensations, often those which are stimulated by the sights of the journey" (Edensor 2008, 135), my memory walked to my childhood summers with my late grandmother at our village of Kwahu-Daah in the Eastern Region, Ghana. She had many farms that we visited every morning during our vacation. We usually left the house early in the morning and made a slow ascent past a stream that has since dried up. My grandmother cleared the path through the dense undergrowth with her cutlass (machete) as we moved through the bushes. The morning dew on the leaves soaked our clothes as we tried to avoid the sting of the *ésa* plant. We filled our clay pots with water from a stream. At the farm, we cleared the field, planted crops, uprooted plants, picked vegetables and fruits, and gathered firewood. After hours of working, we cooked on a makeshift stove and ate lunch. I remembered our travel back home through a network of paths, balancing a tray or basket with fresh produce on our heads. On one of these return trips, I hurt my leg and dragged myself *Kum! Ko-ko-gya, Kum! Ko-ko-gya, Kum! Ko-ko-gya, Kum! Ko-ko-gya* . . . through the winding, bushy path.

On this walk to the death pit, I had a clear recollection of the smells and bodily sensations of the past—the fresh produce, the smoke from the stove, the sound of the boiling cocoyam and plantains, and the spicy *nhyerawa* hot peppers, my tongue salivating and preparing itself for the food, my body cringing from the thought of stepping on a snake or coming face to face with a monkey. The hooting sounds of the owl brought memories of my grandmother hollering to communicate with her relatives at neighboring farms. Unlike this walk through the Owumena, our return trip from the farm did not involve more climbing. It was a downhill trend on slippery and clayey ground. We walked with or passed others; sometimes, we passed women walking alone with children on their backs. Sometimes we passed men walking alone with their machetes on their shoulders. Other times we passed by families. Back at home, we cooked dinner, ate, cleaned the dishes, washed up, and sat around the fireside to hear *Ananse* stories. My grandmother was a member of the *Akosua Tuntum* female vocal band. She taught us *Akosua Tuntum* songs.

While the Owumena walk did not end in a folktale and songs around a fire, it was still a walk to remember. I became knowledgeable about the landscape "creating situations in which one can grow intellectually while travelling trails under the guidance of predecessors who have both followed and left footprints" (Legat 2008, 35). It validated the "reality of the past in the present and in so doing . . . re-established the relation between place, story and all the beings who used the locale" (ibid.).

When we arrived at the top, I put my slippers back on and walked with Maame Sackey to her house. I looked back down into the depths of the pit. I understood then how the place got its name, *Owumena*—"death hole." Some call it *Abor mena*—"disaster hole." No one running into this pit, slowly or at full speed, would survive, especially if one is oblivious to it being there. Is this what happened to the Asante, according to the popular narrative? One could even sustain severe injuries if care is not taken on a walk into it. With this and other walks, our steps traced out the "everyday routines of the previous habitués of the path, and were in a sense possessed by them." According to Edensor, "This spectral aspect extends to walking along well-marked paths, where we follow in the footsteps of numerous others" (137). I thought about what this site symbolized for Kormantse residents: their sense of pride derives from how this hole served as a death trap for the strong Asante army seeking their gold and enslavement. On my walk away from the pit, I hummed the Asafo song that Nana sang and wrote down for me months earlier: *Wadweoo waadwe waadwe . . . Wenyi ayεw bi* (see figure 3.1). I was exhausted.

    Aaba!
    Asafo
    Nea onnim no sua a, ohu
    She who does not know, knows by learning
    I keep learning about you
    Meresua momma menhunu
    I am studying let me know
    From beautiful women
    Maame Poli, Tekyiwa, Esuon, Aprokuwa, Sackey
    Ebuei, ebuei, ebuei, ebuei
    Tén-té
    Is it true

    Abofra bɔ nwa na ɔmmɔ akyekyerεε
    The child cracks a snail, but she does not crack a tortoise
    However, *Abofra hunu ne nsa hohora a, ɔne mpanin didi*
    When a child knows how to wash her hands, she eats with Elders
    I am still washing my hands
    Peeling away your many layers
    Deep in the Owumena death pit
    To the rocky landscape
    Banning of the drums
    Funerals
    Every step taken
    Reveals
    Your greatness
    Entanglements with society

    You are *fapem, nyinado*
    Foundation
    Tue nkyen ano

The family is like a forest
On approaching it
You discover that each tree has its own location
Still *Nsateaa baako ntumi mpopa animu*
One finger cannot effectively wipe the face
Fingers of witty and beautiful Kormantse women join mine
To find you
The walker knows more than her mother and father
Nyew osenkyir ɔreba o
ɔko wɔya, wɔya, wɔya
Cry . . . y
For yourself
Death ladder, one person does not climb it

Ama Poli, Ama Aprokuwa, Ama Esuon, Ekua Tekyiwa, Aba Sackey
Speak their truths
They are lying; they are lying
Akromanti or Kormantse
Asubontene Pra
Owumena
Spirited Kormantse women
Ki-kim! Ki-kim! Ki-kim! Ki-kim!
Hri-di-di-di-di-di, sru!"
Aaba!

CHAPTER FIVE

"It Was Too Sweet!"

Walking with Two Kormantse Women

Hu m'ani so ma me nti na atwe mienu nam
(Blow the dust off my eye is the reason why two duikers always move together)

—Akan proverb

In this sense, then, African feminism is a tautology

—Oyéwúmi

If you only hear one side of the story, you have no understanding at all

—Chinua Achebe

Abowa kɛse ahaw wura
Odziamon
Ebusua asɛnkyera dzi a
Sɛ ihu a, nna abɔ birim
Bɔdzafo, wodzi amon
Na Twidan ebusua
Odziamon, odziamon
Ebusua asɛnkyerɛ dze a
Sɛ ihu a, nna abɔ birim
Bɔdzafo, wodzi amon
Twidan ebusua
Wodzi amon
(Big animal master of the hunt
Its eats fresh
Lineage symbol when you see it you get startled

Bodwa people they eat fresh
Twidan lineage eats fresh)

—Twidan Ebusua lineage song, *"Odziamon"*

Krebuu!!! with My Own Eyes and Body

My walk with one elderly lady at Kormantse Lower Town taught me important lessons about Asafo *ndwom* performance and how to enjoy it, how to ask questions, how to sit, how to present myself, and how to speak with Elders. Maame Ama Owusuma, who does not leave her house due to her poor vision and arthritis, is a retired caterer and a successful entrepreneur. She always sits on a stool on her indoor patio with a bucket beside her. Inside the rubber bucket are her medications, cosmetics, and accessories. Seven months into my research, I asked if I could stay with her. She agreed. At the time, she lived with one of her daughters and granddaughter. Her daughter had taken over the catering business, so every evening she mixed the flour at a *nika-nika* milling place at the neighboring town, kneaded the dough, cut and shaped each piece into a loaf, placed them in large wooden cartons, and covered them up with a white cloth overnight. At dawn, Maame Owusuma woke up, lit the oven, and baked the bread with her daughter and granddaughter. Other entrepreneurs came to the house and picked up their share of the bread for sale.

A Digression . . .

Before I stayed with Maame Owusuma, I had walked through Kormantse Upper and Lower Towns in search of lineage houses. *Ebusua fie* usually display images of the first Ancestress and a symbolic animal or plant to convey their history, the importance of women in the various societies, and the lineage's ideals (see chapter 2). Before I stayed at her house, I had visited Maame Owusuma on different occasions to ask about the image on their Twidan house.

Like many Akan societies, the Fante are matrilineal.[1] The matrilineal *ebusua* is the key unit in the social structure. Membership in this exogamous grouping is accorded at birth, although adoption into it can occur. Membership ensures inheritance, use of land, a proper naming, a suitable funeral, and burial. According to my teacher's oral accounts and documented sources on Akan culture, "This relationship is based on the belief that all members of the matrilineal are blood relatives by virtue of their descent from a common Ancestress from whom they inherited the same blood" (Christensen 1952, 1).[2]

According to Mercy Oduyoye, most migration stories of the Akan do put women at the center, with women leading the community to freedom and prosperity. She shared an ancient migratory narrative, one that I had not heard, especially since the Fante credit three men, *Oburmankoma* (Eagle quality), *ɔdapagyan* (Whale quality), an *ɔson* (Elephant quality), as the spiritual leaders who led them on their migration:

> The ancients tell us that as the Akan, the Children of Anowa, progressed south from northern Africa toward the savannah and the Atlantic, they became thirsty and there was no water for miles around. [Walking] with them was a priestess named Eku who had a dog. They came upon a lake, but they were frightened to drink the water lest it was poisonous. Eku let her dog drink of the water. Nothing happened to the dog. Then Eku herself, as leader, tried to prove to the people that the water was drinkable. She drank and nothing happened to her. Whereupon all the people shouted *"Eku aso"* (Eku has tasted) and they ran forward to drink. The place where the incident happened is known to this day as Eku-Aso. (Oduyoye 1997, 8)

Oduyoye's narrative makes no mention of men as leaders of the Akan; it confers the leadership to a woman. ɔbaa na ɔwo barima.

Therefore, in these societies, unlike in patrilineal societies, a woman "never becomes a member of her husband's family. She remains a member of her own family and so do the children that she bears. This means that what her own family loses on her getting married are her services on the farm, for example, but in the place of this, it is understood by her family that the husband is going to help her have children who will ensure the continuity of her own lineage" (Oppong 1991, 9). Furthermore, as Oppong continues,

> Marriage in a matrilineal one is, on the whole, less stable than marriage in a patrilineal one, but it also means that a woman in such a society is less likely to put up with ill-treatment from her husband. This is because she continues to enjoy the protection from members of her own family and may even continue to live in her family house

TABLE 5.1. Fante Lineages and Totems*

Lineages/Ebusuakuw	Totem/Asenkyeredze	Subgroup
Nsona	Crow or fox	
Twidan	Leopard/Tiger	Eburotuw
Konna	Buffalo or bush cow	Ebiradze
Anona	Parrot	ɔyoko, Agona, Eguana
Aboradzi	Dog	Tekyina
Ntwea	Fish	

*Mensah Sarbah (1897, 5), quoted in Christensen (1954, 21). The Nsona, Twidan, and Anona have more members. Tensions among members and migration have led to divisions and breakaway groups. The totem on the Nsona lineage houses that I photographed is a crow with white marking around its neck. See Christensen for further discussions regarding the origins of the Nsona and Aboradzi and their totems. Although lineages do not regard themselves as descended from the *akyeneboa*, the *akyeneboa* embodies the ideas and represents the qualities the lineages must live up to.

after marriage. That confidence that such a woman has is reflected in the Akan (Ghana) saying which translates as 'If you divorce me I will not eat stones.' (Ibid.)

Since through the centuries it has been only the maternal Ancestors who mattered, the succession and inheritance has remained strictly in the female line, the children belonging to the *ebusua* of their mother (Meyerowitz 1951, 29).

The Fante, like other Akan people, have seven to eight *ebusua* and groupings (*ebusuakuw*). Many of them have subgroups that sprang up because of migration or tension within the main lineage. Each *ebusua* lineage has a totem (*akyeneboa* or *asɛnkyerɛdze* among the Fante), and if this takes the character of an animal, this animal must not be trapped, killed, or eaten.[3] The Twidan have *twi nndzi twi*, "kurotwamansa does not eat kurotwamansa," to stress the idea that people of the Twidan lineage do not eat, trap, or kill their totem, a leopard.

During my search, I came across lineage houses at Apam, Anomabo, Abandze, Cape Coast, Elmina, Kormantse, and Obokrom. At Kormantse, whenever I saw one, I knocked on the door, asked permission to take a picture of it, and asked about the significance of the various symbols, as

TABLE 5.2. Kormantse *Ebusua* Lineages and Totems

Ebusua/Lineage	Ahyensew/Symbol
Anona	Ekoo—Parrot
Kona	Ekó—Deer
Twidan	Sebɔ—Tiger (image more like a leopard)
Aboradze	Awenadze—Lion
Nsona	Akonkoran—Crow (with white collar)
Dehyena	Parrot
Domna	Edom—Fish

well as any songs associated with them. One *Aboradze Fie* (Aboradze clan house) had two lions standing on a stool between two swords and a plantain tree said to be the original crop. It did not have the image of the Ancestress. Another Aboradze house displayed more symbols: a seated Ancestress, totemic symbols—plantain tree and lion, and a young hunter arriving from a successful hunt. *(A)Kona Ebusua Fie* featured a woman seated on a stool and an antelope with a leaf in its mouth and a bird's nest in its antlers. The Kona totem, the deer, represents *abotar* patience because the deer allows birds to lay their eggs and hatch. This artwork on one house has the deer with a nest in its antlers and a woman, with the wisdom knots hairstyle, seated on a stool holding a sword. The three captions, from top to bottom, identified (1) the Kona as an original lineage dating back centuries, (2) the great-great female Ancestor, Nana Gyaahyewa, a warrior and Asafo captain, and (3) the name of her lineage.

All the images have a woman seated on a stool, wearing beads around her neck, earrings, and a *nyansapɔ* wisdom knot hairstyle. One woman is breast-feeding a child; one is holding a gold-weighing scale; another is cooking; other women, like Nsona and Kona Ancestresses, are holding swords to show their warrior status. What do these images tell us about African women, Ghanaian women, and Fante women? How does their "presence" unseat the centuries-old myth about "African women as impoverished helpless victims?" (Aidoo 2006). I was equally interested in any *ndwom* that expressed the spirit and character of the Ancestresses and their lineages.

One day, I asked a woman seated outside the Twidan house about the significance of the images; she did not know. She asked a boy to take me to one of her Elders, Maame Ama Owusuma. We crossed the Accra-Takoradi Highway and walked to the house of Maame Owusuma, a beautiful elderly woman with an animated spirit. She was advising a young girl about some mistakes the latter had made. The girl did not seem happy. The Akan say, *Sɛ wo te sɛ obi retu ne ba fo a, tie bi fa hyɛ wo ho,* "If you hear someone advising her child, listen to it for your own good," so I stood at the doorstep for about five minutes and listened. Maame Owusuma punctuated her words with *anwensɛm* proverbs and *ndwom* in a manner that I had not experienced before (what I have attempted to accomplish here.)

When I finally knocked and entered her house, she looked at me from head to toe; her eyes moved down to my ankles and paused at the beads around them. She stared at me, then the beads for a moment. Then she offered me a seat and asked about my *amandzeɛ* mission. I told her about my search and asked her about the significance of the Twidan image and the role of the woman in it. She was surprised that the image had a woman and insisted that there was no woman in the image. She said it was only a leopard, and that she had the cloth with the image of the leopard. While she dismissed that a lady was in the picture, she admitted that she had heard of a lady, Esu Esha. I showed her all the pictures I had taken of the lineage house. She directed me to her nephew, the artist who drew the image, to ask about the woman in the image. She instructed me to ask for the woman's name and to come back to her with the answer.

The nephew, Teacher Asebir, was a teacher at the junior high school and a visual artist who drew many of the images on the Kormantse lineage houses. He insisted that the woman in the image was *Abrewa Tsia*, Matured Short Lady, and her grandson.

> Teacher Asebir: "If you look at the drawing, the top of it, it has been written that *Odziamon Nananom*, Descendants of those who eat fresh meat. It is on the top. At the bottom it has been written *Twi Nndzi Twi* (Leopard does not eat leopard). How that happened was that the family itself is called Twidan, Twidan—*wɔdan Twi*.
> Ama: "*Wɔdan twi?*"
> Teacher Asebir: "*Wɔdan twi. Wɔdan twi ana woeedzidzi.* They depend on *kurotwamansa* tiger before they can get something to eat. So Twidan, that is how it came to be. People who depend on tiger. The story is that there was once an elderly woman and her grandson who rested under a tree. The grandson was a hunter. Every day, he would

FIGURE 5.1. Twidan *Ebusua Fie*. Photo by author.

go hunting before he gets meat to bring home for them to eat. One day, when he went hunting, he could not get any meat. He wandered a lot but could not find any meat. If you remember in the drawing, there is a pineapple and a kurotwamansa also standing there with meat in its mouth. There is another piece of meat on the ground that the animal did not eat. Since the boy could not get meat, he went and stood under the tree. The tree is also in the drawing. He was standing there, and he saw that there were some ripe pineapples on a hill, so he was standing there looking at the beautiful pineapples, it looked like gold."

Ama: "Gold?"

Teacher Asebir: "Gold dust. So, they have a proverb that says, *Kurotwamansa a, ɔnam ne sika aborɔbɛ ntsi ɔkɔm nndze n'da,* 'The Kurotwamansa that because of golden pineapple, never starved.' Kurotwamansa is a 'tiger' and because of the golden pineapple, it was never hungry. So, the boy was under the tree looking at the pineapple. What he suddenly saw was that the tiger had come from the bush and to the pineapple. Because the pineapple was ripe, this is where the small animals came to eat. So, the kurotwamansa hid there. That is where it hid so it too can get food."

Ama: "The tiger?" [Some call the animal with spots a leopard.]

Teacher Asebir: "The kurotwamansa gets food to eat by the pineapple. So, the young man was standing under the tree, all he saw was that the tiger had returned. When it came, it caught one of the animals eating the pineapple and ate it. When it finished, it caught another animal and placed it in front of the young man, turned around, and walked away. So, when the young man took the meat and went home, his grandmother asked him, 'Why have you been so long? Today you took too long.' You saw in the picture that she has a pot ready and was waiting for him before she could get meat to put in the soup. The child took the meat home and his grandmother made soup with it. The next day, the boy did not go hunting at all; he went and stood under the tree and waited. When the animal finished eating, it brought him some of the meat again. The young boy took it home. Which means that all the time, when he was just roaming before and could not get something to eat, he did not have to roam. Later, he came to depend on kurotwamansa before he could eat. During the going and coming back, going and coming back, people heard about him and came and joined that family and they named it *Nkorɔfo a, wɔdan twi ana woeedzidzi,* "The people who depend on the kurotwamansa before they can eat." If the kurotwamansa sees that you are a Twidan person, it will not use its mouth to touch you. My grandparent said in the ancient times, when a kurotwamansa died, during that time, there were no towns, so they lived in the bush. So, when a kurotwamansa died, they took it and buried it. They sewed a box and buried it just as they bury a human being. And I myself when I matured, when someone died, one of my grandmothers, her name is Esi Abba, she did not go to school, but she knew how to draw very well. So, she was the one who, every day when a Twidan person died, before they put the box (coffin) down, she would use *ntwoma* red clay to draw the spots on it. . . . You see because of the kurotwamansa's dotted skin, she would take *ntwoma*, then she would use charcoal and whitish clay and draw on the box. She would take her time and place the dots on it just like the kurotwamansa to show that the kurotwamansa's grandchild is the one going. People who depend on the kurotwamansa before they could eat. That is the Twidan family. It is a story that I read, and I developed it into an artistic project" (Teacher Asebir, personal communication, December 19, 2016, Kormantse, Ghana).

Teacher Asebir went on to describe the woman's hairstyle, which, according to him, was a typical style in the olden days for mature or elderly women who were knowledgeable and respectable. "You don't leave your hair *basa-basa*, disheveled. Every day, you tie it with thread to show your *nyansapɔ* wisdom knot." I asked him if he knew of a song that referenced this story. He did not. However, he advised, "You can develop it in a musical way." I thanked him and walked briskly to Maame Owusuma's house.

> *Twidan ebusua*
> *Nkorɔfo a wɔdan twi ana woeedzidzi*
> People who depend on the tiger before they could eat
> *ɔbaa Sima*
> You don't leave your hair *basa-basa*
> Your hairstyle shows your *nyansa* wisdom
> Your knowledge
> Don't put it up carelessly *basa-basa*
> Unkempt
>
> Aaa
> *Kurotwamansa a, ɔnam ne sika aborɔbɛ ntsi ɛkɔm nndze n'da*
> Kurotwamansa that because of golden pineapple, it never starved
> *Twidan ebusua*
> Young man do not roam
> The golden pineapple is there
>
> *Abrewa Tsia* Ancestress
> Plait your wisdom knots
> Take a thread
> Wrap around your hair
> Wear your wisdom knots
> It is because of her beauty/fashion, that is why the beautiful Black woman
> Holds her breasts when she runs, not that they will drop off

> Show off your hairstyle
> Kurotwamansa does not eat kurotwamansa
> *Twi ndzi twi*

I showed Maame Owusuma the picture again. I told her what Teacher Asebir shared about the woman in the drawing. She started a Kormantse Twidan Lineage *ndwom* song, "*Odziamon*" (see chapter epigraph). This is one of many Twidan songs, she indicated. She corroborated her nephew's explanation that the totem is kurotwamansa, which they used in a song. She sang the song again. "Every *ebusua* has its song," she added.

> Ama: "So please, who sang this song for you? Who taught you?"
> Maame Owusuma: "I came and met it. They taught me. Because I was a child, I met and walked with the Elders." She continued her response with another song, "*Wɔse menkyerɛ m'*" "They say I should explain" (example 16 ♫).
> Ama: "What is the meaning of your name?"
> Maame Owusuma: "You don't know Owusuma, you see?" She looked away.
> Ama: "No."
> Maame Owusuma: "Maame [Mother], as you are sitting here right now, if you are dying right now, would you know it?"
> Ama: "If I am dying? No."
> Maame Owusuma: "That is how death comes. That is what I was saying. My mother birthed ten children; it was left with four. You are recording this? This, don't record."
> Ama: "I should not record?"
> Maame Owusuma: "No."
> Ama: "OK."

I stopped recording and listened to her explanation of her mother's misfortune. When she allowed me to record again, she sang a song from a different lineage, "*Ye fi Abo m'ee*", "We are from rocks" (example 17 ♫). She explained that the song belonged to the Kona lineage:

> They say they are from stones. Ahondze, it comes from the earth, these very same beads. At first, the Elders, they had many beads that came from the earth. They come from rocks. The stones are rocks. So, the best beads originate from rocks. *Yɛ fi abo m'ee eee, Kwɔna aboradze yɛfi abo m'ara yɛyɛ ahondze papa yi a.* They are the Kona

clan. So that is the little that I know. I am not part of the clan, so this is gossip that I am engaging in. If you find someone who is part of it, she can sing it very well for you to hear.

I thanked Maame Owusuma and returned to the seaside. I spent more times with Maame Owusuma and learned many lessons from her. I was especially impressed by how she merged conversations with songs and proverbs. It seemed she had a song for every issue she talked about. I planned to use her conversational evocative style in my own work. *Aboa kɛse aha wura . . . Odziamon . . . Twidan ebusua odziamon.*

Back to Krebuu! with My Own Eyes and Body

So, before I stayed with Maame Owusuma, I knew she could sing. I knew she loved Asafo and had a lot to say about it. I knew she was feisty and straight to the point. We cooked together; she talked and advised me as she would her granddaughter. A lot of her advice was shared as proverbs, because "The wise individual is spoken to in proverbs but not in plain language," *ɔba nyansafo yɛbu no bɛ, yɛnka no asɛm*, and song. I came to know Maame Owusuma as a fierce, witty, and honest woman, who truly embodies the spirit of the kurotwamansa, the totem (*akyeneboa* or *asɛnkyerɛdze*) of her Twidan *ebusua*. A lot of people know her for her ferocity, and I heard that some people avoided her because she "tells it as it is." Her voice is powerful and, like the women I grew up with at Accra, she is direct and does not "hold her tongue." At the same time, she would sit and listen. She is caring and kind. She shared many recollections of Asafo and Kormantse matters that have come and gone and her perspectives on a lot of people in the town. She told me about a lady who used to live with her. According to her, Maame Ekua Atta is a great singer who knows a lot about Asafo *abakɔsɛm* and *ndwom*. Maame Owusuma arranged for Maame Atta to come to the house. When Maame Atta came to the house, Maame Owusuma told her about my search and Maame Atta agreed to share her memories of Asafo with me. We gathered on Saturday, July 15, 2017.

To avoid "the problem of speaking for others" but not quite "retreating" from speaking for them (Alcoff 1992), and to maintain, to a degree, the colorful, complex, and sophisticated nature of their ways of talking and remembering, and as I have done in previous chapters, I share their words as they were related to me. Like Abu-Lughod and others—who

FIGURE 5.2. Maame Ama Owusuma. Photo by author.

decided to explore how the wonderfully complex stories of the individuals they came to know in a community in Egypt might challenge the capacity of anthropological generalizations to render lives, theirs and others', adequately (1993, xvi)—I decided, as in all the chapters, to maintain the dialogic nature of our chat and to focus on my interactions with Maame Owusuma and Maame Ekua Atta in order to avoid the trap of smoothing contradictions, flattening out their experiences, and homogenizing them (ibid., 9). I situate their detailed descriptions of ritual and their storytelling to show how "The vividness and style with which [they] recounted stories impressed me. The rhythms of their conversations, the voices dropping off . . . and then rising to dramatic pitches in enactments of reported speech, the expressions, the exaggerations, the detail—all lent intensity, even urgency, to the tellings" (ibid., 2).

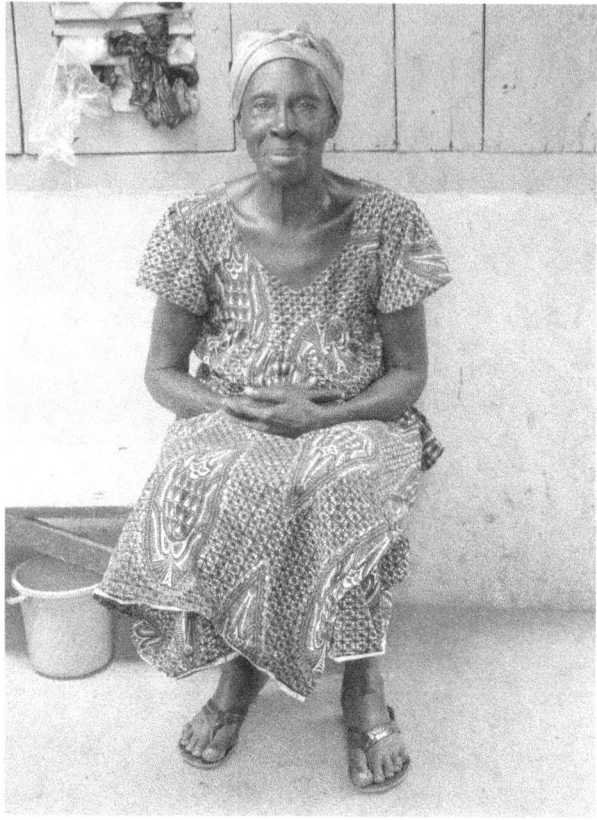

FIGURE 5.3. Maame Ekua Atta. Photos by author.

Since *ndwom* in general—and in Africa specifically—is not an isolated art but happens interdependently with other forms, is multimodal, and because Asafo *ndwom* and culture are integral to all aspects of Kormantse society, our discussion touched on *ndwom*, *abakɔsɛm*, religion, politics, myths, and proverbs in true oral tradition style. They completed each other's thoughts. Sometimes, insults hurled at the other made me uncomfortable; I would often pause to see how the other would react, but they kept moving along as if they were not affected by them. I gathered that their friendship had endured tougher issues than mere affronts. After all, *ɔyaw yɛ mframa,* "Insult is borne by the wind." Their interactions were performative acts—colorful and vibrant, blending different oral features, ceremonial chants, drum rhythms, proverbs, appellations, sounds, and songs performed through footwork, facial expressions, and bodily gestures. Their storytelling and remembering led to topics that I had not considered addressing, such as when Maame Ekua Atta raised an *adzewa* song while we were discussing Asafo. Furthermore, that strategy illustrated how connected and integral Asafo was to the various segments of Kormantse society, culture, and life.

One of my favorite oral features during this conversation was repetition: the repetitions, the repetitions, repetitions, whether in song, words, phrases, or gestures. The same songs came up at different points in the talk; sometimes when that happened, it shifted the topic or added to it. This means that the discussion was not always direct; it shifted and moved as their minds and memories moved, allowing them to control the conversation. It was their story, and they had the right to tell it as they wanted. Furthermore, *Woyɛ nkɔmmɔmim a, wohwere sɛmɔdɛbɔfoɔ,* "If you dominate conversation, you lose the company of good conversationalists."[4] I found this approach helpful, enjoyable, and aesthetically pleasing because it opened more windows into the complexity of the two women's lives, their thoughts, their interests, their lived experiences, and the depth of their knowledge. When words and phrases were repeated, they were done to stress a point, to reflect, or to show their excitement for the topic under discussion. It often changed the rhythmic flow of the conversation, and it resembled the patterns, tonality, and sounds of the Asafo talking drum. It was a true oral event "with sound effects, playing on a complex set of rhythms, (images) symbols, ideas, sounds, etc." (Ogede 1992, 76), and senses. It was too sweet; it was too sweet, too sweet! I have organized the discussions into different sections based on how the conversation evolved.

Unearthing the Roots of a Conflict: Kormantse na Abandze *Ndwom*

Maame Owusuma started the conversation with "*Kormantse na Abandze,*" an Asafo song, a version of which I had heard earlier and one that had been popularized by Ghanaian Hi-Life singer C. K. Mann and his Hi-Life band (example 18).

> Maame Atta: "The hill is up there. Kokoado, if they divide our town into two, one half is here; the other is there."
> Ama: "But why do they say 'Nkum rosu a Bentsir a?'"

Maame Owusuma: "This is Bentsir (Kormantse No. 1). This is where they first settled, slept first. Until Nkumfo came; they should come and play *Ténté*; we brought them to stay here."

Maame Atta: "Ténté is *Akɔmfo* ayer (drumming/*ndwom* for Priest) . . ."

Maame Owusuma: "It is not *Akɔm* ayer (Priest ndwom)!"

Maame Atta: "It is not *Akɔm* ayer?"

Maame Owusuma: "*O, fi hɔ*! (Go away you!)"

Maame Atta: "Ténté is not *Akɔm* ayer?"

Maame Owusuma: "It is played for Eminsa."

Maame Atta: "Our eldest *bosom* Goddess is up there, when the year ends, they remove . . ."

Ama: "Three years or one year?"

Maame Owusuma: "They reroof it three years, three years. When the three years arrives, then the wooden frame that they do it with is rotten. So, they must, since the wood is spoilt, they must go and take some at Eminsa's mouth/edge, and they will get bamboo, and cut Eminsa's wood that stands in it . . ."

Maame Atta: ". . . the tree is called *Esu dur*. The tree is there. They stand around the lagoon. It is called *esu dur*; that is what they cut and tie and stand them by the Bosom (structure). They stand it very large, and they use *ehun* (raffia) to roof it aaaa . . ., until kim, kim! When they do that, the old one, they take it off and throw it away in a pit over there. So, the old, when they uproot it and they remove it, they carry it; those beneath it, big and strong men under it are more than thirty. When they are taking it, the thing it is big; it would encircle itself like this, encircle itself like this, big like this. When they are taking it, then it is encircling itself. Then the women will sing *awo nye, awo nye, awo nye*. [Owusuma joined with excitement] *Awo nye eee nsu o, ɛnam o* . . . What is it?"

This led to *ndwom* 2 and its explanation; Maame Owusuma continued with another Asafo song, "*Awo nye*" (example 19 ♫). She did not remember other parts to the song: "Something, something, something before they threw the old, thatched roof into the pit."

Maame Atta: "The men, the Asafo song they sing is . . ."
Awo nye, awo nyeee
Nnsu oooo, ɛnam ooo
Ampa, Mbrɛana wo bo efuw a!

"That is Asafommba's own. So, when they take the old roof aaaa . . ., then they will release it into the pit, *ru-lu-ru-lu-ru-lu, ru-lu ru-lu-ru-lu-ru-lu, ru-lu, a-te-yam*! (tumbles, tumbles, tumbles, tumble, falls!) If it lands belly-up, looking up [she demonstrates], Hey! We have caught fish already! That year, they will catch abundant fish aaaa . . ., till it overflows. Then, they would sit and play Asafo. They would sit and play Asafo. While some are playing the Asafo, others are putting up the new roof."

Maame Owusuma: "That is what those playing the drum came to do; the women were dancing; priests were in it . . ."

Maame Atta: ". . . the shrine itself has a Priest . . ."

Maame Owusuma: ". . . So, the drum, when they were playing the drum, this place Bentsir, they did not know how to play it. Some of the Nkum people are at Abora side. It is they who our Elders invited to come and play. So, when they came and finished playing, they would go back to their town. They played for about three days and then they would go back to their town. When they go, three years, they would come again. When they came one, two, three times, our Elders told them, 'Don't go; we will give you some place to stay, so that all the time, you will not go and come, go and come, go and come. That is why Nkum got stuck. So that today, they have rather taken everything out of our hands. Our Elders underestimated them and they have taken everything from our hands. Today, it is they whom people listen to when they talk." [Maame Owusuma was upset.]

Maame Atta: "So today, they don't take off the roof again. They have made it block. It is aluminum. Which when it goes bad . . . it is not aluminum?"

Maame Owusuma: "This is some of the matters that have come and gone. They said it; we did not come and meet it. We came and saw its very end. As for us, when we came, the good ones had gone; however, when we came, they did it aaaa . . ., for us to see it. Especially, when they went and took the thing and were bringing it, hah!"

Very early on during our conversations, I picked up on how comfortable Maame Owusuma and Atta were with each other. They talked to each other, at each other, and with each other. Many times, they talked with each other as if I was absent. *Yɛnsiane kokumotie ho mmɔ pɔ*, "We do not bypass the thumb when tying a knot." They went back and forth, arguing back and forth, back and forth, questioning each other, correcting, interrupting each other, and joking. Maame Owusuma did most of the interruptions; Atta ignored it, moved on, or engaged her a bit with a question herself. Maame Owusuma raised a third song. It was in a call-and-response style, and like many songs for the various Deities, it moved freely.

Tribute to Kormantse Gods

They continued to sing a song dedicated to Goddess Eminsa and Odum, "*Odum na Eminsa*" (example 20). The two cheered as they recalled and reminisced about the songs they sang and experienced as children and as young women. They interjected their singing with hand clapping, Pa! Pa! Pa! Pa! Pa! Pa! hand gestures, and foot stomping, Tum! Tum! Tum! Tum! Tum! Tum! to capture their love for Asafo *ndwom*. "*ɔawar Eminsa*" was, certainly, Maame Atta's favorite. She cheered and cajoled while she sang and repeated it again and again. Here I was with two women in their eighties, seemingly weak and burdened with aches, yet enlivened by the songs of their early years. Their muscles remembered the past and refused to stay still. My mind walked to the ninety-six-year-old woman and others who came out of their houses to the Kormantse main street to dance and sing while a group of men performed Asafo songs at a recording session (see chapter 7).

In my excitement, I added, "Hey, hey!" Maame Owusuma called out, "*Gyina hɔ! Gyina hɔ! Gyina hɔ!*" "Stand there! Stand there! Stand there!" and started "*Nana Sesa Kwesi*," a song I had heard about their guardian Deity Nana Sésa, months earlier. Maame Atta joined in the response (example 21).

Maame Owusuma was moving vigorously in her seat from side to side and stomping her feet, stomping her feet. They repeated the song with more gusto about the guardian Deity, personified in the song as someone who is strong, feared, and revered. When he fired a shot, the crowd ran away.[5] It is because of him that the bush and forest is calm, so listeners are instructed to ask him. Maame Atta ended the song with a rhetorical question.

> Maame Atta: "If you are sick, can you heal yourself? If no one comes, you would die!"
> Maame Owusuma: "If I remember some [songs], I will bring them; you too [she told Atta], if you remember some bring it, *ɔawar Eminsa, ɔawar ɔbaapa Na Ama Amina ee*

ɔawar Eminsa ɔawar ɔbaapa Nna Ama Aminee
ɔawar Eminsa, ɔawar ɔbaapa ee
ɔawar Eminsa, waa war ɔbaapa!"

Ama: "What about Eminsa Osuom?"

Maame Atta: "Eminsa, who is up there? That was her song. *Yee, yɛaba oo yee, kɛyerɛdɛ na* Akooku Abaka a, he is up there."

Maame Owusuma: "*Wɔmbom, wɔmbom, wɔmbom, wɔmbom* (Put your hands together; put your hands together; Put your hands together). She stomped her feet." [While she stomped, Maame Atta called out the song they sang earlier, then explained.]

Maame Atta: "There was no time up there. Hah! When they were reroofing her? Hah! *Osuom Ampɔn, ɔkɔtɔ Kuresi, ɔbaa basia, wo tam akron, Awo mber, Okro wɔdan n'* [appellations for Mother Goddess]. Hah! Is it that which we are saying it here ugly, ugly like that (*taan taan yi*)! It was no play at all, at all, at all. Hah! Ebueii! (My goodness!). The first Elders, they were sitting there like something . . . we have come, and we are going. Hah! Ebueii!"

Maame Owusuma: "The world, they have divided it into one hundred; 75 percent of it is gone."

Maame Atta: "It is gone; it is gone . . ."

Maame Owusuma: "These songs, where are some; these songs, where are some?"

Maame Atta: "All the time is gone. With all due respect (*sɛbe tafra kyɛ*), we have worshipped, worshipped God. At first, we were lost, and today, we have seen God, so we don't remember anything."

Their memory walks made my memory walk to the times with my grandmothers at Kwahu-Daah in Ghana when we visited them during the summer vacation. They shared stories and other secrets with us after supper. Here in this shared space, gender did not define my relationship with Maame Owusuma and Atta, and I was careful to not allow gender to define those relationships, because as Oyéwùmí (2003) argues in her edited volume, "Feminism continues to be the most avid manufacturer of gender consciousness and gender categories, inevitably at the expense of local categories such as ethnicity, seniority, race, and generation that may be more locally salient" (4–5). What we shared was more than gender. It was on a level that was familiar and fuller, one based on my childhood memories, age difference, mother-daughter, granddaughter-grandmother relationship, and ethnicity. Not once did I consider our relationship a sisterhood because "the problem with the concept of sisterhood is that it takes political solidarity for granted rather than as a goal to be worked at and achieved" (4).[6] They were my Elders.

> Two beautiful Kormantse women
> Feisty and calm
> Maame Owusuma, entrepreneur
> Maame Ekua Atta, *nwomtonyi* lead singer
> Two women
> Twidan and Kona
> Different but alike
> Hah!
>
> Two women
> *Hu m'ani so ma me nti na atwe mienu nam*
> Blow the dust off my eye is the reason why two duikers always move together
> Memory walking
> Recalling
> Asafo, *adzewa*, Osuom Ampong
> Asafo come back!
>
> Two women
> *ɔyaw yɛ mframa*
> Insult is borne by the wind
> *ɔawar Eminsa*
> *ɔawar ɔbaapa*
> *Na Ama Amin ee*
> *Wɔmbɔm! Wɔmbom! Wɔmbom!*
> Goosebumps
> Sound effects
>
> Ru-lu-lu-lu-lu te-yam
> Hah!

Within ten minutes, they had performed four songs beginning with the song that commemorated a war between Kormantse *Nkum na Abandze* (Kormantse No. 2 and Kormantse No. 3). I would later learn from archival sources that the final line of that first song, "*Nkum rosu a Bentsir a*

("If Nkum is crying, it is because of Bentsir") referenced an old tradition that if there was any trouble between two of the three neighboring towns, Kormantse 1 (Bentsir). Kormantse 2 (Nkum), and Kormantse 3 (Abandze), the third would assist in the settlement. According to a June 25, 1925, document, "Nkum failed to notify Abandze of their celebration. Nkum was in the wrong for not notifying Abandze about holding a custom in connection with elected captains" (PRAAD, ADM 11/1/728). According to that source, a similar event occurred in 1907 between the two towns. While Bentsir was present during the deliberations between Abandze and Nkum at the Saltpond District Office, they could have prevented the conflict before it started by stepping in to help resolve the tensions (ibid.).

Kormantse Bentsir and Nkum Conflict: Safohen Kwame Sackey

I asked Maame Atta and Owusuma about an incident that led to a conflict between their town and the neighboring Nkum. The response touched briefly on Kormantse *abakɔsɛm*, church, and the effect of Christianity on their lives.

> Ama: "Nkum and Bentsir fight that they fought after Aba Sackey's father died; how did it happen?"
> Maame Owusuma: "Be patient, be patient."
> Maame Atta: "Mmm . . ."
> Maame Owusuma: "Listen! Listen! Listen! Ekua, listen! Listen and let me say it, the matter that she is talking; let me straighten it for you-ɛ? Kwame, they did not call him that? Kwame Sackey, isn't it that?" [She sounded irritated; however, Atta did not respond in kind.]
> Maame Atta: "He was at Kokoado. The child's father who died."
> Maame Owusuma: "That is the one I am talking about!"
> Maame Atta: "Kwame Sackey."
> Maame Owusuma: "That is what I am talking about."
> Maame Atta: "Safohen."
> Maame Owusuma: "Yes."
> Maame Atta: "Safohen . . ."
> Maame Owusuma: "His burial, it was during which, whoever, whoever also, Kweku, that child, yesterday, I was mentioning his name and I forgot."
> Maame Atta: "Another person, too, had died at Nkum."

> Maame Owusuma: "So, it was due to his burial [Safohen Kwame Sackey] that brought the war. Hm!"
>
> Ama: "Why did they fight?"
>
> Maame Owusuma: "The plot that is lying there; you, who I came and got you and brought you to come and do my thing for me. I came and got you. But when you came, you said the plot that is lying there is yours!"
>
> Maame Atta: "Even though, you came and met it; even I came and met it."
>
> Maame Owusuma: "Ah! Me, I am putting my thing here, you say, you will not allow it. And he too says, 'If you allow or you do not allow, I will put it here. It is for me. If you allow it or you do not allow it, I will put it here.' That's it."

This conversation helped explain some of the tensions between Bentsir and Nkum. As in this case, dispute over cemetery land led to many tensions and riot between the two towns. According to archival records, a dispute in 1909 erupted because Bentsir cleared the land, beat company drums, which had been forbidden by the district commissioner, while Nkum was at farm and not notified. Others, as indicated in a complaint filed by Nkum, involved No. 1 going to a "forbidden place with military (Asafo) drums and songs."

> Maame Atta: "So, they took Kwame Sackey [his body]; they ran with it and went and buried him and then struck the drum. 'You, beat us.' *Tweaa*! Scare! You did not see one person in town." [She moved her hand from down to up in a quick motion to indicate that they fled, left town].
>
> Ama: "They ran?"
>
> Maame Atta: "They ran. I, myself, I used my own eyes, Ekua Atta, I was alive. Me myself, I tell you. It is not someone who is telling me. Me myself, my eyes *krebuu*! with my own eyes."
>
> Maame Owusuma: "The land is ours" [she chuckled].
>
> Maame Atta: "The town itself, it is Kokoado. It stretches from here aaaa . . ., goes through Nkum to (A)hasowodze. Here, they called it town's child. All this place was bush. This was the only house, and that one, and that one on the thing there. That was the only house here. All of it was bush, *ɛpɔw*, thick forest. Today, it has become a town for a school to come into it."
>
> Maame Owusuma: "And many, many churches."
>
> Maame Atta: "Ao! The only church, no church had come. The only churches that were here were Methodist and Roman (Catholic)."

Maame Owusuma: *"Ebueii é,* these songs, where are they?"
Maame Atta: "We did not attend. Roman, Methodist, we did not attend. We followed our Gods."[7]
Maame Owusuma: "These songs, where are they?"
Maame Atta: *"Ge-ge re, ge-ge-re, ge-ge-re* . . . [she laughed]. Lord, we thank you, Father [She went on her knees]. It is you who change. *Ampa* (True)!"

Asafo Through Women's Bodies: It Was Too Sweet

I finally had the opportunity to ask about Asafo *ndwom.* Prior to this gathering, I had heard and read about Asafo; I had attended funerals where Asafo performers performed; I had paraded with Asafo drummers through the street mourning with deceased family members at Cape Coast; and I had recorded about fifty Kormantse Asafo songs. Asafo is portrayed as a male tradition in which men do the fighting. Men occupy most of the offices, play all the accompanying instruments, call the songs, and clear the paths. Though women are members of their father's Asafo and serve as captains, priests, and warriors, they have been written out of Asafo. I was interested in learning about Maame Owusuma and Atta's memories and thoughts on it because even among people of the same age, gender, ethnicity, and culture, *ndwom* can be experienced differently. The two women corroborated a lot of what I had heard and sang most of the songs I had learned to sing. They also added their vibrant and colorful interpretations of it.

Ama: "So, the Asafo, when they played it, how was it?"
Maame Atta: "The Asafo, they used three drums . . ."
Ama: "Do you know their names?"
Maame Atta: "The drum itself is *Asafo kyen.*"
Maame Owusuma: "She says, the drums that they play, there are three. This one plays this; this one plays this."
Ama: "The three, do they have names?"
Maame Atta: *"Dawur,* you know *dawur* (bell)? It is different from the one playing the *dawur.* That one, it is only him playing the *dawur.* The very small drum is called *tenteba*; it reverberates more than the big one."

Maame Owusuma: "*Me na* (My mother), I am coming. You see at school, they too, they have their drums."

Maame Atta: "But the Asafo one is tall. If it is standing, it is about this high." [She raised her hand to indicate its height.]

Ama: "So, did you see them play Asafo?"

Maame Atta: "Yes, isn't it what I am telling you?"

Ama: "So, when they played Asafo, what was it like? What did it do?"

Maame Atta: "*Gyae!* Stop! It was too sweet. Goosebumps. Goosebumps. When they played it, then all the *saman* ghosts, all the dead ones have descended. This one *tsimm*; that one *tsimm*. This one *tsimm*; that one *tsimm*. *Tsimm. Tsimm. Tsimm. Tsimm.* Tsimm. The women would go *hmm . . . hmm . . . hmm . . . hmm . . .* like that. It was no play! Eh! And when they say someone has died and they strike the Asafo drum, if you are not careful, war will descend. As for today, God, all of it, he has cooled it for us. Eh! Hah!"

Ama: "But it was a good thing for the town? Wasn't it a good thing?"

Maame Atta: "It was a good thing. It was ancient ancient times. It was the *ayer* ndwom of our great-great-Ancestors. They did not know God. When they came, they did not know God. Go and buy medicine to do this. Go and buy medicine to do this. If the *ndwom* happens, when an old man dies, *tsimm*! be prepared. Like that, Aba Sackey's father matter that we were talking about, Hah! When they played. Hm! Even the police people were afraid of this town."

Maame Owusuma: "But you provoked him to come and settle."

Maame Atta: "Hoo! This town, police folks were afraid of its inside."

Ama: "Because of what?"

Maame Atta: "If you come and you don't come well, you will not go back. If you come and you do not come very, very well, you yourself, you will not go."

Maame Owusuma: "*S'abotar. S'abotar.* Be patient! Be patient!"

My inquiry took their "memories on a walk" that showed their love for each other, resilience, and knowledge about Kormantse and Asafo *abakɔsɛm* and *ndwom*. Some of this information I already knew from my walk with other mentors. I was excited about their use of sounds, smells, tastes, and bodily sensations to describe their experience of Asafo *ndwom*, validating Connerton's observation that the past is sedimented in the body (1989). Their ways of telling reminded me of Stoller's advice to anthropologists:

It is especially important to consider the body's smells, tastes, textures, and sensation, especially in those societies in which Eurocentric notions of text—and interpretations—are not important. It is representationally and analytically important to consider how perception in non-Western societies devolves not simply from vision (and linked metaphors of reading and writing), but also from smell, taste, touch, and hearing. In many societies, the "lower" senses are central to the metaphoric organization of experience; they also trigger cultural memory. (1992, 57)

The use of sounds, *tsimm tsimm tsimm tsim, ru-lu-lu-lu-lu, a-te-yam, hmmm...hmmm...*, warm and cold body sensations, and "rush on the body" such as "goosebumps" and taste, "sweet," communicated how much their bodies had "soaked up" Asafo drumming and other traditions. Asafo had touched their bodies, senses and emotions and evoked very strong feelings of joy, fear, and even sadness.

Samantaadze

The conversation quickly turned back to Maame Aba Sackey, the lady who walked with me into the Owumena death pit. Maame Owusuma was still preoccupied with Sackey.

> Maame Owusuma: "You yourself, you were in the stomach, and you are coming to say . . ."
> Maame Atta: "Aba Sackey herself, does she know her father? They said it for her to hear."
> Maame Owusuma: "Didn't she . . ."

Then there was an argument between them about Maame Aba Sackey's mother and her *ebusua*.

> Maame Atta: "So, when the father died, and Aba Sackey was in the stomach, then they gave birth to Aba Sackey and named her *Samantaadze*; they named her after her father."
> Ama: "They named her after her father?"
> Maame Atta: "Ehhhh. If he died . . ."
> Ama: "What is Samantaadze?"
> Maame Atta: "They say Samantaadze."
> Ama: "What does it mean?"

> Maame Atta: "The name that your father, you were in the stomach when your father died. So, you do not know your father. And they name you after him. They gave it to her. Aba Sackey."
>
> Ama: "But you said, "Samantaadze," what does that mean?"
>
> Maame Atta: "If you have died, your name has not died. It is alive on earth."
>
> Ama: "Ahh, Samantaadze?"
>
> Maame Atta: "Samantaadze."
>
> Ama: "But they do not call her Samantaadze."
>
> Maame Atta: "No, they call her Aba Sackey. Aba Sackey. In ancient times (*tsetse aber mu no*), if you were in the stomach and your father died, they named you after your father. That is why the Elders, in ancient times they said, 'Samantaadze, even if you have died, your name lives.'"

Samantaadze was a concept I had not heard about from anyone and was glad to learn about it. I would not have learned about this had I steered the discussion back to Asafo *ndwom*. It cut short our discussion on Asafo *ndwom*, but I was glad that happened. Maame Owusuma was upset about a response Maame Atta gave.

> Maame Owusuma: "So why are you arguing with me?" [Owusuma demanded. I was concerned this might erupt into a big fight and end our gathering. Maame Atta remained calm with her response,]
>
> Maame Atta: "I thought you said she was Aba Sackey's mother."

That resolved the issue. Such exchanges, which occurred often, made me uncomfortable. Later, I came to appreciate that as part of how the two women related to each other: candor. They were honest with each other and understood that *Twene anim da hɔ a, yɛnyan nkyɛn,* "When the vellum of the drum is intact, we do not beat the sides."

Back to Asafo

After a brief discussion on Kormantse *abakɔsɛm*, in which they corroborated the other narratives, they went back to Asafo. Atta raised a song about an Asafo captain who is revered by Kormantse leaders.

> Maame Atta: "Then the Asafo is in it . . . *ke-kre-ke-kre.*"
>
> Ama: "Please can you sing it again?"

Maame Atta: "*ɔhen Gyesi e.*"

Ama: "You say *ɔhen*, a Safohen?"

Maame Atta: "*ɔmanhen. ɔhen Gyesi, gyina hɔ*. It was like, he and his people, he was walking with them, and he stopped. When matter comes, what will you do? *ɔhen Gyesi e, igyina hɔ afor yɛ dɛn*? There was a building there and he was standing there. And he took a walk and came to his children's side." (example 22 "*Gyesi Mbo*" 🎵 🔊).

I had not heard this song prior to my meeting with Maame Owusuma and Atta. I heard it later from the Kormantse song leader, my voice teacher, and a pickup group that I called the Kormantse Five (see chapter 7). According to them, Safohen Gyesi was an important Asafo captain who led many successful wars against their enemies. In this song, the singers gloat about not being afraid (*Yɛ nsuro*) because they were in the company of Nana Gyesi. Singers brag about the war being a day's affair, an easy war (*Dakor asɛm a!*). There were some variations between different interpretations of the song. However, *Obi nkɔ kurom nkɔfrɛ ne ho Agyeman*, "One should not go to another person's town and call herself a Liberator," so I did not challenge them. Furthermore, knowing that *obi ne ne yafunu ntwe manso*, "One should not be at loggerheads with her stomach," I avoided the temptation to cross them. Most importantly, I was happy to hear the different version of songs and *abakɔsɛm* as an indication of what our Elders say, *Ani a ehunuu tetehɔ na eni hɔ, na aso a ɛtɛɛ tetehɔ asɛm deɛ na ɛwo hɔ*, "The eyes that witnessed events of the past were not there, but as for the ears that heard them, they were there."

Ama: "Is that Asafo song?"

Maame Atta: "Asafo song."

Maame Owusuma: "Part of it."

Maame Atta: "They embellish; the Elders, they embellish (*kenkan*) aaa . . ., until they come to the actual song."

Maame Owusuma: "You did not come and meet the Elders. We did not meet them. These young ones, their mouths do not allow them; they are all about money or they are disrespectful."

Maame Atta: "We have forgotten them; we know a little, but there are some . . ."

Maame Owusuma: ". . . but the mind."

Ama: "I am here so if they come let me know."

Maame Atta: "You have not gone yet." [She laughed.]

Religion: Seventy-Seven Gods and Christianity Fighting for the Soul of Kormantse

In his chapter about the "archaeology of memory and spiritual genealogies," examining how the Cromanti/Kromantin' communities in the Caribbean and South America used the memory of Kormantse in present-day Ghana to generate discourses and practices of resistance against slavery and fight for freedom, as well as to create an autonomous African identity in the Americas, Agorsah notes that "the history of the migration to Kormantse is often tied to the founding of Kormantse's deities and their contributions to the survival of the historic Kormantse settlement and people" (2014, 91). The seventy-seven Deities, each with its specific songs, according to Kormantse Elders, continue to provide and protect them. There are no gender-specific pronouns for the Supreme Being in the Akan language; however, the Deities in traditional religions have specific genders. About half of the thirty-five deities whose names were shared with me were female, while the other half were male. Interestingly, what we often associate with male and female entities are reversed; the warrior Deities at Kormantse are female—such as *Bohimahi, Eminsa*—and the protective and guardian ones are male—*Dzerma, Sesá*.

Still peeling the layers off Asafo, the topic switched back to the Mother Goddess and the other Gods. I had heard Her song many times, so I was curious to hear their version of it when I asked Maame Owusuma and Atta.[8] Maame Atta called it and helped with the chorus in a manner that I had not heard before. They sang it twice.

> Atta: *Eminsa Osuom o obi frɛ hɛn o*
> Atta/O: *Hɛn ara yɛdze hɛn man*
> Atta: *Eminsa Osuom o obi frɛ hɛn o*
> Atta/O: *Hɛn ara yɛdze hɛn man*
> *Yegor maa*
> *Aboa bi nyi beebi a na waa fa hɛn yɛdze*
> *Osuom a ɔdzi ne man*

The second call had a slight variation and in ways that resembled how my ten-minute tutor performed it. Here, she replaced Eminsa's name with one of Her many appellations, ɔ*koko Kɛse* (mighty mountain), which shifted the rhythm and flow of the song.

> E: *Eminsa Osuom o obi frɛ hɛn o*
> E/O: *Hɛn ara yɛdze hɛn man*
> E: *ɔkoko kɛse o obi frɛ hɛn o*
> E/O: *Hɛn ara yɛdze hɛn man*
> *Yegor maa*
> *Aboa bi nyi beebi a na waa fa hɛn ɛdze*
> *Osuom a ɔdzi ne man*

Ama: "Is that an Asafo song?"
Maame Atta: "*Adzewa* song. We the women, we sing it."

I was confused by Maame Atta's response that this was an *adzewa* song because I had been told time and time again that it was *abosom ndwom*, a song for the Gods. Before I could probe further, they raised another song. I did not intervene. This is their story.

Maame Owusuma: "*Ke-ye-re-de yaa boo oye, ke-ye-re-de* . . ."
Maame Atta: "We have a gourd, a hoe, and a stone in her hand and she plays it. That one is even better than Asafo. Especially, our ancient Elders. Me, myself sitting here, my mother was *ɔsahen* (leader of the group), so when she went, I followed her. That is how it is." [She sang *koo-koo-de-dee, koo-de-dee, koo-koo-de-dee, koo-de-dee*—a variation of Ghanaian Ewe *agbeko* rhythm. Maame Owusuma placed the back of her right hand in her left palm and clapped the down beat, Pa! Pa! Pa! Pa! . . .]
Ama: "So, did you also sing with them?"
Maame Atta: "Me myself? Me myself, I became a *nwomtonyi* (lead singer)."
Ama: "Really?"
Maame Atta: "I am telling you. Because of Jesus, all its message has left my head. I don't take it anywhere. At that time, this our God Eminsa, She is our Elder God so, we don't leave Her name out when we sing Her song. All the Gods here, She is the Elder. They cleared the path with Her and came there. So, we don't play around Her" [we do not take Her for granted].
Ama: "*ɔkoko kɛse*."
Maame Atta: "*ɔkoko kɛse obi mfrɛ hɛn. ɔkoko kɛse* (the great mountain) is over there."
Ama: "Aaahh . . . *ɔkoko* (mountain, hill)!"

Prior to this gathering, three women and my primary mentor, Nana, had shared some names of the various Gods at Kormantse. Nana identified only thirty-five Deities by name and would not give out the rest because, he said, "They don't like their ending [all their names and identities] to be revealed." I had also had the opportunity to visit some of the shrines, the largest of which belonged to Nana Eminsa. Her abode was a circular cement structure with a thatched roofing. A white cloth (*krádá*) draped the entrance. I learned later from Nana that the priest who sits at the entrance of the shrine bathed Eminsa during this ceremony. According to him, "When she is being bathed, one cannot open the eyes and look at her. If one opens the eyes and looks at her, the person will go blind. It has happened before. When she is bathed the person places all the bathing items beside her/him. The items that were gifted to Jesus are those same things that are used on Nana Ama Eminsa" (personal communication, July 19, 2017, Kormantse, Ghana). I asked him why they used gold, frankincense, and myrrh on Eminsa. "Nana Eminsa is as pure as Jesus," he replied.

Ama: "*Osuom*, what does it mean?"
Maame Atta: "*Osuom Ampɔn*?"
Ama: "Yes, *Osuom*."
Maame Atta: "*Osuom* is the God Eminsa, her appellation (*mmran*)."
Ama: "Aaaahh . . . her appellation?"
Maame Atta: "Her appellation, *Osuom Ampɔn*. She is a Deity. ɔkoko (mountain). When they were coming [the early settlers], they brought Her with them. Emintzimadze . . ."
Maame Owusuma: ". . . this water. . ."
Maame Atta: "Her lagoon is over there; a town is there . . ."
Maame Owusuma: "Mankessim . . ."
Ama: "The water, what do they call it?"
Maame Atta: "Eminsa."
Ama: "The water, too, they call it Eminsa?"
Maame Atta: "Yes. Everything that they do for her, they take it from there. The straw and the bamboo, and all the wood, they get it from the lagoon, and they bring it. When they go and they are coming, it is beautiful *kɛ-kɛ* . . . beautiful beyond belief!" [She laughed out loud].
Maame Owusuma: *Gyɛe, gyɛe, gyɛe, gyɛe*! ("Stop, stop, stop, stop!")
Maame Atta: "If they go and they are coming, stop . . ."
Ama: "I am listening to you."

Maame Atta: "As for the wood, they have to cut it long. You cut six, then you tie it. You cut six, then you tie it. People aaaa . . ., about fifty, young and older men . . ."
Maame Owusuma: "Weren't they more than fifty?"
Maame Atta: "They were more than fifty. They are walking by the seaside. Everyone."

Maame Owusuma picked up a stick from behind her and placed it on her left shoulder to demonstrate how the men carried the wooden poles from River Eminsa back to Kormantse.

Maame Atta: "You see what she has done? They tie it and place it on their shoulders, so when they . . ."
Maame Owusuma: "That is what they are walking with and they step and step and step." [While seated, Maame Owusuma demonstrated how they walked, stepping one, two, three . . . then Maame Atta picked up the stick and demonstrated.]
Maame Atta: "They are walking by the seaside, you see? So, carrying the thing they have tied it, all of them."

Atta managed to get up, cried out *"Egya-ee* (Ouch!)," and took the stick from Owusuma. She continued.

Maame Atta: "All of them, they have on *lanta*, a big cloth that they wrapped around their waist, through their legs and around their buttocks (*mo lanta*), and they were wearing shirt on top." [She placed the stick on her left shoulder and managed to stand upright, straight, and with both hands on the stick. Only Nana had demonstrated this walk earlier.] "The stick is on their shoulder like this. They have tied it. Everybody . . . so when they get here, they are walking by the seaside, o! They walk by the seaside and go and walk by the seaside and come. The lagoon (*baka*) is by the seaside. So, when they are coming, when they have passed Saltpond [Akyemfo, another neighboring town], and they all step like this." [I imagined a group of over fifty men in a line, wearing *lanta*, walking along the sea with long poles on their shoulders, stepping slowly: left, right, left, right, left, right, left. Maame Atta missed a step and was thrown off balance. She did not fall, but Maame Owusuma warned her.]
Maame Owusuma: "You will fall-o. When they are walking, they don't overtake someone." [Maame Atta agreed to this and added to it.]

Maame Atta: "They don't overtake or pass someone. You don't step on your friend's heel."[Atta corroborated Maame Aprokuwa's description of the Asafo men's walk along the coast with Eminsa's wooden poles].

The reroofing of Eminsa, the mother of all Kormantse Deities, was a common reference and narrative that most of my teachers talked and reminisced about. Not only did they talk about the tradition with pride and excitement, but they also lamented its demise. I learned that the last reroofing occurred over two decades ago. That Maame Owusuma and Atta corroborated the description of the walk along the sea by my other mentors, Ama Aprokuwa, Maame Ama Esuon, Nana Odum, and others, was crucial. Because now, rather than referencing it as "isolated knowledge" or "individual memory," I could reference it as part of the people's collective memory, one that helps to situate the role and importance of Nana Eminsa and this tradition in Kormantse society.

Ama: "You don't step on your friend's heel?"

Maame Atta: "No, no. Oh, no. You don't step in the space between them. So, like this." [She demonstrated]. "They will come from the seaside aaaa . . . till the seaside town. They will bring it and climb the hill; they will bring and climb the hill. So, while they are climbing the hill, the wooden poles are on their shoulders, then the song is inside; the song is inside; the song is inside; the song is inside. [She repeated this statement to the pulse of her step as she stepped, stepped, stepped, and stepped.] As soon as they appear on the hill [she put the stick down], then our Ancestors and mothers will call out her appellations: '*Osuom Ampɔn o, Osuom Ampɔn o, Ama Amina eei, Ama Amineei, ɔkɔtɔ Kuresi, ɔkɔtɔ Kuresi, ɔbaa Basia wo tam yɛ akron, ɔbaa Basia wo tam yɛ akron, awo dooo, awo dooo . . .*'" [She hoisted her cloth up and down and stepped throughout the house, toward the front entrance and back, back and forth, back and forth, flapping the cloth.] "Maame, you yourself, Hah! And the Gods have descended like that, *a-ge-ge-ge-ge-ge-ge-ge*. It was no play at Kokoado there. It was no play. The older women, what they needed to hear was the song, '*Wo mbo no aho nyi e!*' ('Give Her Praise!') Then they would respond:

Maame Owusuma/Atta: "*Aho nye, aho nyeeee, nsu oooo, enam ooo, apa, mbrɛana wo bo efuw a abowa!*"

Maame Atta: "Hah! Ebueii! Then our mothers and Ancestors, Ebueii! Na *Ama Amin ee, ɔbaa Basia ne tam akron, ɔkɔtɔ Kuresi, ɔkɔtɔ*

Kuresi, Osuom Ampɔn, Osuom Ampɔn, Osuom Ampɔn, Awo mber, Awo mber . . ."

Maame Atta took off the cloth around her waist and hoisted it like a flag, fanning it up and down, a practice done to congratulate and praise. She stepped around in rhythm, on slightly bent knees, bouncing up and down, bouncing from side to side, all the while flapping her cloth in excitement. She continued.

> Maame Atta: "Maame, I swear to you, then it was no play. Our Ancestors, the appellations are they all of them? I, myself, do I know them? We the children, tiny, tiny, we too, following them. We are following them; we are following them. Then they are coming; then they are coming. And then someone calls out, *"Wo mbo no aho nye e!"*
>
> Maame Owusuma/Atta: *"Aho nye, aho nyeeee, nsu oooo, enam ooo apa/aboa, mbrɛana wo bo efuw abowa!"*
>
> Maame Atta: "Hah, it is us going. It is us going. It is us going. E! e! e! e! *Maana wo bo efu a. Mbrɛana wo bo efuw a . . . Abowa, mbrɛana wo bu efuw a . . . eh, eh*! (Now that you are angry; now that you are angry)!"

Maame Atta continued to dance with the cloth, hoisting it up and down and moving in excitement and jubilation, stepping from side to side, stepping from side to side, stepping from side to side. I could not help but wish I had witnessed and experienced this event.

Back to Asafo

Maame Owusuma called another Asafo *ndwom*, *"Wɔmfa nyɛ hɔn nanom"* (example 23 ☙ see audio sample 3).

> Maame Owusuma: *"Wɔmfa nyɛ hɔn nanom, wɔ mfa nyɛ hɔn egyanom."*
> Maame Atta: *"'Mfa nyɛ hɔn egyanom, mfa nyɛ hɔn nanom."*
> Maame Owusuma: *"'Mfa yɛ hɔn egyanom, 'mfa nyɛ hɔn nanom."*
> Maame Atta: *"'Mfa nyɛ hɔn egyanom, 'mfa nyɛ hɔn nanom."*

They both danced, Maame Owusuma seated and Maame Atta slightly bent over and stepping, both pointing their fingers as if to poke someone in the eye and moving to the rhythm of the *ndwom* like a group of women did in December 2016 when I made my first Asafo recording in front of the chief's palace on main street (see chapter 6). They were energized, smiling, reminiscing. This was a performance of childhood memories on a walk, dancing—a celebration. Maame Atta embellished the song, "*Ke-ga, ke-ga, ke-ga!*" stepping to the beat. "'*Mfa nyɛ hɔn nanom, mmfa nyɛ hɔn egyanom . . . 'Mmfa yɛ hɔn nanom, 'mmfa nyɛ hɔn egyanom.*" "Our Ancestors have poured on the floor" (left a wonderful tradition, footprints, behind). Out of the excitement, Maame Owusuma, while still dancing on her stool and with a smile on her face, said to me, "Ama Oforiwaa, you are going to make us waste our time. Take your matter and go! *Oye!* That is enough."

I had nudged their memories of the past and taken their memories on many walks with Asafo songs, *adzewa*, their Deities, history, and traditions, many of which according to my mentors have fallen into disuse. It brought back, from what I surmised, good memories. I helped bring back beautiful memories—powerful memories that defined their identities as Kormantse women, matured, wise women who once walked and danced with Asafo. Therefore, they liked to talk to me. I was happy and laughed out loud that they were happy and enjoying themselves. Memories: What do they do for us? Who are we without our memories? As Joseph Ki-Zerbo articulates, "Unless one chooses to live in a state of unconsciousness and alienation, one cannot live without memory, or with a memory that belongs to someone else. And history is the memory of nations" (1981, 2). The essence of who we are is steeped in our memories. I watched the two women in their eighties—one who could hardly walk and on her stool, the other slightly bent over and with squinted but intense eyes—come to life with the performance of these Asafo songs that they participated in and witnessed as children. One would never guess they had complained earlier about aches and pains in their joints that morning! I, on the other hand, with camera in hand, moved to the beat of the song with excitement. *Wo foro dua a, foro tenten na wote hwe a, atumpan ama wo dammirifua*, "When you climb a tree, climb a tall one, so that when you fall, the talking drums would play condolences for you!" This moment was golden. I am still climbing.

I had used a different version of the song in my performance art piece, *Walking with My Ancestors* (2014, 2019). It was taught to me as a declamatory, free-moving Asafo song of dissent that protested slavery and treatment by white colonial officers. I enjoyed their rendition of this song; it was metered, upbeat, and lighter. I hummed along to their rhythm. In the performed moment of the song, our background did not matter; our age differences did not matter. That I was a music professor at a university in the United States of America, and they, retired entrepreneurs, did not seem to matter. Music and performance transcended those barriers or differences. We shared a moment where age did not matter. Still, I was aware of the power differentials between us because though we were Ghanaians, my status as a professor in the United States, earning far more than they did, placed me on a different level. In my mind, however, they were my Elders, deserving of respect. Money is not everything. *Abɔfra hunu ne nsa hohora, ɔne mpanin didi*, "When a child learns how to wash her hands, she eats with the Elders." In their eyes, I was a child, slowly learning how to wash my hands.

Maame Owusuma and Atta gathered to share and support; to reminisce and to compare experiences, to celebrate their lives, and to share their love for Kormantse, Asafo, and culture. They gathered to find strength in each other's lived experiences. They were lifelong friends who shared a life, culture, age, and ethnicity. At times, their exchange felt like one between siblings. They are beautiful, not only in the physical sense—their dark, glowing, semi-wrinkled skin, piercing eyes, and pursed full lips like the other women I walked with. Beauty is also about their character, such as the Akan say, *Ne suban yɛfɛ*, "Her character is beautiful." In them, I experienced the way beauty unveils opposing standards. They were confident, respectable, and had agency. Maame Ekua Atta was thoughtful, kind, calm, polite, but dramatic, fierce, and outspoken. She belongs to the Kona *ebusua* and epitomizes their totem, a deer with a bird's nest in its antlers—patience. *Abotare tutu mmopɔ*, "Patience moves mountains." *Asu a ɛtaa ho dinn na ɛfa onipa*, "It is the water which stands there calm and silent that takes (drowns) a person." Maame Owusuma, on the other hand, was outspoken, raw, combative, and would snarl in a second, like her *ebusua* totem, *kurotwamansa*, if you crossed her—fierce. But she could be calm and remain quiet if she wanted to. *Aburuburo nkosua, adeɛ a ɛbɛyɛ yie nsɛe*, "Like the doves' eggs, what will succeed will never fail."

> Memory
> You who move the crippled to dance
> You summon Eminsa
> That mother of all Kormantse Gods
> Osuom Ampɔn
> Ama Amin ee
> ɔkɔtɔ Kuresi
> ɔbaa Basia ne tam akron

Nkaa
Memory
You took them
Two eighty-plus-year-old women
On a walk
A walk with songs
Dance
They mimicked the dawur bell
The ɔdabɔ drum
Dankan gourds
Step, step, step, step
Hmmm…. Hmmm…hmmm

Memory
Hu m'ani so ma me nti na atwe mienu nam
Blow the dust off my eye is the reason why two duikers always move together
When an orphan sees a gravesite
She cries because she remembers
You made two women laugh
Memory, memory, memory
You can hurt
But you also heal
You heal
You can heal

When the discussion turned to Christianity, the tone shifted to a serious mood. My mood changed as well as they lamented the effects of Christianity on their traditions.

Maame Atta: "Yes, worshipping God has changed things."
Maame Owusuma: "We have left all of our traditions . . ."
Ama: "But worshipping God does not mean we have to stop, or . . .?"
Maame Atta: "But . . ."
Ama: "It is God who created it, or . . .?"
Maame Atta: "The ancient people, there was God."
Maame Owusuma: "They did it with a clear mind. Today, we use dirty mind and wrongdoing. That is all the matter. Dirty mind and bad mind, all that . . ."

It is interesting to note that while they denounced the effects of Christianity on their traditions, they, and all my mentors, are faithful Christians who attend one of the twenty-five churches at Kormantse every Sunday. Still, as Agorsah notes, "Despite the waning observation of indigenous religious practices in Historic Kormantse today, due to aggressive Christian activities in the area, almost every compound in the town has at least a family or lineage shrine. Many of them claim to be ancient to the historic settlement" (2014, 91). Maame Atta picked up the refrain to the Asafo song.

Maame Atta: "'*Mfa nyɛ hɔn nanom, fa nyɛ hɔn egyanom ɔdze ye kyirem e . . . 'Mfa nyɛ hɔn nanom, fa nyɛ hɔn egyanom, ke-gem . . .ke-gem . . . ke-gem . . .*"

Seated, she stepped to the beat and pointed her two forefingers. Again, Maame Owusuma stomped both feet on the ground to the beat of the song and pointed her two forefingers while she swayed from side to side.

Both: "'*Mmfa nyɛ hɔn egyanom, fa nyɛ hɛn nanom*"
Owusuma: "*wɔdze yɛ Tuafo*"
Atta: "'*Mmfa nyɛ hɔn egyanom, fa nyɛ hɔn nanom*"
Owusuma: "*wɔnfa nyɛ* Bentsir"
Atta: "*Mmfa nyɛ hɔn egyanom, fa nyɛ hɔn nanom*"
Owusuma: "*wɔdze yɛ Tuafo a*"
Atta: "'*Mmfa nyɛ hɔn egyanom, fa nyɛ hɔn nanom*"
Owusuma: "*wɔdze yɛ Tuafo a*"
Atta: "'*Mmfa nyɛ hɔn egya nom, fa nyɛ hɔn nanom*"
Owusuma: "*wɔdze yɛ* Kyirem e"
Maame Atta: "'*Mmfa nyɛ hɔn egyanom, fa nyɛ hɔn nanom. Ah! Aboa mprɛana wo bo efuw* a. *Eminsa Osuom o obi frɛ hɛn o. Hɛn ara yɛdze hɛn man* (I sang the refrain with her). *Hɛn ara yɛdze hɛn man na yɛrgor mu aa. Aboa bi nyi beebi a na waa fa hɛn yɛdze.* You yourself, your grandmother, she is going to climb the hill and come there; she is climbing the hill and come there. You yourself, you are going to catch who? You yourself, you are going; you yourself, you are going pa-paa-pa! (for real, real). *Mmfa nyɛ hɔn egyanom, fa nyɛ hɔn nanom, wɔdze yɛ kyirem e.*"
Maame Ama: "You say, *Wɔ mfa nyɛ hɔn nanom, mmfa nyɛ hɔn egyanom.* What does that mean?"

> Atta: "All of it is *kasa twii*, 'talk that scratches.' Instigating talk. There are two Asafo, Nkum and Bentsir, ɛh-heh. So, everybody is used to instigation. It is like you are causing pain or picking a fight. If you are bringing a sin, go and do it to your mother; go and do it to your father. As for us Kyirem people, as for that one, you cannot do it to us" [Owusuma shook her head]. "They too, their Asafo *ndwom*, the moment they sing, they will mock us. So, that is it. It says, 'The evil things that you are doing to us, may it be done to your father; may it be done to your mother. Don't do it to Kyirem, one of our Asafo battalions.'"
> Maame Owusuma: "No."
> Maame Atta: "Don't do it to me. If it is a bad thing, go and do it to your mother and father. Don't come and do it to Kyirem."

This song attested to Esi Sutherland-Addy's contention that many Asafo songs are effective vehicles "to convey social sentiments and those implicated in the institution" (1988b). The seventy Kormantse Asafo songs I had collected thus far aligned with the six thematic categories that Acquah (2008, 62) provides: (1) identity-related songs, (2) war-related songs, (3) *kasa twii* (talking to scratch your heart/mind) or provocative/rivalry songs, (4) recreational songs, (5) morality songs, and (6) songs expressing the heritage of Asafo ensemble.[9] Of these, inter-Asafo conflicts or implicit and explicit provocations and those like *Wɔ mfa nyɛ hɔn nanom, mfa nyɛ hɔn egyanom* were the most common.[10] The songs are derogatory and offensive; they ridicule their enemies about their weakness, their cowardice—likelihood to run and hide, immaturity, and their lack of morality. At the same time, they gloat about their company's prowess. I would say about 70 percent were insults to their neighbors. I was surprised to learn about the connection with their neighbors, especially since I had learned it as a song protesting the harsh treatment by European colonial masters. It pointed to the malleability of a song and how songs can be contextualized and recontextualized by its users. Our discussion turned to *adzewa*, a style that I had not considered as part of my research, though I was aware of its existence at Kormantse.

> Maame Owusuma: "Ebuei, all the many songs are gone."
> Maame Atta: "Doing God did not help us."
> Maame Owusuma: "Oforiwaa, take it like that for the songs!"

Adzewa: "They are Better, They Walk with Asafo"

Kormantse women are members of an ensemble called *adzewa*, an all-female ensemble accompanied with gourd rattles, a drum, and a bell. Months prior to this session, I asked about the Kormantse *adzewa* group and was told they had disbanded because their gourds were broken, but mostly because many of the women stopped participating due to their membership in church. *Adzewa*, like Asafo and many other traditional practices, had been branded fetish by churchgoers. Nana and I talked about meeting with the group to discuss plans to reinstate the group and record some of their *ndwom*. That, I was told, would also involve buying new gourds, for which I did not have the resources. So, I was grateful for this opportunity to learn about *adzewa* and hear a few songs from the two mothers. To help me understand this tradition at Kormantse and my discussion with Maame Owusuma and Ekua Atta, I recalled the search I conducted with a group of Ga women in Jamestown at Accra.[11]

Nlesi Adowa is a Ga women's performance genre based on the Fante *adzewa*, in which a single drum accompanies women singing in a call and response style (see Aduonum 2017).[12] The genre is performed at the installation of chiefs, funerals, naming ceremonies, and marriage. The accompanying instruments include the *mfobah* (gourds) and the *ampae* drum. Nlesi Adowa uses the *adaawu*, a canoe-shaped bell with a slit running down its center, *mí* or *dzo*, a goblet-shaped drum with tuning pegs, and *tò*, a gourd with an opening at its anterior end, enmeshed with colorful beads. Hand clapping and dancing are major components in Nlesi performance. Performers dance, sing, and/or play instruments. Membership is predominantly female and, at the time, consisted of about thirty women between the ages of sixty and eighty-five. The only male member of the group was the drummer, who drummed and did not sing, dance, or play the gourds. The music is organic and involves complex interlocking patterns, call and response singing, hand clapping, and dancing by the group members and audience. Like most traditional African expressive performances, it is a celebration of mind, body, and soul. Instrumentalists sing and move their bodies as they play their gourds; dancers sing and clap while they move their bodies gracefully; and the various jagged counter-patterns from the gourds clash, interlock, and overlap to form one dense composite sound. They interact and weave around each other into this tapestry of sound and movement, multiple parts defining the others in a sonic experience in which one part is only meaningful within the context of the whole.[13]

> Ama: "You said, Asafo, its *akyerɛba* (younger sister) is . . .?"
> Maame Owusuma: "*Adzewa*."
> Maame Atta: "*Adzewa* walks with Asafo. The women play it."
> Maame Owusuma: "Like the Asante play *adowa*."
> Maame Atta: "The *dankan* gourds that they play in their hands, during the time, the elderly women in this Kormantse town created *adzewa*. When the Asafo walks, they go with them."
> Ama: "Did they fight?"
> Maame Atta: "No, they did not fight."
> Ama: "So, what did they do when they walked with Asafo?"
> Maame Atta: "Sometimes, if something happened, like when a King dies and they are looking for someone who plays *ayer* (*ndwom*) and understands mature issues, they invite us. They talk and when they sing the songs, you understand. No, they don't go and pick a fight; also, there is happiness inside. When you get to the town itself, they won't know you, but when they experience your singing and what you are doing, then they say, 'Oh, those people, they know how to do things very well.' That is how it is. So, when they go, they go with their women. They won't go and pick a fight. However, if you are a resident and you bring a fight, then, as for us we did not come to fight, but . . ."
> Ama: "So, what do the women do when the Asafo men go?"
> Maame Atta: "When the men play the Asafo, the women do like what I was doing here."
> Maame Owusuma: "When they finish, they give women a chance to do their thing. They will always play the *adzewa*. They play aaaa. . . . That is what the women do to help Asafo."
> Maame Atta: "The *adzewa* songs are elderly matters, and the Asafo is elderly matters. 'I don't have any, Efua Krowa, where do I get it from?'"

Maame Ekua Atta demonstrated her role as *adzewa* lead singer and raised "*Efua Krowa*" (example 24 ♫).

She reflected on the song and elaborated: "They are getting it today, fresh. I have a debt and they want it right now, but I don't have it. What should I do? Efua Krowa's daughter Efua, right now where do I get it? They are getting it today. So, the *adzewa* songs address all issues like the Asafo songs." Since she was a *nnwomtonyi* (song leader), she did most of the talking and led the songs, which kept coming. She called *"Efua Odondo"* (example 25 ♫). She repeated more animatedly. Maame Owusuma elaborated with a reference, "Like Aba Sackey's mother. . . ." Maame Atta responded, "Ahh! Maame, stop it." I did not understand what was said. However, Maame Atta became sad, so I did not probe. She placed both hands on her head and dropped her head as a sign of reflection and mourning. She choked with sadness and her voice cracked. The song had become a memory archive and those memories hurt. We paused. This moment with Maame Owusuma and Atta helped clarify why *adzewa* groups perform at funerals—they can evoke sadness for mourners. After the brief pause, they sang six more *adzewa* songs.

As I think and write about my encounter and experience with Maame Owusuma and Atta, I recall their nurturing tone and the care with which they shared.[14] The two eighty-plus women, seated on stools beside each other, one with poor vision and the other with rheumatoid arthritis, epitomized my ideals of motherhood. At times, they, especially Maame Owusuma, chastised me for not knowing, for asking the obvious, but I never felt attacked because as the Akan Elders say, *Akokɔ nan tia ba, na ɛnkum no*, "The hen's leg treads on the chick, but it does not crush it to death." Furthermore, *Obi se bɔ wo brayie a', ɔnnidii wo atɛm*, "If someone tells you to lead a good life, the person has not insulted you"; *Obi se hyɛ wo sapo mu nsuo a ɛnyɛ yaw*, "When someone tells you to fill your sponge with water [reinforce your resources], it is not an insult."[15] I took those as ways of developing deeper relationships, walking further, and connecting with me. Sweet mothers!

Maame Ekua Atta raised *"Daano Wɔnye Hɛn Yɛ,"* another *adzewa* song that a group of five men had performed the day before (example 26 ♫). "It says, when you are confronted with a tough or stressful situation, you look for someone who is strong to fight to save or help you, but when you have it good, you ignore us or don't praise us."

Maame Owusuma: "When you get something good from it . . ."
Maame Atta: ". . . Then you alone you take it." She repeated the song.
Ama: "Please say it slow, I can't hear what you are saying. What does that mean?"
Maame Atta: *"Daano wɔnye hɛn yɛ."*

Ama: "What does that mean?"

Maame Owusuma: "Last time you did not praise us. You took us for fools."

Maame Atta: "Eh-heh!"

Ama: "*Daano wɔnye hɛn yɛ?*"

Maame Owusuma: "The last time we came, they made fools of us. When they went and got the thing and they were eating, as for that, they did not call us. They alone ate their thing. Even though we made ourselves available when they called us to help them; they did not praise us or acknowledge us."

After a back-and-forth exchange between the two women, I concluded that the song was about ungrateful and unfaithful people, opportunists who seek favor and help when they are in difficult positions but do not help others when they are in need. In other words, *Akokɔ di wo yɔnko ayuo a, pam no, na dabi ɔbedi wo deɛ*, "When a chicken eats your neighbors' grain, drive it away for it will eat yours another day." It is about those who forget that *Onipa yɛ adeɛ a, ɔyɛ gye ayeyie*, "When someone performs good deeds, she deserves praise."

Birth Stories

This question about birth date always brought a moment of silence to my mentors because many births were not recorded. Instead, they used past events—an earthquake, the death of a prominent person, a plague—to mark their births or to calculate their age. Some had their names etched onto their arms (usually left arm) in dark ink. Others referred me to Nana to help estimate their age. Most, though, either guessed and gave a ballpark number or referred to past events.

Ama: "Please, how old are you?"

Maame Atta: "Owusuma would know. Sister, eighty what, eighty, or what?" she asked Owusuma.

Maame Owusuma: "She says she is how many years old?"

Maame Atta: "I am eighty-five years old."

Maame Owusuma: "Five? She has not reached five. She has not reached five [eighty-five]. Let's make it four [eighty-four]. As for me, I am ahead of you."

Maame Atta: "You came before me?"

Maame Owusuma: "You say, I am what?"

Maame Atta: "You are older?"

Maame Owusuma: "I am ahead of you, for what I saw, you did not see. It means when they birthed Ekua Mansa and the earth shook. They had given birth to Ekua Mansah when the earth shook."

Maame Atta: "As for me, I . . ."

Maame Owusuma: "When they gave birth to her, then the earth shook. As for me, when the earth shook, I was around eight years. As for that, I saw it. The earth shakes. All we saw was that we were at my father's house; all of us were there to go and eat. We were eating and we saw that 'Ah! the floor, what is it doing? What is it doing?' The chairs that we sat on were *pom-pom-pom-pom-pom-pom-pom-pom*." [She bounced on her stool in rhythm to the sound.]

Maame Atta: "The first one was bigger, than the latter one."

Maame Owusuma: "By far! You say, 'Let's sit here,' and then it will be walking with you *kim-kim-kim-kim*. You are standing, but you are going *kim-kim-kim-kim-kim-kim-kim-kim*. During the first earth shake, they had built this house. That is why there is a mark on the mud house [she pointed to a crack in the wall]. All the mud cracked. So, when that happened, Abanyin Kwame said, 'Everyone, get outside.' So, all of us, we left the house and stayed outside in the yard. It did like that aaaa. . . . It was about fifteen minutes past 7 p.m."

Maame Atta: "It was in the afternoon?"

Maame Owusuma: "At night. *Kim-kim-kim-kim-kim-kim-kim-kim* and it did it like that aaaa . . ., till about 9; no, it did not get there. The thing shook for only fifteen minutes. It was harsh. So, when it finished and we opened the gate, all the soil on the ground had come to settle in front of the door. Every plant/leaf came and settled in front of the door. So that is the little that I saw."

The first earthquake in Ghana occurred in 1615, and the earliest recorded one occurred in 1636; subsequent ones were recorded in 1862 and 1906. The most destructive one occurred at about 7:20 pm in 1939 and was "recorded teleseismically at various observatories around the world" (Amponsah 2004, 542). According to Amponsah, citing Jumer (1941), the 1939 one "caused a lot of damage and a loss of life and property." Though it felt like fifteen minutes to Maame Owusuma, it is recorded to have lasted "about 20 to 30 seconds" and was "assigned a magnitude of 6.5 on the Richter scale and a maximum intensity of IX."

The *"Kim! Kim! Kim! Kim! Kim! Kim! Kim!"* and *"Pom! Pom! Pom! Pom! Pom! Pom! Pom! Pom!"* that Maame Owusuma experienced at her tender age of eight years occurred around 7:15 p.m. and was indicative of the magnitude of that "earth shake." Such a description and corroboration of experiences during this earthquake places her birth year as 1931, since she was eight when the earth shook. This calculation made her eighty-six years old at the time of our conversation in 2017. Her calculation was correct. If Maame Atta was a year old during the earthquake in 1939 as they estimated, then she was seventy-eight at the time of our interview. Maame Owusuma was indeed older than her, but her statement, "Let's give her eighty-four," did not seem reasonable. In response, Maame Ekua Atta picked up *"Asamankama Aba"* (example 27 ♫).

> Maame Atta: "Asamankama Aba, she does not have a boy; she does not have a child; she is coming to find some place to sleep, so give her some place to sleep. You understand?"
> Ama: "Yes."
> Maame Atta: "OK."
> Ama: "The Asamankama, who is she?"
> Maame Atta: "She is a woman, but she did not give birth."
> Maame Owusuma: "She gave birth to one boy (later); she did give birth to a girl to add to it."
> Maame Atta: "Give her some place to sleep. She is coming to find a place to sleep. So, give her some place to sleep, Ama Asamankama Aba.
> *Wɔmma m'beebi ara ma menda*
> *ɔrepɛ beebi ara na ɔada da o*
> *Asamankama Aba e*
> *Wɔmma m' beebi menda o!*"

"When you see a stranger, give her a hearty welcome. Give her some place to sleep; honor will touch you. It would touch you too." Our Elders say, *Onipa nnyae mmɔborɔ yɛ a, yɛnnyae no mmɔborɔ hunu*, "If a person is in constant need of sympathy, we don't deny her sympathy."

Because the songs kept coming, I stated, "As for this, I may have to follow you everywhere you go so that when you remember, you can bring it out." Maame Owusuma and Atta performed more *adzewa* and songs for Deities, including "*ɔawar Eminsa*," the song for Mother Goddess that they had sung many times before. Maame Owusuma was excited on her stool, stomped her feet, and exclaimed, "*Wɔmbom, wɔmbom, wɔmbom, wɔmbom!*" (Put your hands together Pa! Pa! Pa! . . .!)

        Memory
        You who move the crippled to dance
        Two women who witnessed
        Krebuu, with their own eyes
        You summon Eminsa
        That mother of all Kormantse Gods
        Osuom Ampong
        Ama Amen
        ɔkɔtɔ Kurase
        Obaa Basia ne toma akron
        A woman who wears nine bands around her waist

        Memory
        Nkaa
        You took them
        Two eighty-plus-year-old women
        On a walk
        Hu m'ani so ma me nti na atwe mienu nam
        Blow the dust off my eye is the reason why two duikers
        always move together
        Birth stories
        A walk with songs
        Asafo
        ɔnantefoɔ na odi adɔdɔdeɛ
        It is the walker who eats sweet things
        It was too sweet

        Asafo kyen
        Dance in chairs
        Mimick the dawur bell
        Asafo
        Adzewa
        Asamankama Aba *Wɔmma m'beebi ma menda*
        Dankan gourds
        There is happiness inside

CHAPTER FIVE

> Walking with Asafo
> Tsimm, tsimm, tsimm, tsimm
> Hmmm . . . Hmmm . . .
> Ru-lu ru-lu ru-lu te yam
> *Kim! Kim! Kim! Kim! Kim! Kim! Kim!*
> *Pom! Pom! Pom! Pom! Pom! Pom! Pom!*
> *Pom*
> *Wɔmbom, wɔmbom*
> *ɔnantefoɔ na odi adɔdɔdeɛ*
> *Wofeefee asɛm mu a, wohunu mu yie*
> *ɔbaa na ɔwo barima*
> Aaa!
> It was too sweet!

Our session ended after about fifty minutes, though it felt longer, considering all the songs and information that Maame Owusuma and Maame Atta shared with me. I walked away with new knowledge about Asafo, *adzewa*, its songs, and function in Kormantse society; I learned more about the Goddess Eminsa, her traditions, and *ndwom*. Between these two women who challenged and filled in each other's recollections, the Akan saying, "*Etikorɔ nkɔ ɛgyina*" ("One head does not go into council"), or the idea that wisdom is not in one person's head, became very clear. Walking with people allows us to pick pieces of information on the way; walking gives us knowledge and helps us fill in the gaps. *ɔnantefoɔ sene oni ne ɔse asɛm*, "The walker knows more than her mother and father." Indeed. There was too much happiness and sweetness inside.

During my stay at Maame Owusuma's house, I made small contributions to her household for her time and accommodation. So, after my chat with them that day, I offered Maame Atta a token to show my appreciation for her time and effort. She accepted with gratitude. The next morning, I left the house early to run an errand. When I returned, Maame Owusuma informed me that Maame Atta came looking for me. I walked over to her house, about a block from Maame Owusuma's house. She handed me the gift I gave to her. I asked why. She told me about a dream she had the previous night in which a voice asked, "The message that we gave to you, did we sell it to you, and you are selling it? Did we sell you the *abakɔsɛm*?" The voice accused her of selling the message. She could not sleep, so she said she woke up and prayed. Then she added, "I should not have taken the money from you. I came there in the morning to bring you the money." When she went to church at night, she told the pastor about the dream and they asked her, "Did you sell the *abakɔsɛm*?" The Elders chastised her for accepting a monetary gift from me for sharing her knowledge about Asafo *ndwom* and matters that have come and gone. I asked if it was okay to share a meal sometimes. While we sat, I raised her favorite song, "*ɔawar Eminsa.*" She joined in.

The brief encounter with Maame Ekua about compensation led me to assume and to generalize that Kormantse women did not expect anything or ask for anything in return for their knowledge, especially since the women at Kokoado Upper Town also refused my tokens of appreciation. They saw sharing their knowledge as an investment in the community and future generations. One woman responded, "Pass that on and help our grandchildren one day."

Most of my male mentors expected monetary tokens for their time and effort—understandably so, especially since many depend on the sea for their employment. At the time, their fishing expeditions yielded nothing, to the point where many had to travel to neighboring Ivory Coast, Togo, or Benin to fish. I was always happy to compensate because they shared of themselves and time, their truth, their memories, and their love for Asafo. They spent their time and energy, just as they would on any paid job. It was not until I had a different experience with another woman that I refined the conclusion I had made about Kormantse women and men regarding compensation. It also caused me to pause and reflect on how we easily generalize and flatten the experiences and perspectives of our mentors; how *mmaa* women and *mmarima* men define working and walking with others; how our relationships with others define working and walking with others. Is it contractual for others, while a labor of love for some? I was still learning. Here is an entry in my journal.

I came back exhausted and just out of it today. While I walked down main street, a beautiful elderly woman called me. She sat on a stool. Other people stood or sat around her. When I got to her, she mentioned that she had seen me all over town and asked what I was doing there. I told her about my search on Kormantse Asafo ndwom and abakɔsɛm, matters that have come and gone. By this time, I had played some Asafo songs at their communication center for all to hear, so I mentioned that I was the one who played those songs in the wee hours of the morning. She told me, "Abakɔsɛm, they sell it. It is not free." I had not asked her for anything. I tried to tell her the importance of recording our matters that have come and gone; otherwise, when someone dies, the knowledge would die with the person. She was not moved. She said their abakɔsɛm did not need to be written down because they had written them all down. Later, I told Nana about my encounter with the lady. He contradicted her assertion that all the abakɔsɛm had been recorded. Still the encounter bothered me (July 20, 2018).

Later that night, after I had walked away from the lady in silence, I reflected on my encounter with the lady. *Who am I to tell a society how to record their abakɔsɛm? Who made me the saving knight, an accusation that has been leveled at ethnomusicologists and anthropologists? Are research and documentation a colonialist endeavor to define, write, and claim ownership of other's realities? And why was I rattled? This was not about me. This was about a society that had existed for centuries and was still alive, without my intrusion, questions, and disruption of their daily lives. What would my petty search do for them? After all, not much has been documented and they are still here. Why am I really conducting this search? Is it really for them? Or I am really doing this to boost my own career?* Our Elders say, *obi nkɔ obi akuraa nkyerɛ n'ase*, "One does not go to another person's village to tell the latter her roots!" *What am I doing? What are we doing? Why are we in this business of ethnomusicology? Who is our audience? How does our audience shape our search, our ways of walking, sharing, and mentoring? ɔbra te sɛ ntentan yɛtete no nyansofoɔ*, "Life is like a cobweb, it takes wisdom to handle it."[16] I started late the next day and walked slowly, cautiously, and mindful of how I framed my questions and *amandzeɛ* mission. I thought deeply about my search.

Three days later, on my way to see another mentor, I ran into Maame Ekua Atta. She was in her usual attire, a beautiful colorful blouse, a wrap around her waist down to her feet and another wrapped around her shoulder. I mentioned that I did not understand some of the words to the *ndwom* they performed. She told me to ask Maame Owusuma. "Her father was a good lead singer (*nnwomtonyi*); he studied and was taught. He would extemporize, extemporize, extemporize (*kenkan, kenkan, kenkan*) before he raised the *ndwom*." She told me she was raised at Tamale (in northern Ghana). "If I remember some of the songs, I will come and sing for you."

I accompanied her to her house to hear her life story. That, too, was too sweet, kwa! Tsim, tsim, tsim, tsim, tsim, tsim, tsim, tsim. *Mbrɛana wo bo efuw a. Mbrɛana wo bo efuw a.* Kim! Kim! Kim! Kim! Kim! Hmmm . . . hmmmm. . . . Ru-lu-lu-lu-lu-lu-lu te-yam!

> Both: "*Mfa nyɛ hɔn nanom, fa nyɛ hɔn egyanom*"
> Owusuma: "*wɔdze yɛ Tuafo*"
> Atta: "*Mfa nyɛ hɔn nanom, fa nyɛ hɔn egyanom*"
> Owusuma: "*wɔnfa* nyɛ Bentsir"
> Atta: "*Mmfa nyɛ hɔn nanom, fa nyɛ hɔn egyanom*"
> Owusuma: "*ɔdze yɛ Tuafo a*"
> Atta: "*Mfa nyɛ hɔn nanom, fa nyɛ hɔn egyanom*"
> Owusuma: "*ɔdze yɛ* Tuafo *a*"
> Atta: "*Mfa nyɛ hɔn nanom, fa nyɛ hɔn egyanom*"
> Owusuma: "*ɔdze yɛ* Kyirem"
> Both: "*Mfa nyɛ hɔn nanom, fa nyɛ hɔn egyanom*"

ɔkɔtɔ Kuresi, Osuom Ampɔn. Two beautiful, proud, and independent women. *Mmarima nyɛ sumyɛ na yɛ de yɛ ti ato so.* Maame Owusuma and Maame Ekua Atta. Kurotwamansa and ɔko. Memories. Asafo *ndwom*. *Onipa yɛ adeɛ a, ɔye gye ayeyie*, "When a person performs good deeds, she performs them for praise." *Wɔmbom, wɔmbom, wɔmbom, wɔmbom*! Pa! Pa! Pa! Pa! Pa! It was too sweet.

PART 3

Walking with Asafo Music

CHAPTER SIX

The Listening and Musicking Walk

Obiara a obedzi asafomba hɔn fun ho agor nnkɛfa noho tɔtrɔtɔ koraa
(Anyone who plays with an Asafo company's dead body will not take himself/herself for free)

—Aggrey

Mayɛ kwansin m'abɛ 🔊
Tuafomba mayɛ kwansin m'abɛ
Abɔfra sɔɛr a, ɔrobɔ m'mpem
ɔpanyin sɔɛr a, ɔrobɔ m'mpem
Hɛn hen Gyesi ee dabi
Minya owu a mɔbɔ abɛn
Mɔbɔ abɛn, mɔbɔ abɛn
Hɛn hen Gyesi e
Asafo san kɔhwɛ w'ekyir
(I have become a palm tree at the junction
Tuafo children I have become a palm tree at the junction
When a child gets up she strikes me
When an adult gets up she strikes me
Our Chief Gyesi one day when I die I will blow the horn
I blow the horn; I will blow the horn
Our Chief Gyesi
Asafo go back to your roots)

—Kormantse Asafo *Ndwom*, *"Mayɛ Kwansin M'abɛ"*

I learned very early on that funerals for Asafo members are the best places to experience live Asafo *ndwom*; they are very important for Asafo companies and have become one of the few occasions where members continue to play *ndwom* without being chastised by some members of the society.

TABLE 6.1. Funerary Rites Outline

Day	Event
One week after death	*Dahyɛ,* date setting to set the date for the funeral. Celebrated with live Asafo *ndwom*.
Tuesday before funeral	*Eyi-eyim* for prominent figures in the community. Celebrated with Asafo drumming, if Asafo member.
Thursday	*Egwuaradze* presentation at deceased's lineage house; involves parading "last bath" items through the streets; accompanied by live *ndwom* performers.
Friday	Deceased brought from morgue and bathed at lineage house. Deceased laid in state. Wake-keeping. Celebrated with live Asafo *ndwom*, other *ndwom*, live or otherwise.
Saturday	Funeral celebrations at deceased's lineage house. Burial. Widow/widower cleanses in the sea. Socialization. *Nsawa* (gift giving) Celebrated with live Asafo *ndwom*, other *ndwom*, live or otherwise.
Sunday	*Aseda*/Thanksgiving/Church service. Sometimes the heir for the deceased is appointed. Celebrated with live Asafo *ndwom*, other *ndwom*, live or otherwise.
Monday	*Adapɛn-Esia* for females. Attended mostly by lineage members. Selection of an heir to the deceased. Accounting of funeral costs and settling of deceased's debts or accounts of money owed to deceased.
Tuesday	*Adapɛn-Essuon* for males. Attended mostly by lineage members. Selection of an heir to the deceased. Accounting of funeral costs and settling of deceased's debts accounts of money owed to deceased.

They have *Dahyɛ* when the date for the funeral is fixed; the fisher folks do it on Tuesdays when they do not go out to sea, and the general population do it on Saturday. Another event, *eyi-enyim* ("the face of the funeral"), is held on the Tuesday before the funeral for prominent figures such as Kings, Queens, Asafo Elders. This is the official opening of the funeral. According to my dance mentor, ɔdomankoma Kyerɛma Kwamena Pra, wake keeping occurs on Fridays, burial on Saturdays, and Sundays are for church service and thanksgiving. The following day, Monday, they have *Adapɛn-Esia* for females, and *Adapɛn-Essuon* for males on Tuesday. Table 6.1 outlines some of the activities following a death.

Egwuaradze! Performing Spectacle and Grief for the Dead

In many Fante societies, when someone dies, family members—the wife, husband, children, and/or grandchildren—purchase, package, and present final bath items to be used on the deceased, as well as alcohol to pray. If a man dies, his wife and children arrange the egwuaradze and present to his family. If a woman dies, the husband arranges it and gives to his family to present. Egwuaradze is considered the "final or last respect" for the deceased and is presented on Thursday morning before the corpse is brought home for wake keeping on Friday.[1] It is an event that announces or raises the upcoming funeral (*ma eyi do*). These days, some families accept money in place of the egwuaradze. I participated in three of these—observing two and walking with a heavy basin filled with bath items on my head through the streets of Cape Coast. The first egwuaradze I witnessed did not have Asafo drumming, but it prepared me for what to expect in the ones for Asafo members.

Egwuaradze One: Two *kɔtɔkorba* L-shaped Sticks

I experienced my first *egwuaradze* while staying at Cape Coast. I was at the house one Thursday afternoon when I heard Akan *Kete* drumming outside. I rushed to the balcony. When I looked down the street, I saw a line of people walking up the street carrying trays of items and a coffin on their heads. Kete drummers, other performers, a call and answer singing group, hand clappers, and a group of children and adults followed them.

I had never seen anything like it, so I rushed to my room, grabbed my camera, rushed down the stairs, and followed the parade; sometimes, I stood aside as the procession filed by; other times, I ran ahead of them. The bell rang, *ken-ke-ren ken ke-ren*. The master drummer played patterns on the black-and-red plaid-covered Kete drums with his *kɔtɔkorba* L-shaped sticks, *pu-tuu pu-tuum, pu-tuu pu-tuum, pu-tuu pu-tuum, pu-tuu pu-tuum, pu-tuu pu-tuu pu, pu-pu pu*; *pu-tuu pu-tuum, pu-tuu pu-tuum, pu-tuu pu-tuum, pu-tuu pu-tuum, pu-tuu pu-tuu pu, pu-pu-pu pu*, then with variations of those phrases. We turned a corner and entered the *ebusua* lineage house of the deceased. The moment we turned the corner, live *fɔntɔmfrɔm* drumming, indicative of the high status of the deceased, welcomed us to the compound. Then, almost as if on cue, one of the porters started to shake vigorously, destabilizing the items on her tray. The tray and items fell to the ground. Then . . .

>Snowball effect
>Two
>Three
>Four porters
>Eyes shut
>Eyes dazed
>Rolling eyeballs
>Shaking
>Back and forth
>Side to side
>*Egwuaradze*
>Jumping
>Hopping
>Final respect
>Dancing
>Dancing
>Showing off status
>Disgrace does not befit the Akan child
>Shaking
>Dancing
>Wailing
>Cryyyy . . .

The *fɔntɔmfrɔm* drums continued to thunder. It felt like Maya Deren's (1985) *Divine Horsemen* had descended on the porters. While the *fɔntɔmfrɔm* drums thundered, people rushed out of the house, held on to both *egwuaradze* and porters. One porter fell, scattering items from her tray, shaking vigorously, and convulsing. Chaos and order. Wailing. Sensory overload. The deceased had descended. Caught off guard, I almost dropped my camera. Another porter collapsed onto the ground. Minutes later, someone gave him some water; he poured the cold water on his head; then, as the water moved down other parts of his body, he slowly came back to what appeared to be his normal state. He danced with his tray.

Fɔntɔmfrɔm drums continued to thunder. *Pu-tu, pu-tu, pu-tu, pu-tu, pu-tu.* The bells rang. *Ken-ke-ren, ken-ke-ren.* The two drummers exchanged phrases, calling, and answering, exalting, and consoling. A group of men placed the coffin under a tent where lineage members of the deceased sat. The porters took the items to a room and presented them to a group of women. I walked slowly behind them, careful not to upset the intensity of their walk, but ready to step aside should another cosmic transmission occur. Speak. The layered patterns and sonic textures of *fɔntɔm-frɔm* drumming, bells sounding, Kete lines, and soundless soundscapes filled the room.

> *Ken-ke-ren, ken-ke-ren, Ken-ke-ren, ken-ke-ren, Ken-ke-ren, ken-ke-ren*
> *Pu-tuu pu-tuum, pu-tuu pu-tuum, Pu-tu, pu-tu, pu-tu,*
> *Pu-tuu pu-tuum, pu-tuu pu-tuum,*
> *Pu-tu, pu-tu, pu-tu, pu-tu, pu-tu pu-tuu pu-tuu pu, pu pu pu . . .*
> *pu-tu pu-tuu pu-tuum, pu-tuu pu-tuum*
> *ke-ka-ka, ke-ka-ka, ke-ka-ka, ke-ka-ka, ke-ka-ka, ke-ka-ka . . .*

After a long *amandzeɛ* mission statement from the presenters, the women chastised them for arriving late (they were supposed to have arrived at 9:00 a.m. but got there at 1:00 p.m.). The *ebusua* inspected the items and told the presenters that some of the items on the list that they had been given were missing. "A nail pricked me," remarked a lady who inspected the coffin. After more negotiations, money was accepted to make up for the missing items, the *egwuaradze* was accepted, tensions were resolved, and the community and families were reconstituted. I walked up to the drummers and listened. One drummer walked up to me and handed me a *kɔtɔkorba* L-shaped stick. Not sure what I was supposed to do, I asked.

Obisafoɔ nto kwan, "The seeker does not get lost." He told me to make a monetary offering to the drummers or play. I could not play, neither did I have money on me to pay, so I promised to do so the next time. I stayed around for some time till the drumming stopped. The drummers packed up, loaded their instruments onto a truck, and drove away.

Take 2: "Won't You Give Him Another Bath?"

On Thursday, February 23, 2017, I went to No. 1 Bentsir Asafo territory at Cape Coast to witness the arrival of the porters carrying the final bath items for the deceased. When I arrived, a tent had been set up to welcome and receive the bath items; the widow and some guests were seated under the tent. I sat beside the King of a neighboring town, a Muslim who said he prefers to be buried a day or two after his death and refuses to be kept in a fridge at a mortuary. Based on my experience of the lengthy funeral preparations even for ordinary citizens, which could take up to four months while the body stayed at the morgue, for a prominent man in the society such as a King, I doubted his wish would be granted. He and I discussed the Asante invasion of the coast in their search for two Kings, Venture Smith (an enslaved African who was taken from Ghana to the American colonies), American politics, the 1854 gathering of Fante Kings, and the signatures that gave the British massive control over Fante land and traditions.

> Ama: "Where did egwuaradze come from? Why is it necessary?"
> King: "We came and met it."
> Ama: "What is the purpose? Why is it necessary?"
> King: "If someone comes out of the bathroom and falls down, won't you give him another bath? When food is eaten, it is gone. . . ."

I did not quite understand the analogy, but he moved on. Recently, my dance mentor, ɔdomankoma Kyerɛma Kwamena Pra, explained the origins of *egwuaradze*:

> In the olden days, there was nothing like *egwuaradze*. A dead person would be embalmed with herbs for two or three days. He or she would be dressed in clothing from his or her own boxes. The most important thing was money which would be used in the cause of the journey, as the Akan believe. Aside that, messages from the deceased family on barrenness, prosperity etc., would be in a form of libation by

the linguist [spokesperson] before burial on the third day. The funeral would be arranged after the burial. After the independence of the country [Ghana], things started changing. That is, for fathers who took very good care of their children, the children had to reciprocate this gesture by bringing items which would be accepted by their father's family. Some of these items would be used on the death and the rest shared by those who bathed the dead body. It was the changes of time that brought about this *egwuaradze* and it was accompanied with coffin and drinks. (ɔdomankoma Kyerɛma Pra, email correspondence, June 2020)

Neither he nor the King stated whether the event is reserved for Asafo members only or every Fante. However, I had seen so many of such final bath parades on Thursday mornings, riding and walking through Cape Coast and along the other coastal towns such as Biriwa and Anomabo, including the first one I witnessed, that I concluded they are reserved for all Fante people. I also learned that sometimes, families keep the remaining items so that if someone—God forbid—does not give birth or have children and she or he dies, they would use the items for her or him. As far as who decides what items to be presented, I learned that the town or lineage members make the decision. If the items fall short, the family will accept money to make up for it; however, if a family presents more items than required, especially at Kormantse, the family will be fined.

While I sat waiting for the *egwuaradze* to arrive, I overheard some women talking about going to the house where the *egwuaradze* was being arranged. I asked if I could come along. They agreed. I followed at a distance. It was a long walk, up and down the hill, through the streets and by makeshift stores, and people's houses. Thinking . . . I met up with a gentleman who said he was a brother of the deceased. I took the opportunity to conduct a brief walking interview. According to him, "The parade through the city helps advertise the funeral (*ma eyi do*) and draws a big crowd to the funeral." He told me briefly about his deceased brother, the greatest Asafo flag dancer at Cape Coast. As we got closer to the residence, he stopped talking. His mood changed. Somber. When we entered the compound, no one or nothing was ready, only a coffin wrapped in brown paper.

I recognized an Asafo flag dancer from a previous event. I took out my computer and showed him the footage that I had recorded of him dancing. He talked me through some of the movements he performed, from the rubbing of his heels by the flag guardians, his running through the dance ring, going to the drum, taking the flag to the Elders, pausing, reflecting, and touching people with the flag three times. He corroborated my description of the dance movements. Kwamena was trained by the deceased, Nana Ekow Sekyi; his training was rigorous. According to him, the *asekambɔfo*, those four or more men who guard the flag while the flagbearer is dancing, have a difficult job. They must be always alert: they have to ensure that the flag does not fall or touch the ground. Importantly, they must ensure that the dancer is not kidnapped by dwarfs or the rival Asafo members. That signals a defeat of that Asafo organization. So, those who guard the flag dancer must know the movements and sense his mood. They must be alert enough to know when a cosmic energy is attempting to overtake the dancer. When they foresee this, they step into the ring, "rub and massage the dancer's heel, to soothe and pull out the negative energy before it takes over the entire body." He agreed to meet after the funeral to share details about the dance movements. We continued to wait for the *egwuaradze* workers.

The women started to arrive with the bath items. I joined them in the room where they wrapped the items. With a list in hand, they started to arrange the items in metal basins. First was a tray with eight pieces of twelve-yard cloth placed along the edge of the basin. The cloth was not enough, so there was a suggestion to bring one or two more. Next were the toiletries—bars of soap, four bottles of pomade, powder, cologne. The pillow was wrapped separately; the sheets and chewing sponge were also wrapped. The mat was not. Garments and undergarments and other accessories—scarves, silk underwear, handkerchiefs, and so on—got wrapped. The drinks—soft drinks, beer—were placed in another basin. The schnapps was not wrapped or placed in a basin. In all, there were about fifteen basins filled with items. While they worked, a pots, pans, and cutlery ensemble, calling and responding melodically, and a hand clapping group outside filled the room with their sounds.

After everything had been wrapped and placed in basins, each of the women picked up a basin, placed it on her head, and formed a line outside. Four men grabbed the coffin and walked to the back of the line; the *ndwom* performers formed behind them. Before we started the parade, a lady came up to the front of the line, holding the bottle of schnapps. She would lead the parade. Following her were the basin carriers, the coffin bearers, a flag dancer, several *asekambɔfo* (guardians of the flag), the pots and pans ensemble, onlookers, and supporters. The *ndwom* had already drawn a crowd of onlookers before we started to walk.

While we waited for everyone to get in line, I looked at the silver basins filled with items wrapped in colorful paper. While we were waiting to walk . . .

> I am *Egwuaradze*
> Final bath items
> The Elders brought me
> I am
> Cloth, scarves, silk underwear
> Soap, lotion, powder, perfumes, chewing sponge
> Towel, mat, bucket, a crate of soft drinks,
> Alcoholic beverages, water
> Placed in trays
> Wrapped in colorful plastic
> Adorned with a bow
> I am beautiful
> Women carry me
> Like a newborn
> Show and tell
> My coffin is grand
> Fit for Royalty
> What is nice is shown
>
> I Am
> *Egwuaradze*
> Last physical bath
> On Mother Earth
> Final respect

Egwuaradze presentation is a staged performance. "Put your hands on your heads! Take off your shoes!" Someone instructed us as we waited for the other porters to join the line. This was an egwuaradze presentation for the greatest *Frankaahuntanyi* flag dancer of No. 1 Bentsir Asafo company. With camera in hand, I took off my shoes. The tarred road was very hot and burned my feet. If it burned the porters' feet, they kept it to themselves and did not show their discomfort, while I stood on one foot, then on the other, wincing and sounding my distress, *agyaeish, agyaeish, agyaeish*. Again, my peripatetic practices gave me away as a stranger. The porters continued to look ahead without any display of irritation. I learned to disembody.

The procession followed; I trotted along, sometimes ahead of the procession, other times behind with the coffin bearers and *ndwom* performers. Another command came in. "Look sad." The women did. I tried to. My feet continued to burn. At one point, even some onlookers offered their instruction: *Wo'nsu ooo, wo'nsu,* "Cry-oooo, cry!" Some of the women started to cry. I could not cry. We went through business streets, market, and residential areas, uphill and downhill, sometimes deep into the rival group No. 2 Anaafo Asafo Company territory, perhaps to make a point. The streets were loud with onlookers and motorists honking their horns in support. Our pots and pans performers combined *ngyegyee nsisido*-layered sounds with call and response singing, hands in the air clapping layered patterns. Pa! Pa! Pa! Pa! Pa-paa pa-paa! Pa-pa-pa! Pa-pa-pa! Paa-pa! Paa-pa! All this contributed to a dense overlay of sound that enveloped the parade. Sometimes, sounds from residents' blasting *ndwom*—hiplife, Hi-Life, gospel—added to the soundscape. *Ndwom* was everywhere. It was a musicking walk, indeed. Some onlookers danced. Sometimes the coffin danced too. "Zirrrrrr!" "Zirrrrrr!" "Zirrrrrr!" the coffin bearers hissed as they moved synchronously in a counterclockwise direction, bouncing the coffin up and down, up and down.

At one point, those of us in front were asked to wait for the coffin. My feet continued to burn, sweat dripping, tears running down others' cheeks, blisters. It was a long walk. Some of the porters looked tired. A woman threw candy into the street; children and some adults ran into the street, scrambling for a piece. I learned later that throwing candy was all part of the presentation. Some of the porters started shaking back and forth, like I witnessed at my first *egwuaradze*. One shook so much that she had to be held in place. Another ran through the streets and had to be restrained. A lady held onto her pants to control her. "Calmly. Calmly. It is Ok," she comforted. Who is she talking to? I was told that the spirit of the deceased had entered her. How did she know what was happening? How did she know what to say? Ah! *ɔhɔhoɔ ani akɛseɛakɛseɛ nso ɔmfa hunu kuro mu,* "The stranger has many eyes, but she can't see what is going on in the town." "Let's pour some coke on her," someone recommended. We continued to parade. People asked, "Whose funeral is it?" "Whose funeral is it?" We gave them the name of the most famous Asafo *Frankaahuntanyi* of Cape Cast No. 1 Bentsir Asafo Company, Nana Ekow Sekyi. After about a five-mile walk through the streets of Cape Coast, we arrived at the house of the deceased. The Asafo performers had assembled with their four drums, two bells, and singers. The moment they saw us approaching, they started playing to welcome us: the two bells, two small drums, and master drummer in the front row; the second master drummer and the singers behind the first row, filled the space with *ndwom*.

The porters presented the *egwuaradze* to the gathering of *ebusua* members who sat waiting under a tent. *Amandzeε* mission statements were exchanged back and forth. The carriers took the items to a room where women inspected every basin to ensure that all the items on a list were there. They approved and accepted the items.

Egwuaradze exhibits many features of a spectacle. They are meaningful for the Fante and occur at regular intervals. The emotional response from the bystanders and observing public is key to the success of the *egwuaradze* presentation. The throwing of candy, the dancing of the coffin, the sad faces, the singing, the instructions given by bystanders, and the public's response contribute to the success of the event. The viewing public is as much a part of the performance as the porters and *ndwom* makers. The crowd dancing, offering advice on the staging, and playing roles are expected and appropriate in the community. They are participants, witnesses, and evaluators at the same time. Their good opinions and commentaries help shape the event and influence its success. Parading through the street is equally about displaying status. The size of the procession—number of porters, the coffin, musicians, and other tokens—affirms the value and status of the presenters and the standing of the deceased.

Entering the Bodies of Others: A Haptic Way of Knowing

The Akan say, *Etua wo nyɔnko ho a, etua dua mu,* "When it's pricking your friend, it's pricking a tree," or *Nea adeε awɔ no na ɔham,* "She who has been pricked, yells," to stress the importance of experience and how experience, especially bodily experience, allows one to feel and to acquire a deeper level of understanding. I wanted to experience what it meant to carry the bath items for myself, so I participated in one for the wife of an Asafo captain, also a King. When I arrived at Gyegyem District of Cape Coast, all the items had been wrapped and packed into about a hundred basins.[2]

The parade was as much about displaying status as it was about showing final respect. First, there were over a hundred people in the procession, including about thirty or more of us carrying the *egwuaradze* in heavily

FIGURE 6.1. *Egwuaradze* parade through Cape Coast. Aduonum is second in line. Photo by Ben.

packed basins, six coffin bearers, supporters, announcers, and *ndwom* makers. It was a highly choreographed and stylized event. Each of the female porters wore the same black wrap, a red wrap around the upper torso, and a white handkerchief tucked into the top right. I was the last to be added to the list of porters, so I did not get the costume. Therefore, I stood out since my "costume" did not match theirs. Two young girls, holding a wreath and a photograph of the deceased, led us. We started to walk.

The parade was long, exhausting. I carried a heavy tray of silk and lace and walked with about thirty other carriers; my neck hurt under the heavy basin; the basin pressed on the scar from my brain surgery; it hurt (figure 6.1). My feet were tired, tingly. My arms were sore. I was thirsty. The tarred road was very hot. We walked and walked. Sometimes we trudged if the climb was steep. Several of the porters complained about the weight of their trays; one forgot her inhaler; I was in front of her and hoped she did not have a crisis; another complained that her tray was caving in due to the weight. We stopped for her tray to be adjusted. We conversed, bonded, forged new relationships with the other female carriers, connected by our experiences under a tray of last bath items for the deceased—the sociability of walking together, connecting rhythm and beats to the sounds of *ndwom*, footsteps, conversation, and commentaries from onlookers. Indeed, "sharing or creating a walking rhythm with other people can lead to a very particular closeness and bond between the people involved" (Ingold and Vergunst 2006, 69). Some of the carriers became important for my research on Asafo *ndwom* and culture.

One of the ladies who organized the parade announced as we filed by:

> ɔyɛ fɛw
> Adze a ɔyɛ fɛ na wɔdze kyerɛ
> ɔabor do
> ɔyɛ Nana Kweku Arhin dze a
> W'enyiwa nnyɛ a, mma nnhwɛ

> (It is nice.
> It is what is nice that is displayed
> It has exceeded the limit
> It is for Nana Kweku Arhin
> Fit for a King's wife
> If you don't have good eyes don't look)

Onlookers commented as we paraded through the streets and by houses, asking questions and giving suggestions and instructions on how we should look. This part of the parade was performed to affirm the status and worth of the deceased and her family. Furthermore, it spoke to the class and social standing of her family. Parading through the streets with that many items, porters, and followers spoke to how important the deceased was in her society. It also showed that *nekyir yɛ dur*, "She has weight (support) behind her." Ultimately, it drew a huge crowd to the funeral.

So, what happens when some families are not able to present their *egwuaradze* in a such a grand style? Would they lose respect in the community? Will it put a stain on the family image? Could a family go bankrupt after such displays? How stressful are such presentations on the family and society? Could this be why in Kormantse, *egwuaradze* presentations are heavily monitored, and a family is fined if it exceeds the prescribed items? However, this is Cape Coast's Gyegyem District; residents here are known for showing off and for being pompous. At the same time, our Elders also say, *Wo te puu-puu a wɔ bi di*, "If you hear puu-puu [like someone is pounding fufu], pound some and eat." They could be pounding rocks or cement on the ground. Looks and ears can be deceiving. This *egwuaradze* was not one of those pretentious fufu poundings.

As a scheduled, temporally bounded, spatially bounded, and programmed event, *egwuaradze* is a cultural performance, those coordinated public occasions "open to view by an audience and to collective participations" (Bauman 1990, 285). At the same time, owing largely to their reflexive nature, they are heightened occasions for the community. Cultural performances like rituals, festivals, carnivals, folk stories, ballets, staged dramas, novels, and epic poems mirror a society's beliefs and ideas about itself and the world around it. *Egwuaradze* is a complex performance in its staging of various elements of the other intellectual traditions noted. Its presentation not only helps to reconstitute a community; it allows the community to display respect and honor the deceased.

After about a five-mile walk in the hot sun, through various districts in the city, uphill and downhill, crowded and empty streets, we arrived at the lineage house. Dignitaries and ordinary citizens in black and red sat under tents. Under one of the tents, the widower, an Asafo captain and King, sat with his family and the deceased's lineage members. They sat behind a table in front of which stood a pole with a wooden replica of a leopard, the *akyeneboa* totem for the Twidan lineage. (see chapter 5). I hummed the Twidan song Maame Owusuma performed, *Aboa kɛse aha wura . . . Ebusua sɛnkyerɛ dze a . . . Twidan ebusua odziamon* (see chapter 5 epigraph). Pieces of different fabrics were wrapped around the pole beneath the totem. The number of pieces indicated the number of lineage members who had died. After the fiftieth death, they bury all the pieces, then the count begins again.

Though the husband of the deceased is a Safohen, Asafo drumming did not welcome us to the house as I experienced at the *egwuaradze* presentation of the flag dancer; *fɔntɔmfrɔm* drumming and Kete drumming welcomed us. Each porter placed her basin in a room where women inspected the items. While we waited, the drummers continued to drum; singers sang. A master of ceremonies introduced each of the gifts. He spent more time on the coffin, showing and bragging about its multiple compartments, and pointing to its inner silk lining. The crowd clapped and cheered as he described the value of the coffin, making the coffin and death enviable.

The next day, Friday night, I arrived at the house to attend the wake keeping. It was a huge gathering because of the family's status in the community. Food was being served. Before I entered the house, I walked by different groups playing—a brass band, a jazz band, a drumming ensemble, and a gospel choir. Each group waited its turn and played after one had stopped playing. People mingled with the crowd; some danced and danced. I walked around, stopping at each group and taking in the different *ndwom*. Portraits of the deceased were mounted everywhere. I took some pictures, then entered the house to people mourning and wailing. In one room where we presented the *egwuaradze*, the deceased, dressed in very fine clothes and lace that we presented the day before, laid on a bed. Her face was made up beautifully like a bride. The room smelled of cologne and powder. A few women sat by her as one stood by and fanned her. I peered through the room as people filed in to view her, talk with her, and pay their respects. They walked around the bed; some stopped and wailed; others stood in place and wailed continuously, talking with and to her (see chapter 5). Live *ndwom* from outside filled the space. The lady with whom I traveled sensed my hesitation and encouraged me to go in and view the deceased. I hesitated but went in anyway. I stood at the foot of the bed and watched as others filed by. Some stood by the deceased and had long conversations, asking her questions, wailing and sobbing. I took some pictures of the room and of the deceased. I walked slowly, closer to the bed, and stood by her. When the lady who fanned the body sat down, I took the fan and fanned the deceased. I had never done anything like that. After a while, I stepped out of the room, stopped by the table, offered my condolences to the widower, whom I had visited before the funeral, and walked outside to the *ndwom*. It was getting late, so I made my way home and went straight to bed. I was exhausted.

Around dawn, I woke up suddenly to a sweet smell like the one I smelled in the viewing room. I looked over at my children; they were asleep. I laid still and took in the smell. *Where is the smell coming from? It is too early for anyone to be taking a bath in our community bathroom.* The room felt heavy. After lying still for a while, I managed to get up and went out of the room. I walked to the bathroom to see if any of the residents was taking a bath. No one was taking a bath or had taken a bath, because the floor was dry. No one else was awake. I went back to the room and sat. I could not go back to sleep. Now, I was afraid. *Did she follow me home? Did she visit me? Why? Was it because I fanned her? Was it because I carried her egwuaradze? Was she angry that I took so many pictures of her? Maybe if I had taken a bath before going to bed or placed a bowl of water outside our door, she couldn't have visited. This did not happen after I viewed the two male Asafo members. Are women's spirits stronger than men's spirits? Although I must admit, the night I viewed the flag dancer's body, it rained torrentially. Maybe that kept him away. Water cleanses and keeps spirits away.* I rose, grabbed my camera, and deleted all the photos I took of her lying in state and of her images on posters. After a while, the scent dissipated. At daybreak, I asked my children if they smelled the scent. They had not.

I walked to the church service before her burial that Saturday morning, thinking about my experience with the scent. I sat very far from the casket. After the church service, a hearse drove her to the cemetery for burial. Later, I shared my experience with one photographer who also took pictures that night. He suggested that she may have visited to "thank me" for carrying the *egwuaradze* and for fanning her body. After this incident, I stopped viewing bodies of the deceased; if I did, like when I attended a pre-burial event for two sisters, I did so from a distance. Our Elders say, *Ahunu yenhunu no mprenu*, "A calamity should not be experienced twice" (one bitten twice shy); they also caution us, *wofeefee funu ani a, wohunu saman*, "When you probe the eyes of the dead, you see a ghost." *Deɛ ɔwɔ akano suro sonsono*, "The one who has been bitten by a snake is afraid of a worm."

> Eh! Egwuaradze! It is Thursday, your day to show final respect for the deceased. Here you come. A parade of final bath items. Women and men carry basins of cloth, soap, lotion, perfume, and powder. Crates of soft drinks. A casket. Black and red plaid covered Kete drums follow. Two *kɔtɔkorba* L-shaped sticks play tu-tum, tu-tum, ta. Bells' ngyegyee sounds overlap: ken-ke-ren ken-ke-ren ka. Singers call and answer. Egwuaradze, welcome; you have arrived-o. "Wash, clothe, pamper. Lay her in state. Bury her in style. Cry-oo cry." Are you a spectacle, a ritual, a musical-dance-drama? Grieving or displaying status? Egwuaradze, the Akan say, *ɔnantefoɔ sene oni ne ɔse asɛm*, "The walker knows more than her mother and father." I walked with you; listened to your ndwom to know you. Egwuaradze Adze a ɔyɛ fɛw na wɔdze kyerɛ. Ampa!

Asafo Death Matters: Toward a "Musicking Walk"

Andra McCartney defines soundwalking as a "creative and research practice that involves listening and sometimes recording while moving through a place at a walking pace. It is concerned with the relationship between soundwalkers and their surrounding sonic environment" (2014, 213). While McCartney lumps both the listening aspect and the recording aspect together, Greg Wagstaff makes a clear distinction between the two:

"Soundwalk in essence is quite simple—one walks and one listens . . . there are two types of walk. Soundwalk encourages those on it to sound or voice that space by promoting interaction with the objects and your surroundings. A Listening Walk asks you to listen and make as little sound as necessary during the walk" (2011).

Others have also made a distinction between the Listening Walk as a "walk with a concentration on listening" and a soundwalk, which, according to Westerkamp, consists of "orientation, dialogue, and composition" (1974 [2000, 4]). Soundwalk artists focus on everyday noises of a place and their interactions with it; they take the everyday actions of walking and sounds and bring them to the attention of the participants or the audience. Some use those sounds, recorded or not, to initiate and encourage their audience in discussions about issues of gender, class, technology, varied listening experiences, and so on (Corringham 2013; McCartney 2014; Schaffer 1974; Wagstaff 2002, 2001). The Listening Walk, thus, involves walking alone or with a group and paying attention to the different sounds in the environment without talking; what becomes of that experience depends on the varied goals of the participants.

Only a handful of musicologists and ethnomusicologists have written about their process that might be compared to or characterized as a soundwalk or, more specifically, a Listening Walk. Musicologist Kofi Agawu credits his appreciation of the music by different groups to a walk at a funeral: "What began as a sideshow would increase intensity and begin to compete with the main event. I walked around the funeral grounds and was able to tune in and out of the different kinds of music being made 'locally,' but for a listener seeking a synoptic view of the event, the outcome was an irreducible plurality. This was a powerful manifestation of simultaneous doing. . . . Standing back from this plural environment, one can appreciate the gift of simultaneity" (2016, 301). While Agawu may not have taken the walk at the funeral intentionally to listen to the music or may not label himself as a soundwalk artist, he does acknowledge that it was through the walk that he was able to take in the individuality of each music group. "Standing back (*walking away* or) through this plural environment, one can appreciate the gift of simultaneity" (ibid.).

Ethnomusicologist Michelle Kisliuk's performance-based ethnography about the BaAka of the Central African rain forest is replete with references to walking: walking to the dance space, walking to a hunt, walking alone, walking with others, walking on the various textured landscapes.

According to her, each of these walks taught her important information about hunting, history, music, dance, performance, cosmology, and negotiating BaAka society. Many of her walks were very crucial to her understanding of BaAka vocal polyphony, as she "often heard BaAka sing bits of melody while working near a camp or walking along a path."

> This being my first time so deep in the forest, I was enchanted when I heard a falsetto BaAka melody (*dingombi*) right through the trees as we approached one camp. A few steps later I saw the man, singing from high in a tree where he was cutting palm nuts. This is it, I thought, this is that romantic "pygmy-singing-in-the-forests" image I had come to expect from reading Turnbull, Lomax, and Arom.... As we approached to cross the stream a teenage girl who had not seen us coming sang a brief, open-throated song that echoed on the water and into the tress. I made sure I memorized the melody on the spot and thereafter thought of it as the water melody. (Kisliuk 1998, 37)

In other parts of her book, she writes, "We walked for about twenty more minutes, nearing the dance at around dusk, at a camp just at the edge of the thick forest. Along the path we could hear from afar overlapping melodies echoing through the trees and shooting gently into the night" (80). Later, she references another walk: "One day, I was walking to our camp on my way from the village. Along the path, I came upon Djongi's daughter, Mokoti, and some younger children. As they scurried along in front of me, Mokoti sang out the phrase of a song. I recognized then that it was the main theme of one Mabo song very popular at the time, 'Makala.' Soon after this epiphany of sorts, I inquired more about the song" (98).

While Kisliuk does not credit her process of learning about the intricacies of BaAka music to a Listening Walk or connect it to the work of soundwalk artists who listen to and analyze sounds in the environment during a walk for creative work and other benefits, one could connect her process to those of soundwalk artists. Both Agawu's and Kisliuk's experiences do not rely on paying attention to everyday sounds in the environment or the everyday sounds of walking—they heard people deliberately making music, either singing parts of a melody or performing in an ensemble. These were not "everyday noises of a place." Also, from what I gather, they did not deliberately take a walk to listen to the music; it was an outcome of their actions, possibly a coincidence, though it contributed to their process.

A "musicking walk," as I describe, define, and use it in this work, captures the experiences of Agawu, Kisliuk, and other musicologists and ethnomusicologists who may have benefited from a walk. Building upon Christopher Small's (1998) helpful formulation about "musicking", "a musicking walk" is one in which participants, deliberately or accidentally, "walk into" and/or deliberately engage with the music in their surroundings while walking, standing away from the music event, or running with others as the music unfolds. One is engaged with the music on multiple levels. Depending on the participant, the level of engagement could be different; it could

- raise the participant's awareness to the intricacies of the music;
- help the participant tease out the multiple parts to a music;
- amplify a participant's appreciation of the music;
- connect the participant to the event more profoundly;
- move one to dance or sing along;
- be applied and used in various ways;
- be enjoyed without necessarily having to engage in any critical analysis of its multiple parts;
- be accidental or planned;
- involve walking with music, sounds, and silence that are performed by humans and nonhumans;
- provide knowledge gained from the experience that could be verified during subsequent performances and interviews.

The musicking walk is a multisensory experience. Depending on the locale, our ways of walking, listening, the type of *ndwom*, and knowledge sought, it produces different forms of information. Because all our five senses reinforce each other to provide the intricate ordered and emotion-charged world in which we live (Tuan in Wunderlich 2008, 128)—how we feel, how we see, how we listen, and how we connect with the land and people—it is critical to pay attention to our senses and those of the people we walk or meet (Pink 2009) during a musicking walk.

Anthropologists Ingold and Vergunst's study on the phenomenology of walking (2008) offers important perspectives on the extent to which walking allows us to engage with the land, our environment, with other people, and ourselves. Our ways of walking add more depth to the experience gained and how we experience music. Ethnomusicologist Angela Impey's discussion about how crucial walking was to her method in her study of the music of women in western Maputaland is instructive. Walking allowed her to experience and connect with the women's music and songs as they strode the different paths the women had traversed in their youth (2018). Hers was a "musicking walk." The "musicking walk" helped me understand the organization of the throbbing and infectious interlocking patterns of the Asafo *dawur*, drums, and singing.

My Musicking Walks

One cool Friday night on February 10, 2017, the woman with whom I stayed told me about a wake keeping at the Anaafo side of the city. The woman belonged to the No. 1 Cape Coast Asafo Bentsir Company and had arranged a recording session with an Asafo Bentsir group.[3] I hesitated to go, but at the time, two months into my research on Asafo *ndwom*, I had not experienced any live performance with all the Asafo drums, bell, and singing. About 8:00 p.m., I decided to go. I walked through the city, asking for directions to the Aboradze lineage house. After about a three-mile walk, the sounds of live drumming led me to an area where the wake was being held for the greatest Asafo master drummer in Cape Coast. This was Asafo No. 2 Anaafo territory. The street leading to the house and adjacent ones were blocked off. Huge tents and a crowd of people in black or black and red attire filled the streets. Under the tent was a group of performers playing three *dawur*, two large drums, and two smaller drums. One of the two small drums was played with bare hands, while the other was played with two small sticks. The two large drums were wrapped in white cloth. One of the drums was center stage and in the front row together with the players of the three *dawur* and the two smaller drums. I would later learn that the large drum is *Asafokyen kɛse*, the master drum. The drummer for the second large drum, the *agyegyedo* (the responder) sat behind the master drummer. They both played with L-shaped *kɔtɔkorba* sticks. A group of singers sang behind the drummers.

I stood and listened for a while, amazed by the ease and energy with which they played the different pieces; after every three or four fast ones, they played one slow one. To signal the end of a sequence, the master drummer played with two drumsticks. I would later learn that this was typical of Asafo instrumental *ndwom* playing at funerals and that the fast style was ɔ*sor* (high/up) style and the slow one was *famu* (slow/cool/on the ground) style. I also learned that there are five Asafo *ndwom* styles: lively ɔ*sor* (high/

TABLE 6.2. Asafo Instrumental *Ndwom* Types

Music Type	Description	Context
ɔsor (Up)	Vigorous, hot, and fast, performed at high speed.	Used for festive occasions, festivals, at which men dance.
Famu (Ground)	Slow, cool, soft, and allows for chiefs and women to dance.	Commonly performed at the installation of chiefs, welcome ceremonies, and at festivals.
Atoprɛ	Musical style for the dead. It is slow.	It is performed at the annual Akwambo festival in memory of the dead; it is also performed during procession to the graveside and burial.
ɔwombir	Medium tempo and performed leisurely.	For procession of Asafo through the streets.
Asafoesi	It is medium to slow tempo.	Performed for the various Gods during ritual celebrations. It is also used to provoke enemies.

hot) for festive occasions; *famu* (slow/cool), *atoprɛ* (for funerals); ɔwombir (for Asafo processions); and *asafoesi* (for the Gods during rituals).[4]

Dancers took to the floor and moved in ways that I had not experienced. They hopped on one foot, crouched low, or pranced around the dance floor as if to evade, attack, and taunt. I was tempted to join the dancers, but resisted. Rather, I stood by and listened to the songs, taking in the complexity and overarching density of the three *nnawur* bells of the Cape Coast Anaafo Asafo Company. The drum patterns did not coincide with the songs; rather, it was a kind of "simultaneous doing" (Agawu 2016, 267) in which the drums and songs did not always align perfectly. The drum patterns floated above the pulse, and as I experienced them, they did not seem to link themselves to the songs. When I asked one of the drummers why the songs and the *nnawur* did not align, he responded, "They do unite, a lot. *Pa-paa pa*." Perhaps I had not heard the music enough and did not get it, or I had a different sense of musicking and experiencing the patterns.

After a while, I walked around and away from the action. It was while I walked away and around that I was able to isolate the intricate rhythms of the three *nnawur*. I could not tell which specific bell played what part, but

FIGURE 6.2. Cape Coast No. 2 Asafo Company drum ensemble. Property of ɔdomankoma Kyerɛma Kwamena Pra. Left to right. Bells *Dawur Mfae, Amponsa* (largest), and *Nguedo*. Drums are *Asafokyen, gyegyedo, ampae,* and *ansarba*. Photo by the author.

I was still able to distinguish between the distinct patterns. Away from the context, I was able to isolate and identify the parts by their different tones, a process that would have been more challenging to accomplish had I been around the various activities involved in the performance. Floating above this complex unit were the multiple lines of the singing and hand clapping. I would later learn the names of the three bells from my dance scholar. They are *Dawur mfae* (caller), *Nguedo* (response), and *Amponsa* (mother).

Continuing to walk and surrounded by the *ndwom* from the live drumming, I entered the lineage house to where the drummer was laid in state. I joined a long line with adults and children who had come to see the deceased and pay their respects. A woman yelled at the children to leave. "Go away from here! Today's children that have come, they are not afraid of anything." "They are witches!" another woman exclaimed. Before I climbed up the stairs to the room, I had a brief conversation with a gentleman who, noticing my hesitation, urged me to go in.

Gentleman: "Go inside. Go!"
Ama: "Can I?"
Gentleman: "Yes, go and look at him."
Ama: "I am scared."
Gentleman: "It is not scary."
Ama: "Can I take a picture?"
Gentleman: "Yes!"

I walked up some steps and entered the room. Since this was my first close viewing of a dead body in my adult life, I expected to see the deceased lying in bed like I had witnessed when I was much younger. Women and men in a sea of black and red clothing sat and stood around. I recognized a woman from a previous recording engagement. She smiled at me. I relaxed. An area had been sectioned off with white and blue ropes and colored wreaths. In this space, a man stood behind a big black-and-white, cylindrical-shaped carved drum, a replica of the Asafo *kyen kɛse* master drum. He was holding a *kɔtɔkorba* L-shaped stick in one hand and the other hand was atop the drum. This was the deceased drummer. He was propped up with metal wires and stuffed with newspaper. He looked alive. He was wearing cotton shirt and trousers in classic No. 2 Anaafo Asafo Company colors—blue and white, and a white scarf around his neck. Their Asafo flags were hung on the walls behind him. As the famous drummer of all Cape Coast, Divine Master Drummer ɔdomankoma Kyerɛma Nana Ekow Abakah stood behind what he played best, an Asafo*kyen kɛse* master drum, which would later serve as his casket. I stared at him for a while; then I walked around the blue and white ropes that separated him from his viewers.

The drum and bell patterns from outside filled the room, creating an eerie atmosphere. Some Asafo performers came in with more drumming, bells, and singing for him, addressing him, pointing at him, and talking with him. Some of the singers had smiles on their faces, while others appeared melancholic and shocked. I hopped onto a chair to make room for them as they filed by the corpse singing; some were wailing. Led by a gentleman who held a folded Anaafo flag, the players of the three *dawur* bells, the drummers on the master drum and responder drum, and singers walked slowly around the deceased. The players held up the bells in their left hands and played. The two drummers followed. At a point, the master drummer stopped by the group of family members. He talked to them through his drum patterns, probably giving them his condolences;

the second drummer answered his calls. Others moved in silence. The three Anaafo bells interlocked their patterns. *Ken-ke-ke-ken. Ton-ton san, san. Ken-ken-ke.* The gentleman playing the *Asafokyen kɛse* master played proverbs, spoke to him, lauded the deceased. The *agyegyedo* drum answered. The deceased ɔdomankoma ɔkyerɛma played along in silence. Singers sang songs that spoke of bravery and pride—calling, responding, evoking, sustaining war songs. The ensemble of bells, drums, hand clappers, and singers surrounded the deceased with sound: *ndwom*, applauding, honoring, mourning, conversing, wondering. Is he really gone? "*Ndwom, ndwom, ndwom!*" ("Song, song, song!"), a lady called out. Someone started another song.

In this moment when we declared our shared humanity, I, as an Akan Kwahu female, an outsider to the Akan Fante culture and Asafo tradition but a performer nonetheless, felt connected and awed at the same time. I tried to sing along one of the songs that I had heard at Kormantse, "*Kormantse na Abandze/Wombisa hɔn ko yi ase ɛ/Abora wombisa oo/Nkum rosu a Bentsir a*." I would later learn that Asafo musicians are allowed to sing songs of other companies, especially if they are not foes. I also learned that during a funeral, Asafo companies in the town or city could help other companies.

I wanted to leave, but I stayed. *Will I be able to sleep at night? Will the Divine Master Drummer ɔdomankoma kyerɛma's spirit follow me home? Maybe if I put a bowl of water outside my door his spirit cannot enter my room. They say spirits cannot cross water to other worlds unless they pay the ferryman or boatman who takes them to the other world. Since he has not been buried, he has not paid his dues, I stayed.* Still, I was petrified. The singers urged him to drum.

>ɔdomankoma kyerɛma
>Master drummer
>Drum
>Alternate stick
>and hand techniques
>Your flag dancer is waiting
>To dance

>ɔdomankoma kyerɛma
>You whose Ancestors led Asafo warriors

> To victory
> You who brings the dead antelope to life
> To speak
> Drum
> We can hear your
> Silent interlocking patterns
> In Akan land we say
> *Wo bɛn ɔkɔtɔ a, wote sɛ ɔbɔ wa*
> It is when you get close to a crab
> That you can hear it cough
> *Pinkyɛ asu, na wo pinkyɛ asu a, na wote sɛ kɔtɔ bɔ wa*
> Approach the stream, it is when you approach the stream that
> You hear the crab cough
> We are near
> We want to
> Hear you
> Talk to us
> Drum

The Asafo historian J. E. K. Aggrey is right! *Obiara a obedzi asafomba hɔn fun ho agor nnkɛfa noho tɔtrɔtɔ koraa*, "Anyone who plays with an Asafo company's dead body will not take himself/herself for free" (1974, 49). In Asafo territory, and indeed in many societies in Africa, the dead is guarded, cherished, drummed, performed, and danced. *Obiara a obedzi asafomba hɔn fun ho agor nnkɛfa noho tɔtrɔtɔ koraa* (1974, 49), "Anyone who plays with an Asafo company's dead body will not take himself for free." Again, *Obiara a obedzi asafomba hɔn fun ho agor nnkɛfa noho tɔtrɔtɔ koraa*, "Anyone who plays with an Asafo company's dead body will not take himself for free." The *ndwom* continued to fill the room. Songs of past wars came to life. They lived, thrived, and were sustained here at the funeral, though they are frowned upon by some in the outside world. But can funerals alone serve as viable platforms for *the Safeguarding of Intangible Cultural Heritage* (UNESCO 2003), especially since it involves someone dying? How else might Fante societies curate and encourage creativity to sustain that performance tradition? If performance is key to sustaining *ndwom*, could funerals alone help sustain Asafo *ndwom* and other intellectual traditions?

I looked at the deceased, then looked away. I looked at the deceased, then looked away. I looked. Is he dead? *Wohunu kɔtɔ ani a wose abaa, nanso n'ani ara ne no,* "When you see the eyes of the crab, you say they are sticks, but those are its eyes." *Hyiee!* He looked so alive. I walked behind him and stood for a while. Here, in this safe space, I allowed myself to be carried away in the *ndwom*. At the same time, I was alert, for if *ndwom* and dance can raise the dead, I could dash out the door. *Animguasee mfata Kani ba*, "Disgrace does not befit the Akan child!" One gentleman attempted to dance, but his moments were restricted due to the tight space.

As I walked around the space and heard the *ndwom* inside and from outside, I took in all that I had learned thus far about Asafo *ndwom*—solo and group, declamatory, evocative, raw, free moving and measured, punctuated by drum patterns, singing, dancing. *Ngyegyee nsisido*. Sounds overlapping. As people mourned, sang, chatted, and comforted each other amidst the pulsating *ngyegyee* rhythms of the lead drummer and evocative songs by the singers, my memory walked to the first funeral I attended as a child, bringing back those locked memories and the live drumming that accompanied it. Furthermore, I was reminded of Meki Nzewi's postulation, "African music is feeling and communal therapy, a humanizing communion, a sharing of human-being-ness" (1997, 23). Not only did the musicking walk allow me to hear the sounds and rhythms away from its context (dance, theater, etc.) and crowd and to configure and reconfigure it in new ways, it allowed me to embody the *ndwom* in ways I had not imagined. It was a humanizing communion, a sharing of human being-ness.

A musicking walk, then, is also conceptual walking, "a reflective mode. It is a creative response to our interpretation of the place or simply a way of gathering information, or critically building awareness of . . . environments" (Wunderlich 2008, 131–133). It shares some elements with the qualitative (see Olmstead) or discursive (Wunderlich) in that it allows us to interpret space and gather information; it is also choreographed in the sense that we think before we actually go about performing it, and it allows for critical assessment of the environment and soundscape. I was in complete awareness of my surroundings and consciously explored the landscape and soundscape while sensorially experiencing it. In this type of participatory walk, my familiarity with the environment was deepened, allowing me to envision and experience the landscape and soundscape differently, evoking my senses, heightening my sense of place and space, and connecting me deeply to the *ndwom*.

I left to go back home around 11:30 p.m. The Asafo ensemble outside had packed up and a new group, The Point Group, performed a mixture of gospel and Hi-Life *ndwom*. I listened a bit, danced briefly, and then returned to the house. On my way, I reflected on what I had witnessed.

>ɔkyerɛma master drummer
>Standing
>Drumming
>Asafo
>Four drums
>Three bells
>High and low drumming
>Dance
>Asafo flags
>Callers and responders
>*Obiara a obedzi asafomba hɔn fun ho agor nnkɛfa noho tɔtrɔtɔ koraa*
>Anyone who plays with an Asafo company's dead body
>Will not take herself for free
>Singers
>*Ndwom, ndwom, ndwom*
>Woo
>Parade
>Mourn
>Wail
>Bué!
>
>ɔkyerɛma master drummer
>Royalty
>Standing
>Our Elders say
>Woforo dua a, foro dua tenten, na wo te hwe a
>Atumpan ama wo dammirifua
>When you climb a tree, climb a tall one so that when you fall
>Talking drums will play condolences for you
>You climbed a tall tree
>Condolences!
>Dammirifua due!

The next day, Saturday, February 11, 2017, I went back to Anaafo Asafo territory to attend the funeral for the late ɔkyerɛma master drummer. I stopped by the lineage house first. The deceased was lying on a bed this time. He wore a traditional *kente* cloth and gold jewelry on his neck, fingers, and wrists. When it was time to place him in the casket, they asked all viewers to leave the room. After about thirty minutes, they brought out the drum casket draped with the company's blue and white flag. Lineage members prayed by making an offering to Ancestral Spirits, and speaking to him, asking him to remember the Aboradze lineage. The three *dawur* bells played. Final farewells were intoned. Asafo members carried the casket to their *posuban*.

After securing the casket in a wooden brace, they lifted it up and danced it three times around the posuban to the rhythms of the talking drummer and the three bells. *ɔbosom anim yɛkɔ no mprɛnsa*, "Appearance before the priest is made three times." Again, standing away from the bells and drums, I could decipher their distinctive patterns easily. *Tete ka aso mu*, "Repetitive listening leaves an indelible mark in the ear." I was getting used to the different tones and patterns. After that they carried the casket to the community grounds where the drummers, singers, and the community assembled for the funeral proper.

Ahahrata mmienu kabom a, ɛyɛ ɔpepe," When individual leaves come together, they form thousands." Therefore, as Ruth Stone (1982) observes of the Kpelle of Liberia, the music event envelopes "units of songs as well as other types of interaction such as dance and speeches given during pauses in the music by the audience or performers as evaluation of the performance. The event consists of the participants' dynamic processes of evaluation and action, creating the interaction from which the event's meaning is derived" (2).[5] In every performance situation, as in this one, the audience is directly involved in the evaluation and creation of the art. A silent audience speaks volumes about the effectiveness of the performers. In so doing, the performers and the audience engage in a reciprocal relationship to create a memorable and shared experience, a celebration of lived experiences. This funeral was full of color, laughter, cheers, humor, dancing, drumming, singing, and theatrical enactments. It was live pa-pa!

>ɔdomankoma kyerɛma
>Divine master drummer
>Your final day with the mortals
>Is here

Flag bearers dance
Take turns
Ring of liberation
Leaps and crouches
Leans forward, rocks back and forth
Back and forth, back and forth
Slightly bent back
Quick footwork
Back and forth

Flag bearer
Twists and turns
Jumps and squats
Circles
He runs
Dives
Waves the flag
Twirls it
Throws
Catches it
Sound patterns
A fallen flag signals defeat

ɔdomankoma kyerɛma
Obisafoɔ nto kwan
She who asks for directions never misses her way
Two *kɔtɔkorbakutaafo* dancers
With *kɔtɔkorba* L-shaped sticks
Move from side to side
Crouch
Dash
Lead the path
Clear the path for you
Sweep away evil spirits
Kɔtɔkorba L-shaped sticks
Lock
Path is clear
Safe for entry

Lady seizes casket
Sits
Dances on it
Rocks back and forth
Back and forth
Women are not supposed to touch casket
Obiara a obedzi asafomba hɔn fun ho agor nnkɛfa noho tɔtrɔtɔ koraa
Anyone who plays with an Asafo company's dead body will not take herself free
Tweaa
She does
Family must pay
For release of casket
It is part of tradition
Amandze

Divine master drummer
Aaa
Death ladder, one person does not climb it
Dammirifua due
Due ne amanehunu
Condolences
ɔbaatan na onim nea ne mma bedi
It is the mother who knows what her children will eat
Nana what will your children eat
Who will articulate your children's dreams
Their *abakɔsɛm* and memories
With you gone
The tortoise is crawling
The child is crawling
Who will carry the other
Buooo, buooo
Buooo

3 *nnawur* bells
Ke-ken-ren-ke
Ken-ka-ka ken-ka-ka

Four drums
Pu-tum-pa
Pu-tum pu-tum
All for you
Honor you
Bué
Family wailing
Asafo drums
Walking
Master drummer talking
Cajoling
Crowd roaring
There is joy in this dance
If dancer falls with flag
Taboo
Enemies seize the flag
Audience must dance it or pay
They pay

Hwɛ
Flag bearer dances aaaa . . .
Stops in the ring
Not a good sign
Flag guardian *asekambɔfo*
Step in
Massage dancer's heel
Pull out negative energy
The trap to trip him
The trap to overcome the dancer
The witches trap
Must not weaken
Trap him

People wailing
Chatting
Eating
It is not real Asafo some say
It is folkloric

It is not the real thing
Asafo captains
Female
Male
Control crowd
With sticks
Move back
Supi Asafo leader
The overseer
Eh it is the walker who eats sweet things

Divine ɔkyerɛma
Drummer goes for two sticks
The end is close
He switches back to
One stick
It is not time
Ebueii
Musicians take turns
Divine master drummer
An old man
The old are buried much later
More time with the living
Final respect

Nkwanpa twetwe adwa
A good soup attracts chairs
Anaafo streets are alive
Awake from its quiet days
Six Fante ebusua
Aboradze, Anona, Nsɔna,
Twidan, Kɔna, Domna ebusua
Gather to pay homage
Master drummers play
Dancers take turns
Flag guardians take turns
Anaafo kyerɛma
Divine master drummer

Aaaa
ɔyɛ fɛ do-do!
It is nice
Pa-pa!

Divine master drummer ééé iii
Tɔn-tɔn-te ne tɔn-te: Yɛrenom nsa no na yɛrefa Adwene
The blind and the cripple: While we are drinking we
are considering our strategy
You have paid your dues
Time to rest
Time to enter the spirit world
It is time Junior Ancestor
To join Senior Ancestors
Your last taxi ride
You a newborn Ancestor
New today
Matured next season

ɔdomankoma kyerɛma
Aaa
Owuo kura adeɛ a, nkwa ntumi nnye
Death has something, life cannot wrestle it for it
Owuo atwedeɛ baako mforo
The death ladder is not climbed by one person
We shall meet
Dammirifa due
Due ne amanehunu
Mesrɛ Nyame ma mo
Twereduampɔn Kwame nhyira mo
ɔne wo ntena
Nante yie
Walk walk slow
Go mu brɛbrɛ brɛbrɛ brɛbrɛ
Brɛbrɛ brɛbrɛ brɛbrɛ
Sleep
Well

FIGURE 6.3. Asafo flag dancers at No. 2 Anaafo Asafo funeral. Photo by author.

After a taxi drove the casket to the cemetery, the crowd started to disperse. The *ndwom* makers packed up; Asafo members dismantled the wooden frame that held the casket. The streets returned to their normal—tabletop shops, makeshift kiosks, cars speeding, people scurrying across the streets, and children playing. A small boy who danced Asafo earlier on grabbed the three L-shaped sticks with which the *kɔtɔkorba* dancers performed. Another group of three boys picked up the wooden frame that encased the casket and walked away.[6] I followed them toward the Anaafo *posuban*. As the boy turned a corner to enter a house, I asked him if I could take a picture of the sticks. I learned important details about the instrumental *ndwom* of Asafo— their instrumentation, styles, structure of a performance, and function. Significantly, through the musicking walk, I learned how to listen to the *ndwom* and watch the players for cues on when to end a performance.

Women Speak and Take Charge: *ɔbaa na ɔwo barima*

I enjoyed watching the beautiful women, who were just as active, at this funeral. It was the women who commented on how the events unfolded.

Women have been silenced, written out of Asafo, their roles overlooked and ignored. Yet, it was the women who commented on the performance. The style of the *ndwom* was not the "correct" version, they commented. It was "folkloric." It was the women who cheered the flag dancers and drummers. The female Asafo captains, with their commanding sticks in hand, were as active, if not more, at directing the crowd. The crowd seemed to pay more attention when the women gave the orders to move back from the performance space. Perhaps this had something to do with women's role at funerals (Nketia 1969), their *ɔbaatan* mother status, or their powerful presence. They were stern, but their sternness had a loving touch. *ɔbaa na ɔwo barima. Akokɔ nan tia ne ba, na enkum no.*

My favorite part of the event occurred when one woman jumped onto the casket, refusing to get off until the family paid a fee. She started to dance on the casket! Moving her legs, flailing her arms, rocking back and forth, and bouncing to the sounds of Asafo drumming and singing. Her facial expressions were priceless: smiling, teasing, cajoling, taunting. "I dare you to get me off!" When some people tried to get her off the casket, she wrestled from their grip and shouted, "Oooo ah! Leave me alone!" "Oooo ah! Leave me alone!" *ɔkoterɛ a ɔtare pɔɔdɔ ho boɔ yɛ to-na,* "It is difficult to throw a stone at a lizard lodging on an earthen pot." If you throw a rock, you might hit the pot and crack it. *ɔbaa na ɔwo barima.* So, the men did not dare touch her, left her alone, and watched her dance. She enjoyed all the attention she was getting from the crowd around her, theorizing through her body. It was "play" at its best, because even at funerals we eat and laugh. She continued to dance, moving her arms and legs to the beat, rocking back and forth, enjoying the *ndwom*. "Oooo ah! Leave me alone!" By this time, the drummers were playing the *ɔsor* fast section, so her movements were fast and moved to the pulse of the drums. She rocked it through her body, offering a "veracity not offered by other concepts" (Probyn 1992, 83).[7] She stalled the process for a good ten minutes, and they could not get her off and take the casket until they fulfilled her demands. "Oooo ah! Leave me alone!"

Juggling Musicking Walks

Wode w'ani hwɛ tua mienu mu a, baako bɔ, "If you look into a bottle with two eyes, one could break," provides a useful framework for my experience at a Kormantse homecoming for the deceased husband of my friend, Ama Aprokuwa, a week after I attended the Anaafo Asafo funeral at Cape

Coast. It was a Friday morning. I had gone to help Ama Aprokuwa carry her *egwuaradze* final bath items to the lineage house of her deceased's husband whose body was being brought home from the morgue that afternoon. Our *trɔtrɔ* transport got stuck in traffic, so I arrived late and missed the porting of the items. When I asked to see the bath items, I was taken to the lineage house where the items had been inspected and received (see chapter 3). While I stood in the room with the Queen Mother of the lineage and other women of the lineage, the sounds of the sole Asafo drummer and singers outside filled the room. I could not fully engage with the *ndwom* as I was focused on the women weeping and singing to the bath items. I stepped outside after a while and walked to the Asafo performers singing some of the songs they performed for me months earlier. While they performed, a few cars and three packed busloads of mourners, including the deceased's children, traveled to Cape Coast to meet the hearse carrying the deceased back to Kormantse. Some, including a brass band, *osode* band, and an impromptu group of musicians, walked toward Cape Coast. All this while, the Asafo performers and a Hi-Life band continued to sing and play. A sole master drummer stood by the roadside and played appellations for the deceased, awaiting his arrival.

Around 1:00 p.m., after what seemed like hours of waiting, we heard the sirens and *ndwom* players miles away. The sirens and *ndwom* got louder as they got closer to the town. The blaring horns from the cars added a different sonic layer to the event. With my camera in hand, I rushed to the street to meet the hearse and mourners. I saw a huge crowd, a sea of red and black clothing, running, jogging, skipping frantically toward us on both sides of the streets; red also, because this is Asafo Bentsir territory: danger. No cars came through the town for hours. I crossed the street to the other side. Brass band players blared their horns while running; the *osode* performers sang and played while they ran along with the hearse; the impromptu performers on pots and pans added to the synchronous soundscape. People in the cars and buses hung their heads and arms out of the windows, screaming; some sang hymns. The children of the deceased hung onto the sides of the hearse, running and peering through the window to catch a glimpse of their father's lifeless body.

Our movements were characterized by walks, brief stops, brisk running, and jogging as family members screamed and cried out loud to their beloved. Bué, bue, bue, bue iiiii . . . mmmmmm, mmmmmm. I stopped to take photos or video the parade; I walked to peer into the hearse. I ran to stay ahead of the crowd. I tripped once, but there was no time for falling, so I balanced myself quickly and kept moving. This was no time to offer condolences. Everybody and everything was moving, sometimes to the beat of the *ndwom*, at other times out of sync with it. Our bodies and senses were fully engaged. My body reacted to the loud sirens, the drumming, cries, and paths that we traversed from the tarred highway to the dusty main street. It did not matter that they did not coincide. Our physical copresence, emphasized by common movements, was crucial to how I experienced this walk with the mourners. My body in motion reacted to their screaming, shouting, wailing; frantic bodies in motion, wailing. *Wo te sɛ obi abɔgye rehye a sa nsuo si wo deɛ ho*, "When you hear that someone's beard is burning, fetch water and place it by yours." They also say, "When you go to someone's funeral, cry for yourself," for one does not know what one's funeral will look like or if one's lifeless body would be found for burial. I sobbed for myself and for my children. Bué, Bué! *Bueeeeeiiiiiii! Agya-é! Ena-é! ɔdekye-é! Eno-é! ɔdeyeɛ-é! Abrewa-é! Hmm . . . Cry . . . y.*

While we ran, the sole Asafo drummer continued to play his proverbial passages. He did not run with the hearse. Rather, he walked up and down the Accra-Takoradi Highway with the drum slung over his left shoulder, his drum patterns piercing through and over the other *ndwom*. It throbbed. It rang. It echoed through the town. I could hear when he played with the *kɔtɔkorba* L-shaped stick, when he played with his hand, and when he combined both stick and hand. His patterns blended with the other *ndwom* to create the synchronous, dissonant, and beautiful sounds one hears at festivals. Each walker or runner seemed to move to their own beat. Some moved to the beat of the brass bands, others to the impromptu pots and pans band; still others moved to the *osode ndwom* and Christian hymns. After we left the dusty Kormantse main street and made our way to the lineage house, I ran ahead of the crowd and arrived at the lineage house. The sole Asafo drummer had joined the singers; another group had assembled and was singing their songs. Each group did its own thing, irrespective of what the other was doing. As the mourners got closer, the *ndwom* of the gospel group, brass band, *osode* band, Asafo, and impromptu pots and pans band overlapped and interlocked. No group tried to silence itself or play softly. Each group played at full volume. Cacophony or not, nobody cared. It added to the excitement and the mood of the day. Some danced, because *Twene nyɛ dɛ a, yɛ sa no saa ara*, "Even if the drum does not sound melodious, we dance to it all the same."

I stood and waited in one corner closer to the house, overwhelmed with emotions. I mourned quietly. I could not hold in my emotions. I allowed the tears to run down my cheeks. Cry. Researcher or not, this is a human experience. Cry. Connections. Cry. Away from the performers, I took in the plurality of the *ndwom*. The resulting soundscape and musical copresence was similar, though probably denser than the macroharmony Agawu describes about Asafo *ndwom* performance at an Ewe town.[8] He compares this phenomenon to what "happens in certain contrapuntal practices in which resultants between phrase beginnings and phrase endings are underspecified, allowing singers a degree of flexibility, and producing in the process a chain of 'dissonances'" (303). My experience at this musicking walk was a dense-textured concurrent happening. I did not have the same experience as I did at the Asafo funeral at Cape Coast or at other funerals that I witnessed later during my *nhwehwɛmu* search. In those situations, one music group performed at its allotted time, stayed silent, or packed up, while the other group performed. Or if the ensemble happened to play various styles, it played the styles sequentially. At this funeral, there was no time for taking turns. Perhaps it was due to the run along the street with the hearse; perhaps it was because the deceased had been away at Abidjan and had missed all this *ndwom*; perhaps, it was what the mood required.

Finally, the hearse arrived at the house with the mourners still hanging onto it. When the hearse stopped, the children of the deceased and others rushed to unlock the hearse. With a lot of screaming, pushing, and shoving, the bearers brought him out. I turned off my camera and stepped onto a chair. He was wrapped in a mat (one of the final bath items). After all the wealth he must have accumulated, here he was, wrapped in a small mat. *Ah, onipa yɛ mɔbɔ! Ah, mortals, is this our end! Whoever wishes death on someone, threatens to kill someone, or kills has not seen a dead body, has not experienced death in the African sense. Wo to adubɔne a, ebi ka woano, "When you give bad medicine, some touches your mouth." No one grows to be as old as a mountain. Death does not spare anyone. We will all climb death's ladder one day. Owuo safoa, "Death has the key." Rich or poor, we are pitiful.*

The mourners got more frantic and tried to snatch him, but the *Asafommba* (Asafo members) were stronger and held onto the lifeless body. They worked briskly. It seemed they had done this many, many times to ensure a dignified funeral for their member. *Obiara a obedzi asafomba hɔn fun ho agor nnkɛfa noho tɔtrɔtɔ koraa*, "Anyone who plays with an

Asafo company's dead body will not take himself free." *Obiara a obedzi asafomba hɔn fun ho agor nnkɛfa noho tɔtrɔtɔ koraa.* The children tried but could not get to it. They carried the lifeless body through the palm frond roofing and the floor covered with cocoa leaves. The master drummer, who by this time had entered the house, continued to announce his arrival, praising him, praising him, consoling, welcoming him with intermittent drum patterns. Welcome, welcome. *Damirifua Due, Damirifua Due!* Condolences! They took the body to a room where the bath items had been set up for his last bath. On my way out of the house, the widow, my friend Ama Aprokuwa, supported by five women from her Domna lineage, entered the house to see her husband. She was wailing and asking, *Wo daber nyi*, "Is this your resting place? Ah, Kɔbena, is this your resting place? ´Eééé iiiii i-iiiii-mmmmmm. . . ." Wailing. Witnessing my friend in such pain and distress was unbearable. Aaba! "When you go to someone's funeral, cry for yourself." *Wo te sɛ obi abɔgye rehye a, sa nsuo si wo deɛ ho*, "When you hear that someone's beard is burning, fetch water and place it by yours." Death does not spare anyone. I cried for myself, my children. I stepped outside to a sea of red and black clothes, tents, and a cacophony of sounds from wailing, screaming, and musicking. Sadness loomed large. In one corner, a group of women sat quietly, rubbed, rubbing and disentangling and disentangled the *saawe* chewing sponge that the women who watch over the body at the wake will chew.

Adding to the already dense soundscape, the Asafo drummer continued to play; the brass band players blared their horns and roared; the pots and pans band banged on their instruments; the *osode* group played as dancers took to the floor. They found joy and consolation in the *ndwom* and moved their bodies to the different beats. Even at funerals we eat. I walked to where Uncle Bedu and the Kormantse Asafo group were performing their Asafo song, "*Dua No Ebu!*" (example 28 ♫ 🔊). It was a sensory-filled musicking walk with so much to see, hear, and feel, a community of running mourners.[9]

When we walk, experiences we encounter help "conjure up other times and places that disrupt any linear flow" (Edensor 2008, 137). It also helps us make connections and place the experience in a broader context. Amidst *ndwom* making and dancing, my own sadness swelled as I walked among the grieving children and family members. My mind traveled to my uncle's funeral in Ghana. While the Asafo drumming at this funeral did not in any way resemble the *ndwom* at my uncle's funeral, the emotions I experienced were very strong. The experience at this funeral helped recall a song that, still today, conjures up my uncle's funeral. Together we grieved, though across different times and spaces and generated multiple rhythms of the experience. I had to attend another wake at Cape Coast and could not stay for the wake at Kormantse.

When the Deceased Is a *Frankaahuntanyi* Flag Dancer

"Where were you? Where were you? Where were you? We were looking for you to take pictures of the hearse when they brought him from the morgue," the family of the deceased flagbearer at Cape Coast, whose *egwuaradze* presentation I accompanied, asked. I told them I was at a Kormantse funeral awaiting the arrival of another hearse. "You would have taken pictures aaaa . . ., when they brought the body." I sat by the widow and waited while the deceased's body was being dressed up in a sealed-off area. After a while, I walked down the hill to where a group of Asafo singers had gathered to sing and mourn their deceased dancer. I recognized two of the songs: "Akwansima Gyedu," which my dance mentor had taught me, and "Kormantse na Abandze," which I head at Kormantse. The performers sang unaccompanied, adding colorful variations of the main lines, creating sameness and difference. I stood at a distance and listened for a while. The pasts of Asafo *ndwom* are still alive at funerals. I trudged back up the hill and sat with the mourners.

The curtains came up and people lined up to see and pay their respects to the deceased. One of the brothers asked me to go in and take pictures. I turned to the widow for approval, but she blinked at me and shook her head, a sign that said, "Don't go." I stayed back as mourners continued to file into the room. Later, she told me to go and take pictures. I was afraid. I peeped through the crowd and took a few pictures of the room. It was decorated with wreaths and lots of red accents. Red: this is Asafo Bentsir territory. Asafo *frankaa* (flags) hung on the wall. A huge bed stood on one side of the room. I was eager to meet him. I looked on the bed for him. It was empty. Where is he?

I saw him standing upright against a wall next to the bed. He was dressed in a laced shirt, a pair of trousers, and holding a *frankaa*, his hair beautifully coiffed. Like the deceased Asafo master drummer of No. 2 Anaafo Asafo, the No. 1 Bentsir flag dancer was propped up with wires and newspapers. Of course he was standing! Why would a dancer who once danced the flag, jumped, and twirled the flag, the greatest dancer, be lying down? We were asked to leave the room. They shielded the space again. When they opened it back up, *asekambɔfo* (those who guard the *frankaa* and dancer) placed four flags on the wall. This time, the deceased was sitting down, bejeweled and beautifully dressed. His children came in and spoke to him, asking, telling, touching him, wailing. Some placed both hands behind their back, on top of their heads, bouncing up and down and wailing (see chapter 4). I stopped taking pictures. This walk is difficult. Tears streamed down my face. This time, I joined the mourners and cried my own cry. I had planned to walk with this famous frankaahuntanyi, but never got the opportunity.

> Never met you
> Your frankaa, voice, dance
> Smile
> I, Ama Oforiwaa Aduonum
> Wanted to talk with you
> Learn from you
> Illness wrapped its ugly cloth around you
> I asked *Nananom* Ancestors to heal you
> Dinnn . . . . silent
>
> You who made the *frankaa* dance
> Dive, twirl, jump
> Now still
> Buooooo
> I missed the opportunity to sit at your feet
> Walk with you
> Nana
> Aaaaa
> *Dammirifua Dué*
> *Du-é ne amanehunu*

The master drummer came in and talked with him, consoled him, praised him with intermittent drum ngyegyee sounds. He played a phrase, paused, played a phrase, paused, played a phrase, paused. Later the *asekambɔfo* came in with two poles that blocked the entrance. It was part of *amandzeɛ* tradition. The Asafo drummer continued to play from outside. The wind started to blow; it got stronger and started to rain. I waited around for a while and walked back to my residence. KoJo and MaAdwoa, who stayed home with a neighbor, were asleep when I got home. Though the deceased's spirit would not follow me home because it had been raining, I could not sleep. I tossed and turned all night. *Aaa. Death! You like what humans like. Life! Why don't you find your own thing? A*!

>ɔdomankoma Frankaahuntanyi
>Bentsir Asafo flag dancer
>Aaa
>*Owuo kura adeɛ a, nkwa ntumi nnye*
>When death has something, life cannot wrestle it from it
>Du-é
>*Owuo atwedeɛ baako mforo*
>The death ladder is not climbed by one person
>Your *frankaa* flags are downcast
>Lonely
>Silent
>Still
>Aaaa
>*Dammirifa due*
>*Due ne amanehunu*
>*Mesrɛ Nyame ma wo*
>*Twereduampɔn Kwame nhyira mo*
>*ɔne wo ntena*
>*Nante yie*
>Walk walk slow
>Walking slow has never stopped the *akyekyerɛɛ* tortoise
>The *nwa* snail
>*Go mu brɛbrɛ brɛbrɛ brɛbrɛ*
>*Brɛbrɛ brɛbrɛ brɛbrɛ*
>Sleep well
>*Sleep well*
>**Sleep, well**
>Nana

Ebusua ɛnyɛ Asafo, na yɛ kɔ egyae, "Family Is Not Asafo That You Can Leave": When the Deceased Is Your Sister

At 3:00 a.m. the next day, Saturday, February 25, the day of the funerals for the flag dancer and Aprokuwa's husband, KoJo, MaAdwoa, and I left Cape Coast to attend my older sister's (my mother's oldest sister's daughter) funeral at Accra. My mother insisted I attend: "She is your sister. What would people think of you if you do not attend your own sister's funeral when you have been busy attending those of strangers?"

> Family
> Could I say, No
> *Opanin bi se ebusua nyɛ Asafo ɛna yɛ akɔ ɛgya e*
> An Elder said family is not like a group that we can join and leave
> Ah! Family you can be a burden sometimes
> *Yɛtoatoa mu sɛ nkɔnsɔnkɔnsɔn, nkwa mu a yetoa mu*
> *Owuo mu yɛtoa mu, ebusua mu nte da*
> If we are linked together like a chain, in life we are linked
> In death we are linked, family links are never broken
> Two opportunities to witness Asafo live
> The burial rites of two Asafo dancers
> Once in a lifetime opportunity
> *Obi nkura nanka, nnyae nanka, nnyae nkɔse sɛ, 'Mehunuie a anka'*
> One does not have the opportunity, dismiss the opportunity to declare, 'If I had the opportunity'
> Had the opportunity
> Dismissed it

I missed the two funerals at Kormantse and Cape Coast for the Asafo members, missing also the grandeur, fanfare, and Asafo musicking that accompanied them. Nana Kwame Ampadu, one of the greatest Hi-Life singers, sang a popular song, "*Opanin bi se 'Ebusua ɛnyɛ Asafo ɛna yɛ ako ɛgya-e-oo*,'" "An Elder said, 'Family is not an organization that you can just join and leave.'" I would have left mine so that I could stay and experience the two Asafo funerals. I traveled to Accra.

My sister's funeral was a Christian event and very different from the Asafo ones I attended at Cape Coast. It was solemn. People in a variety of black and red clothes sat under black tents or walked around. There was no live drumming or dancing, though people mourned. The program was long, with lots of talking, prayers, Bible reading, obituaries, and the singing of some hymns. When I got up to walk around to stretch my legs, the hymns and prayers blared over loudspeakers. The gospel songs that the group performed were very moving and reminded me of a funeral I attended for a middle school girl during my secondary school days.

I felt sad. It also triggered the memory of my uncle's death. It was a different musicking walk from those at Cape Coast and Kormantse. I went back to my seat and viewed my sister's body lying on a bed from a distance. *Nea ɔwɔ aka no suro sonsono,* "The one who has been bitten by a snake is afraid of a worm"—even if the worm is a sister. They sealed off the entrance to the tent where she lay and placed her body in a white casket. Her daughter was a police officer, so a police van drove her to the cemetery. Her children and a few Elders in our family accompanied her. As they drove her away, I felt a sudden rush of sadness. I will never see her again—her smile, experience, her fire, resilience. Tears were in my eyes, again, at another funeral.

> *Dammirifa due-ooo*
> *Onua Abena Dedaa*
> *Ogyaba*
> *Due ne amanehunu*
> *Mesrɛ Nyame ma wo*
> *Twereduampɔn Kwame nhyira wo*
> *ɔne wo ntena*

I stayed behind with my mother and other family members. After the mourners arrived from the cemetery, we had catered meals and conversed for some time. I returned home and went right to sleep.

"You Would Have Taken Photos, Pa-pa!"

At 3 a.m. the next day, Sunday, February 26, I woke up my poor children, KoJo and MaAdwoa, boarded a *trɔtrɔ*, and traveled back to Cape Coast. I had intended to stop at Kormantse to witness their *nnase* thanksgiving service for Aprokuwa's husband, but the funeral grounds were deserted when we drove by. Later that day, we attended the *nnase* for the *frankaa* dancer at Cape Coast. As we approached the house, we heard gospel songs. KoJo and MaAdwoa—who complained that I spent too much time at funerals—and I started to dance. They had been laid back since we left Accra, so, I was relieved to see them enjoy the *ndwom*. They danced. They imitated the movements of the *frankaa* dancer. KoJo twirled, dashed, hopped on one foot, jumped, and kicked. MaAdwoa leaped into the air, crouched, and rubbed her heal. They threw imaginary flags on their backs and rolled them. "Mama, this is nice," KoJo smiled. MaAdwoa smiled and kept prancing. It was precious! Dancing Asafo.

Most people wore a combination of white and black: merrymaking, joy, and sadness. The widow was dressed in all white—white top and long skirt (slit), white earrings, and white bead-necklace. Since I missed the funeral, I concluded she was wearing white because she had been taken to the sea for cleansing on the day of the funeral and burial. She sat next to an empty chair, also draped in white. The Asafo ensemble had gathered and continued to play and sing. Under another tent, a gospel group performed different gospel songs, accompanied by congas, bells, rattles, and wooden clappers.

> Mourner 1: "Where were you? He came down. He was angry because they did not throw the ezuzu [a rope that is thrown out before the flag is danced] or bring out the akatamanso flag [the company's longest flag]; the door was locked because they said they could not find the key to the room. He demanded that they knock down the door and bring out the flag."
> Mourner 2: "He said, 'Knock down door. Get it out!'"
> Mourner 3: "Dancers danced on the coffin. They danced the flag. They had the coffin at Victoria Park."
> Mourner 1: "Lots of donors and other visitors left. There were no donations."
> Mourner 3: "You would have taken photos, pa-pa!"

The family gathered to thank well-wishers, select heirs for the deceased, two men who would function as fathers for the children in case one could not perform his duties, and an *ebusuapanyin* lineage Elder, since the deceased was a father and an Elder in his *ebusua*. When the heirs were announced, the mourners rushed to them, grabbed them, and sat them onto seats; people poured white powder on their heads and bodies; women fanned them with cloth, *ɔno nyi oo, ɔno nyi oo, ɔno nyi oo*! ("Here he is-oo; here he is-oo; here he is-oo!"). The children of the deceased rushed to them, hugged them, and cried. Some sat on their laps and rocked back and forth. The Asafo players and gospel group continued to play. I joined the group of dancers, watching their steps and following them closely. I had performed this type of dance before. My body remembered those moments and gave in. Occasionally, a caller in the gospel group would call the group's name, "God reigns as King" (*Ewuradze dzi hen*); the chorus would respond, "In everything" (*Wo adze nyinara mu*). I sat with the widow and chatted with her for a while, listening to the Asafo drummers from a distance.

KoJo, MaAdwoa, and I walked around and then started our slow walk back home, reflecting on how I juggled three funerals that long weekend: receiving the hearse for the *kɔtɔkorba* L-shaped stick dancer at Kormantse, missing the wake and funeral for the *kɔtɔkorba* dancer at Kormantse, missing the hearse and funeral for the flag dancer at Cape Coast, attending the wake for the flag dancer at Cape Coast, driving to Accra for my sister's funeral, attending the *nnase* for the flag dancer back at Cape Coast, dancing to gospel *ndwom*, listening to Asafo drumming, taking photos, and chatting with the widow. *Ebusua dɔ funu*, "the family loves the corpse!" "Where were you? You would have taken *mfoni* photos, pa-pa!"

Musicking Walk with the Asafo *Frankaahuntanyi* Flag Dancer

On Monday, February 20, 2017, my dance teacher called to inform me about Asafo drumming scheduled for the next day, Tuesday, between 1 and 2 p.m. It was *eyi-enyim*, a prefuneral event for prominent people. This event was for the greatest Asafo flag dancer at Cape Coast, noted earlier in this chapter. Around 12:30 p.m., I headed to Bentsir territory. The house was about a twenty-minute walk along the sea. I had taken the route many times, so I knew all the landmarks—Victoria Park, makeshift stores, houses, the Emintzimadze Palace for the Cape Coast King, Cape Coast Castle (former dungeons for enslaved Africans, now a museum for tourists), the Anglican Church, artifact shops, a courthouse, the Methodist church—so though *Obisafoɔ nto kwan*, I walked without asking for directions. Since this path was familiar, I had developed a "deeper, non-cognitive, sensual form of appreciation for the terrain, experienced through the feet and legs, promoting adaptation to the environment through a heightened sense of corporal balance" (Edensor 2008, 132).

I entered red territory, No. 1 Asafo Bentsir. Bentsir means *aban no tsir*, "the structure or building's head/top," so part of the community was on a hill. When I arrived at the deceased's residence, two drums, wrapped in *krada* white cotton cloth, leaned against a wall. Nana Ekow Sekyi, the deceased, was a ninety-year-old man who danced the Cape Coast Asafo Benstir flag. He was known as a great dancer at Cape Coast and surrounding towns. In fact, I learned that he participated in Asafo activities at Kormantse Bentsir. A lady whom I had come to know through my walks along the sea told me I had arrived too early. So, I ran back to my residence for more batteries and a cable cord.

As I returned to Bentsir territory, I heard a lone drum talking. The drumming, intermittent with long and short phrases, rang through the city to summon people to the event. While he played, someone asked the young man to "play louder and call them." The house and street had been blocked off and transformed into a ritual space, a "site of memory" where past events would be reenacted, knowledge and ideas about Asafo and the community shared, and harmony brought to the community through *ndwom*, dance, theater, and other artistic events.

With the drum slung over his left shoulder, the lone drummer continued to play, moving from one corner of the house to another, reminding people that the big day is coming on Saturday. Another gentleman arrived. He picked up the other drum, slung it over his left shoulder, grabbed the sticks, chewed on some kola nuts, offered a quiet prayer, and then started to play. I found out from someone that he was the master drummer, a priest, and *nunsin* herbalist. After playing on the master drum for a while, the other instruments of the ensemble joined him. According to the *ɔkyerɛma* lead drummer, the ensemble consists of the *Kwesi Atobo* master drum, *agyegyedo* master drum supporter, *ampaa* small supporting drum, *aburukuwa* small supporting drum, two *nnawur* two conical-shaped bells, and the chorus of singers. One of the supporting drummers played with two small sticks, while the other played with his bare hands. The two larger drums used one *kɔtɔkorba* L-shaped stick each. The ensemble had the same formation as the No. 2 Anaafo Company: the master drummer, two small drums, and the *nnawur* were on a bench in the front row, while the second master drum and the chorus sat behind. The second drum was located slightly behind the lead. The *nnawur* players either sat or stood, holding the conical-shaped bell by its conical end in the left hand, with elbow pointing downward, and playing with the right hand. Playing the bell seemed exhausting. Both arms moved up and down to the rhythm of the patterns.

Bentsir members are proud of their company because according to them, as Number One, they hold the keys to the town, a symbol that is also sown

The Listening and Musicking Walk 241

FIGURE 6.4. Cape Coast Bentsir No. 1 Ensemble. *Kwesi Atobo* lead drum in front, *agyegyedo* supporter drum second row, 2 *nnawur* bells, *ampaa* and *aburukuwa* small drums. Embodied call and responders standing in back. Photo by the author.

onto their flags. It was with such pride that they answered my question as to why they use only two *nnawur*, while Anaafo uses three, and another company uses five: "We need only two bells because we are strong; we don't need more than what we have. Anaafo Asafo uses three; another company uses seven bells. We don't need too many bells to be loud or effective." They described Anaafo Asafo *ndwom* as "culture" (just as the women at the Anaafo funeral had declared), while their playing is closely aligned to the traditional way. The gentleman who started playing the drum initially, switched to playing one of the *nnawur*.

Since the deceased was a flag dancer, several dancers danced the flag, including those from other companies, to honor him. Some danced with more vigor than others, moving the widow and others to tears. One woman, who had been dancing earlier, was taken over by a cosmic energy and led into a room. At various points during the dancing, the *frankaa* flag dancer walked up to an audience member and touched her with the flag three times. When this happened, the person either had to dance or give money to the dancer. They donated money. I had never seen anything like it, read about its significance, or the significance of the dance movements. Some of the onlookers took to the ring and started to dance, darting, crouching, kicking, prancing, squatting, and leaping to the left and to the right. After a while, a gentleman, whom I learned was the leader of the Bentsir Asafo Company (*Supi*), walked up and prayed to venerate the Ancestors and to call the spirit of the deceased to descend. "Your day is coming," the gentleman ended the invocation. This signaled the official opening of the event. N*kwan pa twetwe adwa*, "A good soup attracts chairs," or *hwerɛma na ɛtwetwe ndwom*, "Whistling induces singing," so, by this time, a huge crowd had assembled to bear witness and to celebrate the life of the greatest Asafo flag dancer at Cape Coast. Bentsir Asafo flags were everywhere.

Each Asafo company has numerous flags; many of these are commissioned by Asafo captains during their inauguration. They use various symbols, images, and proverbs to depict scenes from wars, communicate other messages to taunt their enemies, placate their company, and to showcase their personality. These are embroidered or cut up and sewn onto the flag. Each flag has a smaller flag sewn onto the right-hand or left-hand corner of the Asafo flag. Before Ghana's independence from the British, it was customary to have the Union Jack (British flag) sewn onto it. Today, postindependence, the flag of Ghana is added to it.

The origin of Asafo flags is debatable. Some scholars posit that they were adopted from Europeans. For example, in the short description accompanying an exhibit of Fante flags by Peter Adler and Nicholas Barnard at Tatham Art Gallery in South Africa, Allison Drew notes,

"Asafo flags are the merger of two cultural traditions, the Akan tradition of combining proverbs and imagery, and the European heraldic tradition, which used flags and banners displaying arms in regimental colours. . . . Asafo companies adopted the European flag and used to display designs symbolizing proverbs about security and social welfare" (1994, 58). Kwame Labi also concurs that Asafo flags were originally fashioned after European flags. He notes, "Asafo adopted certain European military practices such as marching in formation, identifying companies by name and number, and carrying and saluting" (2002).[10] Others, including my dance teacher, Divine Master Drummer Nana Kwamena Pra, assert that Asafo flags predated the arrival of the Europeans to the Gold Coast in 1471. According to him, "Before the Europeans came, there was *frankaahuntanyi* flag dancer." He added,

> The truth is that, before the advent of the Europeans, we were performing our Asafo with our flags. They saw it and because there were inter-tribal wars which were not allowing them to trade, they decided to settle cases by introducing peace treaty flags to those factions. This helped to continue with their trade. . . . Before the white man came, Asafo members used to weave beaten *kyɛnkyɛn* [chechen wood], a type of creamy white or light-yellow brown wood, into cloth and then displayed Asafo symbols on it to perform victory dances and for the community to see. The whites brought the cotton through trade, and we used that instead of the *kyɛnkyɛn* wood. (ɔdomankoma Kwamena Pra, phone conversation with author, May 24, 2020)

In fact, several chiefs and traditional rulers along the coast of Ghana unanimously agree that the flags used in Asafo were not introduced by the British.[11] *Ani a ehunu tetehɔ ɛnni hɔ, na aso a ɛtee tetehɔ asɛm deɛ na ɛwɔ hɔ*, "the eyes that saw ancient times were not there, but the ears that heard the past were there."

The variations in these narratives do not negate the consensus about the sheer artistic and symbolic nature of the flags (Adler and Barnard 1992; Labi 1998, 2002; Miscots 2012). "The flags of each company are of immense importance to the company, whose members guard them as a sacred trust. They generally have worked in them emblems with symbolic meanings" (Sarbah 1903, 114). They are the most visual and most decorated elements of Asafo companies and "the kinetic counterparts of the posuban and also for the most powerful and unifying expression of Asafo creativity" (Adler and Barnard 1992, 100). Their intricate, colorful appliqued and embroidered designs have drawn attention from art connoisseurs around the world and have been displayed at museums all over the world. They are so symbolic that in addition to swearing an oath to respond to any call from their company either by day or by night, initiates into a company must swear to protect and defend their flags. Sarbah notes, "the honour of their company flags [was] their first consideration and their service to their company was their indispensable service" (quoted in Labi 1998, 102). Like the Kormantse Bentsir flag (fig. 6.5), each flag has images, proverbs, and other phrases that speak to the status of the Asafo association or mock its foes.

FIGURE 6.5. Kormantse Asafo Flag. ɔsono kokuroko, nso ɔkɔtɔ na oku no, "The elephant is monstrous, yet it is the crab that kills it."[12] Shown by Kormantse Asafo Supi Kobena Wobir and King's Spokesman Kweku Suapim.[13] Photo by author.

Flag dancing, with its acrobatic moves and turns, has received sparse attention in the literature (Kwabom 2018; Miscots 2012), yet as the highlight of many Asafo ceremonies, together with the accompanying drumming and singing, it creates a public show of vigorous dancing. "A vigorous dance with qualities of aliveness, high intensity, and speed characterizes an African ideal of artful muscularity and depth of feeling." This vitality, or playing the youthful body with "percussive strength," is what draws the attention of the crowd.[14] At the same time, it serves as a ritual offering for the Ancestors and a display of pride, strength, and perseverance to other companies.

The *frankaakitanyi, frankaahuntanyi* (pl. *frankaakitaafo*) is the only person who dances the flag. In the past, he would dance the flag to enact movements from wars, their victory, and display the symbols of the Asafo to the community. His movements consisted of war tactics and those that depicted victory. His athletic performance "involves somersaulting, spinning around, leaping in the air, and twirling the flag" (Labi 2002, 30).

According to Ọbádélé Kambon's interview with several Kings along the coast of Ghana, the dance-like aesthetics of the Asafo flag dancing (1) were due to "sunsum" or spirit possession, (2) had practical combat applications, and (3) showed joy or demonstrated a dramatized version of actual movements that were used to succeed in war (Kwabon 2018, 340). He dives to signal evasion from the enemy; when he rolls the flag on his back and spreads the flag, he is displaying the symbols on the flag; when he kicks to the left and to the right, he is kicking his foe. Some of his movements are intended to antagonize and ridicule, while others are playful and celebratory.

The featured flag dancer at the *eyi-eyim* event was the same gentleman who started the drum call earlier in the day. He had on a raffia skirt and two long, beaded necklaces crisscrossed across his naked torso and around his upper arms like a priest. Amidst intense drumming and singing, he stepped into the ring without the flag; he stood quietly in one place for a minute, listening to the *ndwom*, studying the space, the audience; then he began to shuffle his feet slowly, back and forth, back and forth, back and forth. Then he hopped on one foot, facing and moving in one direction, then he moved in the other direction on the other foot. One of the *asekambɔfo* who guarded the ritual space threw him a flag. Then,

    Aaa
    Frankaahuntanyi
    Dance that flag
    Jump, crouch, low
    Twirl
    Give flag to audience
    Give flag to audience
    Give flag to audience
    Touch, touch, touch
    Roll the flag
    Roll
    While twirling flag
    Up
    Jump
    Release
    Spread flag
    Dance it on your back
    Display its beauty

Quick footstep
Hop on one foot
Leap
Twirl it
Stop, pause
Survey your surroundings

Roll on the floor
Show your struggle
Your difficulties
Jump to show victory
Anibere a, ɛnsɔ gya
The eye gets red, but it does not ignite fire

Asekambɔfo flag guards
Clear the path
Clean his path
Guard him
The flag
Lest he drop the flag
Falls
Disgrace does not befit the Akan child
Panes nim adeɛ pam nanso ne to tokuro
The needle knows how to sew, but its bottom has a hole
So
Massage the dancer's heels
Rub his heels
Lest the spirits take him to *mmotia krom*
Land of the dwarfs
Daabi da!
Oh, no

Frankaahuntanyi
Okyerɛma master drummer talks to you
With
You
Calls you
Summons you

Advises you
Wave the flag
Dive
Evade your enemies
Stop, think, move!
Low, low, low
Dive
High

Ei

Frankaatunyi
You who move the widow to tears
Your dance brings memories
You who once brought
The *kyɛnkyɛn* wood
To life
Revive the dead
Celebrate victories
Symbols

Aaba!
Heart of Asafo company
Anomaa mfa dua ho abufu
The bird cannot be angry at the tree
Dance that flag
Hey!
ɔaba oooo
Hah!
Breathe
Breathe
Breathe
You have done well
Mbo-na-yɛ!

After about an hour of watching the *frankaa* flag dancing and listening to *ndwom*, I left to pick up KoJo and MaAdwoa from school. When we returned, the *frankaa* dancer had been taken over by a cosmic energy. The deceased had descended and taken over the dancer's body. He was shaking in place, not talking, but making high-pitched sounds. He looked dazed, tongue tied, withdrawn, darting his head from side to side. The spirit had descended. The drumming and singing continued, sounding louder and more urgent. I learned later that one of the *asekambɔfo* flag guards who was drunk, though it was a taboo in the sacred space, tried to touch the flag when he had been asked not to; he also followed the dancer when he had been asked not to. He contaminated the ritual space by entering it with alcohol and touching the flag, defiling it. People were angry at his behavior and were talking. *ɔpatafoɔ di abaa*, "One who intervenes sometimes gets hit," so, my children and I followed slowly at a distance while they led the dancer upstairs into a room. He stood at the entrance of a room, still making high-pitched sounds, Hm! Hm! Hm! Hm! Hmmm! Hm! Hm . . . and shaking. When one of the flag guards tried to touch him, the dancer pushed him, and he fell down a flight of about eight stairs. He laid there still; no one helped him up. When people finally helped him up, blood covered his face, and an open wound scarred his cheek and mouth. Another gentleman came up and was furious at what happened. When people explained why the dancer pushed the *asekambɔfo* flag guardian, he retorted, "So you are happy that happened?"

This incident put a slight pause in my walk. My attention had been diverted from the musicking that was still happening. It was a musicking walk, nonetheless, as all this happened while the *ndwom* enveloped the atmosphere. I recalled a statement by one of my mentors: "At funerals, anything can happen, but the show goes on." I was told other dancers were still dancing the flag. The flag dancer did not come back out before we left. KoJo and MaAdwoa were confused about the whole incident and asked what had happened. Still musicking walking, we trudged away into the darkness toward my residence. In the two-kilometer distance from the ritual space, during our walk back to the apartment, amidst the throbbing patterns of the drummers, *nnawur* players, and the songs of the singers, Kojo and MaAdwoa told me that they had a rough day at school. I held them close while we walked to sounds of the Asafo. When we got home, I read them an Ananse story. Afterwards, we danced the *frankaa*! Asafo is a spirit.

You!
Heart of Asafo company

The Listening and Musicking Walk

Frankaatunyi
Entire ensemble
Kwesi Atobo—master drum
Agyegyedo—second master drum
2 *kɔtɔkorba* L-shaped sticks
Ampaa—small supporting drum
Aburukuwa—small supporting drum
Two Bentsir *nnawur*
Embodied callers and responders
Dancers
Have assembled
For you
Show must go on
No matter what

Aaaa
Asafo
Anomaa mfa dua ho abufu-oo
The bird cannot be angry at the tree
Show must go on
No matter what
Dance that flag
Hey!
He has descended
ɔaba ooo!
ɔaba ooo!
Hmm! Hmm! Hm!
Hm . . .
Ebueii
Musicking walk
ɔpatafoɔ di abaa
Slow
Breathe
Breathe
Breathe
You have done well
Mbo-na-yɛ

CHAPTER SEVEN

"Kenkan Makes it Sweet"

Walking with Asafo Ndwom

Tete ka aso mu
Repetitive hearing leaves an indelible mark in the ear

Wopɛ danka mu ahunu a,
wo kɔ deɛ yɛsene no na wompae mu
(If you want to see the inside of a *danka* drum/gourd rattle
you go to where it is carved, you don't split it open)

—Ghanaian Akan Proverbs

Nwomtonyi: Wontsei asɛm a ɔaba 🔊
Wontsei asɛm a ɔaba Tuafo mba e
Ama woo hom ntsei asɛm a ɔaba
Okura akɛkyer egyinambowa ne ba
Asafommba: Ama woo Bentsifo e
Hom ntsei asɛm ɔaba o!
(Embodied Call: Listen to the matter that has come
Listen to the matter that has come Tuafo's children
Goodness listen to the matter that has come
A mouse has caught a cat's baby
Embodied Answer: Goodness Bentsir people
Listen to the matter that has come)

—Kormantse Asafo *Ndwom,* "*Wontsei Asɛm a ɔaba*"

I performed my first Asafo song in the late 1980s as a student at Mfantsiman Girls' Secondary School at Saltpond in the Central Region of Ghana, though I did not know at the time. Mfantsiman Girls' Secondary School, founded by the first president of Ghana, the late Dr. Kwame Nkrumah, was established in 1960 as a polytechnic to empower girls in the town. We learned that it also served as a gesture of gratitude to the town for its role in the country's political life. A year after construction began in 1958, the late composer and music teacher, Mr. Joseph Maison, composed the school's ode to commemorate its inauguration. The ode, "ɔbra Nye Woara Bɔ!" (Life is What You Make It, 1959), inspires the students to be diligent and hardworking and details the numerous benefits of hard work, commitment, and compassion in one's life. The introduction is in typical Asafo style—an evocative exchange between a lead singer who is answered by loud statements from the chorus. In this case, however, the entire chorus performs the call and response. The song is declamatory and moves freely with the intensity of the call, whose articulations and projections set the pace and mood for the performance; it uses shouts, drop-offs, and exclamatory endings to emphasize the theme.

After the rousing Mfantsiman Girls' Secondary School Ode Call (example 29 ♫), the piece turns to a verse structure, alternating between measured, longer-phrased stanzas and chorus. It is in this section that the composer outlines the importance and benefits of hard work and diligence (example 30 ♫).

Unlike Asafo *ndwom* that is performed either a cappella or accompanied by an ensemble of up to four drums and five bells, the Mfantsiman ode is arranged in four-part harmony and accompanied by the piano. It did not have the embodied call and answer that I would later experience. Furthermore, unlike the Asafo *ndwom*, the call and the response are performed by a chorus in stepwise movement downward. That Mr. Maison borrowed indigenous Ghanaian *ndwom* genre for the ode is no coincidence. That he specifically used Asafo *ndwom* structure as a template for the school's anthem is strategic. It served as an important symbol to re-memory the past. Importantly in this case, it served to celebrate the role and importance of the Asafo tradition in Akan societies. At the time, I did not know any of this. I did not know that the song was inspired by Asafo.[1] I also did not think much about the words or their reference to the leadership and bravery of the three spiritual leaders —Oburmankoma (Eagle), ɔdapagyan (Whale), ɔson (Elephant)—who allegedly led the Fante during their migration from Tekyiman to Mankessim in the 1300–1400s. I do not remember any discussion about these spiritual leaders, their relevance to Fante *abakɔsɛm*, or their connections to the lessons about hard work and perseverance. Neither do I remember an occasion where our *ndwom* teacher, Mr. Thompson, offered an analysis of the song's features and source. I do remember being encouraged to sing the song with energy and pride. Decades later when I decided to search Asafo songs, "ɔbra Nye Woara Abɔ" did not come to my mind.

Neither did I know that Asafo songs are powerful, declamatory, or metered; evocative, raw, using chest voice; exciting, expressing the pride, resilience, solidarity, and strength of its performers. I learned about most of this at my first live experience of Asafo drumming, dancing, and singing, six days after I arrived at Kormantse. We gathered at the King's palace on their main street after a beautiful group of seventeen men agreed to perform for a token. Altogether, they performed seventeen songs, sixteen Asafo, and one Hi-Life song, for about thirty-five minutes. Following the session, we had an interesting discussion about the role of Asafo and the effects of its demise on the society. An elderly man in the group reflected on the demise of the tradition: "We are dying, dying. It is killing us."

By this time in my process, my dance teacher had already lectured me on the integrated nature of Asafo, that it involved drama, dance, song, drumming, spirituality, poetry, and other features. As an organization, the group seemed like an opera company or all the other companies around the world that merge different performing arts in their musicking. At the same time, as an art form, it seemed like one of those musical forms that combined theater, dance, music, costuming, and staging—*wayang orang*, Western European opera, Peking opera, *bunraku*, and so on. So, while I set out to investigate this tradition in Fante society, I was interested in some of the resonances it shares with other art forms. I wanted to learn about the unique features about Asafo *ndwom* and what it shares with other art forms, including those of the West, especially since music of Africa has been "Othered."

The process was long and difficult. But *Kwan tia yɛ musuo*, "Shortcut is an omen." Because *Nsateaa baako ntumi mpopa animu*, "One finger cannot effectively wipe the face," it was also multilevel and multicentric. It involved organizing performance sessions, attending performances, having private discussions and brief singing lessons at the seaside with a Kormantse Asafo lead singer, undertaking analyses of songs, taking lessons in the Fante language, and studying proverbs. Nigerian Ibo Elders say, *Aka aja aja na ebute onu mmanu mmanu*, "A hand soiled with sand leads to a mouth soiled with oil." I soiled my hands *and feet*. Because Asafo is connected to other domains in Kormantse society, many times these "lessons" veered into issues of gender, politics, Asafo *abakɔsɛm* and membership, their Gods, conflicts with others, socio-aesthetics, and even rap music.

Embodied Call, Embodied Response: What Some Kormantse Men Sang and Said: "Oye, Oye, the Women Bring Trouble to Us"

The performance on main street started with a call from an older gentleman, who may not have projected well because after the first call, another gentleman picked up the call and performed all the calls after that. The song *"Adende"* (example 31 ※ 🔊) will become one of my favorites. The lead, Kobena Bedu, called each song in chest voice, gesturing with his hands, and the group of sixteen men answered, some gesturing with their hands, hopping around, or just moving their bodies in their seats. At times, one of the chorus members picked up the call and traded it back and forth with another singer or the lead, before the chorus answered. This part was my favorite.

Altogether they performed seventeen songs including *"Adende"* ("Alas, Alas!"), *"Oye, Oye"* ("It's good"), *"Nkum na Abandze"* ("Nkum and Abandze"), *"Okura akɛkyer egyinambowa ne Ba"* ("The Mouse Has Caught a Cat's Baby), *"Yɛkɔr Akyemfo nyimpa nnyi hɔ"* ("We Went to Saltpond, People Were Not There"), and many more. At the time, these titles were not clear to me because of the pace at which they were performed, but also due to the overpowering sound of the drum. The songs were melodic, declamatory, and loud, mixing grunts and other calls. They were vigorous, energetic, and full of life. At times, the lead partly spoke his words very fast, like he was rapping. Each song ended with a stop, an exclamation, a practice I surmised was a way to assert their strength and pride, but also to end the phrase—a period, a full stop. It was too sweet.

One of the women who was watching from her house across the King's palace came out dancing; she leaped into the air, taunting, and teasing. She kicked sideways after each movement forward; she crouched, rose, shook her legs, pranced, and kicked sideways again with her right, then her left leg. She was fierce, but she was also smiling. A University of Cape Coast professor who helped organize the group, Dr. Kwadwo Nnuroh, commented that she was mocking and taunting their rivals. The quiet town became alive. After a series of twelve Asafo songs, there was a suggestion to switch to a Hi-Life style. After some deliberation about how to play that in the absence of the *dawur* bell and whether it was appropriate to play it on the Asafo talking drum, one of the town's leaders sang out the pattern to the drummer: *"ge-ge-ge-ge-ge."* Another drummer took the drum from

Kofi Abbam, the drummer, and played a different drum phrase. It was a three-stroke pattern played over the two-beat pulse. Everyone clapped the down beat. Pa! Pa! Pa! Pa! Pa! Pa!

Unlike the Asafo songs that sounded serious and did not seem to have a regular pulse, everyone clapped to the beat of this Hi-Life song. It was lively, fast, and energetic. However, it was nothing like the Hi-Life *ndwom* by Kwame Ampadu, E. K. Nyame, Teacher Boateng, A. B. Crentsil, Yamoah, and others I grew up listening. Those had a constant feel and a jagged pattern that began after the second beat on a bell or another percussion instrument. The dancing lady, who had been taking a break on the sidelines, stepped back into the space and changed her movements. This time she pointed her index fingers towards another dancer who performed those same movements toward her, all the time stepping to the beat of the song with their gestures and intricate footwork. The pulse of the song and drumming coincided; they matched. An eighty-five-year-old woman, who I later learned had been sick in bed, emerged from her house and started dancing happily in the street. She bounced on one leg, then on the other, moving from side to side to the beat of the only Hi-Life song that the group played. Her body remembered. As she danced, another lady fanned her with a piece of cloth to congratulate and encourage her. *Nkwanpa twetwe adwa*, "Good soup pulls chairs"; *Hwerɛma twetwe ndwom*, "Whistling brings songs." More children, men, women, the old and young gathered on the main street to listen, observe, and/or dance. With camera in hand, I started to sway from side to side. It seemed as if even the dust rose from the ground to join the celebration, which made me think about whether the spirits of the Ancestors had joined the celebration. After playing the Hi-Life style for about three minutes, they switched back to Asafo songs. It was too sweet. Because *ɛdɛ nka anomu*, "Sweetness does not remain in the mouth permanently," after some time, someone yelled, "We are done; we are done." Another gentleman agreed, "We have gone far. We have gone far" (We have played for a long time). Then it was over. Three gentlemen, one of whom happened to be my friend Aprokuwa's son, took turns playing the *gyina hɔ hwɛ* talking drum with a *kɔtɔkorba* L-shaped stick. Each of them strapped the drum across his left shoulder. With the drumhead facing out, the stick in hand, and the other hand on the drumhead, each player talked through different drum strokes.

The drum patterns floated above the pulse of the music and were not meant to coincide. This was partly because such "patterns provide a groove but are not always organically linked to the songs themselves." It is "a laxity that contributes to a feeling of multiple temporalities unfolding simultaneously" (Agawu 2016, 302–303). During the short breaks between one song and the other, the drummer continued to play his intermittent patterns. Not once did the drumming stop. Later when I asked him what he was playing, he admitted that he did not really know what he was saying on the drums. He had just started learning to play. The Asafo songs were like nothing I had experienced before. They were unapologetically raw, energetic, involved grunts, shouts, partly spoken, and partly sung. I could not make out the structure of the song, the lyrics, or the performance form. The only feature I made out was the exchange between the lead singer and the group of men, though it seemed as if he was commanding them.

The use of the term "call and answer, call and response," or "responsorial" to describe the performance is inadequate because the exchange between the lead singer and the group was more than that. The singer did more than call or raise the song; the group of men did more than respond or answer. The lead called, asked questions, gave instructions, made claims, or stated facts. It was an "embodied call." Every part of his body was as involved in the singing as his mouth. He walked around, gestured with his arms, feet, eyes, head, and other parts of his body. For their part, the responses were similarly embodied, an "embodied response." Some of the men standing behind the group on the bench were hopping around with smiles on their faces, bright eyed, pacing back and forth, or interacting with the other singers. It was a full body engagement and communication among the chorus members. "Call and response," as a descriptor, is not enough.

The performance of these songs expanded my palette of African *ndwom* that I had experienced during childhood—in my family's drumming ensemble, at funerals, festivals, what I had observed at the Institute of African Studies at the University of Ghana, and in my adult years. Like most people in Accra, I had been exposed to many Western-influenced musical styles—church hymns, Nigerian and Ghanaian Hi-Life, brass band music, jazz music, Congolese soukous, Nigerian Afrobeat and juju, South African *kwela* and *isicathamiya*. I had musicked to *ndwom* from the African diaspora—capoeira, samba, vodou, calypso, steel drum music, reggae. At the same time, I had received training in Western music theory, performance practices, and music history, and been exposed to or performed some of the musical styles—opera, symphonies, Christmas carols. The "colonizing force of western tonality" (Agawu 2016) was strong on my musical palette. For someone who, during my undergraduate years at Fisk University at

Nashville, was trained to sing in the Italian bel canto style (and was actually advised by my voice teacher to refrain from singing my Ghanaian songs because they were ruining my voice) and performed arias during which I learned about the diaphragm and head and chest voice, voice placement, coloratura passages and recitatives, the tonality and performance style of the Asafo songs were raw and beautiful. *Will I ever be able to perform these songs with such passion and gusto?* Furthermore, my knowledge of the Fante language was also put to the test, leaving me to conclude that I needed more training, and that my understanding of African *ndwom*, though extensive, required other exposures. One cannot know all the *ndwom* traditions of the Akan, let alone the *ndwom* of an entire country or continent!

When the drummer sounded his last stroke on the drum, my colleague, the University of Cape Coast professor who helped organize the group, Dr. Nnuroh, and I engaged the performers in a discussion.

> Dr. Nnuroh: "Ama, did you see the old lady come out and dance?"
> Ama: "Yes, paaa! (Very well). I saw her. So why have they have stopped performing?"
> Dr. Nnuroh: "Let's ask them."

For the next thirty minutes, we engaged the group in a vibrant dialogue. I use Asafommba (Asafo members) for different performers who spoke at various times; otherwise, I use specific names and titles.

> Dr. Nnuroh: "Hi-Life is sweet. So why have you stopped performing it? Give me two reasons why you have stopped playing Asafo."
> Asafommba: "Why so?" Some of them laughed.
> Asafommba: "The incentive has not come." [He was referring to the compensation we agreed on.]
> Dr. Nnuroh: "I know we use power to play Asafo. We will come to that. I am asking why Kormantse town stopped playing Asafo." [The power we referred to was alcohol. Some believe that to perform the raw sounds of Asafo songs, one needs to have something in the "pit" (stomach).]
> Asafommba: "Aaa . . ." [Apparently, we did not word our question properly.]
> Egya Nako: "The reason why we have stopped playing Asafo is because a lot of people say this thing is fetishism and it is God who owns the earth, so we should stop and worship God. If you go to the big

cities—Cape, Accra, everywhere—they play Asafo. As for them, don't they know it is fetishism? So, it has made a lot of things *sekyew* in our town. People are dying, dying. There are some Elders in this town for whom every week or month, we performed certain customs. Because of worshipping God, we have stopped all those things. So, a lot of the people are dying, dying."

Dr. Nnuroh: "Father, you said because you stopped, everything has stopped short."

Egya Nako: "A lot."

Dr. Nnuroh: "When you say something has sekyew, what does that mean?" [The gentleman did not answer the question directly. Dr. Nnuroh rephrased our question.]

Dr. Nnuroh: "How does the stress that the town has gone through hurt the town?"

Egya Nako: "It bothers us."

Dr. Nnuroh: "Give me only two reasons."

Egya Nako: "One is that lots of people are dying, dying."

Asafommba: "Things are not going well for us."

Asafommba: "Things are not going well for us. Even when we go to sea, we don't bring back anything. At first our Elders used to do *apetse* [serving food to the Gods and sprinkling mashed yams throughout the town], all those things they have stopped. So that when we go to sea, we don't get anything. It brings trouble to us." [There had been a lot of talk about drought in the fishing industry along the coast.]

Dr. Nnuroh: "So now that we have all agreed that because we stopped doing these things it is bringing us troubles, how are we going to lift it up again?" [There was mumbling and discussion in the background.]

Asafommba: "It has to be our Elders."

Dr. Nnuroh: "But those of you here are not children. You are all Elders."

Asafommba: "At first, we used to have priests here . . ."

Dr. Nnuroh: "Let me revise the question. What are some of the benefits of having Asafo here?"

Asafommba: "When something happens, they sound the Asafo drum so that everyone knows that something is going on. Let's suppose someone gets drowned, when they sound the Asafo drum, then everyone knows that something has happened. They will all come out to see what it is."

Dr. Nnuroh: "What is another benefit?"

Asafommba: "At first when someone died, they sounded the drum, so that everyone knew that someone had died. Nobody should go to sea. If someone's wife or mother disappeared for a while, maybe she has gotten lost in the woods, they sounded the drum and we went together to find her. It was used to protect and secure the town."

Dr. Nnuroh: "So why have we allowed this to happen?"

Asafommba: "Our Elders ignored these things and they fell apart and the town has regressed." [Blaming the Elders and blaming Christianity had become a common parlance and for a moment seemed like a convenient excuse. *Abrewa hwe ase a, ɔde hyɛ ne poma,* "When an old woman falls down, she blames her walking stick."]

Dr. Nnuroh: "So, if I say, I am going to leave it up to those of you here to ensure that the Asafo lifts up, and puts on its best clothes, what would you do? What one or two steps would you take to make that happen?"

Asafommba: "We will gather and deliberate and suggest that we do the things that we used to do so that our town 'puts on its best clothes' [will progress], so that we can be safe and peaceful."

Asafommba: "Asafo is culture. I go to church, but when they called today, I came. There may be someone who goes to church and so they are shy. This is not fetishism. As for me, I can sing. Even if I can get someone, I could teach him before I die. It is culture. So, the Elders and lineage leaders should ensure that we teach some people before we go [die]," [the lead singer spoke for the first time].

Dr. Nnuroh: "You did not say your name."

Asafommba: "They call me Kobena Bedu."

Dr. Nnuroh: "Kobena Bedu, you say Asafo is culture; it is not fetishism, and if you had the opportunity, you would teach someone. We must lift this up. This is all we have. I am particularly fascinated by the women dancing." [We turned to the King of the fisherfolk's association, Apofohene, for his perspective. He spoke at length.]

Dr. Nnuroh: "Nana, when you go to sea do you play Asafo?"

Apofohene: "When we go to sea, we don't play Asafo; however, if someone drowns, then we will stand by the sea mouth and call the Spirit to help it come home. It is the Asafo that they used to draw the Spirit of the victim home." [One gentleman added that they don't take the drum with them to sea; rather, if someone drowns while they are at sea, on their return back, they would sing Asafo songs till they got to land, so people knew that something had happened.]

I had learned from a brief chat with someone prior to this gathering about the role of the drummer. The drummer was the most important position in the Asafo tradition. This was before I read De Graft Johnson's description of the master drummer as an important person who was regarded as the "wife" of the Asafo company, and in the olden days, someone was sometimes bought to hold the position (De Graft Johnson 1932). So, I asked:

Ama: "What effect does the demise of Asafo and its drummers have on Kormantse community?"

Asafommba: "They are cutting our necks. They are beheading us" (Wɔrotwa hɛn kɔn).[2]

Dr. Nnuroh: "What is the difference between what the drummer plays when someone drowns and when someone is missing in the bush? If I say someone has died so play the rhythm, can you play it?" [We asked the young gentleman, Kofi Abbam, who played the drum. Some people mumbled that he did not know how to play it because he was new to the instrument. I would later learn from Aprokuwa at Kokoado that all the drummers had died. They do not have one, though her son, Kofi Abbam, Kobena Carpenter, and Ekow Nunsin play. They are not lead drummers. About Kofi Abbam, Nana said, "They have not taught him. To learn how to play, Safohen would sit behind him and teach him by tapping his shoulders how to play and talk."]

Bedu: "Asafo, when someone gets lost in the bush, they have what they play; if someone is coming to fight us, they have what they play. So, everyone should prepare themselves and get ready . . .

Dr. Nnuroh: "So, when the ɔkyerema drummer is playing, he is talking . . .?"

Asafommba: "He is talking with it."

Dr. Nnuroh: "So, when you hear it, you know someone has drowned. Is it for entertainment?"

Asafommba: "No, just for emergencies."

Dr. Nnuroh: "But you had Hi-Life; that is fun."

Asafommba: "Yes. We have a tradition each year where we wear red attire. That is the Afahyɛ time. That is when we play Asafo to celebrate. But we don't normally play Asafo for entertainment."

Dr. Nnuroh: "Are women part of it? Women were the ones who were dancing when you were playing."

Asafommba: "They know it."

Dr. Nnuroh: "Do women play Asafo?"

Asafommba: "Some can play. They support us. Some of them are on the hill; they know how to play it."

Asafo has been presented by scholars as a warrior association for able-bodied men, in which every male member of society belongs to his father's Asafo.[3] The *ndwom* has also been constructed as masculine, where only men do the drumming and singing. The role of women within the Asafo is glossed over in the works about Asafo. At this session, all the singers were male, including the three men who played the drum. Thus, I was surprised by their statement, "Some [women] can play. They support us. Some of them are on the hill; they know how to play it." What exactly does "They know how to play it" mean? Do they play the drum? Could they play? When do they play? Are they allowed to touch, see the Asafo drums? Francis Bebey claims that

> Because the drum is, in certain circumstances, equated with a man (and a rather exceptional man, at that, whose powerful voice is capable of sending messages far and wide), women must consequently treat it with the same respect that they show towards their menfolk. No woman would dream of beating her husband in public (even though she may occasionally do so in private!), nor may she beat the drum in the village square. In some African societies, women are not even permitted to touch a drum under any circumstances. (1975, 14)

De Graft Johnson's remark that a woman must not get too close to an Asafo drum, far less look inside it, lest she becomes barren (De Graft Johnson 1932), seemed more far-fetched than Beby's claim. Nannyonga-Tamusuza's own experience of trying to learn a drum is also telling. She writes,

> My Kiganda music teachers, who had been mainly men, had always discouraged me from learning how to drum, but always praised me as a highly talented dancer. I remember, when I was in high school, I asked a fellow student (who is male) to teach me what he performed in the previous rehearsal. He dismissed me and said there was no way I could learn to beat the drum since I was a woman. He said it was a 'men's thing' to drum. Similarly, during my field research, as part of my research methodology, I had to enroll as a drum student. One of my drum teachers could not overcome the fact that a woman wanted to learn how to beat the drums. (2005, 137)

Bebey, De Graft Johnson, and the other writers who have drawn such conclusions were probably oblivious to the fact that women play drums among the Baganda of Uganda, Wolof of Senegal, Venda of South Africa, and so on.[4] Among the Baganda of Uganda, Sylvia Nannyonga-Tamusuza's teacher informs her that "When walumbe killed many people, a virgin girl would beat the drum and its sound would reduce Walumbe's anger." We also learn that "The most important ritual for women to beat the drums within the palace occurs when the king pays homage to the royal shrines (*masiro*) of his predecessors" (2005, 99). They probably were also not aware that among the northern Ewe of Ghana, "Gabada," a recreational music style that uses two bells, a small rattle, and three drums, "is played exclusively by adult women who may be in some kind of association" (*Traditional Women's Music from Ghana* 1981).

I wanted to learn more about the men's statements and wanted to inquire. I even thought about inviting the women who danced earlier to participate in the discussion. I recalled a discussion I had with members of the all-female Nlesi Adzewa group at Accra, Ghana, in 2003. When I asked the women why they did not play the drums—they played the gourds, sang, and danced, and the sole male member played the drum—the leader of the group answered, "Drumming is boring. Singing and dancing are more fun!" (Gladys Allotey, personal communication, July 26, 2003, Jamestown, Ghana). At this discussion with the men, I thought, *Are we making a big deal about women and drumming? Could we observe women's political stances and power through other means? There are many. Who is prioritizing drumming over singing, dancing, etc.? Why? Are there other ways of appreciating women's work and their politics without comparing them to what men do? There are many. Do labels or tags help us define women's positions and contribution to society? ɔbaa na ɔwo barima.*

Nnaemeka suggests tags do not always help us assess African women's political stance because what they do and how they do it are critical ways of constructing certain frameworks: "The majority of African women are not hung up on 'articulating their feminism'; they just do it. It is *what* they do and *how* they do it that provide the framework'; the 'framework' is not carried to the theater of action as a definitional tool. . . . Attempts to mold 'African feminism' into an easily digestible hall of pointed yam not only raise definitional questions but create difficulties for drawing organizational parameters and unpacking complex modes of engagement" (Nnaemeka 1998a, 5).

TABLE 7.1. Kormantse Asafo Bentsir Divisions per Uncle Bedu

Divisions	Color	Role
Kyiremfo	*Duawusu*/Blue-Black	Vanguards
Adzewafo		Middleman
Amfɛrfo		Rearguard

We moved on to discuss membership, structure, and division within their Asafo company. During our discussion about the divisions within their Asafo, women's role came up again. Bedu provided this information:

> Bedu: There are three divisions of our Asafo. They each have songs that they sing. We have kyiremfo, adzewafo, and amferfo. Kyiremfo are seventy-year-old men. When we go to war, they lead the group. They have lived a long life, so they are experienced. After them, we have the adzewafo. They are the fifty-year-old men. They follow the kyiremfo. Then we have amferfo; they are the children, between twenty and twenty-five years old. The real fighters are the kyiremfo and adzewafo; then the amferfo follow and observe.
>
> Dr. Nnuroh: "If the Asafo rises up and takes off, how would I know this is the kyiremfo, adzewafo, and amferfo? Do they have something that tells them apart from one another?" [There was some mumbling and quiet discussion among the men. Bedu came up to the mic to speak.]
>
> Bedu: "At first, kyiremfo wore a certain black cloth called duawusu; it had designs on it."

Out of nowhere, someone remarked, "The women who bring the trouble wear *lanta* and follow along."[5]

> Dr. Nnuroh: "You say women go and bring trouble, what would make women go and bring trouble?"
>
> Asafommba: "Like the women who were dancing today. They were kicking with one leg, as if to insult our enemy. Sometimes, the women would put cloth in front of their stomachs to say our neighbors, our enemies, have swollen and oversized prostates. That is what brings the trouble." [Oooo . . . now I understood why the one dancer kicked and kicked while she pranced across the floor. She was kicking their enemies and hurling insults. ɔhɔhoɔ ani akɛseakɛse nso ɔmfa nhunu kuro

mu, "A visitor may have big eyes but she may not see what is going on in town," and Nigerian Ibo Elders also say, *!gba anya hara hara abughi ihu uzo*, "Opening eyes very widely does not mean seeing very well."[6]]

I wanted to continue the discussion about how women "go and bring trouble." How would women have responded had they been part of this conversation? Who spoke for women in the company of men? Ideas about femininities and the representations of women in many Akan proverbs, some of which blame women for the troubles in society, came to mind. While some provide positive images of women or are neutral, others are negative.[7] We left this topic unresolved and went back to talking about *ndwom*.[8]

> Dr. Nnuroh: "Are there songs for heading to war, during the war, and returning victorious or defeated after the war? Could you give us one of each?"
> Asafommba: "Yes!"

Then, as our Ghanaian Akan Elders say, ɔ*ba nyansa foɔ yɛ bu no bɛ, yɛ nka no asɛm*, "For the wise child, we use proverbs, we don't use plain language,"

> *Dua no ebuiii*[9]
> *Hɛn dua no ebu oo Tuafo mmba e!*
> *Hɛn dua kakra na daano osi hɔ n'*
> *Onnyi hɔ!*
> *Dua kakra n'a osi hɔ n'*
> *Onnyi hɔ*
> *Dua n'ebu a*
> *Dua n'ebu a*
> *Onnyi hɔ*
> *Dua n'ebu a*
> *Dua n'ebu a*
> *Oonyi hɔ*
> *Agyensɛm' dua*
> *Yɛakyer banyin agye ne nsa m' dua e!*
>
> (The tree has broken/fallen
> Our tree has broken Tuafo children . . . ééé
> Our big/mighty tree that once stood there

> Is not there!
> The big tree that stood there
> Is not there!
> The tree has broken; the tree has broken
> Taker of a stick
> They have seized a man and taken a stick from him [He has died/been defeated])

Bedu: "That means that someone has died."
Asafommba: "It could also be performed for the death of an Elder, a family member, or a King."

The song can be performed for the death of a man or a woman, though the text references *banyin* (man). Though declamatory, evocative, and free moving like all the others they performed, this song was solemn. Poignant. I could see why it is performed to announce a death at sea, at the hospital, or at home. The singer stretched and suddenly cut short ("dropped") the end of the two first lines to express pain and loss, wailing.:

> *Dua no ebuiiii!*
> *Hɛn dua no ebu oo Tuafo mmba ee!*
>
> The tree has fallen . . .
> Our tree has fallen Tuafo children . . .

He repeated the phrases for emphasis, relied on textual extemporization, mixed spoken and sung texts, and used symbolic language, because *ɔba nyansafoɔ yɛ bu no bɛ, yɛ nka no asɛm*, "For the wise child, we use proverbs, we don't use plain language."

> "The mighty tree has broken/fallen" (An important, revered person has died)
> "Taken a stick from him" (Taken the person's symbol of authority, strength, life)

This performance style of moving from spoken speech to a song or proverb is also common in other African orature and speech. It was a practice that I was familiar with, and yet when it happened in this context, it was still too sweet. The drummer punctuated the text with short rhythmic phrases, playing interludes during brief pauses. It was one of the few songs I heard that did not end with the stop or exclamation. Rather, it slid downward and ended on a melancholic tone.

The group referred to the songs they performed earlier to demonstrate their victories at war and their valiance:

> Asafommba: "Nobody fought with us and conquered us! That is why we are Great Ngyedum. I*gya biara yɛ dum no*, "Every fire, we quench it!"

They repeated the Hi-Life song to which the old woman danced earlier, "People of Tuafo are coming. We are red-eyed [serious]."

They also performed another song that ended with a phrase, "We will never run from a crowd!" (*Yɛ renguan dɔm ara da!*). Indeed, many of the songs they performed that day described their enemies as weak and fearful cowards who ran when Kormantse people went after them. Songs like "We went to Akyemfo, nobody was there" and "The servants have gone/The people, we looked everywhere for them/We did not find them/We found them hiding in a ladder" were typical. About 70 percent of the songs they performed that day used *kasa twii*, speech that hurts, instigates, insinuates, gloats, and disses their enemies,[10] what the late Akɔdeɛ Afful of Elmina had termed earlier as *nsaa*.[11] In one song that recounts an 1883 fight between Kormantse Nkum and Abandze/*Ya ara nkyɛ* 🔊, two neighboring towns, they belittle their neighbors while aggrandizing themselves:

> *Ya ara nkyɛ, ya ara nkyɛ, ya ara nkyɛ, ya ara nkyɛ, ya ara nkyɛ*
> *Ya ara nkyɛ na Nkum na Abandze*
> *Hɔn edzi nkwaseako*
> *Ya ara, ya ara*
> *Etsiwafo mbanyin e*
> *Etsiwafo mbanyin mbɔsom!*

> (Had it been us, had it been us, had it been us, had it been us, had it been us
> Had it been us this Nkum and Abandze fight
> Was a stupid fight
> Had it been us, had it been us
> Strong soldiers would have had to intervene!)[12]

My favorite song, which they sang again during the focus group, "*Oye, Oye Kofi Dedu mba e*" 🔊 ("It's good; Children of Kofi Dedu"), recounts their war with the Asante at Edena in the early nineteenth century when the Asante stormed the coast to bypass the Fante middlemen to have direct contact with European slave traders. In this song, they paid homage to and proclaimed their relationship with one of their revered Asafo captains and one of their female warriors, Ekua Yaaba, the younger sibling of the town's founder, Komer. "We went to Edna war/To cause trouble/Hold your guns/We will force the enemy to eat white clay/Depart with white clay!" Here are people who defend their territory, against outside and inside aggression. Ebueii! Didn't our Akan Elders say, *Sɛ woankasa wo tiri ho a, yeyi wo ayi bɔne*, "If you do not talk about your head, they give you a bad haircut." They sing to diss their enemies, defend their territory, signify, gloat, glorify themselves. Here are people who assert. Kormantse lives matter.

After going through the songs many times, I still needed more exposure to understand what makes them "sweet." These Kormantse songs were raw, rough, at times dissonant, organic, and intimidating. The Kormantse Asafo singers, through their walking together, charged through their lyrics and gesturing to intimidate. The performance was a sensory overload with so much to hear, see, and feel. It was overwhelming. However, as they continued, it started to expand my socio-aesthetics of what "sweet" *ndwom* is. I was learning to appreciate and enjoy Asafo *ndwom* in local ways. *Tete ka aso mu*, "Repetitive hearing leaves an indelible mark on the ear!"[13]

> Oh! Asafo
> Come back!
> Nananom
> Come back
> This place is hot
> You are the glue
> That cements the town
> Us
> You
> Are sweet
> Our anchor
> We are lost without you! (Journal Entry, December 12, 2016)

What Nana Odum III, Asafo Captain, Sang and Said: "Asafo Is Military. The Women Saved Asafo"

Nana: "We have Asafo Akyerɛ, that is a woman. She also has a stick and a sword. She also uses it to mobilize the crowd. It can be anyone who is smart and feisty; they must carry you, appoint you. Maybe this one is feisty; they must appoint you. Not all the women are feisty, but if you are or if your Elder dies, then they will put you in her place."

I found out through talking with Nana and others that, in fact, women play significant roles in Asafo. They are not troublemakers as the men had portrayed them. That women were Asafo captains challenged many sayings by our Akan Elders, like ɔbaa tɔn nyaadua na ɔntɔn atuduro, "A woman sells garden eggs, but not gunpowder," and ɔbaa yɛ ekyɛm a, ɛtwere ɔbarima dan mu, "When a woman makes a shield, it is stored in a man's room." In fact, some of the women led wars, including the one at Edena with the Asante army in the early nineteenth century. According to oral narratives, Asafo Akyerɛ Nana Gyaahyewa, a rich woman of the Kona lineage, led the war; she also purchased cloth and gave them to the warriors to cover the rifles to prevent the gunpowder from getting wet. Whoever wove the proverb ɔbaa yɛ ekyɛm a, ɛtwere ɔbarima dan mu probably forgot about or was unaware of ɔbaa Hemaa Nana Yaa Asantewaa of Egyeso, Asante, who led the war of the Golden Stool against the British, the Yaa Asantewaa War, when the men were afraid to fight, and the many other female warriors. ɔbaa na ɔwo barima! Ancestresses. Warriors!

> Ama: "Do you have songs that memorialize the various events?" [Nana replied with a Kormantse Asafo ndwom, "Akyem Esuantse" (example 32 ✳).]
> Nana: "It means that when the fight came, when we pushed them [the Asante] into the bush, we seized their golden stool, and their King, Nana Karikari, went and told Dwaaben King that they should come and beg us to return the stool.'"
> Ama: "So, did he come?"
> Nana: "The Dwaaben King was afraid to come. Later when he got the stool for them, they turned around and fought the Dwaaben people. It is a song we sing to tease them to come back. We taunt and insult them with it. They said, 'If you kill a thousand, a thousand would

come!' (Wo kum apem a, apem bɛba!), so we are taunting them to come back."

Ama: "Do you have any more songs? What else goes on while they are singing?"

Nana: "We use the drum to accompany. They talk with it; they say proverbs on it aaaa . . ., and you have goosebumps. Then the spirit descends, very, very hard."

I met Mr. Victor Albert Kwesi Hammond, Safohen Nana Odum III, alias Teacher Hammond, three days after the gathering at the King's palace. After asking around about Asafo matters that have come and gone, a lady asked a young boy to escort me to Teacher Hammond's house. We walked between people's houses, by store fronts, through the dusty main street, by a water reservoir, unleashed dogs, many uncompleted houses, a lineage house, and smoked fish industries. The smell of raw, smoked, and fried fish, the dust from the paths, the sound of sewing machines emanating from the seamstress' shops and from the roaring sea filled my lungs, ears, and eyes. The smoke from the fish-smoking ovens made my eyes water. It was a sensory-filled walk (Pink 2009). During subsequent trips to the house, I relied on my senses to guide me through the convoluted pathway. Unlike all the other destinations, I repeated this walk almost every day and formed very close relationships with the people along the way and the land.

We arrived at an unpainted and partially completed cement house wedged between the highway and the Atlantic Ocean. Two women and a man greeted us. When we asked for Teacher Hammond, someone went and knocked on a door. A square-shaped wooden plaque with his full name and date of birth hung outside his door. On the small porch, a poster of an obituary of a woman hung on the wall. A beautiful petite elderly man emerged from the room and greeted us. This was Teacher Hammond, or "T" as some referred to him in the compound. I recognized him because he was with the assembly of Kings with whom we talked about Kormantse chieftaincy and other issues. He was the one with dates and the one who asserted that the British got the idea for their military from Asafo. He was the one most people I spoke with about my interests in Asafo recommended I contact.

After I introduced myself and articulated my mission, he agreed to mentor me. Teacher Hammond was a petite Elder, calm and laid back; he giggled often and was humorous. Like our Elders say, *Twene anim da hɔ a, yɛnyan kyɛn*, "When the drumhead is there, we do not beat the sides": he

FIGURE 7.1. Safohen Nana Odum III (Teacher Hammond).

was candid. He seemed calm, but as I would experience later, *Asu a ɛtaa ho dinn na ɛfa onipa,* "It is the water which stands there calm and silent that takes [drowns] a person." We agreed on a token. He would offer a prayer and ask for guidance and protection from the seventy-seven Gods in the community. He would also call on the spirit of Nana Odum, his Ancestral Spirit, who according to Nana, after they went to war at Elmina, returned walking on "the sea like Jesus—all medicine." Nana inherited his Safohen title from this warrior.

Teacher Hammond, Nana Odum III (henceforth Nana), was ready, holding a sheet of paper with the texts of Asafo *ndwom* he had handwritten, when I arrived. He referred to this occasionally as we talked. We started our talk with a brief biography. He was eighty-three years old at the time. He is a member of the Kona lineage and had lived at Kokoado Upper Town on the hill, before moving down the hill to Lower Kormantse. Nana has the equivalent of a high school diploma and is considered highly educated by the townspeople. Because he writes things down, he keeps records of historic events in the society, people's birthdates, and other matters that require recording. He is also the timekeeper for some people in the community. People ask for the time when he walks through town. Once he asked me to help get a battery for his watch. The wristwatch did not work well after replacing the battery. When I purchased a new watch for him, he mused, "This is the community's watch."

As one of the few remaining Asafo captains at Kormantse, Nana shared his firsthand experience with Kormantse Asafo.

Ama: "What is the meaning of Asa-fo?"
Nana: "ɔsa is a fight. A fight is ɔsa. 'We have left our town behind; we are going to Kokoado to fight.' That is ɔsa."
Ama: "What about the 'fo' that is attached?"
Nana: "They are many of us, many."
Ama: "Please, what is Asafo?"
Nana: "Asafo is military. They defend the town. They fight to protect the town."
Ama: "Is that all they do?"
Nana: "When someone dies, we play Asafo, to accompany him or her. We play Asafo for anyone who dies."
Ama: "For everyone?"
Nana: "Yes. If you are a man, a woman, and an Asafo member, then we must play Asafo to send you off. If you are a woman and a member, we have to play Asafo for you."
Ama: "What if a person is not a member of Asafo?"
Nana: "Then we will not play for the person. Maybe the woman is in front of a God [Priest], then we have to play Asafo."
Ama: "Besides fighting and funerals, what else does the Asafo do?
Nana: "We have Afahyɛ. When we fought with the Asante, every year, we must wake them up and ka gu hɔn do ['knock them down'] into the Owumena [death pit]. It happened in the first week of July when they pushed them into the hole. So, every year July—it happened on Friday—so every Thursday, we have to wake them up and 'throw, throw.' By this time, about 12 noon, they brought the Asafo; the groups—battalion no. 1 amferfo, they wear danger (red), battalion no. 2 adzewafo, they wear yellow, the Elders, battalion no. 3 kyiremfo,

TABLE 7.2. Kormantse Asafo Bentsir Divisions per Nana (Safohen Nana Odum III, Teacher Hammond)

Divisions	Color	Role
Amfɛrfo	Red	Vanguards
Adzewafo	Yellow	Middleman
Kyiremfo	*Duawusu*/Blue-Black	Rearguard

they wear duawusu, it is a cloth with images of trees on it. It is dark blue. So, there are eku-asa, three groups. The amferfo, they are the young men; they lead; they go and survey; then the adzewafo, and kyiremfo stay in the back during the fight." [This was different from what I learned from Bedu with the group of men.]

Ama: "Do you have posts in the Asafo?"

Nana: "Yes, we have different posts."

Ama: "Which is the first?"

Nana: "It is the Supi. When they are going to war, he leads the war; he and the Safohen. The Supi, when the matter happens, they go to his house to meet and pray and then go."

Ama: "What does the Safohen do?"

Nana: "When they play the Asafo, I direct the crowd; if you are not with the crowd, I have to roam aaa . . ., when I find you, I have to beat you up and instruct you, 'Go back to where they are playing the Asafo.' I do that; I roam aaa . . ., and I bring them together. If someone is doing any foolish things, I must beat him and tell him to stop doing those foolish things. When the fight comes, I also lead."

Ama: "So, your role is to lead and beat people?"

Nana: "Yes, I lead and beat people, mobilize them." [Nana giggled.]

Ama: "So far, we have Supi and Safohen. What other roles are there?"

Nana: "We have Asafo Akyerɛ; that is a woman."

Nana was also one of the first people to complain about the negative effects of Christianity and the church on Kormantse society and was resentful toward the pastors of the churches. "The church is too much. It has spoiled things and we keep dying, dying. We have stopped performing our traditions and rituals. There used to be four churches. Right now, we have thirty-six in this little town. [He later revised the number to twenty-five.] They keep bringing them!" he added. Yet, Nana organized the congregation for the first church, a Methodist Church, in the neighboring town, Nkum, and another church, Zion Church, years later after he left the Methodist Church. He continued to serve as Safohen and was very active in the Asafo company.

He sang all the Asafo songs he mentioned, provided the *abakɔsɛm*, significance, and context for each, like the song "*ɔkɔtɔfo Gyesi*" (example 33 ≋ 🔊).

> Gyesi is a Safohen. When the fight happens, if the Amferfo battalion do not guard the town, if the people come, then they will destroy the town. So, they must stand firm. Before they went to war, they had to ask their fate (*Bisa hɛn tsi*). They called the priest. After she prayed, she smeared some medicine on their bodies; and they had to dip their hands in the medicine seven times. Another priest marked their bodies with white clay. If yours does not turn red, you stand aside and you take your gun. If yours turns red, no matter what you do, they will not let you go because you would die if you went. A gunshot will hit you.

During our conversation, the other gentleman was so moved by Nana's singing that at one point, he remarked, "He has sung, and goosebumps have showered me. When they sing then the Spirit has arisen." He sang it again.

Nana claimed that they were victorious in all the wars they fought. "If we don't bring a person's head, we have to bring back a live person. That is why the Europeans looked and said, in the whole world, they have Great Britain, then they will also name us Great Kormantine. In the whole world, only two countries have the titles, Great Britain, Great Kormantine, because of our bravery." Then he sang "*ɔdɔm Kyirem*" (example 34 ≋).

According to Nana, every Asafo captain has a song and a flag that he commissions to showcase his qualities. Nana Odum sang his Safohen song, which according to him referenced a time when Safohen Odum, his predecessor, was directing a war. His voice echoed with pride and force as he sang his song:

> *Nyew o Odum ee* 🔊
> *Sɛ yɛyɛ ebisa tsir a*
> *Hyia hɛn sarmu*
> *Nyew Odum ee*
> *Odum ee bisa tsir a*
> *Hyia hɛn sarmu oo*
> *Asafo Amferfo yenya amandze ampa o*
> *ɔyɛ a tsie w'asowa m'!*

> (Yes, Odum ask
> Meet us in the forest
> Asafo Amfer we truly have issues
> Listen carefully with your ears) (Kormantse Asafo ndwom, "*Odum*")

I listened quietly and tried to mimic his voice and line in my mind.

Nana did not sing any of the songs that the group of men performed; neither did they perform any of the songs he performed, indicating the breadth of Asafo songs. Nana sang specific Kormantse songs, including those for the three battalions and those of other Asafo companies at neighboring towns. Neither did his performance evoke the same passion, rawness, or the rough quality that the group performed. His rendition was mellow. Still, they were declaratory, free moving. The breadth of his knowledge was incredibly large.

Nana placed women in a respectable role when he discussed their contribution to Asafo; they were not the troublemakers or war mongers as the group of men portrayed them. They were collaborators in the fight against the enemy. He shared the story behind one *ndwom*:

> A man from Asaafar came to marry a Bentsir (Kormantse) woman. The man died and had been buried a long time ago. Before he died, he helped and accompanied our warriors to war. So, they [our people] had to go and fire shots to remember him. When they got there, their Asafo company had cut weed all over so that when our people went, they could claim that they fought with them. That is when Abanyi, he was a very rich man, had built a two-storied building. When our people went, their flag is called, "Old man I am tired" (*Akwaadaa maa fena*). They can jump on top of the house and dance. He told the Asaafar people that if they did not fire a gun and fight the Bentsir people, then he would not like it. Someone came and told our people, 'This is what is happening.' Our women who were going to toilet saw that they put guns on it. They picked up all the guns and brought them to our men. When the people went to collect the guns, there were no guns. 'Fight and let's see.' Our Elders studied the situation and sang. (see "*Abanyi*" example 35 ❊)

"The women saved the Kormantse warriors from being slaughtered," Nana concluded. Do the male singers who accused women of bringing trouble know about this history? The women saved Asafo.

Like many of the Asafo songs that I had heard thus far and served as archives, this song and others memorialized the past in ways that other forms of orature—folklore, myths, folktales, proverbs, and written sources—did not. For through the song performance, they comment on the main event while incorporating other references and connections, proverbial language, and other oral forms to "sweeten it." A song is not just a song; it is a complex array of references, sounds, and images (see Knight 1976; Saboro 2011).

Nana referenced the death pit multiple times.

Ama: "Do you have any songs about the Owumena?"
Nana: "No, we do not."
Ama: "While they are singing is there anything else going on?"
Nana: "Yes, they use the drums to accompany. They talk with it; they say proverbs on it aaa . . ., and you are sitting, and goosebumps pour on you. Then the Spirit comes very, very hard."
Ama: "How many drums do you have?"
Nana: "We have two big ones and two small ones. One is what we talk with.
Ama: "What is that called?
Nana: "It is called Atoapentsin. That one, when war/fight comes, you who are playing the drum, you don't have to hide it. If you hang on the side, they will fire at you; they will fire at you to die. So, you don't have to hold it on the side. You must hang it in front of you. That is why it is called Atoapentsin."
Ama: "Atoapentsin, what does it mean?"
Nana: "It is *gyina hɔ hwɛ,* 'stand there and see.' The drummer does not run to go anywhere. Even if the war is coming towards him, he stands there. He does not run to go anywhere. The drum hangs on him, and he drums to call his people. He does not run anywhere."
Ama: "What is the next one?"
Nana: "The next one is *ekumtawia.*"
Ama: "What does it do?"
Nana: "It answers. As for him when they play the Asafo, it answers."
Ama: "What about the other two?"
Nana: "They are *dɛnkyerɛma* and *ampaa*. You play the ampaa with hands and play the dɛnkyerɛma with two small sticks. The ampaa answers that Asafo drum. The two big drums are played with two kɔtɔkorba sticks."

Ama: "Are there other instruments?"

Nana: "There is a dawur. The dawur is what starts the thing. If you sing the song to go high, it is ken ken ken, ken ken ken, ken ken ken.... It means you are singing the song to invoke energy: "Akyem Suantse, wɔ mbra oo, ee ee" the drums goes, and the dawur goes ken, ken, ken.... If we play at a time when kaa ka-ka ka; ka-ka-ka-ka, that is for the women. The women dance it the most. Like in

> *Beseadze kyiremfoe, beseadze kyiremfoe*
> *Yɛkɔr enyamanmu yɛkotu ɔhon (2x)*
> *Nyimpa atɔ nsu mu (abɔyɛfo) wɔnyi n' ma hɛn*
> *Nyimpa atɔ nsu mu (abɔyɛfo) wɔnyi n' ma hɛn*
>
> (Beseadze kyirem group, beseadze Kyirem group
> We went to cut some hay
> A person has fallen into the river
> Deliver him for us) (Kormantse Asafo *ndwom*, "*Beseadze Kyiremfo*")

Ka-ka-ka-ka, ka-ka-ka-ka; then the women go like this" [he moved his hands in a swimming/rowing motion while he sang a pattern like the kpanlogo.]

Ama: "So, it means someone has fallen into the sea?"

Nana: "Yes, they were going to gather some hay and one person fell in the sea. So, our people, they said they were going to uproot ɔhon there; they don't know how to swim like our people, so our people went and pulled the person from the sea. He did not die. So, our people used it in a song. Beseadze too has a kyirem group/battalion.

Ama: "What is Beseadze?"

Nana: "It is a town; if you are going to Ajumako, you branch and go there. It is Beseadze. ɔhon is the hay that we use to roof a hut. It is the one that you saw roof Nana Eminsa's shrine.

Ama: "So, they went to cut some hay and someone fell into the sea?"

Nana: "Yes! Nyimpa atɔ nsu mu (abɔyɛfo) wɔnyi n' ma hɛn; nyimpa atɔ nsu mu (abɔyɛfo) wɔnyi n' ma hɛn!

Talking to Nana was like watching a performance. He rarely answered "Yes" or "No." A typical answer to a question moved through short or long direct responses, proverbs, a song, rhetorical questions, and other oratorical references. As performances, these conversations combined different oral features, facial expressions, and bodily gestures: For example, when I asked about a song connected to the death of one Asafo captain, Nana Gyesi, Nana's response moved from one modality to another. These multimodal registers were typical of the many conversations I had with him and others.

> Ama: "Why did they shoot him?"
> Nana: "They were fighting with Nkum people; they shot him. That is the song, Gyesi mbo/ ɔhen Gyesi mbo/ɔama ma Mfantse/asaase kyir hɛn/ɔhen Gyesi mbo/ɔhen Gyesi ee ɔkó esi oo/ɔhen Gyesi mbo! They chased the no. 1 people aaaa . . . [He got up, raised his hand to gesture how long they chased No. 1 people, then sat down.] If they got close, won't they shoot him?"

Blending these performative features with different literary styles—including but not limited to proverbs, praise poems, songs, *ndwom* transcriptions, Fante and English languages, and conventional prose—mirrored the works of African literary critics whose "double writing," or interweaving of various personal and peculiar African oral features into the European-derived written form, allows them to traverse the European and African forms (Adu-Gyamfi 2002).

We had focused group discussions with the town's spokesperson and other people in the community who came to learn from Nana. Other times, Nana and I took memory and history walks while I accompanied him to his farm, trudged up the Kokoado hill to photograph his Asafo sword and stick, or through the sand to where a whale was washed ashore. Most destinations were marked by *ndwom*.

One day, I asked Nana, "How did you learn about all these songs and matters that have come and gone?" He explained: "I walked with the Elders a lot. When they needed something, they would ask me to do it. I ran errands for them and when I came back, they would sit me down and share some historical facts, hidden knowledge, and songs with me. 'When you are close to a crab, you can hear it cough'" (Nana Odum III, personal communication, February 10, 2017, Kormantse, Ghana).

He continued, "When they carried me as Safohen, my Ancestor, the Spirt that was on him, he left it in me too, I am walking with it." He added that through his walks with the Spirit of his Ancestor, he experiences vision quests and receives answers to questions in the middle of the night. When that happens, he wakes up and writes down the information. Once, when I

FIGURE 7.2. Aduonum and Nana on a history walk, walking interview. Photo by Joe.

visited him, he complained that the battery in his lantern had burned out, and he could not write down the answers to questions that came to him in his sleep. So, I helped with some batteries. *Wosum borɔdeɛ dua a, sum kwadu nso dua*, 'When you provide support for the plantain tree, provide one for the banana tree also."

"When they carried me as Safohen, I had to learn all the songs, their meanings, and *abakɔsɛm*." Nana became my go-to person. Walking with him helped shape my search and put me in good standing with Kormantse residents who later taught me songs. One day, during our discussion on Kormantse Asafo Gods, he described one of the protective Gods through song. Before Nana sang the song, the gentleman, Jojo, interjected, "We don't sing that song recklessly [*basa-basa*]." I asked if I should not record it. Nana replied, "It's OK. Let's sing it." So he sang Kormantse Deity Nana Dzerma *Ndwom* "*Kweku Anankor ei*" (example 36 ❦).

> Nana: "He has one leg, one hand, one eye is also squinted" (*kyew*).
> Jojo: "Teacher, you are getting too far." [Jojo tried to stop him, but Nana continued.]

Nana: "Yes, the water is over there. The water is there right now. People come from Tekyiman and other places to visit it. Women who trade bring their cars, and at night, they fetch the water and take it with them. All the money they have is from here. When they come, they bring offerings because the water helps them."

Jojo: "Goosebumps have showered me."

I never understood Jojo's statement, "You are getting too far," until I asked Nana to write down the names of the seventy-seven Gods at Kormantse. He wrote down only thirty-six names, their qualities, and their role in the society. When I asked about the remaining forty-one, Nana replied, "*Wɔ mpɛ dɛɛ ye yi hɔn ewie i*, 'They don't like us to reveal their end'" (reveal all their names). "Being close to a crab does not necessarily mean one can always hear all of its cough!"

Nana shared many songs. However, he did not differentiate between Asafo songs and songs for the various Gods. Also, since I did not ask, he did not discuss the structure of a song performance. Still, the information he shared, the walks we took, and the *ndwom* he sang were enough for further probing. Our Akan Elders say, "*ɔhonam mu nni nhahoa*, "No part of the human body should be regarded as marginal," or *ketewa biara nsua*, "No offering is too small." Every interaction and walk took me deeper into Asafo aesthetics. Nigerian Ibo Elders say, *The nzo ukwu biri ogologo njem*, "A step taken marks the end of a long journey." Every step taken took me closer to the end of my journey. I continued to listen to my mentors and Elders. "If you dislike listening to the lengthy talks from the Elders, you may be bereft of oral traditions," *Wosuro asɛm ten-ten a, wonte mpaninsɛm*.

What the Kormantse Five Sang and Said: "It Makes It Sweet," "Men Ran"

Seven months later, on Friday, July 15, 2017, I arranged a session with a group of five Kormantse men: Egya Kobena Bedu, Egya Kwame Atta, Agya Yiiyii, Egya Kwame Nako, and Egya Kwesi Kom. Four of them were of the Domna clan and referred to themselves as siblings; the other was of the Anona clan. Three of them performed with the group I worked with seven months earlier; the other two, Egya Kwame Atta and Kwesi Kom, were new to me. At the time, I was staying with Maame Owusuma and I sought permission from her to perform in one of her rooms because the organizer, Egya Kobena

Bedu, hinted that some of the men were uncomfortable because *Hwerɛma na ɛtwetwe ndwom*, "Whistling induces singing," and they did not want to attract a crowd. They feared chastisement from their pastor and congregation. So, we gathered at a spot in Maame Owusuma's basement.

Before they performed, I asked a few questions to contextualize the performance and to verify information that I had gathered so far about the role of Asafo.

> Ama: "You were saying when someone drowns or gets lost, you play Asafo; so now that you don't play Asafo, what does it do for the town? What happens when someone drowns? Is it disturbing the town and in what way? Is it good for the town that you don't play Asafo?"
> Egya Nako: "They say it is worshipping God; it is fetish, so you should not come close to it. We have used religion to tie it up aaaa . . ., even if you are going to do it, you are afraid."
> Egya Yiiyi: "Because if you go to chapel, you can't go and play Asafo."
> Egya Nako: "So, we have stopped and look up to the religion (Christianity); we have stopped, but when something serious happens or a man dies, if it is a peaceful death, we can do it . . ."
> Bedu: "We have people who will play. Sometimes it is a child who plays. They tell him not to and the child will stop. So right now, what we want to know is how much you will give us so we can start. Because the Asafo ndwom that we going to sing, we sing and then explain it."

Bedu started with an Asafo Rousing Call [There are multiple versions of this call.]:

Call (C):	*Asafo ko eyi hɔn!* (3x)
Answer (A):	*Ko eyi hɔn!* (3x)
C:	*Asafo ko eyi hɔn*
A:	*Ko eyi hɔn*
C:	*Ebiasa a*
A:	*Yɛ tse hɔn do!*
C:	*Dombi botum hɔn*
A:	*Oo-ho!*
Call:	Asafo war has birthed them
Answer:	War has birthed them
C:	What about the three

> A: We conquer them
> C: Can a multitude defeat us
> A: No!

They did not perform this opening call when I met with them at the King's palace.[14] I learned that it was the rousing call to get the group hyped and ready, and that all Asafo song performances start with a version of this call.

The leader repeated the first line three times. When I asked why he said the line three times and why he referred to *ebasaa* (three) in his call, he referenced the number of mounds on the cooking stove (*foonoo/mukyia*), which according to him makes the stove stable and firm. Then he added a biblical reference: "Everything is three. God the Father, God the Son, and God the Holy Spirit. It is in the Bible. It is not four. It is three."

> Ama: "So, is that where *ebiasa* comes from?"
> Bedu: "Yes, that is where it comes from. Everything that is three is dangerous. It is in the Bible."
> Ama: "Where in the Bible is it?" [He laughed.]
> Egya Bedu: "You see, God the Father, God the Son, and God the Holy Spirit. It joins to make one, just like we say, ɔbɔsom enyim yɛ kɔ ebaasa, "We appear before the Gods three times."

With this rousing call, the group performed a series of songs from identity-related songs, war-related songs, provocative/rivalry songs, recreational songs, morality songs to songs expressing the heritage and history of Asafo. Others were meant to instill pride and a sense of patriotism in the people and documented past events. The songs moved in stepwise motion with no sudden leaps, though when the Asafommba sang together, the texture was similar with a few variations, because some singers varied the tones. They listened to each other's variation and adjusted accordingly and came right back to the main melody of the chorus. They told me it was a deliberate strategy to make the songs "sweet"; in some ways, it amplified the notion that "Harmony in African [music] emerges spontaneously rather than being assigned to particular members of the ensemble.... Each member of the ensemble sings whatever part he chooses to sing, and he may even move from one part to the other during the singing. This style is quite common in singing Asafo songs" (Adjei 1999, 89). Most of the songs the group performed used homophonic parallelism— moving parallel to the melody in thirds and sixths, a practice that A. M. Jones (1962) and later Nketia (1974)[15] and Agawu (2016) attribute to the Akan and other groups in Africa. Not all the chorus members sang variations a third above the melody; only one did. Yet, it stood out from the other line, blending nicely to "sweeten" the entire embodied response. The leader called out a song; the chorus responded. Sometimes, the "one who sweetens" added his contribution in certain parts of the chorus; other times, he came in with his "sweetener" from the start of the chorus to the end. In one song, "*Nkum na Abandze/Ya ara nkyɛ*," Bedu began with a long-winding declamatory call; the chorus answered, with the "one who sweetens" adding his sweetener a third above the main line. There was a brief instance when his voice dropped slightly lower, but he quickly moved back to the sweetener.

As lead soloist, Bedu has a greater ability to express emotions in song than do the responders. Like the Dodo lead singer that Patricia Opondo (2002) describes, he is expected to be eloquent and, above all, knowledgeable (207). A Dodo soloist, according to Opondo, "distinguishes herself from the other singers by the capacity for expressing herself through the effective use of images and idioms" (208). Whenever Bedu raises a song, his responders listen to him intently, paying attention to his mood, energy, facial expressions, gestures, and the idioms he inserts; then they respond accordingly, sometimes mimicking his expressions and gestures.

> Ama: "Why do you sing the song three times?" [I was hoping he would repeat his reference to the Bible and the symbolism of three he referenced earlier.]
> Egya Nako: "The second time if you stop, it slips, so every *ndwom*, we sing it three."
> Ama: "What about four?"
> Egya Nako: "You can sing it four times also."
> Egya Bedu: "If the song is sweet, you have to repeat it. The reason why we are singing it three is because you are recording, so we must make the *ndwom* short, otherwise, we would sing it aaa. . . ."
> Ama: "I have noticed that one person raises the song (*ma ndwom no do*); why is that? What do you call him?"
> Egya Nako: "They call him *nwomtofo/nwomtonyi* [singer of *ndwom*]."
> Ama: "What do you call the others who answer?"
> Egya Nako: "Asafommba [Asafo children]." [Nako is the oldest among the group, and from what I gathered, is quite knowledgeable about

the Asafo tradition. Egya Nako could sing the lead and "sweeten" the *ndwom*.]

Ama: "So Asafommba answer, and the *nwomtofo* raises it?" [They all responded in the affirmative. During a short break, I asked about when they perform Asafo since it is considered fetish by Christians and people are discouraged from getting involved.]

Egya Nako: "If an issue comes, we will play. At our Afahyɛ, we will play in October. There was a Bentsir man; his wife was at Anloga; she lived with Anloga people, so he went to look for her. The Anloga woman made a report that we have stolen from her, that the town has stolen her money and broken into her house. So, all of us we fled . . . the police surrounded the town . . ."

Ama: "You ran? Men ran?"

Egya Nako: "Yes, if they come, they would arrest you. For four days, no one set foot here."

Ama: "So, nobody was here?"

Egya Nako: "Only women were here. Only the women were here. They [police] took the whole town. No cars passed through, if they caught up with you, they arrest you." [I thought about our Elders' saying that suggests that men are strong and reliable: *ɔbaa yɛ akyem a, ɛtwere ɔbarima dan mu*, "When a woman makes a shield it is stored in a man's room"; or one that says when trouble comes, it rests on man's chest. And yet, the men ran! Hm! *Sɛbe sɛbe, mmarimma nyɛ sumyɛ na yɛ de yɛ ti ato so*, "With all due respect, men are not pillows for us to put our heads!"]

Ama: "When did this happen?"

Egya Bedu: "2005."

Ama: "Is there a song that you sing about it?"

Egya Bedu: "When someone dies, that is what we are going to sing, if you are standing alone and you fall down, you say" [Bedu sings]:

> *Dua no ebuiii*
> *Hɛn dua no ebu oo Tuafo mmba eeee*
> *Hɛn dua kakra no a daano osi hɔ no*
> *Onnyi hɔ!*
> *Dua kakra no a osi hɔ no*
> *Onnyi hɔ*
> *Dua no ebu a dua no ebu a onnyi hɔ*

Dua no ebu a dua no ebu a onnyi hɔ
Agye nsɛm dua
Yɛakyer banyin agye ne nsɛm dua e

(The tree has broken/fallen
Our tree has broken Tuafo children . . .
Our big/mighty tree that once stood there
Is not there!
The big tree that stood there
Is not there!
The tree has broken; the tree has broken
Taker of a stick
They have seized a man and taken a stick from him)

Egya Bedu: "Right now, nothing is there; the tree has broken; it has been uprooted. That is the song that we have sung."

Ama: "When someone dies, then you sing this song for the person? You were saying that the woman was an Anloga person. I did not understand how the conflict occurred."

Egya Nako: "His wife was an Anloga woman." [Nako explained why the incident upset them. Anloga was the name given to descendants from the Volta region who lived on the outskirts of Kormantse, on the boundary between Kormantse and Saltpond. They speak the Anlo Ewe language and work as fisherfolk.]

Ama: "He was a Kormantse man?"

Egya Bedu: "He was our brother. Our family. Our Uncle's son. A Domna man, like us."

Ama: "The wife's husband died?"

Egya Nako: "The husband, our brother, went and stayed with his wife for about four days and he did not return. They had plans for him—that if they catch him, they will kill him. We waited aaa . . ., we did not see him at home. It became a missing person's case. Then we sounded the drum and set out to look for him at his wife's place. When we got there, all their houses were on fire."

Ama: "You put fire in them?"

Egya Yiiyii: "Their mud houses, we put fire in them."

Ama: "Why?"

Bedu: "Because they killed our person."

Egya Nako: "They had our person, and when we inquired, they said they did not know where he was."

Ama: "Where was the man?"

Egya Nako: "He was dead. They killed him and buried him, and we did not find his body even till today."

Ama: "Did you burn the building?"

Egya Yiiyii: "No. Our children went and did that thing."

Egya Nako: "We did not send them. We sounded the drum and sounding the drum is serious matter. The police came so everyone had to run." [The police did not choose between the guilty and innocent, did not discriminate, so they all ran. ɔbofoɔ nnim aboa yarefoɔ, "The hunter does not recognize (care about) a sick animal."]

Egya Nako: "It was serious matter. If we were still drinking like we did in the past, we would have drunk a lot today."

I appreciated this story because besides Nana's explanations, I had not been able to learn about the contexts for Kormantse Asafo *ndwom*. Thus far, much of what I had witnessed took place at funeral celebrations at Cape Coast. Could the same songs be performed for the dead at funerals as they would be for a drowned victim, a missing person, or a murdered person? From this brief discussion about the same song being used for a missing Kormantse man at Anloga town as it would be used for a dead person, I concluded that the same songs could be used in different contexts, including a loss to the community.

The Kormantse Five performed about fifteen songs without the accompaniment of the up to four drums and one bell that usually accompanied their Asafo song performances. All the songs were declamatory and moved freely with the intensity of the embodied caller, whose articulations and projections set the pace and mood for the performance. Lines were repeated; some of the refrains were exact repetitions; others had subtle variations. Most of the songs had the single melody by the embodied caller and a "sweetened" response in thirds by the embodied responders. Simultaneous doing in four related parts, like in other music, was never used.

All the songs ended with a halt, a stop, an exclamation that testified to the intention of the words they sang—a period. They sounded rowdy and loud. Though I had heard some of the songs before, they were different due to the number of people performing, the add-ons, the cries and shouts, the projections of the lead singer, and the sweetener. The melodic and rhythmic character of the songs was shaped by the tonality and rhythm of the Fante Akan language. At one point, the "one who sweetens" gave out a high-pitched sound like a siren, "waaaahhhhh, waaaahhh, waaaaaah . . ." continuously while the others sang, creating a heavy sound that roughened the edges of the songs and their thick texture, increasing its density. When I asked why the "waaaahhhhh, waaaahhh, waaaaaah," he smiled and said he was "fanning the song" and "praising it." "It makes it sweet," he mused. Rough is sweet, *pá-pá*!

What Egya Afεdze and Me Nyame Said: "It's Like Rapping, Rap"

About three weeks later, on August 5, I had a brief exchange with two men at the King's palace. One was the town's council member, Me Nyame; the other was the King's junior brother, Afεdze. I had gone to seek permission to see their Asafo flags, something I had been asking for some time. While I waited, we discussed the importance of Asafo in Kormantse society. Afεdze intimated that Asafo is a spirit that moves and breathes. They cited and sang a song that they said embodied the spirit of Asafo.

Ama: "Who wrote the song?"
Egya Me Nyame: "They don't write it."
Ama: "But who wrote the words?"
Egya Afεdze: "Right now, they play it on record."
Ama: "But who started the song?"
Egya Me Nyame: "Our Elders brought it. Our Nananom Elders, but they play it on record these days."
Ama: "What year? Can you say it was 19 this or 19 that?"
Egya Me Nyame: "No, no, no, no, no, except for Kwesi Mprah." [By Kwesi Mprah, he was referring to Teacher Hammond, Nana.]
Ama: "You said Kwesi Mprah? Why is that?"
Egya Afεdze: "He is the one who writes things down. Now we have modern Ghana and we used to have Gold Coast Ghana. The drum, when they play it, it means everyone is serious. Nobody is going to have the time to write this or that. Everyone is doing something."
Egya Me Nyame: "Wɔ kenkan aaa . . ." [They read aaa . . .].
Ama: "Kenkan, what does it mean? Do they read from a paper?" [Kenkan in the Akan language means "to read." I did not see the

connection, especially since I had not seen any of the performers read from a script.]

Egya Me Nyame: "They don't read a paper."

Ama: "Is it a book that they read?"

Egya Me Nyame: "They don't read a paper."

Egya Afɛdze "It is like rapping."

Ama: "Rapping?"

Egya Afɛdze: "Yes."

Egya Me Nyame: "The person who starts the song goes around the song and embellishes it until he gets to the actual ndwom."

Ama: "So, the person who kenkan, what do they call him, nwomtonyi or what?

Egya Afɛdze: "So, like me, if I start a song, I will kenkan, then you see that someone else will add to it."

Egya Me Nyame: "Another person, based on his knowledge of the event, what has been told to him by his Elders, he adds to it."

Egya Afɛdze: "They all sing it. Sometimes what someone's Ancestor has told him. We are all one people. If your Elder has shared some with you, mine will also share some with me. What has been told to you is different from what has been told me. They exchange all this before the actual song. He adds to what I am doing; another will also add to it. That is how it is. So, everyone has something in his mind that when someone raises a song, he sings it. When it gets to a certain point, then he will add what he knows or has been told. That is how Asafo ndwom is. It goes ge-ge-gege, ge-ge-gege."

Ama: "You said rap. Why rap?"

Egya Afɛdze: "Yes. They rap. Something like when they [rappers] are singing the song, they say a lot of things aaa . . . until they sing the song; if someone is on the side, you see, he too will sing the song. You see, he will be saying a lot of things, then you know this is the song he wants to sing.

Ama: "How is that like rapping?"

Egya Me Nyame: "He is making an analogy. It is a comparison. It is also speaking in proverbs, kasa twii, insulting, provoking, insinuating."

Egya Afɛdze: "You see, rap too they do that. They insinuate and insult other rappers. They are using kasa twii to insult their foes."

The comparison with rap or rapping caught me off guard because I had not considered it at all. Usually when people say something is rap or rapping, they are usually comparing it to an aspect of rap for its style or the syntax. People say the flow of some poetry is like rap because of rhyming or the way it is delivered.

According to the book *Hip Hoptionary*, rap "is a verbal spot—word play competition . . . [it] tells a story or offers a message through lyrics, usually over music" (Westbrook 2002), and according to the *Encyclopedia of Rap and Hip-Hop Culture*, rap is defined as the "spoken element of Hip Hop and its most elementary level, rap is speaking to the beat of music" (Bynoe 2006). Cheryl Keyes defines rapping as "talking in rhythm over music (1996, 225). From what I heard about Kormantse Asafo *ndwom*, delivering text over drumming or live *ndwom*, and the brief description the gentlemen gave of kenkan, some of the similarities and the analogy were becoming clear. Their explanation that before the lead singer starts the song, he will kenkan aaa . . . and give background to the song before the chorus answers seemed to share some elements with rap. That sometimes while the lead singer is performing his kenkan, another singer will pull out his kenkan based on stories that his Elders have told him, rapping back and forth, made the comparison even stronger.

Though I did not think about this then, singers going back and forth with kenkan in an embodied call and response, or "exchanging kenkan," is very similar to how rap artists "trade phrases." According to Cheryl Keyes, trading phrases is "the exchange of rhyming couplets of phrases between emcees in a percussive, witty fashion, and in synchrony with the DJ's music" (1996, 230). She cites the performance of the rap song "Freedom" by the Furious Five, the group that set the stage for rapping in rhythms to music (231). The exchange between the different artists in Public Enemy's "Don't Believe the Hype," and many other rap songs in which artists go back and forth exchanging snippets or inserting their narratives into the larger theme of the song, captures this style.

Egya Afɛdze and Me Nyame explained further that rap is also like *kasa twii*. *Kasa twii*, in the Akan language, literally means "speech that scratches or hurts." In the Ghanaian Akan language when we say, *obi akasa atwi wo*, it means the person has insulted you; the person has used words, proverbial or otherwise, against you, to antagonize, offend, or provoke you. "Signifyin'" came to mind as the gentlemen explained. Artists who employ signifyin' use indirect talk, code switching, metaphors, gestures, and metonyms to hurt, intimidate, and antagonize. Like signifying, *kasa twii*, in Asafo *ndwom*, functions as a critical rhetorical strategy in which singers mock, belittle, or confront another person/group, a foe. The singer(s) can also use it to gloat and brag about their qualities and wealth. Hip-hop artists such as Public Enemy, Kendrick Lamar, Tupac, Cardi B (Okurr), Nicki Minaj (the Queen), and Megan Thee Stallion use figurative and implicative speech, tropes of marking, loud talking, testifying, and calling out their intended target.[16]

Kasa twii or *nsaa* (chapter 1) is like a specific genre of rap called *diss tracks*. A diss track is a song in which the artist argues, insults, teases, or expresses her or his "beef" with another artist or artists. When two artists crash, they can argue in person, through social media, or most often through their music. Diss tracks are the worst things to happen to artists because in those songs, a rival usually exposes the other's weaknesses. Everything artists try to hide from the public, their pretense or soft spots, could be used in the diss track, exposing them to their fans and making them vulnerable to other attacks. J. Cole's "1985" is directed at all young and new rappers like Lil Pump, Lil Xan, 21 Savage, Young Thug, and others who think they have the integrity to diss him. Drake's "Charged Up" and "Back-to-Back," were aimed at Meek Mill; while Lil Kim dissed Nicki Minaj with "Black Friday."

There are also rebuttal diss tracks where artists who are instigated make a song to strike back at their opponents, sometimes leading to a back-and-forth "kasa twii" between artists, such as when Cannibis released "Second Round K.O." against LL Cool J, and LL released "4,3,2,1" back at Cannibis. These beefs can result in physical violence—even death. Drake's "Back-to-Back" (2015), Snoop Dogg's "Pimp Slapped," Nicki Minaj's "Roman's Revenge," NAS' "Ether," Roxanne Shante's "The Roxanne's Wars," Remy Ma's "shEther," and Common's "I Used to Love Her" are illustrative of this style of rap.

In their provocative song, "*Yɛkɔr Akyemfo nyimpa nnyi hɔ*" (example 37 ⏸ 🔊), Kormantse Asafo "humiliate" their enemy by asserting their strength and courage against their foes. The tension between Kormantse and Akyemfo (Saltpond), their neighbor, dates back over a century. Some of the friction was caused by where each of the two towns fish in the Atlantic Ocean. Saltpond has been using their nets on the beach past Great Kormantine and up Abandze (Little Kormantine). Furthermore, the land from the fishing boundary pillar to the stream (Zerma) near Kormantse is claimed by both Saltpond and Kormantse. The tension got to a point where Kormantine fisherfolk destroyed the boats of Akyemfo fisherfolk. Thus, there was a request to build a fishing boundary pillar between the two towns. In an April 25, 1908, report by the commissioner for Central Province signed by E. C. Elliot, a tentative one was arranged but did not seem satisfactory. The boundary pillar was eventually constructed and still stands today. Other conflicts resulted because of riots. According to a report dated January 21, 1891, ten prisoners at Akyemfo Saltpond were convicted of rioting at Cormantine.[17] Thus, in the song, Kormantse Asafo insist that they went looking for their foes, but the latter had fled. Their foes' settlement had been deserted, only ten heads were left. The inference here is that their foes are cowards. Many diss tracks taunt and tease their targets as cowards who either run or avoid confrontation.

How did these Elders in this fishing town on the coast of Ghana know about rap and rapping, enough to make such remarkable comparisons? They were not talking about hiplife, the Ghanaian version of hip-hop/rapping; rather, they referred specifically to rap, a musical style whose origins remain beyond the Black Atlantic. How do we account for the similarities between a musical style in two seemingly disparate worlds? Is Asafo, with its declamatory and intoned speech over drumming and whose singers kenkan aaaa . . ., a progenitor of rap music, whose emcees showcase verbal dexterity? Indeed, rap is on a performance continuum in which the Africanist aesthetic continues to reflect musical, dance, and oral practices that resemble those (*jeliya* tradition in Senegambia and *oriki* in Nigeria) in West and Central Africa, the source of the Atlantic slave trade. They both share the "Processual mode of expressivity that privilege the negotiation of the self (and community) in the moment through a complex rhythmic timing, verbal or non-verbal rhetorical strategies, and multiple layers of meaning that draw from its socio-cultural context and its audience (and performers)" (Ousmare 2011, 12).[18] Rap is a part of a larger diasporic/Black Atlantic performative discourse that uses the power of the word and music to accomplish specific agendas.

What Egya Kobena Bedu, the Lead Singer, Sang and Said: "Kenkan Makes It Sweet!"

I sat alone with Egya Kobena Bedu, the embodied lead singer, at the seaside on August 6, 2017. He is the one who raised all the Kormantse songs I had heard thus far by virtue of his experience and singing ability, his knowledge of the songs, and his ability to recall the words. The structure of the song and the duration of the performance depended on how long he kept calling the songs, the length of the kenkan, and the variations he introduced, all of which varied from one performance to the other. He plays an important role in Kormantse Asafo performance. Our Elders say, *Wopε danka mu ahunu a, wokɔ deε yεsene no na wompae mu*, "If you want to see the inside of a gourd/danka drum, you go to where it is carved, we don't split it open." *Pinkyε onyina, na wo pinkyε onyina a, na wo hunu n'adukuro.* (Ampem, 148). "Go nearer a silk-cotton tree, when you go nearer it, it is thus you see its buttresses." So, I went to Egya Bedu.

At first, when Egya Bedu suggested we meet at the seaside, I thought it was a good idea. As a fisherman, the seaside was also his home, since he spends most of his time there.[19] It was convenient for him to meet there. I also thought he preferred the seaside because it was a "safe space." Yet, the roaring sea and its crashing waves made it difficult to hear Egya Bedu's answers and singing. I was also distracted by the children running around and playing. People who knew Egya Bedu stopped by to greet him and asked him questions, thereby interrupting and slowing down our progress. I must admit, sometimes these "interruptions" contributed to my learning, as I share later.

> Ama: "Please, the song that you sing, where did you learn it from? Who taught you?"
>
> Egya Bedu: "When they played Asafo, I stood there; I was about twelve years old like your son. I would stand there and listen; I listened aaaa . . . and then one day, when they were playing Asafo, I started to pick up [raise] the song. After I heard it for so long, I absorbed it. I did that for about three months. One day when they were playing, I was standing in the back. When they play Asafo, they arrange benches, one here, one here, and one there [in a U-shape]. And the person raising the song would stand in the middle. So, while I was standing in the back, the Elders asked me to come to the center and sing. So, it is not like somebody taught me; it was like the spirit . . ."
>
> Ama: "You say 'spirit'?"
>
> Egya Bedu: "It is not like anybody taught me; it is like a gift; You understand? It is not a situation where someone taught me. I can sing it very well. There are lots of very good songs. Many songs are there."

Within Asafo tradition, as in many *ndwom* traditions in Africa, one does not need special training to become a singer, either in the chorus or as a lead singer. The skill is acquired through enculturation, repetitive exposure, and walking with the Elders. One must be present during Asafo performances, pay attention, and listen to the different songs as they are performed. It helps also to consult with an Elder who can teach the context and specifics of the song texts. Though it could happen, the art is not passed down from father to son or hereditary as among the *jeliya* tradition of the Senegambian regions, where learning through apprenticeship is also key to the artist's training.[20] Sometimes, it is also believed that the talent is a gift from the Gods and Ancestors, as Egya Bedu noted.[21]

After this brief introduction about his biography and Asafo *ndwom*, I played back the songs from the first session in December 2016 and the other session I had with him and the four men—the Kormantse Five. I asked about the lyrics, the structure of the song, and the meaning of the songs.

> Ama: "Please let me ask you, how do you sing the song? How do you start it? Do you sing it directly or do you say something before you begin?"
> Egya Bedu: "That is the kenkan."
> Ama: "What is kenkan?" [I wanted to confirm what the two gentlemen had shared with me the day before.]
> Egya Bedu: "When I am going to begin a song, I have to say some things that will help the Asafommba responders know that this is the song that I am going to sing. If you just pick it up and sing, maybe the person who hears it will not know it, unless I start to kenkan. When I kenkan, you know it is this song that I am going to sing. The moment I pick this song, then you know this is the matter that I am going to say. That is how it is. Some of it you must kenkan; some too, if it is a serious time, then you sing it very fast. Some of them, if you don't kenkan and you sing it, it would not be sweet."
> Ama: "So, the kenkan is not like a book that you are reading?"
> Egya Bedu: "No. It is part of the song. If you are going to sing and you do not kenkan, if they answer, it won't be well. You understand?"

Kenkan are narrations of the story or past events that the soloist or leader improvises before the actual song and before the chorus responds. They weave poetry, sounds, and proverbs and borrow texts from the main song. As my high school music teacher, Mr. Awotwi Thompson, explained, "Kenkan are like recitatives to an aria, providing the context for the upcoming song or performance" (Thompson, July 18, 2018, Saltpond, Ghana).[22] The revelation that the structure of Asafo song in a Ghanaian fishing town shared elements with a western European music style challenged the idea of "Other" that is often assigned to the *ndwom* of Africa and a useful critique of "Otherness."

The lead singer kenkan aaaa ... gives background to the song before the chorus responds. In the provocative song, *Nkowa no wɔkɔ* ("The Servants Have Fled"), the soloist begins with the call, inserts the title of the song, moves to the kenkan, then the chorus by Asafommba. Bedu demonstrated the kenkan and actual song in his usual evocative, raw, and sweet style like this (one possible version of the song):

C:	*Nkowa no wɔkɔ ei Tuafo mba ei* 🔊
Kenkan¹:	*Koakoa n'moa dɔ nsu enyi dzi Akɔ-na-aba, akɔ-na-aba yɛ mbusu*
C:	*Yɛahwewhɛ ahwehwɛ a yennhu hɔn*
	Yɛakɔ siwdo yennhu hɔn
	Yɛkɔr atwer mu a, wɔ hyɛ hɔ
Kenkan¹:	*Akɔmfo adadaw wɔamma obiara annkyerɛ hɔn akɔm*
Kenkan²:	*Wonya abɛbrɛsɛ a wɔfrɛ Tekyi*
Ans:	*Yee Tekyi, yee Tekyi ei*
	Nkowa no wɔkɔ!
C:	The cowards/servants have gone, Tuafo children
K¹:	Crows hover on the sea
	Back and forth, hovering is dangerous
C:	We have searched everywhere we can't find them
	We have gone to their headquarters they are not there
K¹:	An old priest did not allow anyone to teach her dancing
K²:	When they get trouble, they call us
A:	Yee—Tekyi
	The servants/cowards have gone!

The song describes who or what a coward is. Cowards are those who provoke a fight and then run or hide. Then it goes on to the first kenkan, using proverbs to compare cowards to crows that go back and forth over the sea; The lead describes cowards as those who, after several search expeditions, are found hiding on a ladder (lines four and five).[23] As exemplified in this song, sometimes multiple kenkan can be inserted midway through the song

TABLE 7.3. Some Kormantse Asafo Performance Structures

Performance Structure	Who	What
Structure 1	Lead	Call
	Chorus	Response
Structure 2	Lead	Kenkan
	Lead	Call
	Chorus	Response
Structure 3	Lead	Kenkan 1
	Member	Kenkan 2
	Lead	Kenkan 3
	Lead	Call
	Chorus	Response

where the lead singer exchanges kenkan with another singer in a back-and-forth manner, trading kenkan, like rap artists "trade phrases." (Table 7.3). As Keyes explains it, it is "the exchange between emcees in percussive, witty fashion in synchrony with the DJ's music" (1996, 230). The chorus restates the theme of the song as their answer, the only time they sing and ends the song.

The structure of the performance is not fixed and could change in other presentations.

I was finally "walking" with Asafo songs and beginning to appreciate their performance practices. ɔnantefoɔ sene oni ne ɔse asɛm, "The walker knows more than her mother and father." It was getting too sweet.

At the time of this meeting, Egya Bedu was a fifty-four-year-old fisherman. He called most of the songs at the first recording session with a group in December. We sat down in the sand and started chatting. According to him, he is a *nwomtofo* and the other group members are *agyedofo* or Asafommba; they answer when he calls the songs. Everyone calls him "Uncle Bedu." He considers himself the best singer/soloist at Kormantse.

Ama: "So, when you saw them play Asafo, how was it?"
Uncle Bedu: "They don't play it by heart or recklessly [basa-basa]. It is culture. It is like when they play the drum, then it means someone has died. Or something has happened."
Ama: "Do they have drums with which they play Asafo?"

Uncle Bedu: "They are four."

Ama: "What are they called?"

Uncle Bedu: "Dabɔ kyen. All the four, that is the name. The set of four drums is called Dabɔ kyen because the drumheads are skins from the dabɔ deer. One is ampae, dɛnkyerɛma, and the one that talks. The big one. That one that they played when we performed for you the first time. That is the big one. That is the one that they brought out the other day . . . Dabɔ kyen. It is the one that hangs around the neck that you took a picture of the other day."

Ama: "Is there a dawur?"

Uncle Bedu: "Dawur is part of it. The day that you came, had the Asafommba played, you would have seen all the drums that I have mentioned and the dawur; they are all part of it." [Ah, akɔm kɔ! The good old days are gone.]

Two days later, on August 8, I went back to the seaside to meet with Bedu. The seaside is where most Kormantse action happens during the day, so I walked there almost every day. Men gather and mend their nets and boats, discuss politics, argue over trivial matters, or play board games; women socialize, trade cooked food, fruits, and vegetables on tables; women spread cloth on the sand and relax; children play soccer, run up and down, giggling and feeling safe. All these activities occur while the sea rolls, thunders, moans, and crashes its waves at the mercy of the sand. The smell of raw, fried, and smoked fish fills the air. The sounds from a nearby pub add to the soundscape of this space. When the wind blows, it lifts the sand, swirls it in the air, and clouds the atmosphere, sometimes getting into people's eyes. Anyone who wants to have a peek at Kormantse life and society must visit the seaside.

I always started my walk to the Kormantse seaside from a particular spot on the Accra-Takoradi Highway. I walked through the local market, whose entrepreneurs had come to know me enough to point out changes in the sea level or ask about my search. Sometimes, I stopped to purchase fresh fruits and vegetables, for a petty chat, or the latest gossip. They also taught me how to prepare the staple dishes, *gari* or *ɛtsew* and *ntsitsii*, fresh fish stew.[24] Women are the primary economists in this space. They determine the price of the items and whether any new traders can join the space. Like the women at Makola who control the markets at Accra, this was their space:

stockbrokers. They also have a banking and loan system, *susu*, through which they collect and circulate money for the members of the cooperative.

From the market, I walked between a series of houses, three of which are lineage houses displaying images of their first Ancestresses. Right before the dusty path turned to sand, the smell of raw and smoked fish filled the air and one's nostrils, a sign that I was getting closer to the sea; popular music blasted from a nearby pub. I always wondered, when I passed by, if clients would patronize it if they played Asafo *ndwom* at the pub instead of the popular Hi-Life and hiplife.

Since this path was familiar, I developed a "deeper, non-cognitive, sensual form of appreciation for the terrain, experienced through the feet and legs, promoting adaptation to the environment through a heightened sense of corporal balance" (Edensor 2008, 132). I traveled this path so much in the daytime that I could walk it in the dark and still find my way around. *Dee yɛni no awia no, sɛ yɛnsɔ kanea nhwe n'anim anadwo*, "When you know someone in the daytime, you don't need light to look at her face at night." The walk required a rhythm that is full of variation, long, legato walks or short punctuated ones, structured at times, or improvised depending on what I was carrying, the weather, the temperature, the shoes I had on, who and how many people I met on the way. It also required that I notice and acknowledge the people, an audience, whose houses I walked by and whose kitchens I trod through. I had learned from Nana, who advised, "The earth does not belong to you. So, you shouldn't walk on it prim-prim-prim, prim. You must take your time and walk. If you walk prim-prim-prim, then it means the earth belongs to you. It does not. So, when you are walking, you must take your time and step, step. The land holds peoples' dreams and memories." I stepped with care also because, though walking broadens the mind, *ɔnantefoɔ hunu amane*, "the walker suffers," the walker could trip and fall.

Over the weeks and months, walking to the seaside became a performance, a "place-ballet" (Seamon 1980). I came up with a way of walking and engaging it, talking with it and to myself as I meandered between the houses. I developed a relationship with the land. Of course, if I stepped foolishly and did not consider the rhythms and curves, I could trip, slip, or fall. Starting from a place of familiarity enabled me to relatively get my feet on the ground, gain some level of confidence and allow me to engage with the town, its landscape, and people rather quickly.[25] Phenomenologist Tim Ingold's observation that we inhabit spaces through active participation with and contribution to the world is instructive. Walking bridges person and place by providing a unique opportunity to belong to that environment (2010).

As I trudged through the sand to meet Uncle Bedu and thought about what I had learned about Asafo *ndwom* that day, I sensed that something was wrong. It was Tuesday, when fisherfolk do not go out to sea. It is believed, among fisherfolk, that Nana Bosompo, the Spirit of the Sea, rests on Tuesdays and would reveal herself or seize anyone who went out to sea on that day. On this day, however, the seaside was unusually quiet; there was something different about the stillness, the mood of the people and environment. I learned that a twenty-two-year-old fisherman had drowned the night before at Cape Coast, about thirty kilometers east of Kormantse. His boat came back on its side without him. "We are in mourning," someone remarked as I walked up and stood by a group of men seated on a bench; some of them played a board game, while others sat idly.

> Ama: "Did you play the drum?" [A chorus of voices gave different answers.]
> Responder 1: "We have prayed at the seaside."
> Responder 2: "That was our Elders."
> Responder 3: "They have all gone."
> Responder 2: "As for us, we don't know how to do it."
> Responder 3: "We did not learn."
> Responder 1: "We used to have all those things."

I learned that they did not and could not invoke the Ancestors by pouring alcohol onto Mother Earth because it was considered fetish. Furthermore, the family of the deceased had decided they would not invoke the spirits.

What happened to all the songs that these warriors once sang when someone drowned? In the past, by this time, the Asafo master drummer would have patrolled along the seaside with the *gyina hɔ hwɛ* master drum, played proverbial passages to coax the Spirit of the Sea to relinquish the body of the deceased. The sea would have delivered the body then. This would have been a perfect occasion to see and hear the *ɔkyerɛma* lead drummer in action; it would have been an appropriate time to experience Asafo songs about rescuing a victim of drowning. However, since the invocation had not been made, the body was missing in the sea. Someone added that the sea was too high, so they were waiting for it to come down. They will get on a boat and try to find him.

Indeed, the sea was very high, rolling and tumbling, throwing huge waves onto the shore, flexing, furious. Each time, the waves got louder and stronger and came closer to the houses, rocking the few boats that were still moored close to the shore. The sea was gray and dark in some areas and swollen at its seams—angry and ready to drown the entire world. She had been defiled with a dead body: a curse. It was terrifying. The fishermen had moved all their boats farther away from the shore and closer to their houses. Some of the boats had already felt Nana Bosompo's fury and had been crashed into pieces, parts floating on the sea.

I wanted to sing the song that I had learned from Nana about rescuing a victim of drowning, the refrain of which states, *Nyimpa atɔ nsu mu a wɔ nnyi no ma hɛn* ("Someone has fallen in the water, deliver him to us"). Our Elders say, *Abɔfra hunu ne nsa hohoro a, ɔne mpanin didi*, "When a child learns how to clean her hands well, she eats with the Elders." Have I cleaned my hands well enough to eat with the Elders? Have I spent enough time and learned enough about Asafo *ndwom* to sing it? Could I? Should I? The Asafo that once saved their lives; the Asafo that brought pride to their fathers and grandfathers, mothers and grandmothers, their Deities; the Asafo whose vitality they experienced in their youth; the Asafo in which they participated as *dawur* player, flag dancer, drummer, lead singer, chorus, or captain; the Asafo that helped coax Nana Bosompo—all this is becoming a thing of the past, and the men seemed to have lost control and could not help it. The newspaper that once announced someone's death, their medium that announced an impending danger, had been silenced. I understood now why the elderly man at our first recording session lamented, "We are dying, dying." Even the dead could not be coaxed by Asafo.

How could I help sustain this dying tradition? What right do I have as a searcher to insist that the group of men, their society, sustain their traditions? Could the United Nation's many resolutions on intangible cultural products help save a tradition in this small fishing town? Who would implement them? At one point, I had thought about contacting the UN body at Accra about Kormantse Asafo. As I stood by and watched the men move cards on the board, I reflected on some of the attempts by Kormantse Elders and other Fante communities to sustain Asafo. I considered UNESCO Sustainability Development Initiatives, Article 5 specifically; UNESCO's Convention on Cultural Diversity (2005); the Ghana Cultural Policy (1975 and 2004); models by Schippers (2015) and Titon (2009); and other attempts to help curate and encourage creativity that could help sustain the Asafo tradition.[26] Titon suggests that the best reliant strategies come from within the community rather than from above (2009b).

I thought about a discussion I had months earlier with the King's spokesperson and Nana about reviving Asafo. The spokesperson was skeptical:

> One thing that is killing us is the God worshipping that has come here. One thing that is killing us is the church. The church is plenty. We can find someone who can play the drum and someone who can sing and as you are here, we will perform. But when they leave here, the church will call them. That is the disease we have here. The pastors have destroyed our Kormantse. Young, young boys sing them very well, that if we say, we are going to raise it (Asafo), it won't be a joke. Our *Frankaatunyi* [flag dancer], when he is dancing the flag, it is no joke. But because of the church if you go and do it, they will preach against you. They will come to your house; sometimes, they will call you inside the church. They will tell you that you have done worldly things. Meanwhile when they came, they used Asafo to protect the town. (Okyeame Kweku Suapim, personal conversation, March 15, 2017, Kormantse, Ghana)

Is the church the only reason? *Abrewa hwe ase a ɔde hyɛ ne poma*, "When an old woman falls down, she blames her walking stick." I hummed the refrain to the Asafo song that Nana sang.

> *Nyimpa atɔ nsu mu a wɔ nnyi no ma hɛn*
> (Someone has fallen in the water, deliver him for us)

After humming the refrain several times, I started to trudge away.

> People are dying
> Nobody seems to care
> Men
> Playing cards
> Apathy
> 4 men went to sea
> 3 returned
>
> Ahhh!
> Young man!
> Who will cry
> Play Asafo for you

Brother, husband, father, son
A student, friend, or uncle perhaps
Fisherman
Alone in the belly of *ɛpopɔn* Nana Bosompo
Atlantic Ocean
Pouring her fury onto you
Rolling, tumbling, tossing, growling
Furious
Defiled

Kormantse Bentsir
Has it come to this
Ahhh!
Asafo
Akɔm kɔ, aka sukuu!
Mysticism has given way to Western schooling
Cry
Cry . . . y
Asafo (Journal Entry, August 8, 2017)

America the Beautiful, Got Me Trauma Ghosted

I walked to another side of the seaside. A group of 150+ beautiful men had assembled, mending their nets, patching their damaged boats, assessing their loss, and strategizing. A gorgeous woman about sixty years old, a true *ahoɔfɛ* beauty, sat behind her tray of *ahwer* sugarcane under the coconut trees, next to several damaged boats, next to men whom she hoped would buy her *ahwer*. Others, with trays on their heads, peddled their valuable merchandize. I bought three stalks to support the *ahwer* business. I mingled among, talked with, and listened to the group of beautiful Black men.

>
> Black men together
> Gathered
> Talking loud Laughing loud
> Bonding
> Supporting
> Walking with beauty
> With permission from No body
> Mending nets

> Boats
> Strategizing
> Home

Walking while thinking . . . once in a while I scanned the area nervously to see if any white person was watching the beautiful Black men. I looked out for whoever might be watching, policing, accusing, or trying to harass them. Any of these beautiful Black men could have been Philando Castille, Alton Sterling, Eric Garner, Danté Price, Derrick Jones, and the many other unarmed black men killed by police officers. My body was on edge. My heart started to beat fast. The result of my experiences as a Ghanaian woman, a Black mother of Black children, living in America, has me "trauma ghosted,"[27] that recurrent or pervasive sense that danger is around the corner, or something terrible is going to happen because you are Black. My memory walked to the day my son asked, "Will they kill me too, when I grow up Mama?" Muscles tensed, heart sunk, eyes twitched. Ghanaian Akan Elders say, *Nea ɔwɔ aka no suro sonsono*, "She who has been bitten by a snake is afraid of a worm." My body was on edge. The effects of "white-body supremacy" that lived and breathed in my own body[28] had walked with me home, Ghana, Kormantse. Feeling connected and disconnected at once. *What is walking in America, the beautiful, doing to me, my senses, creativity, mental health, body? The Dilemma of a Ghost.*[29] *ɔnantefoɔ sene oni ne ɔse asɛm*, "The walker knows more than her mother and father." But *ɔnantefoɔ na ohunu amane*, "The walker also suffers."

> Flash back
> America the beautiful
> Where the proud sons and daughters of Mama Africa
> Are Orphaned
> Devalued
> Criminalized
> The New Jim Crow
> 13th
> Police patrolling
> Red, blue, and white lights
> Flashing
> Intimidating
> Laws against gathering of Black bodies
> Policing Black bodies
> Decentered Black bodies in America

America the beautiful
Where walking while Black
Jogging while Black
Gets you killed
Black bodies can't breathe
Akokɔba sa kyerɛ akroma sɛn ara a, ɛnyɛ no fɛ,
"No matter how gracefully the chick dances, it does not please the hawk" (Ampem, 23).
Racial battle fatigued
Trauma ghosted
Things have fallen apart-oooo
Gaps!
What will the orphan do
Agyanka bɛyɛ dɛn
A royal in one place, may find herself enslaved in another place
Baabi dehyeɛ yɛ baabi dɔnkɔ
Trauma ghosted
Cry . . . y

Unbelonging
Child of the new African Diaspora
Back and forth
Back and forth
Diasporic intimacies

Flash forward
This is *not* America
This is Kormantse
Home
The Soul of Black folk
The Center
150+++
Bebree kwa
Black men can assemble
Talk
Gather
Bond
Console

> Walk freely
> Breathe
> With permission from No body
> Mend nets
> Strategize
> Black Lives Matter here
> εpopɔn Nana Bosompo
> Protects
> Even in her fury
> Gods will trouble the waters
> *Pa, puum, pu-puum, pa*
> *Pu-puum, pa-pa*
> Will they kill me too, Mama
> Breathe Ama
> Breathe
> This is *not* America
> *This* is Kormantse

I trudged to the seaside and stood at the edge of the sea, then paced back and forth, pretending to be the Asafo lead drummer with the *gyina hɔ hwε* drum. *Pa, puum, pu-puum, puum, pu-puum, pa-pa, pum, pu-pa-pa, pu-pa, pu-pa-pa, pu-pa, pu-pu, pu-pu-pa, pu-pa-pa-pa, pu-tum pa pa,* invoking and pleading with Nana Bosompo to deliver the body of the drowned fisherman. The waves crashed, rolled, tumbled, and splashed onto my feet, washing them. I dug my toes into the heavy, wet sand to stay grounded. Pacing up and down the coast while thinking, I stepped on a seashell—stabbed my foot. I hobbled along. *Ko-ko-gya, ko-ko-gya, ko-ko-gya, ko-ko-gya.* Thinking 150+ Black men. *Baabi dehyeε yε baabi dɔnkɔ. Ko-ko-gya.* What will my feet remember? This is *not* America. *Ko-ko-.* . .

I stopped by Nana's house and accompanied him to his farm. On our walk down the Accra-Takoradi Highway, I asked him about the drowning victim. Amidst his telling me more about the role of Asafo in the past, I sang the refrain to the song:

> *Nyimpa atɔ nsu mu a wɔ nyi no ma hεn*
> (Someone has fallen in the water, deliver him for us)

"*Naa-nyin! Naa-nyin!*" ("That's it. That's it"), he giggled. "We have forgotten about all these songs," he lamented.

Who Is a Good Nwomtonyi Singer?

In the evening, I went back to the seaside. Uncle Bedu was there waiting. We sat under a different coconut tree. I asked what it meant to be a good singer.

> Uncle Bedu: "A good singer must be able to articulate and have a carrying voice. She must know the meaning of songs; know how the drum rhythms match with specific songs."[30]
>
> Ama: "When we say someone can sing a song, what does it mean? What does the person have to do to show that she can sing? 'She can sing; she can sing.' What does that mean?"
>
> Uncle Bedu: "It depends on how she comports herself for praise."
>
> Ama: "What does she have to do to deserve such praise?
>
> Uncle Bedu: "You see, there are plenty of songs in the town and lots of people can sing them. When someone sings it and another person sings it, and when the people in the town say 'Ooo . . . this person sings better than anyone else,' then you know who sings well."
>
> Ama: "Why will they say one person sings better than another person?"
>
> Uncle Bedu: "Then it means she learned the song better than the others."
>
> Ama: "She learned it better how?"

By this time, another gentleman, Paapa, had joined us and was listening to the conversation.

> Paapa: "It means that the person learned it well; it means that when she sings the songs, she explains them very well. It is like being able to explain English. It is like the person has learned it and is able to explain it. So, they would say, 'Let's find Uncle Bedu. Bedu is the one who can sing the song and explain it.'"
>
> Uncle Bedu: "The Asafo song, you see, if I am walking and I hear someone sing it, I will go and stand there and listen. If the person does not sing it well, I will tell him that it is not sung like that." [He gave an example of a boy who sang a song. According to him, the boy did not sing it well, so he corrected him. Before concluding that a good singer is one who can sing the words correctly and understand its meaning, I asked for other qualities of a good singer.]
>
> Ama: "It also depends on the person's voice. What else?"

Uncle Bedu: "The voice is not part of it. All it is, is that you have to sing the song correct for people."

Ama: "Voice is not part of it? But doesn't the person have to sing so that we can hear what she is saying?"

Uncle Bedu: "Yes."

Ama: "So, what happens if you know the song, but your voice does not carry?"

Paapa: "You see, if someone is singing, and the person's voice does not carry, then someone with a stronger voice will pick it up . . ."

Uncle Bedu: "If I you are singing it correct, like I am singing and my voice does not carry, and he can sing like me, he [Paapa] can pick it up and take it high."

This is probably what happened at the first recording session when an older gentleman, one of the Kormantse Five, started the first song. He must not have projected well, because after the first phrase, Uncle Bedu picked it up.

Ama: "So, the voice has to go up?"

Uncle Bedu: "Yes. The Asafo song, you see, if you don't let your voice go up, if the drum is playing and your voice does not go up, it is not sweet."

Ama: "It is not sweet?"

Sweetness, it appeared, was not limited to aesthetics, taste, or the texture and quality of sound. It also implied "volume," being able to project.

Uncle Bedu: "The last time when we performed with the sole drummer, you saw that the song went up paaa . . . [very loud]."

Ama: "Do women raise a song?"

Uncle Bedu: "Yes, some women can raise a song. Sone of them can sing fine. You see, when our town first came, they settled at the top first. So those up there, the women, some can sing it." [Paapa added he could not sing because he did not walk with the Elders like Bedu did.]

Paapa: "If you had to select, among the young men here, who can sing Asafo song and explain it, only this one [Bedu] can do it. Because his father was in the Asafo; also, when he was young, he used to walk with them. So, he learned it. In the morning, when they are deliberating an issue, he would go and sit there, so the thing *dwiri no.*"

Ama: "*Dwiri no*, what does that mean?"

Paapa: "It is like a Spirit has showered you; you have inherited the Spirit or energy or qualities of another person."

Uncle Bedu: "It is like what you are doing; when you die one day, your daughter will pick up those qualities or that energy. We say she has inherited or taken over your interests and qualities. It is like our Elders say, ɔkɔtɔ nwo anoma, "The crab does not give birth to a bird.""

Ama: "When some people sing, they say they exercise their voices. They learn how to place the notes and project it. They take lessons to breathe and develop the voice. Did you do something like that?"

Uncle Bedu: "No."

Ama: "Did you go to someone who said, 'Sing it like this: a a a a a a or hmmmmm . . . aaaaa . . .?'"

Uncle Bedu: "Nobody taught me like that."

Ama: "So where is the voice from? Who dwiri you with it?

Uncle Bedu: "Some of it is a gift. This one is a gift. Nobody taught me or showed me. It is a gift."

Ama: "I heard that four people went to sea. One did not come back?"

Uncle Bedu: "He has not come back."

Ama: "He has not come? They have not rescued him still?"

Uncle Bedu: "No."

Ama: "In the past, when something like this happened, they would have sounded the Asafo drum. Why don't they sound the Asafo?"

Uncle Bedu: "If you do, they will say, 'You go to church and you play Asafo. My uncle's son, he can Asafo very well. Nowadays, he does not play. He goes to church. And if he plays, they will say, 'You go to church, why are you playing Asafo?'"

Paapa: "Asafo is a Spirit. Wherever the person is, when the Asafo drum sounds, we use it to call the Spirit; they would call him. And the Elders, whoever is playing the drum, and the Safo captains would take alcohol, talk, walk, and pray along the edge of the sea. Today, it has all passed. He drowned around 7:00 p.m. last night and it is about 2:00 p.m. today and still he has not come back."

Uncle Bedu: "Young boy, very beautiful."

Ama: "Do you have a song that you would sing when someone drowns?"

Uncle Bedu: "If someone drowned, those who went to sea, even if someone could not sing, they would go and call someone in the town who could sing Asafo songs. And they sing and walk along the mouth of the sea and walk to town and walk back aaa. . . . ."

Ama: "What song would they sing? Don't you have a song that says Nyimpa atɔ nsu mu a wɔ nyi no ma hɛn?" [I wanted to verify the song and was eager to hear its rendition by the "caller of songs" himself. He may add some kenkan.]

Uncle Bedu: "No. the song, you see, we have songs that when you sing, we know what has happened. When I sing a song, even if someone has not drowned, if you are sleeping and you hear the song, you know someone has died. If you are sleeping aaa . . ., and you hear . . .

> ɔrokó e ɔannyɛ yie 🔊
> Yeee!
> ɔbanyin a ɔrokó e
> ɔannyɛ yie
> Osee!!! ɔannyɛ yie o
> ɔbanyin a ɔrokó e
> ɔannyɛ yie
> (She is fighting
> It did not succeed
> The man was fighting
> It failed)

. . . she is fighting. Then you know something has happened."

Ama: "Can you sing it again?"

While I was waiting for him to repeat the song, a man came by, pointed to a wound on his leg, and asked if I sold medicine. "Me, I am not a doctor." Paapa interjected, "She is not this . . . he thinks you sell medicine."

Ama: "I don't sell medicine."

Paapa: "She does not sell medicine!" [I must have missed something because Bedu smiled but did not say anything. His uncle waited for the gentleman to leave. I did not think to ask why the gentleman thought I sold medicine. Neither Uncle Bedu nor Paapa explained. Uncle Bedu sang the entire song, this time starting with "ɔdɛ nyew ooo, ɔroko e ɔannyɛ yie Yeee! yie o . . ."]

Uncle Bedu: "When you hear it, you know someone has died."

Ama: "Is that an Asafo song?"

Uncle Bedu: "Yes. Like the boy who has died like this, when he fell in the sea at night, in the past, those who were with him . . . even if I did not hear it till this morning, you would hear a song like this and you would know someone has died, and then we would start asking for details." [Bedu sang a second song, "Dua no ebu" (see chapter 4).] Uncle Bedu: "You would hear the women crying. Then you know someone has died."

Entangled Songs, Contesting Memories

I was surprised to hear Uncle Bedu say that they would not sing the song that Nana sang for me, "Nyimpa atɔ nsu mu," for a drowning victim, intimating that there were no specific songs for drowning victims. The two songs he performed, "ɔroko" and "Dua no ebu" were songs that could be sung to announce any death. Did he not know this song? I started to wonder whether Bedu did not know the song, or if it was a case of memory slippage. It turned out the event in the song occurred at Beseadze, a neighboring town. According to Nana, "They were going to cut grass and one person fell in the sea. They don't know how to swim like our people do, so our people went and pulled the person from the sea. He did not die. So, our people used it in a song; Beseadze is a town not too far from here."

The variations between what I learned from Nana and Uncle Bedu registered as my search entered its second year. By the thirteenth month into my search for Kormantse Asafo *ndwom* pasts, I was walking mostly with Nana Odum III and Kobena Bedu. Nana continued to sing Asafo songs, provide context, and help with writing and translating song texts. Bedu continued to sing songs, provide the context for them, and discuss their performance structure and style. This arrangement worked well, until the day Uncle Bedu commented that Nana has memory slips and was not singing the songs correctly.

Uncle Bedu and I were leaving the seaside after a session where he listened to the songs I had recorded of him and of Nana on an iPod. As we turned the corner toward the main street to Nana's house, he told me there were many songs he did not perform for me but would do so the next time we met. Then he stated that someone had commented that Nana had altered one of the songs. I asked him if he thought so; he smiled and did not respond. Instead, he performed "Nkum na Abandze" in a way that I had not heard. He started with a long and winding declamatory introduction to the song. When I asked Uncle Bedu why Nana had not kenkan when he sang it for me, he did not respond. I did not tell him that Nana had told me already that he, Nana, could not kenkan. Bedu demonstrated the kenkan again and again. "This is what informs people about the upcoming song if they don't know it." He sang the entire song with details about the event that led to the song's creation.

The next day, I went on a memory walk with Uncle Bedu to a place where he claimed one of their Elders, Safohen Boadum, died after he sang a song. According to him, after Boadum got shot, he dove into the sea and swam like a fish back to Kormantse. He proceeded to climb the hill to Kokoado. When he realized that he would not make it, he sang the song, and afterwards he died. Boadum, according to Uncle Bedu, belonged to his Domna lineage. We walked to a decayed coconut tree between two houses. This is where, according to Uncle Bedu, the Asafo captain died after singing his last sang, the song in which he congratulated their war captain Gyesi. Uncle Bedu sang the song again, "*Gyesi Mbo . . .*" (example 38 ⚫).

I went on a memory walk with Uncle Bedu because Nana said Bedu "did not hear it properly." I did not tell Bedu that. That memory walk did not evoke the same emotions and connections as those that I embarked on alone. Perhaps it was because Nana had told me Bedu did not hear it properly, or because, unlike the Owumena that still exists, the coconut tree and other landmarks that once stood in this location were no longer there. According to Nana, Boadum was shot; however, he hopped on one foot to the Kormantse seaside. When he got there, they called his sister who picked him up. They took him to an herbalist who was able to remove the bullet. The herbalist nursed him for a while before he died. Nana did not remember the song that Boadum sang.

The Akan Elders say, *Anomaa mfa dua ho abufu,* "A bird cannot have a strained relationship between it and a tree," so, I did not muddle the relationship between the two men. I did not share any of this with Nana. I did not tell him about the memory walk. Neither did I tell Uncle Bedu that Nana said that the gentleman in question was Supi Teyin, not Boadum, and that "Boadum is a God in the drum room."[31] *Wo nsa hyɛ obi anomu a, yɛmmɔ n'apampam,* "When your fingers are in somebody's mouth, you don't strike the top of the person's head." What is heard and how that is shared depends on the needs of the people, the place and time of the sharing; sometimes remembering becomes a moral practice (Herzfeld 2001).

What need does Ancestral connection with Boadum serve Bedu? What fulfillment does Bedu get by asserting that Boadum was from his lineage? Nana mentioned that Boadum was a God. He also stated that Asafo captain

Teyim, not Boadum, was healed and died later. How do those assertions serve him? Was it more important that they both sang the song, "ɔhen Gyesi mbo?" or should I have attempted to "describe the competing cultural logic that permits simultaneous production of very different versions of the past"? (Herzfeld 2001, 69).

The use of oral narratives, though validated as a rich source through the pioneering work by Vansina (1965) and our Ancestors, is contested because "tellers" continue to weave multiple and sometimes conflicting ideas in their narratives of place, people, and events. Colorful variations exist in the retelling and recovery of these oral narratives. Some recollections are highly detailed and nostalgic, while others offer brief mention of the issues; some are discarded altogether because they do not fulfill the needs of the people; others are improvised during the telling. How societies remember or choose to remember—sedimented in the body (Connerton 1989) through myths, songs, folktales, and dances, I learned—depends on many factors, including moral, religious, and political issues.

More important for me was the need to maintain my contacts and to learn as much about the different traditions, versions, and *abakɔsɛm* of this culture, even as they were couched in various interpretations. Each twist or bump in the "telling" was an opportunity to learn about the multiple ways that Asafo has impacted lives and the many contexts in which the *ndwom* was used. "Eyes that witnessed past events are not there, but ears that heard historical events are there," *ani a ehunu tetehɔ na ɛnni hɔ, na aso a ɛtee tetehɔ asɛm no deɛ ɛwɔ hɔ*, thus truth is relative to the teller and her efforts to represent the past in the present. Truth claims are filtered through differing interpretations. I did not attempt to "resolve" the differences in Uncle Bedu's and Nana's narratives. For, as Herzfeld recommends, "the fissures may be best kept open so that we can fully discern the ideological and political consequences of both" (66).

Me Buronyi

I continued to walk with both Bedu and Nana. When I returned to Kormantse in 2018, I played back all the songs I had recorded for them to listen and for their feedback. Nana remembered all the songs and sang along. I met Bedu at the seaside. I played all the songs for him, including those that Nana sang. At one point during the playback session, a gentleman stopped by and said he wanted to tell me about his issues with the hope that I could help him. He was serious and contemplative, seemingly bothered by something. I thought he wanted some money, so I told him I could not help him and continued to focus on my work with Bedu. The gentleman left, then came back. He sat next to me. He waited. By this time, Bedu had taken the headphones from his ears, and unplugged them, so the gentleman and others listened to the songs. He hung around for a moment, then he left. After the third time, he left and did not come back again.

Later Bedu told me why the man came: "He wanted you to tell him about, predict his *hyɛbrew'm* destiny. He thinks you are a diviner, a *nunsinyi* herbalist, a *kɔmfo* priestess." I was flabbergasted. I asked why he would think that. "The beads around your ankle." That disturbed me. I was also disturbed because some of the fishermen referred to me as Bedu's madam, his wife. He called me "*Me buronyi,*" "my white woman." *Dabi, Dabi, Dabi*! No! No! Nooo!!! I protested. "I am not a white woman." He proceeded to explain. "I am not one," I interrupted him. As black and brown and proud as I am, a colonialist mentality and image of beauty that I detest, abhor, and resist had been assigned to *me*.

"Me buronyi (buroni–Akan Twi)" is a term that some Ghanaian men, including some Hi-Life singers, use when they refer to their beautiful women. I don't care for it. Sometimes, a slightly lighter skinned Ghanaian is called *oburonyi*. Therefore, some women and men continue to bleach their skins despite the detrimental effects of skin lighteners. In fact, my mother had a sister called Akua Buroni, though she was darker than me! Knowing about the colonial legacy of such definitions did not help. Perhaps it was also due to my experiences in America, with whiteness, and my experience with those who are desperate, desire to be supreme, the white-body supremacy that lives and breathes in my own body, and my attempts to "undo Heidi." My heart skipped a beat. I cringed. I was angry. Period. *I have been called a white woman in my own native land! Should I continue this discussion and appeal to his conscience about the . . . of this label? Is it because I am socially constituted in a global configuration of economic power? How does economic power equate beauty?*

I felt weird and angry. I now understood how Black Americans feel when they are called "*oburonyi.*" *Etua wo nyɔnko ho a, etua dua mu,* "When it is inserted into your friend, it's in a tree!" "*Sorry-oo, my sisters. I did not know. Now, I understand how you feel." Though I had been told I dressed different, walked different, talked different, asked too many questions, and looked like a Black American (I accepted that), I had hoped this oburonyi term would* not *be used on me, against me. But there it was.* After the playback session, I walked away, still upset. Unsettled. Unbelonging. A wayfarer.

"The *Ahweneɛ* Beads around My Ankle": *Kɔmfo* Lady

The process of learning Asafo songs was thus multicentric and multimodal. It veered onto other nonmusical paths that led me to conclude that the "insider"/"outsider" categories are "rarely so pure or simple, but rather, layered with complex and multiple facets" (Wolf 1993, 7). Most of my walks were beneficial; others were challenging, frustrating, and exhausting. That I was never simply "at home" became clearer as I compared my experiences in Ghana through my twenties with those of my later years in the United States of America. My collective memories of times past coincided with and conflicted with my teachers' lived experiences, reminding me daily of the many shades of "at homeness" (Collins and Gallinat 2016, 10), not fully in, and not fully out.[32] My mentors expected me to know certain facts about the *ndwom* and language just because I was a Ghanaian Akan performer. This often made me feel more of an outsider, because I honestly did not know certain facts. Now I comfort myself with Efik Shayak's advice on NPR's *Morning Edition*: "Think of identity as multiple belongings, more fluid, like concentric circles, local, regional, international, and global" (November 15, 2021). It is okay to not know everything about our multiple locations.

The beads around my ankle added to my entangled relationships with some of my mentors. At times, wearing them did not help my situation as an "insider researcher." Sometimes, inquiries about my beads interrupted our conversations and interview sessions. "What are those?" Some observed me with suspicion. Others thought I was a "juju woman," "priestess," a "diviner" and sought medical help from me. Therefore, the gentleman, Uncle John, was convinced I was a diviner and asked me to "read into his future" because he was facing some challenges. Some said they were afraid of me.

Once during a session with Uncle Bedu at the seaside, his uncle, Paapa asked,

Paapa: "Madam, I want to ask you something."
Ama: "Ask me."
Paapa: "The thing around your ankle, what does it mean?"

I laughed because Nana had mentioned previously that people had been asking him about the beads around my ankle and wanted to know whether I was a priest or sold medicine.

> Uncle Bedu: "The friend who came to tell me about you said, 'A sister has come to the seaside looking for you; some beads are around her leg.' When he mentioned the beads, I knew it was you." [I laughed and clapped. Ha-ha-ha-ha-ha-haaaaaa!! Bedu laughed. Paapa was not amused and did not laugh with us.]
>
> Paapa: "I want you to explain it to me."
>
> Ama: "Really?"

He waited for a response and would not go away. He had contributed to our session, so I obliged.

> Ama: "I don't have a reason. I just like it."
>
> Paapa: "Kɛ-kɛ?" ("For no reason?").
>
> Ama: "I like it Kɛ-kɛ. Since I study matters that have come and gone . . ."
>
> Paapa: ". . . Listen, when I was coming of age, I knew we did not just put them there [he pointed to my ankle]; we put them on the hips."

I was aware of what he was referring to. It was true that, for aesthetic and other practical reasons, wearing beads around the hips started at a very early age for baby girls. For babies, I learned, they were used to "lift" the buttocks; but beads were also used to help determine whether the child had gained weight or not. For a woman, they are said to draw attention to the beauty of that part of the body (Lawal 1996), or they add to a woman's beauty and sex appeal, so I was not surprised when Paapa added, "We put them on the hips, and you hold onto them and become happy." Uncle Bedu and I laughed.

I thought of the many dances for which women wear beads to accentuate the hips or add to the accompanying music (Green 1996; p'Bitek 1984; Nannyonga-Tamusuza 2005). p'Bitek's description of preparation for the Ugandan *orak* dance came to mind:

> You adorn yourself in Acoli
> Costumes
> . . . .
> Or bells on your legs
> You wear bead-skirts or string
> Skirts . . .

And a ten-stringed bead
Around your waist. (1984, 43)

Our conversation about the beads around my ankle continued. Uncle Bedu informed me that people had been asking him about the beads around my ankle. He added that some called me his "madam," or "*oburonyi* with the beads." I was not as offended by the "madam" title as I was about the *oburonyi* designation. He sensed my discontent. "They call you *oburonyi* because you are different. Our women are beautiful, but you are also different from our beautiful women here. You have the beads around your ankle; our women do not do that, unless they are *kɔmfo*. Only those who come from abroad do that; *oburonyi*—the white people, the Jamaicans, those who don't come from here."

My memory walked to an encounter I had with one gentleman, to whom I was mistakenly taken during my initial search for Teacher Hammond (Nana). When the gentleman came into the living room where I was waiting, his eyes moved from my head, down my body, and settled at my ankle with beads. He stared for a while and then moved his eyes back to my face. His disdain and disapproval of my appearance were unmistakable. I introduced myself in the local Fante language and stated my *amandzeɛ* mission and search for Asafo *abakosɛm* and *ndwom*. *Akwaaba*. "You are welcome," he replied. Then he said something that caught me off guard: "I thought you were one of those people. A Jamaican, those Black people. I was going to ask you to leave. I abhor Asafo. I am a Christian. I also did not grow up around here, so I don't know much about Asafo, but I can find someone to help you."

I was shocked. I wanted to tell him about how Asafo saved Kormantse from outside aggressors, protected the land, its people. I was rattled. But I was careful not to show it, because I did not want him to label me as an "angry Black woman." *Oh, no. There it is again. This is not America. This is Kormantse, Ghana, Africa. "White-body supremacy you have walked with me with your labels that are meant to silence Black women. Here in this part of the world, African/Black women express, are expected to express their anger and frustration, freely, honest with their emotions. A Black woman can be angry. It is her right! A Black woman can also be glad. Both!"* He was my Elder. *Sɛ ano patrɛ a ɛkyɛn namɔn*, "A slipped tongue damages more than a slipped foot." My eyes were *hyerebahyereba*. *Etire nyɛ borɔferɛ na wɔapae mu*, "the head is not a pawpaw that you can split open." We talked for a while despite my discomfort. We talked about the importance of educating our youth. He said he would ask the Kormantse Queen Mother to help me. After more discussion, I asked permission to leave. I did not go back. *Opoku mfa ne nkuu, sɛ medware a, me ho mpae*, "Let the whale keep its cream, if I bathe, my skin should dry up."

> Colonized personalities
> Dilemma of a ghost
> *Saman twɛntwɛn*
> In-betweenness
> Alienated
> Entangled identities
> Should I go to America
> Or stay at Ghana
> Black skin white masks
> Coloniality
> White-body supremacy
> Desperate to be supreme
> Listen
> Precious beads don't make noise
> We are All born Supreme
> Leave me
> Us
> Alone
> A!

Paapa stated that people would think I was a *kɔmfo*, a priest, or someone who sells medicine. Then he added, "Last time, someone said he was coming to you so that you could help him with his wound." Aaaa . . ., I thought about the gentleman who came to me for medicine. None of this bothered me until another gentleman who had joined us said, "I thought you were a priest. When I got here, I was afraid." How many people have avoided me because they were afraid of me? How many mentoring opportunities have I missed because people were suspicious of me? The beads had become a marker, an identifier for me. "Walking" and the clothes we wear can have profound implications on our search. The conversation about my beads continued for another three minutes before moving back to our discussion on Asafo. The walker knows more than her mother and father; the walker eats sweet things, but *ɔnantefoɔ hunu amane*, "The walker suffers." Bué!

"*Adende*": First Singing Lesson

One of the hallmark methods and, in fact, "respectable" approaches to conducting ethnomusicological fieldwork is active participation. Although collecting, transcribing, analyzing, and walking are comparable means to understanding the music we study, active and live participation in the musical styles is the hallmark.[33] Many ethnomusicologists, including the various writers in *Shadows in the Field* (2008) and *Performing Ethnomusicology* (2006), situate their narratives in this paradigm. However, because *mako nyinaa mpatu mmere*, "Not all peppers ripen at the same time," and we are "samples," my experience was a little different.[34] By the time I met with Uncle Bedu at the seaside, my interactions with Asafo songs had been that of an observer—listening to and recording the two sessions, hearing Nana sing them, hearing snippets of them at funeral celebrations at Cape Coast and at Kormantse. Neither had I witnessed any rehearsals or ad hoc rehearsals that I could join. Although I had hummed it and sung a refrain at the seaside and at Nana's farm, I had not had the opportunity to participate fully with someone or sung an entire song. Neither had I had any direct instructions on how to sing the songs. The style was still new to me, and I was afraid of embarrassing myself trying to sing it. During one of my sessions with Uncle Bedu, I asked him to teach me. He had already assured me that I did not need any voice coaching.

> Ama: "If I came to you to learn Asafo, is there a song that you would begin with?"
> Uncle Bedu: "I would start with the easy one before I go to the difficult ones."
> Ama: "Which are the easy ones?"
> Uncle Bedu: "I would start with "Adende."
> Ama: "Is "Adende" easy?"
> Uncle Bedu: "Yes. There is another one, "*Egya yɛma hom akɔaba o*"— "Elders We Welcome You" [example 39 ※ 🔊].
> Ama: "This sounds more difficult than Adende."
> Uncle Bedu: "Yes, it sounds more difficult."
> Ama: "How would you teach Adende?"

Though this was not how he learned the *ndwom* because he was exposed to them in the context of other activities, and he had heard them sung over and over, he broke it down line by line for me. Since he did not take voice lessons on how to place the voice or how to project, he did not tell me how. He just said, "Sing loud, articulate, project." I repeated each line after him. It felt awkward. The process was long, but *Biribi ansɛea, biribi nyɛ yie*, "If something does not mess up, something does not go well" (there is no gain without pain). First, we focused on the words, then his intonation, then his gesturing. I could not do all three at once. Unlike some of the other songs that blend declamatory, free-moving passages with the measured, the entire song was declamatory. The declamatory style was difficult for me. *Bata bɔne yɛ animguaseɛ*, "When a journey expressly taken to seek fortune becomes a total fiasco, it becomes a disgrace." I persisted. The most difficult part was the projection of the song, singing loud. I could not imagine singing to loud drumming. If what Uncle Bedu said earlier was true, that "If you don't let your voice go up, if the drum is playing and your voice does not go up, it is not sweet," then mine "would not be sweet." I could not "let my voice go up" like his did. Except for the chorus, I repeated each line he performed for me.

Uncle Bedu: *ɔaka bosom nsu e, Tuafo mbaa-e* (call)
Aduonum: *ɔaka bosom nsu e, Tuafo mbaa-e*
Uncle Bedu: *Me na dze memfa* (kenkan)
Aduonum: *Me na dze memfa*
Uncle Bedu: *M'egya dze memfa* (kenkan)
Aduonum: *M'egya dze memfa*
Uncle Bedu: *ɔama ewisu abra m'* (kenkan)
Aduonum: *ɔama ewisu abra m'*
Uncle Bedu: *Ikur n'enyim ɔnnsaa ɔda nsawerɛw* (kenkan)
Aduonum: *Ikur n'enyim ɔnnsaa ɔda nsawerɛw*
Uncle Bedu: *Adende, adende, ɔaka bosom nsu a ya ara e* (call)
Aduonum: *Adende, adende, ɔaka bosom nsu a ya ara e*
Uncle Bedu/Aduonum:
Adende, Adende, ɔaka bosom nsu a ya ara (chorus)
Asɛm ba a ya ara
ɔko ba a ya ara
Adende, Adende ɔaka bosom nsu a
Ya ara yɛsaw!

FIGURE 7.3. *Adende* singing lesson with Uncle Bedu, Aduonum, and Bedu's cousin. Photo by Paapa.

Every line had a different attack and projection. I could not articulate the words with passion like he did. I comforted myself with the knowledge that this was my first "lesson." My voice could not carry as far as his. At one point, he laughed at how hard I was trying. "Just sing. Relax," he instructed.

I could not capture the slips and slides he did so skillfully with his voice. Sometimes, it felt as if I was off key. When I tried to "fix" it, to "clean it," he brought me back to the "correct" way of singing it, the "sweet" way. This went on for some time. He told me to listen to the recordings on my own and rehearse at home. I was not bold enough to try the kenkan. That was more challenging because it involved proverbs that I did not know, and it referenced events that were beyond my comprehension. We spent many sessions on this one song. *Tete ka aso mu*, "Repetitive listening leaves an indelible mark in the ear."

Toward the end of one of our sessions on *Adende*, a gentleman joined us. Uncle Bedu asked me to demonstrate what I had learned. Uncle Bedu had already told me that the young men were not interested in joining Asafo, learning the songs, and would not come and learn if they were invited because, according to him, "The children who have come these days, they like women's issues. They don't have anything to look up to." So, I was quite surprised when the gentleman came up eagerly to sing with us. I thought he was great.

I started gesturing, raising my hand, projecting my voice, and making facial expressions as Bedu does when he performs the song, my attempt at an embodied call. Uncle Bedu joined and corrected my intonation. "You can do it," he assured me. I thanked him. *Akokɔ nom nsuo a, ɔdekyerɛ Onyankopɔn*, "When the chicken drinks water, it shows to God" (to say, "Thank you!"). I left the seaside humming and gesturing. I felt awkward, "impostor syndrome," but people at the seaside encouraged and lauded me.

> Asafo
> Finally
> I
> *Kɔmfo* Lady
> High Priestess
> Ninsin healer
> Ahwenɛ Beads around my ankle
> Getting closer to you
> *ɔnantefoɔ na odi adɔdɔdeɛ*
> It is the walker who eats sweet things
> Hm!
> Your inside is sweet
>
> Many layers
> *Abakɔsɛm* walks
> *Posuban*
> Memory walk
> Death pit
> *Egwuaradze*
> Deceased drummer drumming
> Flag dancing
>
> Entanglements
> Abhorrent

Black skin, white masks
Colonial legacies
Flash backs
This is *not* America
The thing around my ankle
My right to be angry
Claiming
Embracing
Angry Black Woman

150+++ beautiful men
Breathing
Permission from nobody
Pacing up and down
Mending nets
Ampa
You are Spirit
Nana Bosompo
If the voice does not go up
It is not sweet
Kenkan
Makes it sweet
The crows hover back and forth
Exchanging kenkan
Phrases
Waaaaah, waaaaah

Asafo
You who intimidate
Diss your foes
Kasa twii, signifyin'
You who archives
Took memories on walk
Yes
The women know you very well
Beautiful Kormantse women
Tete ka aso mu

Repetition leaves indelible mark in the ear
Adende singing lesson
Repeat
Repeat
Kenkan
Nyimpa atɔ nsu mu a wɔnyi no ma hɛn
You are sweet
Too sweet
Pa-pa kwa
Onipa yɛ adeɛ a, ɔyɛ gye ayeyie
Mbo na yɛ
Ko-ko-gya, ko-ko-gya
Ke-ren Pu-putum, pu-tuu pu
Ko-ko-

CHAPTER EIGHT

Anammɔn

Shadows in the Fields, Leaving Footprints

Yɛpɛ a yɛbɛhunu nti, na yɛkyekyere boa a, yɛde ano sata
(It is for ease of reference that is why we leave ends when we tie a bundle)

—Akan proverb

Right now, if our Asafo tradition would stand or fall,
it would depend on you

—Maame Ama Aprokuwa

Without oneself walking and leaving footprints,
one can only listen to and repeat the
narrative of others who have walked the story

—Legat

ɔman yi abɔ ei
ɔman yi wabɔ Tuafo mba ee
Mena dze memfa
Me'gya dze memfa
ɔama ewiso abra 'm
Wɔ yɛ n'dɛn yɛrokɔ ɔmanko a
ɔman yi abɔ a
Asafo woeguan kɔ!
(Our town has fallen/War is inevitable
The town has fallen Tuafo children
My mother's thing I took
My father's thing I took
It has made a thief out of me

What happened we have gone
The town has fallen
Asafo has run away)

— Kormantse Asafo *ndwom,* "*ɔman yi Abɔ*"

During my search and walk with Asafo, I was also *Walking with My Ancestors* at former dungeons for enslaved Africans at Cape Coast Castle Dungeons. Cape Coast Castle is where captured and shackled proud Africans were imprisoned for months until a ship came to transport those who survived across the Atlantic to plantations in the Americas. I wanted to understand, more profoundly, the magnitude of crimes that were committed when human beings were turned into commodities. Every Monday and Thursday in 2017, for four hours each time, over a period of five months, I sat alone in the dungeons. Each night, before a visit, I did not eat, brush my teeth, bathe, or empty my bowels. I tossed and turned all night and could not sleep. In the morning, I rushed to Cape Coast Castle and changed into clothes I had not washed for months. Then, I got shackled—neck, legs, and wrists. I dragged myself on sunbaked floors, *Ko-ko-gya, ko-ko-gya, ko-ko-gya, ko-ko-gya*, into dark, damp, insect-infested holes underground. I sat. Buried. Scared. Waiting. Four hours alone. For consolation, reflections, and entertainment, I sang lullabies, Negro spirituals, and many of the Asafo songs I had learned. I choreographed dances, wrote songs, and wove poetry.

Sometimes, I walked in the dungeons and at Kormantse the same day. I woke up early in the morning, cooked breakfast for my children, KoJo and MaAdwoa, walked about two kilometers to catch a taxi, dropped them off at school, rushed to Cape Coast Castle Dungeons, changed into my visitation clothes, got shackled, then hobbled, *Ko-ko-gya, ko-ko-gya, ko-ko-gya, ko-ko-gya* to my four-hour immersive visit in either the male or female dungeon. After four hours alone in those dark, damp, algae-covered walls and insect-infested holes, I hobbled back out, *ko-ko . . .*, changed into my other clothes, got unshackled, then traveled to Kormantse. Those were heavy and difficult days, heavy on my heart, mind, soul, and feet. *Wode w'ani mmienu hwɛ toa mu a, baako bɔ*, "When you look into a bottle with two eyes, one gets shut out." My body shut down for a week. The soles of my feet became numb. Heavy. My feet remember. Once, on my way from

Kormantse, my head got smashed into the car windshield when our taxi driver crashed head-on into another car, causing extreme headaches and aggravating my scars from two previous brain surgeries. CT scan. MRI. In the evening, I picked up KoJo and MaAdwoa from school, cooked dinner, helped with their homework, read them stories, and sang lullabies to them. After they went to sleep, I typed up my field notes. I felt disconnected, at times, even from my children. Though I did not share the details about my immersive visits in the dungeons with KoJo and MaAdwoa, they experienced the change in me. The lullabies and stories got shorter. Then stopped altogether. This walk is getting extremely difficult. *Worebedi nankwanse asuro mogya?* "You are going to be a butcher and be afraid of blood?" *Hwɛ. Wosuro abɔn tutuo a, wontu ahini.* "If you are afraid of digging up burrows, you will never reach the striking distance of the rat."[1] I kept walking.

In my most recent nationally recognized solo multimodal performance piece, *Walking with My Ancestors: Cape Coast Castle* (2019), a work based on these immersive visits, I employ Asafo songs. I use them in scenes where the character is defiant, evokes strength, resilience, and pride. I perform Kormantse Asafo songs, *"ɔroko e ɔanyɛ yie," "Oye Oye Kofi Dedu Mba," "Adende,"* and others. I was deliberate in harnessing these songs to express my multisensorial responses to the various spaces—numbed feet, frozen buttocks, tingly toes, hazy eyes, growling stomach, full bladder, shackles eating my skin. For example, I sing *"ɔroko e ɔanyɛ yie"* ("She Fought but Failed) in the scene where I ask, "How did you die?" and "Why didn't you fight?" I perform *"Oye Oye Kofi Dedu Mba"* ("It's good; It's good, Kofi Dedu Children") when I connect experiences of the contemporary Blacks in the Black Lives Matter Movement with those of enslaved Africans who protested their treatment in the dungeons.

I also used the songs, deliberately, as my way of "prolonging their lives" against erasure. In this way, I join Ghanaian Hi-Life artists like the late C. K. Mann and folkloric groups like Twerammpon Traditionals at Cape Coast. I also join art music composers such as the late Ghanaian composer Mr. Joseph Maison, who used elements from Asafo *ndwom*, including its forceful and declamatory and free-moving call, to inspire Mfantsiman Secondary students to work hard in order to excel in life, and the late Dr. Ephraim Amu, whose "Yaanom Abibirimma é" ("Fellow Africans"—1931) draws on the Asafo genre to encourage his fellow Ghanaians to work hard for the country's development.[2] Both Maison and Amu illustrate the importance of Asafo *ndwom* and convey how Asafo continues to occupy Ghanaian composers' imagination, especially as it serves as "pre-compositional models" for various works using traditional genres, a practice for which the late Akin Euba coined "creative ethnomusicology" (2000).

Incorporating Asafo songs in my performance art piece, *Walking with My Ancestors*, is my attempt to help sustain the Asafo songs that I learned during my search. It will become part of the footprints I leave behind on my walking trails with Asafo. *Obi nkɔ obi kurom nkɔfrɛ ne ho Agyeman*, "One should not go to another person's town and call herself a Liberator-o, and *Obi nkɔ obi kurom nkɔkyrɛ ne ho sɛ: 'Meyɛ ɔdehyeɛ*, "One should not go to another person's town and declare: 'I am a royal.'" I went to Kormanste as a student of *abakɔsɛm*, to learn about Asafo *ndwom*. This is my attempt to give back, to show my gratitude for their accommodation and grace my mentors showed me, and to showcase what I had learned.

Footprints I: Entering the Schools

JHS principal has agreed to let me come and read poetry on Wednesday during their morning worship. I learn that Primary has a Speech and Prize on Friday, June 2. (Field notes, May 26, 2017)

I visited Ophelia and Desmond. They read through the poems. They are getting better at them. I am excited. They will wear traditional *kente* with beads. JHS headmistress wants me to come at 8:00 a.m. She wants me to advise them about teenage pregnancy, grades, school. (Field notes, May 29, 2017)

When I asked average Kormantse teenagers what Asafo is, some did not know, others had vague ideas of what it is. When I asked average Kormantse teenagers about the *abakɔsɛm* of the town, one gave me a detailed account because she had consulted with the Elders in her attempts to win the Ms. Kormantse title. The others had vague ideas about that *abakɔsɛm*. The Elders say, *Nea onnim no sua a ohu*, "When she who does not know studies, she knows," so I sought permission from the headmistresses and headmaster (principals) of the Methodist Elementary and Junior High School (JHS), two public schools located on the Accra-Takoradi Highway (see Walking Trails, figs. I-1 to I-4), to share what I learned about the town's *abakɔsɛm* and Asafo. The principals gave me permission to conduct a study. After two weeks, I collected the completed surveys. Most of the students did not know the town's migratory *abakɔsɛm*; some knew basics about Asafo and the various Gods but nothing about the *ndwom* of Asafo.

Because (1) I had learned from the Kings and Elders that since the town had stopped practicing many of the traditions, such as *bragrɔ*, an initiation ceremony for girls, teen pregnancy was on the rise and young girls quit school without completing their basic education, and (2) the school headmistress asked me specifically to speak about teen pregnancy, I wrote a skit about the topic—its effects, the cost of rearing a child, and so on. I also drafted several spoken word pieces on what I had learned thus far about the town's *abakɔsɛm* and Asafo. *Tikorɔ mu nni nyansa*, "One head does not store all wisdom," so one Friday morning, Nana and I visited the JHS school to present a workshop with the students. The room was packed with excited students and a few teachers.

We started with the skit about pregnancy. Two volunteers, a girl and a boy, acted out the various scenes. After the skit, we had an invigorating discussion. Some of the students, especially the girls, commented on how unfair it is for the boys to continue with their schooling while the pregnant girl must stay home. The girls were also upset that after getting a girl pregnant, the boy could desert her and chase after other girls. They wondered why the girl in the skit did not take heed of the saying, *Abaa a yɛde bɔ Takyi no, ɛno ara na yɛde bɔ Baa*, "The stick that is used in hitting Takyi is the same that is used in hitting Baa." The discussion continued for a while. Finally, Nana stood up and shared a few words with the students about teen pregnancy and chastised them for engaging in improper activities.

He told them he sees them leaning against the walls at night like lizards. "You are supposed to be at home studying!" Then he warned them, "If I see you out at night, leaning against the walls, I will chase you with a stick and cane you!" (Odum III, May 31, 2017, Kormantse, Ghana). The students laughed at the thought of an eighty-three-year-old Nana chasing after them with a cane at night, but they knew he was serious and believed he would chase after them with a stick and cane them. Nana shared the town's migratory *abakɔsɛm*, the role of the various Gods, and a few of their songs.

At the time, I was not comfortable singing Asafo songs, so I shared what I had learned about the Mother Goddess, Nana Eminsa. Nana suggested I sing the entire song with refrain and then teach them the refrain, after which I would raise the song and the students would perform the response. When I started "Eminsa Osuom e/ obi mfrɛ hɛn o," the majority of the class replied, "Hɛn ara yɛ dze hɛn man!" Ah. I was surprised, paused briefly, and continued singing. We went through the song several times. Asked afterwards how they knew the song, many replied that they heard their grandfathers sing it, though it had not been taught to them directly. We had

FIGURE 8.1. Aduonum with Nana at Kormantse Methodist JHS classroom. Photo by JHS teacher.

a question-and-answer session after the event. On our way out, several of the students and teachers applauded and thanked us for the presentation.

Next, I approached the headmistress and headmaster (principal) of the elementary school about sharing what I had learned. I told them about my spoken word pieces, and they were eager to see and hear them. They asked for copies of the pieces for use in the classrooms. During a visit to the kindergarten class, one of the teachers mentioned an upcoming Speech and Prize Giving Day and suggested it would be good platform for the students to share the spoken word pieces. The headmistress selected two students—a girl, Ophelia in the fourth grade, and a boy, Desmond in sixth grade—to perform the words. I visited their homes and spoke with their parents about the presentation. Their parents were excited. In my field notes that day, I wrote, "This is a good day! I am helping transmit, preserve a tradition, to sustain a tradition by teaching and engaging the young ones" (May 27, 2017). I read some of the pieces to Ophelia and Desmond and asked each to pick one. Ophelia picked the poem about Asafo's demise; Desmond chose the one about *abakɔsɛm*. They were both excited.

Prior to the event, I shared my spoken word pieces with three Elders in the community, including Nana and his nephew, Uncle "T." They corrected my Fante language and suggested minor details in the write-up. I read the poem about Kormantse's alleged defeat of the Asante. After the line "I called on Nana Eminsa," I started to sing Nana Eminsa's song: "Eminsa

Osuom e obi mfra hɛn o o . . .". Uncle T's wife, the now late Maame Aba Aframba, who was preparing a meal, joined the singing when I got to the part "Yɛrgor maa . . .". She sang it slightly different from how Nana performed it. This would be my first, though unplanned, singing lesson. She corrected my intonation and the tempo of the song. She sang it. She raised it much higher, while the last note ended hanging; she did not release it or end with the "stop."

I sang with her and tried to mimic her embodied style, but I could not produce her nuanced pitches nor embodied presentation. She stood up, came closer to me, and sang it again and again using hand gestures, facial expressions, while evoking the greatness of Nana Eminsa by inserting ɔkoko kɛse (Mighty Mountain), an appellation I had not heard. She insisted that I correct the lines. When I repeated it, she said I was dragging the song. By this time, we had drawn a crowd, because *Nkwan pa twetwe adwa*, "A good soup attracts chairs." Two women in the crowd also said I was dragging the lines. "*Mado; mado!*" ("Pick it up; pick it up"), she instructed. So, I tried and tried. She sang it again and again. I sang it with her. After many attempts, I knew it was still not right by her. She did not seem satisfied. I asked her to sing it again for me to record. She did. Nana and Uncle T did not say anything. They seemed pleased with the outcome. Could it be that women sing it differently? Could it be that the elderly sing differently? Uncle T's wife was much younger. I was nervous. *Aburuburo nkosua, adeɛ a ebeye yie nsɛe*, "As with the eggs of the dove, things destined to succeed will never fail." I was excited and ready for my debut at the Speech and Prize Giving Day.

One Saturday morning and three other days during the school's recess, I met with Ophelia and Desmond to read through the pieces. Two days before the Speech and Prize Giving Day, Ophelia got sick and did not attend the additional rehearsals. The headmistress and I visited her. I took some medicine. She had been throwing up and looked very weak. *Obi nnom aduro mma ɔyarefoɔ*, "One does not drink medicine for the sick person," I would have ingested medicine to speed up her recovery.[3]

June 2, 2017, arrived. The Speech and Prize Giving Day started with long speeches by leaders of the town, the principals, a representative from the district office, and the emcee. Two student cadet groups performed a marching drill, and an ad hoc cultural group performed a choreographed dance. No one performed Asafo. Our presentation was listed on the program, but there was no sign of Desmond. The headmistress assured me that he was ready to perform. Still, I was nervous. Halfway through the program, Desmond came out in a colorful *kente* skirt and designs on his torso and arms. His chest was bare. He performed Spoken Word 1 , "I, Am Asafo. . . ". He did very well and received a huge applause from the Elders, family members, and friends. *Onipa yɛ adeɛ a, ɔyɛ gye ayeyie*, "When someone performs good deeds, she deserves praise." During the applause, the headmistresses suggested I present the version in the Fante language. I walked up to the center of the space, introduced myself, and gave a brief background about my search on Asafo, beginning with Spoken Word 2 , "*Me yɛ Asafo, Wɔ woo me tsetsepɔn . . .*". I also read the version about Asafo's demise in my Spoken Word 3 , "I am Asafo, Today, they say I am fetish, Evil . . .". Ophelia would have performed Spoken Word 4 , "The town has forsaken me, We are dying . . .".

I thought the audience, many of whom knew about my wanderings through town, and "shadows in the field," received it well. They clapped. *Onipa yɛ adeɛ a, ɔyɛ gye ayeyie*, "When someone performs good deeds, she deserves praise." I forgot to sing Nana Eminsa's song that the now late Maame Aba Aframba helped me learn. She would have been so proud. About a year ago, I learned from Nana that Maame Aba Aframba has "gone to the village." Ah! Death, you again! Maame Aba Aframba-éééé. Dammirifua Du-é! *Owuo begya hwan*? "Who will death spare?" *Owuo ne yɛn reko, ɔpatafoɔ ne hwan*? "Death is in a fight with us, who will mediate?" Du-é! *Owuo nnim adeɛ kyɛ.* Death does not know how to share fairly." Nana Eminsa. Eminsa's Royal. Hyiee! Du-é! Mmm . . . (arms on head, bouncing up and down).

Footprints II, Sankɔfa Wonkyir: Adom Communication Centre

It is Friday, July 13, 2018. I am at the Ahenfie, the King's yellow palace on main street, to witness how laws are legislated at Kormantse. It is about 9:00 a.m. A week prior to this date, I had shared my interest in playing Asafo songs at their Communication Centre. Some fishermen at the seaside encouraged me to do it. Someone said, "The women would love it. They will dance in their houses aaaa. . .". I had also asked Nana about it, and he said I should go ahead with it. While I waited for the meeting to start, I approached the King's *ɔkyeame* spokesperson, Nana Kweku Suapim. He asked to consult together with another Elder, Nana Kobena Wobir, who is also an Asafo Supi.

The two men sat with me and asked my *amandzeɛ* mission. I told them I wanted to write about the *prɛkɛtɛ* drum they seized from the Asante and would like to be given the permission to see the drum. I would also like the permission to play Asafo songs at the Communication Centre. The Supi said the second request was good news for Kormantse. He expressed regret for how their traditions had fallen on the wayside. He added, "*sankɔfa wɔ nkyir*," "It is not a taboo to go back and fetch what was left behind." He gave me the go-ahead to play the songs at the Communication Centre.

They also promised to show me the drum; however, that did not happen because as the Supi later explained, *Nkyen dan mu yɛ ɔman no awiei* ("The drum room is the town's head"), and that it was not the easiest space to enter—sheep had to be slaughtered, special prayers offered; the drum room is not entered *basa-basa* (recklessly). Was it their way of telling me, *Me bu me nsa*, like the late Egya *Akɔdɛɛ* told me when I asked to see the Anyampafo drums at Bantuma? Someone had already told me that they will never show it because I am a woman! Ebueii! But Ah, isn't their Principal Deity a woman? *The* Principal Warrior Deity?

> Ah!
> Gender ééé iiiii i
> You
> Again
> Female
> Woman
> Whatever you call yourself
> *ɔbaa basia, Ewuraba*
> You are a pain
> An obstruction
> An abstraction
> *ɛnyɛ ɔbaa na ɔwo barima*
> Isn't it woman who gives birth to a man
> You
> Narrower of experience! (Journal Entry, October 17, 2016)

Footprints IIa—On Air

I went to Adom Communication Centre early this morning at 4:30 a.m. T. Tommy dropped (me off). Like he does each morning, ɔsɔfo David dedicated the town with prayer. He announced my presence. "Our Mother is here to share abakɔsɛm and Asafo songs that our Ancestors left for us. Please stop everything you are doing and listen. Take a pen and take notes. . . ." After the dedication, he gave the microphone to me. I took the microphone and started playing songs. Within a few minutes a man came to take pictures of me. An older lady came to say, the sound was not clear and that it was breaking up. I introduced myself and gave some background. More people came out to listen and to dance. An older man came out and sang all songs; it was very emotional and rewarding. He remembered old times. Three JHS students came out to listen. A young woman came out and danced, doing the gun movements. I joined her in the dance. I shared the background knowledge I had learned so far about Asafo. A man came from across the street and wanted to see me after the program; a young man came and told me that the people were happy and were talking about me and the program. I ended the program with their appellation, "Ngyedum!" The Okyeame (King's spokesperson Suapim) called. (Saturday, July 21, 2018, Kormantse, field notes)

Mindful of the fact that ɔman yɛmmu no anibuo, "The affairs of a town should not be handled lackadaisically," and to not become ɔhohoɔ a ɔto abɔntempono mu, "the visitor who locks the main door," I presented the information without pointing fingers or blaming anyone for the demise of Asafo. Rather, I hailed the town for its abakɔsɛm and Asafo tradition, delivering the information to illustrate the community's valor and genealogy. The sound was clear most of the time; at other times, the recording of some of the songs skipped and was not clear. Outside noise interfered with the playback, causing a cacophonic overload of sounds. At times, the drumming overshadowed the singing and contributed to the distortion of the sound. The speakers in the Communication Centre were not the best quality, though they worked. Overall, the program was okay.

After the program, the pastor summarized the presentation and talked about the importance of "going back to the roots." He talked about what he learned from the presentation. That there were three Asafo groups, *amferfo*, *adzewafo*, and *kyirem*, in the town, and there were Asafo songs for every event in life, he said, was new knowledge for him. He also gave thanks to all the teachers, my mentors who helped with the study. A woman who had come to advertise her medicine on air at the center invited me to come to her town, Asebu, to learn about their matters that have come and gone and give a similar presentation at Asebu. I told her I would consider it.

After the program, the pastor, ɔsɔfo Pastor David, walked with me to the residence of the gentleman who wanted to see me. Finding out that I was a Kwahu Akan, Pastor David asked why a Kwahu woman traveled to the Fante region to study Asafo. I told him about the evolution of my research from the songs of enslaved Africans to Asafo songs about slavery, and, finally, to Asafo because slavery was a taboo subject along the Ghanaian littoral. He did not comment. As we walked the undulating path I had never traveled, I asked the pastor why he thought the gentleman wanted to see me. Though our Elders say, *ɔhɔhoɔ nto mmra*, "The stranger does not break laws" (because she does not know them), I was concerned I may have broken some laws or played some songs that offended him. According to the pastor, the gentleman is a King who had heard the program, was impressed by it, and wanted to see me. This would be one of my most nervous walks because I was not sure what I was walking into. What if he chastised me for playing Asafo songs in the wee hours of the morning? What if he accused me of instigating a fight among the neighboring towns by my *ndwom* selections? I decided that even if he did, I would console myself with the knowledge that *obi se hyɛ wo sapɔ mu nsuo a ɛnyɛ yaw*, "If someone tells you to fill your sponge with water [reinforce your resources], it is not an insult." I would take that as a lesson and learn from it. *ɔyaw yɛ mframa*. "Insult is borne by the wind."

We talked about the importance of matters that have come and gone, how many societies cherish their *abakɔsɛm*, while Kormantse seems to have fallen behind. This was an interesting talk with the pastor because I had learned from many people that the pastors preach against their traditions, including Asafo, as "worldly and sinful," coded "fetish." Christians who sing Asafo songs or perform in the Asafo group are chastised by their fellow Christians and sometimes reprimanded at church for engaging in such "ungodly acts." One mentor had complained, earlier on during my research, "When you sing Asafo songs, the church people will come to your house at night, stand behind your window, and preach against you!"[4] I did not bring this up with the pastor. Then he made a comment that confused me because he seemed to contradict his statement earlier: "There are some people here in this town who do things in the dark, they worship idols, and then come to church and pretend. They are hypocrites." I wanted to ask to him about the church's role in the demise of Asafo, but I was preoccupied with the upcoming meeting, so I just replied, "Oooo . . . mmm . . ." Furthermore, *Wo nsa hyɛ obi anomu a yɛmmɔ n'apampam*, "When your hand is in someone's mouth, you do not strike on top of the person's head."

We arrived at a dark, barely lit house and were asked to enter a room. We entered and sat down. The pastor told the gentleman about our *amandzeɛ* mission. "*Maa nko me sɛmpa*" ("The matter is mine only"), the gentleman replied. He said he had been waking up early of late because he was troubled by events in the town. He was up when he heard the program on the air, was impressed by it, and decided to walk over and inquire. He likes to study *abakɔsɛm*, conduct research, and wanted to know if I could give him a copy of the script for the program, my findings, and a copy of the songs I played. He is the subchief of the Anona lineage and was frustrated by the divisions and the splits in the town. He did not know much about Asafo and its songs. I started the song, "*Ya ara nkyɛ/Ya ara nkyɛ/Ya ara nkyɛ/Ya ara nkyɛ/Ya ara nkyɛ/Ya ara nkyɛ/Nkum na Abandze kó yi hɔn kó nkwasea kó!*" He was impressed because according to him, he did not grow up at Kormantse and knew very little about Asafo. Then he said something that caught me off guard. He said he would gather his people one day and invite me to speak to them. I felt vindicated, but I was mindful of our Elders' saying, *Obi nkɔ obi kuro mu nkɔfrɛ ne ho Agyeman*, "One does not go to another person's town and call herself a Liberator." I joggled this saying with another that says, *Obi nkura nanka, nnyae nanka, nnyae nkɔse sɛ, "mehunuiɛ a, anka,"* "One does not have the opportunity, dismiss the opportunity, and then declare, 'if I had the opportunity.'" I left his house thinking, "I have become an advocate and voice for the town's Asafo." I felt uncomfortable, but proud, nonetheless.

I walked back to Nana's house to ask what he thought about the program. On the way, people called out to congratulate me and asked when I would come back to the center for additional programming. I saw Nana outside his room talking with people about the program. The moment Nana saw me, he called out, "*Abrewa, me Kɔnfo na, mbo ayɛ adze*," "Old Lady, my High Priestess, good job, you have done well!"

Two days later, I visited the Obaa Hemaa Queen Mother of the Aboradze lineage to record Aboradze lineage songs. The moment I walked into her compound, people who knew I had played the songs at the Communication Centre came to me and congratulated me for a job well done. She congratulated me as well. She also said, "When I first heard the songs, I laid in bed very still, shaken, anxious, and listened for the message, to hear people crying, or hear our Asafo warriors marching, drumming, with more singing and provocation. Then I said to myself, 'What matter is this? Who has died? What has happened to someone? What is the conflict?' Then I heard your voice and your explanation. I relaxed. I got up and started to dance. A few of us who were up, danced and danced and danced. We remembered the old times. You did well" (personal communication, Aboradze ɔbaa Hemaa, July 23, 2018, Kormantse Ghana). When I walked from her house, I thought about her remarks.

Her remarks concerned me because I caused her anxiety and worry. That I could have provoked a war scared me. What is my responsibility as a scholar, researcher? How do my walks, my comings and goings and questionings, and good intentions cause pain, anxiety, and conflict? *ɔman yɛmmu no anibuo*, "The affairs of a nation should not be handled lackadaisically." Her remarks also helped validate how crucial Asafo *ndwom* served as archives and communicative tools for the societies. It confirmed for me that Asafo drumming "puts fear in people's hearts" and was not played recklessly; so, whenever the drummer sounded the drum (*si kyen do*), people expected that something serious had happened. I remembered what my late Akɔdeɛ Afful shared early on (chapter 1): "Asafo songs are serious matter. When they sing the songs, then there is serious matter." Therefore, the ɔbaa Hemaa's remarks also helped me understand how serious and profound this art form is to the societies and people. *Ntontom ne hwan na ɔrekɔto onyina kɛsɛ*? "Who is a mosquito to wrestle with the silk-cotton tree?"[5] I went back to her and asked how I could present the program differently next time so that it does not create anxiety and confusion in people. I also asked if she thought I should play the songs again. "It is our *abakɔsɛm*," she replied. I kept walking. Thinking.

Footprints IIb—On Air

Friday, August 3, 2018.
I arrived at Kormantse Communication Centre at 4:30 a.m. today. It was a long three-kilometer walk since the taxi driver did not show. It was dark outside. After the pastor dedicated the town with prayer, I started the program. I announced myself and spoke in Fante about the different offices and instruments of Asafo. Uncle Bedu, Egya Nako, Kofi Abbam, and many others came out. Uncle John and Iron Boy were among the first to come out to listen. Mr. KoJo Sam, the older man who sang along all the songs the last time, came out almost immediately and sang along. He lives right behind the Centre. I joined him in the singing. He said it reminded him of the past. Women were

sweeping their compounds to Asafo *ndwom*, *ndwom* serving as a background for their daily chores. Work songs. New contexts. A taxi driver parked his car and listened to the songs. After the program, I walked home with him (KoJo Sam). His mother had passed away and was being brought home today. The songs touched a nerve. Nako suggested we embark on another recording project. After the program, Uncle John said some people at the seaside applauded me on how well I presented the program. Me Nyame, one of the town's organizers saw me walking through town and congratulated me, *Mbo na yɛ*, "Job well done." (Field notes, Friday, August 3, 2018)

The Program Outline

I. Play songs—start with "Eminsa Osuom" and "Oye Oye"
II. Introduction
Good morning. [They respond "Yaa Ahenewa" to me. They call me Nana Abena Ansahfoa I (I used my royal title).] Today, we are going to discuss Kormantse *ndwom*. Kormantse has many *ndwom*. Some are ampe, sunda, osode, ntsenma, kokoma, twobox, awarbonsei asa, KoJo amba, akɔm kyen, and Asafo.
III. Play Asafo songs
IV. Asafo is a group [that] protected the town. It is not fetish.
   a. Asafo has three groups.
      i. Amferfo—they wear kɔkɔɔ (red)
      ii. Adzewafo—they wear akokɔ ne sradze (yellow)
      iii. Kyiremfo—they wear duawusu (type of cloth, dark blue color)
   b. They have many Elders. Each one has specific duties. Some are Supi, Safo Baatan, Safohen/Safo Akyerɛ, Nwomtonyi, Okyerɛma, Frankaahuntanyi, Asekambɔfo, ɔsɔfo, Kɔmfo, ɔkyeame, etc.
V. Play songs
VI. Asafo *ndwom*
Now we will talk about Asafo *ndwom*. They play Asafo with a set of four drums. The set of four is called "Dabɔ kyen." They use the skin of the deer/antelope to head the drums. The drums are
      i. *Gyina na hɔ hwɛ*. They use it for playing proverbs and for talking. It is played with two kɔtɔkorba L-shaped sticks.

ii. *Ekum tawia*—played with two L-shaped sticks.
   iii. *ɔtoapentsin/ampaa*—played with two bare hands.
   iv. *Dɛnkyerɛma*—played with two small sticks.
   v. *Dawur* bell is also part of the ensemble.
VII. Play songs
VIII. The patterns of the instruments:
   a. Dawur plays
   b. *ɔtoapentsin/ampaa* plays
   c. *Ekum tawia*
   d. *Gyina na hɔ hwɛ*
IX. Play songs
X. End program with words of gratitude.

I left the Centre with mixed feelings. Entanglements. Were these efforts enough? How do we encourage societies to preserve their *ndwom* traditions when the contexts for those traditions no longer exist? Whose decision is it to make those determinations? Researchers? Townspeople? Do all townspeople support attempts to preserve their traditions? What if those traditions conflict with lifestyles, identities, and beliefs—such as religion, especially Christianity? I had these concerns when I initially thought about presenting at the school and on air and still thought deeply about them during and after the programs. Seeking permission and being granted permission to offer the programs did not alleviate my concerns. Who did I offend? Could playing those instigating Asafo songs that reference wars with neighboring towns aggravate tensions between them? Could we, "sustainability advocates," inadvertently pit townspeople against each other?

Who Made Us "Sustainability Advocates?"

I left the Speech and Prize Giving Day and went directly to the Cape Coast Castle for my walk there. On the way, I thought more deeply about my research and my role in this community. Why did I come to Kormantse? Why did people talk and share with me? How else could I give back to the community? Applied ethnomusicologists and sustainability scholars have proposed several measures to promote sustainability of *ndwom* around the world.[6] I thought about producing small booklets explaining what I had learned concerning Asafo and Kormantse history and donating them to the schools. I wondered though, since these narratives have so many variations, which of those *abakɔsɛm* to privilege. I also thought about the Ghana Cultural Policy (1975, 2004), whose fifteen objectives include the following:

1. (1) creating awareness of the traditional values and generate pride and respect for the nation's heritage;
2. (6) creating an institutional framework for the collection, preservation and conservation of tangible and intangible assets;
3. (7) eliminating, through public education, and appropriate legislation, cultural practices that lead to the abuse of the rights of the individual on account of ethnic differences, gender, age, religion, physical challenge or economic status;
4. (8) promoting the arts by enhancing the status of artists and artistes, identifying, developing and rewarding creative talent making artistic products contribute to wealth creation both for creative individuals and the nation as a whole;
5. (9) promoting the cultural awareness of the youth through formal and non-formal education to ensure that they are prepared to play their role in the cultural life of their communities;
6. (10) developing data and resource materials on Ghanaian culture for schools, colleges and the general public; and
7. (11) undertaking and promoting research to create a data base on culture for policy makers, academics, administrators, artists and artistes, embassies, foreign visitors and all other interested persons. (Ghana Cultural Policy 2004)

Their implementation requires the efforts of several stakeholders, including "all civil society groups, business and corporate organisations ... the Houses of Chiefs, District Assemblies, religious bodies, educational institutions, social groups, voluntary associations, artistic groups and associations, non-governmental organisations as well as the media agencies and institutions" (2004, 13). I thought about how these objectives would be addressed at Kormantse, since religion and pastors, according to my mentors, are the major cause of their dying traditions.

I once had a conversation with two Asafo members at Abura, a neighboring town, and with some Elders at Kormantse. Both groups suggested that such initiatives would require funding from outside sources. I wrote the following in my notes after one such meeting at the house of a deceased

Asafo captain at Abura. Like the many conversations I had on Asafo, it moved through different issues.

> I met the brother and uncle of the deceased. They said the Asafohene's position should have been filled; however, it was because of people's mentality and attitude towards Asafo—fetishism. Usually, they move the stool out of the house, but had to "turn it out and place it downwards and prayed." Old people are dying off and the young, because of Christianity, are not interested and shun Asafo. Also, wars are not there anymore. Sponsorship is key. Asafo is about money to pay members who perform, since the state is not obliged to pay them. Members must feed their families because it takes time, just as it takes time to go to work. Police and soldiers have taken over their responsibilities and duties of the state. Sustain the art by curating and creating. Who would they alert about drowning, a death, a wrongful person, Asafo or the police? Asafo used to be the right hand of the King. (Field notes, January 8, 2017)

That they must take time off work to practice the *ndwom* and teach it to the youth to sustain and maintain their traditions required some sponsorship and financial assistance, came up time and time again. When I asked how they intended to implement the objectives of the Ghana Cultural Policy, they said they had not heard of it.

As I walked away from my second program towards Nana's house, I reflected more deeply on the role of the King in these towns, who, according to the Ghana Cultural Policy, "is the kingpin of Ghanaian traditional culture, and its contemporary relevance is generally recognized" (13). Why had the King not taken the initiative to preserve these traditions? I remembered asking an Elder why the King did not encourage creativity and sustainability of these traditions. He said, "Even if he summons people to come to a discussion and participate in these things, they will not show." At this preliminary level of my studies, I thought the entanglements and tensions were far too complex to unravel, so I decided to stick with the little contribution I could manage. If "The applied worker can provide information to communities about their music and its history, and promote their music" (Fenn and Titon 2009), then I have fulfilled some part of that obligation. Still, I continued to think about what the Elders say: *Obi nkɔ obi akuraa nkyerɛ n'ase*, "One does not go to another persons' village to tell the latter her roots," or *Obi nkɔ obi kurom nkɔfrɛ ne ho Agyeman*, "One should not go to another person's town and call herself a Liberator."

> *Biribi reba e, biribi reba e* 🔊
> *Tuafo mba ei*
> *Owu reba ogyina nkwanta*
> *Nna nkwa so ogyina nkwanta*
> *Yɛma hɔn adze a wonndzi*
> *Yeyi hɔn edzi so a wɔnnkɔ*
> *Ntsi hɛnara Kyiremfo yi*
> *Yɛnye hɔn bɔko ana yɛahwɛ hɔn enyim*
> *Hɛn hen Gyesi yɛakra dɛ yɛrokɔ ko aba*
> *Yehyia mbarimba*
> *Hɔn tsir efuw a ma dɔm yi hɔn!*

(Something [war] is coming, Tuafo children
When death is coming it is standing at the junction
When life too is standing at the junction
When we give them something they won't accept
When we expel them, they won't leave
So, we Kyiremfo battalion
We will fight with them before we look at their faces
Our chief Gyesi we have given notice to fight and return
We are meeting strong men
Their hair is overgrown, crowd should shave them)

Nkekaho / Re-Invocation

Tón-Tón-Tón-Tón-Tón-Tón-Tón
Asafo!
Asá-fo
Mekuta ɔkɔtɔ mekuta aserewa
Sought permission
To walk with you
Know you
The Elders say
One should not go to another person's town
And call herself a Liberator
I could not
Aboa kɔkɔsɛkyi se ɔde ne kwasea pɛ nyinkyɛ
I did

How can a Ghanaian Kwahu woman go native
Ghanaians don't dress like that
Balancing many identities
Blurring dichotomies of insider and outsider
New African Diaspora
White-body supremacy rearing its head
Unbelonging At home
Trauma-ghosted
At home
Flashbacks
Ever-shifting identities
Over-doing it
Double native
Or
Concentric circles of identity

I
Kwahu woman of Aduana lineage
Storyteller

Who breaks my hand
Cannot see, touch drum
Though I drum and teach drumming
Cannot see, touch drum
When ɔbaa na ɔwo barima
Tweaaa!!

I
Entered
Inserted myself
ɔhohoɔ nte deɛ ne bɔtɔ reteɛ
The stranger does not hear what her luggage hears
Obisafoɔ nto kwan
Knowing very small about Asafo
Nsateaa baako ntumi mpopa animu
One finger cannot clean the face
Hu m'ani so nti na atwe mienu nam

Ibo Elders say
A step taken marks the end of a long journey
Kwahu woman
Knowing very little
Abakɔsɛm walk
Posuban walking
Memory
Musicking
History walking in beauty
Thinking
W
                              A
                    L
         K
   I
       N
                   G

Interviews
Egwuaradze
Last baths

Funerals
Corpse fanning
Dead men standing
Flags dancing
Spirits visiting
Talking drummer consoling
Memory
S
    L
        I
            P
                P
                    I
                        N
                            G

Kormantse éé iii
Eminsa mba
Tuafo mba
Waaka bosom nsu
Ya ara yɛ saw
Women play Asafo
Know Asafo well, well
Kenkan
Makes it sweet

Wɔmbom, wɔmbom
Dua no ebuii
Adende
Kormante na Abandze singers
Your four drums and bells
Kasa twii
Rapping diss tracks
Aa-ba!'
Your inside is too sweet

Ah!
Asafo
You are Spirit

Fapem
Nyinado
Wó si pi si tá
Tse-tse wɔ bi ka, tse-tse wɔ bi kyerɛ
Our Elders say *abɔfra hunu ne nsa hohoro a, ɔne mpanin didi*
When a child learns how to wash her hands, she eats with adults
Tete ka aso mu[1]
Repetitive listening leaves an indelible mark on the ear
Kwahu woman
Wofeefee asɛm mu a, wohunu mu yie
Walked and listened
Leaving *anammɔn* footprints
Esie ne kagya nni aseda
I still say
Thank you

Death joined the walk
Owu reba ogyina nkwanta
Nna nkwa so ogyina nkwanta
Yɛma hɔn adze a wonndzi
Yeyi hɔn edzi so a wɔnnkɔ
Maame Aba Aframba, Egya Akodɛɛ Afful, Auntie Monica
The walker also suffers
Du-é oooooo.

Asafo
The Elders say one does not go to another person's village
To tell the latter her roots
How to safeguard her traditions
A visitor who locks the main door
Schippers, Titon, Amu, Aduonum, and other outsiders
Champion you
Ei ɛdan ho pae na tɛfrɛ wura mu

A crack in the wall of a building makes way for invasion by the cockroach
Ah! Sɛ yɛnim sɛ mako bɛbre ama ayɛ ya a, anka yɛdii no bunu mu[2]
If we foresaw that cayenne pepper, would on ripening be so hot to the taste
We would have eaten it green
Asafo
Applied ethnomusicologists would champion your cause
Folkloric groups
May back you
UNESCO Conventions
Want to guard you
Ghana Cultural Policy
Gives lip service
Trudging

They aim to sustain
Their goals may be contentious
Unknown to many
Unattainable
Unsustainable for some
A possibility with sponsorship
ɔba nyansafo, yɛ bu no bɛ, yɛnka no asɛm
The wise child is instructed in proverbs not in plain words
Should an outsider go to another person's village
To tell her of her roots
Safeguard her traditions
Dufɔkyeɛ da nsuo mu, da da a, ɛrennane ɔdɛnkyɛm
A piece of log will never turn into a crocodile
No matter how long it remains in the river
Ebueii

Hmm . . .
Asafo

What are our commitments to the lands, Sefa Dei asks
What is good ethnomusicology
Ko-ko-gya
African musicology
Indigenous knowledge
As discursive frameworks
De-center colonial ways of doing
White racial framing

A good conversation never ends
It is the walker who eats sweet things
Our Akan Ancestors say
Nkyene nkamfo ne ho se ɔyɛ dɛ[3]
Salt does not praise itself that it is tasty
You did
Must
Nkwan pa twetwe adwa[4]
A good soup attracts chairs
Grab your chair
Let's keep walking!
You can't be *pɛtɛmprɛm* and be afraid of
ɔsono
Ko-ko-gya, ko-ko-gya, ko-ko-
Kim! Kim! Kim! Kim! Kim! Ki-kim
Hmmm ... hmmmm. ...
Ru-lu-lu-lu-lu-lu-lu-lu te-yam!
Po! Po! Po!
Hri-di-di-di-di-di, sru! Hri-di-di-di-di-di, sru!
Hri-di-di-di-di-di, sru! Sru! Sru! Sru!
Walking in beauty

Asafo
Dancers, nnwomtofo, and warriors
Edna, Bantuma, Anomabo, Oguaa *akyerɛkyerɛfo*
ɛnam dua so na ahoma ɛduru ɛsoro

ɛnam dua so na ahoma ɛduru ɛsoro

ɛnam mo so

Kormantse Bentsir Asafo
Ngyedum
Great Kormantine
Rehuru anaa rehra
Akyerɛma, akyerɛkyerɛfo, anansesɛmfo, nwomtofo,
asafo, nimdeɛ nhwehwɛmu fo ee
ɛnam dua so na kontrofi ehu kwayɛ mu
It is because of the tree that the monkey sees inside the forest
ɛnam mo so ooo
Aaa Asafo
Foriwaa Amanfo ɔbaa kokoɔdurufoɔ
Aburoo bɛtem a me yɛ apata mma má ɛkɔm guo
Reclaiming my voice, creative mobility
My center
Meda mo ase
Mekuta ɔkɔtɔ mekuta aserewa
Daasebrɛ
Da mo ase a, ɛnsa
Meda mo ase
Tón-Tón
Tón!

NOTES

Nnianim / Prologue

1. This piece challenges our understanding of the status quo and gives voice to previously unheard narratives about slavery. Each show concludes with a "talkback," to encourage dialogue about how this overlooked and "silenced" part of our world history continues to define relationships, politics, and policies. The talkback is meant for sincere and critical conversations about how today's racial and cultural problems connect with truths of our shared and painful pasts. The piece has been performed in Illinois, Washington, DC, and Ghana.

2. See William E. F. Ward, *A History of Ghana*, 92.

3. At the time, it was an empty land with no residents. However, as construction began, people walked from surrounding towns to work and trade items. Over time, and as the trek got tedious, workers began to stay overnight, sleeping "under its walls" (outside the building). In the local Fante language, *aban ase* (below the fence/structure), would later morph into Abandze, the town that developed around it.

4. Among the Fante along the coast, especially, slavery is a silent and taboo topic. Some African-Americans—Saidiya Hartman, *Lose Your Mother*, Bayo Holsey, *Routes of Remembrance*, etc.—expressed difficulties finding collaborators along the coast who would talk about slavery. The few who broached the topic, according to them, did so through Ghanaian proverbs (Holsey).

5. Slavery is celebrated only when it relates to the tourism industry.

6. The Late ɔsagyefoɔ Dr. Kwame Nkrumah was the first president of Ghana after its independence from Britain.

7. Shumway, *Fante and the Atlantic Slave Trade*, 144–146.

8. Zhao, "Doing Fieldwork," 189.

Notes for the Reader

1. Last few lines borrowed from J. H. K. Nketia, *Ayan*.

Introduction

1. Asafo rousing call between the lead singer, *nnwomtofo*, and chorus, *asafommba*. This is recited before the actual performance of songs.
2. De Graft Johnson, "Asafu."
3. I conducted most of my research at Kormantse, where I walked with many scholars during my sabbatical in 2016–2017 and then again in 2018. During this time, I also visited several towns along the coast, including Akyemfo, Apam, Anomabo, Cape Coast, Mankessim, and Elmina, to attend funerals, walk by their Asafo *posuban* military posts, talk with scholars, and observe drumming and dancing events.
4. According to one version, warriors invoked the Gods for passage over a river.
5. Ampem, 136.
6. See Ama Oforiwaa Aduonum, "Ethnomusicologists, Keep Walking," and "Walking as Fieldwork Method."
7. Barz and Cooley (2008), Jackson (1987), McCollum and Hebert (2014), Nettl (2015), Rice (2014).
8. See Chapter 3 of Angela Impey, *Songwalking*.
9. Bakan (1999), Dirksen (2019), Kisliuk (1998), or Seeger (1982).
10. Impey (2018) explores the walking and singing experiences of ten women in Western Maputaland. Throughout the book she shares her discovery and rediscovery of the land through their eyes and memories of the land. During one of those walks during which the women played their *isitweletwele* and sang, she writes, "As we walk along the newly resurfaced road, the women point out various landmarks: the new trading store located next to a large tree where they used to congregate for their midnight *isigcawu* dances (121).
11. Urban geographers Pierce and Lawhon (2015), Evans and Jones (2011), anthropologists (Ingold 2010; Lee-Vergunst and Ingold (2006, 2008); Legat (1999); Tuck-Po (1999); social scientists Kinney (2017); Moles (2008); and others; Oppezzo and Schwartz (2014), Anderson (2004), and Edensor (2008, 2010), Wunderlich (2008), and Middleton (2010) discuss walking as an embodied practice affording a creative and critical relationship with space and lead in theorizing walking as method in the last decade. See Joseph Wherton et al, "Wandering as a Sociomaterial Practice."
12. Such as Impey did on many occasions during her research.
13. Bonilla, "The Past is Made by Walking."
14. See Oddey and Wright, *Modes of Spectating*.
15. Maps designed by Illinois State University Cartographer Jill Freund Thomas.
16. Ampem, 152.
17. Jérome Truc, "Places of Memory," 201.
18. Sarah Pink, *Doing Sensory Ethnography*, 151.

19. Bruce Chatwin, *The Songlines*.
20. They told us boys could not have children.
21. See Kwasi Aduonum, "Akosua Tuntum" and "A Compilation."
22. Students at the Institute of African Studies were nicknamed "dondologists" by their peers in the other departments.
23. Bruno Nettl, *Ethnomusicology*, 155.
24. Most of the existing fieldwork and research on Asafo has been conducted by male scholars.
25. Zhao, 189.
26. R. Pain (2001), Pawson e. & Banks (1993), Jennifer Rogers-Brown (2011), and G. Valentine (1990), etc.
27. See Perkins' (1994) about his experience with a group of elderly men while he walked through Cape Coast.
28. See Don Kulick and Margaret Wilson, *Taboo*, and Catherine Appert and Sidra Lawrence, "Beyond #MeToo."
29. See Michel De Certeau, *The Practice of Everyday Life*.
30. See Garnett Cadogan, "Walking While Black." Certain disabilities prevent some people from engaging in the practice of placing one foot in front of the other continuously. This does not mean that they cannot do field research. Riding or driving are parallel areas of inquiry to walking. However, the outcome of such research will be markedly different from those conducted on foot.
31. See Hillie Koskela, "Bold Walk."
32. KoJo is the Akan name for a boy born on Monday. Adwoa is the Akan name for a girl born on Monday. MaAdwoa's middle name is Pokua, named after my mother, thus MaAdwoa.
33. See Buchi Emecheta's novel *The Joys of Motherhood*, 1979.
34. See Pierce and Lawhon, "Walking as Method," 2015.
35. Guba in Pierce and Lawhon, 658.
36. Currently, there are two Kormantse towns, bordering each other, Kormantse No. 1 SN and Kormantse No. 2. This analysis is based on data collected at Kormantse #1. Some even refer to Abandze, another town north of #1, as Kormantse #3.
37. In 1645, two parts of Kromantse (the two parts according to the source) bore the names Bentsir and Nkum which are still used by Kro-mantse Asafo companies today, and, what is more, they were in conflict in a distinctly familiar way (Ratekband, cited in Datta and Porter 1971, 292).
38. On archaeology (Agorsah and Butler 2008; Shaffer and Agorsah 2010; Agorsah 2008, 1996, 1993); diaspora studies (Bilby 1981; Kea 1982; Rath 1993; Thornton 1998; Blake and Blake 1898; and Agorsah 2008); and religion (Agorsah 2014). Passing references appear in various sources about the division of its town (cited in Datta and Porter 1971); flags and art (Datta 1972, Doss 2007, and 2010, Labi 2015 and 2002); and slavery (Buah 1980).

39. See William G. Schaffer and Kofi Agorsah, "Bioarchaeological Analysis," 3.

40. According to the Kormantse Housing census of 2010, their population was 7,911. The projected 2018 census was estimated at 9,284. Courtesy of Saltpond District Assembly (2017).

41. A more recent account by Elders of Kormantse in 2016–2017, however, asserts that they migrated from Sudan and settled at Takyiman before making it to their current settlement with two leaders: Nana Komer Panyin and his younger brother, Komer Kakra.

42. See Ansu Datta and Richard Porter, 281. Pax Britannica was part of the covenant signed in 1844 between the British governor at Cape Coast Castle and chiefs in southern Gold Coast. It mandated that all criminal cases in those societies shall be tried before the queen's judicial officers, effectively erasing or diminishing local legal systems and codes.

43. De Graft Johnson, 313. According to De Graft Johnson, the master drummer's position is so important that in the olden days sometimes a person was bought to hold the position.

44. The shilling (s) was a former British coin. Its purchasing power in the 1930s when DeGraft made this calculation would be equivalent to today's 2.10 GBP; 25s is equivalent to 52.50 GBP, or $66.83 today.

45. They are locked away at the Omanhen's palace, though Nana Odum III insists that Asafo flags are never kept in the Omanhene's palace; the Safohen or one of the Asafo leaders keeps them.

46. At Elmina, many have folded, with the remaining groups performing only ceremonial roles.

47. Datta and Porter, 281.

48. I did not witness the *Afahyɛ*, nor did I see musical instruments other than the *gyina hɔ hwɛ* master drum or witness the installation of new Safohen. The last *Afahyɛ* was performed in 1972.

49. See Per Hernaes (1998) for an extensive list of Asafo historiographic resources.

50. Ampem, 158.

51. Achebe (1958), Aidoo (1987), Anyidoho (1984), Armah (1968), Bá (1982), Chinweizu and Ihechukwu (1980), Fanon, Ki-Zerbo (1981), Mbembe (1992), Nkrumah (1965, 1970), Soyinka (1963), Tamale (2020), wa Thiong'o (1986, 1987), Wiredu (1998), and many others.

52. Agawu (2003), Kidula (2006), Nannyonga-Tamusuza (2012), etc., have also addressed the colonial framing in ethnomusicological discourse about Africa.

53. Ampem, 157.

54. See the use of narratives in Impey (2018), Kidula (2014), Kisliuk (1998), Muller (2011), Nannyonga-Tamusuza (2005), Ozah (2006), Seeger (1982), Shonekan (2020), Stone (1982), Sklar (2001), and Tang (2007).

Chapter 1

1. Hoefnagel 6, and Herzfeld, *Anthropology*, 55.
2. I may have heard it before and did not know at that time.
3. A lady had recommended that I talk to him when I mentioned my interest in learning about Asafo songs of protest and slavery.
4. According to oral narratives and written sources, Kwaa Amankwah was a hunter who led his people to a site where he encountered water. See John Fynn (1971).
5. The Dutch involvement in Elmina affairs occurred after they captured Elmina Castle from the Portuguese in 1637.
6. Abrofonkoa, European servants, were made up of those who worked for the Dutch; while Akrampa consisted of residents who were descendants of the Dutch.
7. "*Hɛn Nananom*" means our Ancestors.

Chapter 2

1. I had audited a few of the classes and with permission from the instructor, I joined the class on a trip.
2. This was the second of such research trips for the class.
3. According to them, the town where the fort is located was named Abandze after the traders from neighboring villages who sold food to the workers of the fort decided to stay at the base of the structure by saying, *Ene meda aban no ase*, "Today I will sleep at the base of the structure." Over time, the area became known as Abandze.
4. They also commented on the symbolism of their Ahenfie *poma* staff, which embodies the spirit of the chieftaincy. It is a wooden stick with a carved image of a parrot and a mother breast-feeding a child; the breast-feeding mother represents the "mother" of the town who feeds and provides for the town; the parrot represents the King and speaks to the people. I learned that the King belongs to the Anona lineage, whose origins involved a mother and a parrot.
5. According to a 1932 document prepared by the Provincial Commissioner's Office dated January 17, 1932, the song is an *esukwa dwom*—the wailing song that was sung to complement the effect of a battle between Kormantse and Abandze at another town, Afrangua.
6. See Gracie Olmstead's (2018) description of her grandfather's walks.
7. Because of schooling for my children, I decided to stay at Abura and traveled to Kormantse; on the weekends, I stayed overnight at Kormantse. Over the months I traveled on public transportation daily to Kormantse from Cape Coast. After dropping my children at school each morning, I took a taxi from Abura to Cape Coast; then rode a bus through several coastal towns—Moree, Akatayiwa,

Biriwa, Anomabo, Abandze, Egyaa I and II, Kormantse Nkum—before alighting at Kormantse Bentsir.

8. Nana mentioned later that Ngyedum is not a town. They came from Sudan; Tachiman came in 1225, they got there in 1228, stayed for three weeks, then left for here. They came to this area forty years before Mankessim. To show that they got there before, today, Mankessim swears Kings at their *Esiw Enyim*.

9. I found out the spokesperson is a staunch Christian.

10. Before I got there, they had stopped at the shrine of Nana Sesá, the God who protects the town, and sang his song; they had also stopped at the shrine of Nana Bohimahi (the warrior Goddess) and their burial site.

11. All Asafo companies have a *posuban* where they store their war regalia, spiritual articles, musical instruments, and other memorabilia (see Samuel Bentum 2006).

12. See Impey, 121.

13. The statue of the female Asafo captain at the *posuban* has a similar *nyansapɔ* hairstyle.

14. Otsir is about half a mile from Kormantse.

15. Public Records and Archives Administration Department (PRAAD), Cape Coast Branch, ADM 23/1/1503.

16. E. C. Elliot, The British district commissioner for the region, described them as a "truculent people" when reviewing a dispute between Kormantse residents and their neighbors that resulted in the former's loss of their fishing trade. (PRAAD) ADM 11/1/748. See also Ward (1948) and Williams (1999).

17. Peggy Appiah et al., *Bu Me Be*.

Chapter 3

1. Ampem, 112.

2. Interviews with scholars at Kormantse and along the coast.

3. According to Ward, three Ashanti invasions occurred at the coast in 1806, 1811, 1814, during which the "Ashanti advance guard was at Kormantine, looking for two Assin Chiefs," and 'The Ashanti advance guard occupied Kormantine, where the Dutch commander surrendered the fort without any attempt at resistance." Fynn has observed that when the Asante went after the fugitive Assin chiefs, Tsibu and Aputei, they camped a short while at Kormantsi, where the Dutch factor traded firearms to them. Fynn explains that "The Great Oath (Ntam Kese) of Asante recalled the death of Osei Tutu who is described by a modern scholar as the 'most venerated person in Ashanti.' But because the event was considered the most disastrous in Asante history, the actual names of the day, Memeneda (Saturday) and place, Kormantse, must not be uttered when swearing the oath."

4. Carl Reindorf, *History of the Gold Coast*, 68. The author hinted at the origins of the name Koromantse when he added, "Hence, when any of the warriors was

asked as to the rumors of the king's death, the reply was, 'Mekoroe na mante' . . . i.e. I joined the campaign, but never heard of it." Such a connection colors Kormantse residents' explanation for the origins of name of their town.

5. A. B. Ellis, *A History of the Gold Coast*, 68. Other scholars, including Margaret Priestley and Ivor Wilks, dispute the place and timing of the event and oath.

6. Ellis' report of the first invasion of the Fanti by the Asante in 1805–1807. This account supports an oral account by one teacher that when residents of Kormantse heard about the Asante presence and destruction of several coastal towns, many Kormantse residents fled the town and settled in neighboring towns.

7. John K. Fynn, *Asante and Its Neighbors*. According to this author, "The 'oath' (Ntam) as an institution is common in Akan society. Every Akan chief, lineage head, and, indeed, every person of importance, had his oath. An oath referred, usually obscurely, to some tragic incident in the past. An allusion to such a misfortune is strongly forbidden for two main reasons. First, it was widely believed that it offended the Ancestors of the community and thus estranged them from the living. Secondly, the Akan feared that an allusion to the incident might lead to repetition of the disaster" (58).

8. Ghanaian popular music style that borrows elements from hip-hop.

9. See James Christensen, *Double Descent*, 31-32.

10. Safohen Panyin Nana Odum III performed the version.

11. See John Mensah Sarbah, *Fanti National Constitution*, and Casely Hayford, *Gold Coast Native Institution*, for extensive discussion of Native Laws.

12. Others have written about walking as an important social practice, aesthetic practice (Bassett 2004; Careri and Picolo 2017), for commemorating the past (Bonilla 2011; Plate 2006), for connecting with the land (Ingold 2000 and 2014; Worley 2016), experiencing oral narratives (Legat 2014; Basso 1984), for experiencing the sounds in the environment (Corringham 2013; Wagstaff 2000; Westerkamp 1974; Schaffer 1974), and "as a form of expression" (Augoyard 2007).

13. See Kisliuk (1998), Seeger (1998), and Bakan (1999).

14. According to Yarimar Bonilla, the Creole slogan *fe memwa maché* literally means to "make your memory walk" or "take your memory on a walk." The phrase refers to the process of thinking back, scanning your memory for past events; when something or someone causes you to recall something, they are making your memory walk" (2011, 313).

15. Steven Feld, "Waterfalls," 92.

16. Chatwin.

Chapter 4

1. In the past, every child, male or female, in Fante society belonged to the father's Asafo. The officers are mostly men; however, women play key roles. Women serve as captains (*Asafoakyerɛ*) within the association, and the priest is usually a woman (*Asafokɔmfo*). She has great powers and, in the past, offered prayers and

sacrifices for the company and directed when warriors should attack their enemies (see Okeke).

2. I had never heard of fried cassava, so I tried it. It was delicious.

3. The president-elect was Akuffo-Addo.

4. Over time, I came to know Maame Poli better, as she walked down to Kormantse Lower Town daily to care for her aging mother.

5. They were wailing for John Mahama, candidate for the National Democratic Congress who lost the election. I found out later that they were supporters of the candidate who won the election, Nana Akuffo-Addo of the National People's Party.

6. She is of the Domna Lineage. She and her children were responsible for bearing the cost of his coffin. See Christensen and Chukwukere for additional discussion on the duties of the children and clan members for their deceased members.

7. Her deceased husband was an Asafo spear holder who taught their son, Kofi Abbam, many songs.

8. She could also wear white beads around the neck and wrist and white earrings.

9. I liken this feeling of "in-between-ness," to what Ghanaians call a "wayfarer," or *saman twetwɛ* (roaming/restless ghost), and similar in concept to anthropologists' "liminal" state (Turner 2011), where one borders or lingers before reaching a definitive state, a threshold.

10. *Adzewa* is a Fante traditional ensemble performed by women.

11. Others said he was a Safohen, Asafo captain.

12. Galamsey is the shortened Ghanaian term for "gather them and sell."

13. These days, as more and more people join the church, people move away, and with the presence of a disinterested youth, many of these ceremonies have ceased to exist. I did not witness the Afahyɛ or a Safohen installation.

Chapter 5

1. See Chukwukere's (1981, 1982) and Christensen's (1954) contentious claims about "double descent" among the Fante. Their analysis of Agnatic and Uterine relations expands our understanding of matrilinity and patrilinity among the Fante and the Akan in general.

2. See also Mercy Oduyoye, *Daughters of Anowa*, and Christine Oppong, *The Emancipation of Women*.

3. Eva Meyerowitz, *Akan Traditions*, 29.

4. Ampem, 124.

5. The archaeologist Kofi Agorsah uses a different name for what was taught to me as Nana Sesa. According to him, "The Tigare shrine that the Bentsir community of historic Kormantse acquired from the north of Ghana for catching witches, for example, was kept strategically at the outskirts of the town ostensibly to ward off the machinations of evil people as they approached the community. Equally,

evil-minded people who had committed wicked acts and were about to flee from the community could be apprehended whenever they passed the altar of the Deity, Tigare (2014, 103). His description fits Nana Sesa, though no one at Kormantse referred to him as Tigare.

6. See Susan Weisser, *Feminist Nightmares*.

7. Today, there are over twenty-five churches, including Methodist, Twelve Apostles, Big Zion One, Zion Church, Apostolic, Presbyterian, Assemblies of God, Nkansah Spiritual Church, Salvation, Anglican, Seventh Day Adventist, Mozama Disco Christo Church, and Christ Apostolic Church.

8. The first song that Nana sang for me belonged to the Mother Goddess Nana Eminsa. According to him, when the fight starts, they use it to evoke and praise her. I had heard the song many times from several people and even received a ten-minute tutorial from another lady who insisted I was singing it incorrectly. When she sang the song, she sped some parts of it, added more embellishments and appellations, and pitched other parts much higher than how Nana sang it. Her version was sweeter than the version Nana performed (see chapter 9).

9. Kenichi Tsukada (2001) has outlined the following categories for Asafo songs: inter-Asafo conflict; songs of interstate; other war-related songs; and songs unrelated to war.

10. Conflicts arise out of disagreements over land dispute, display of flags, drumming, songs, histories, threats, and intimidation. Colonial records provide much evidence about how Asafo songs, drumming, and the display of company flags provoked tension among Kormantse Asafo and its neighbors.

11. Ancestors of this group are said to have settled at Jamestown when they migrated from Anomabo, a coastal town in the Central Region of Ghana.

12. For discussions about similar all-female ensembles, see Aduonum (1975); Ampene (2005); Anyidoho, Nannyonga-Tamusuza (2005); Opondo (1996); and Ozah (2006).

13. I did not pursue my research with the Ga Nlesi Adzewa beyond the initial gathering and recording of songs, so I did not get into lyrical analysis of the songs.

14. "Walking in writing," is mentally revisiting a place to think about what one is describing and taking stock of what was going on at that moment in the narrative. It is how we "walk back to" past moments in order to write about them.

15. Ampem, 118.

16. Ampem, 132.

Chapter 6

1. A few, such as the one at Kormantse Bentsir, are presented on Friday.

2. The egwuaradze my friend and her children presented for their deceased husband/father, what Nana Odum presented for his deceased wife at Kormantse, and

the one presented to a flag bearer were on a much smaller scale compared to this. Nana Odum presented two silk underwear, two silk head wraps, two containers of powder, two bottles of perfume, two towels, two pieces of cloth, a mat, a pillow, and a bottle of holy water.

3. I moved to Cape Coast because I was told its Asafo companies still performed live music. My children, KoJo and MaAdwoa, stayed with my sister, Abena Kyeraa at Accra, and attended school there.

4. See Acquah, "New Trends in Asafo Music Performance, 29."

5. See also Nnanyonga-Tamuzusa, *Baakisimba*; Kisliuk, *Seize the Dance*; and Ozah, "Child Queen."

6. I learned from my dance teacher that Anaafo Asafo is the only company at Cape Coast that secures its casket in a wooden frame.

7. I attended six more funeral-related events that month of February, including a homecoming, wake keeping, an *eyi-enyim* (beginning of funerals for prominent people), a funeral, and *ndase*—thanksgiving. Five of them had live Asafo drumming and dance; some had other styles such as *kete*, *fɔntɔmfrɔm*, gospel music, brass band, jazz, or hymns.

8. Agawu, *Imagination*.

9. See Clifford Geertz's (1975) discussion of his run with the Balinese when they were being chased by the police for their participation at a cockfight.

10. See also Datta and Porter, "The Asafo System."

11. Kwabom's interview was part of a study to support his thesis that Asafo flag dancing was not developed as a means of hiding fighting techniques behind dance.

12. Ampem, 66.

13. The flag was created after Ghana's independence from Britain, hence the Ghanaian flag on the right-hand corner.

14. See Farris Thompson, *Flash Spirits*.

Chapter 7

1. My music teacher, Mr. Thompson, pointed this out to me while discussing my current research project on Asafo.

2. The Ghanaian Akan saying, "When you behead a snake, what is left is a mere rope," sums up the role of the drummer and his demise in the tradition; *Wo so aboa no ti a, na nea aka yɛ ahoma*.

3. De Graft Johnson, "Asafu," and Ansu Datta, "The Asafo System."

4. See Blacking, *How Musical is Man?*, Nannyonga-Tamuzuza, *Baakisimba*, and Tang, *Masters of the Sabar*.

5. *Lanta* is cloth that is wrapped around between the thighs and around the waist like underwear.

6. See Sefa Dei and Mairi McDermott, *Centering African Proverbs*.

7. See Grace Diabah and Nana Amfo, "Caring Supporters."

8. See Ellen Koskoff, *A Feminist Ethnomusicology* and *Women and Music*.
9. See chapter 6.
10. Later that day, when I explained some of the lyrics and role of Asafo to my son, he remarked, "They are gangsters!" I had not made that connection until he pointed it out.
11. See chapter 1.
12. See introduction.
13. Ampem, 157.
14. Godwin Kwafo Adjei (1999) calls "Aho." According to him, "Every asafo performance is preceded by what is referred to as 'aho.' That is before the start of everything, the leader of the group shouts out the appellation of the group or a short phrase which is immediately responded by the chorus. For example, the leader may shout the following phrase, 'oko oeyi hon' [we've fought and defeated them] and the response from the chorus with be 'oeyi hon,' [we have defeated them]" (83–84).
15. Nketia defines this practice of "simultaneous doing" in different terms, including what he calls "polarity," the duplication of melody in octaves, and homophonic parallelism, in which the singers embellish the main melody in thirds, fourths, fifths, or sixths.
16. Other African-American music styles like work songs, blues, spirituals, jazz, rhythm and blues, and gospel music also use signifyin'.
17. Public Records and Archives Administration (PRAAD), Cape Coast Branch, ADM 23/1/1503.
18. Some scholars have posited that rap came from Africa; others have refuted that claim (see Catherine Appert's *In Hip Hop Time*). Cool DJ Herc, the Jamaican migrant who is often credited as the first to initiate emceeing in the South Bronx, says hip-hop has its origins in Jamaica.
19. I learned that some fishermen slept at the seaside overnight, especially since they had to go out to sea at dawn and returned late at night.
20. See the following authors' discussions on the training of African musicians: Aduonum (1975), Ampene (2005), Anyidoho (1994), Bebey (1975), Berliner (1981), Nnanyonga-Tamusuza (2005), Ozah (2006), Stone (1982), and Tang (2007).
21. See Stone's (1982) discussion about Kpelle musicians' sources of talent, competence, and music (84–85).
22. That Western styles share elements with Asafo performance structure in these coastal towns challenges the "Other" signification that is often applied to the music of Africa.
23. This could have been a reference to one of their neighbors.
24. *Gari* is made from cassava root, while *etsew* is made from corn. *Ntsitsii* is stew made from fresh fish cooked in palm oil and tomato sauce with a touch of pepper and salt. Delicious!
25. See Pierce and Lawhon, "Walking as Method."
26. I met with Nana and the town's Okyeame, spokesperson, to discuss how to revive Asafo on two occasions.

27. "Trauma ghosted" is the body's recurrent or pervasive sense that danger is just around the corner or something terrible is going to happen any moment (see Menakem 2017, 8).

28. According to Resmaa Menakem, "white-body supremacy" is a term that describes how the white body is elevated above all bodies. The white body is the ostensibly supreme standard against which other bodies' humanity is measured. The attitudes, convictions, and beliefs of white-body supremacy are reflexive cognitive side effects, like the belief of a claustrophobe that the walls are closing in. These ideas have been reinforced through institutions as practice, procedures, and standards. https://medium.com/@rmenakem/white-supremacy-as-a-trauma-response-ce631b82b975.

29. Ama Ata Aidoo, *Dilemma of a Ghost*.

30. See Nketia, *Music of Africa* and Nnanyonga-Tamusuza, *Baakisimba*.

31. The names come to him when he wakes up at dawn.

32. I liken this feeling of "in-between-ness," to what Ghanaians call a "wayfarer," or *saman twetwe* (roaming ghost) and recalls anthropologists' "liminal" state (Turner 2011) where one borders or lingers before reaching a definitive state, a threshold.

33. Contributors in *Shadows in the Field* (2008) and *Performing Ethnomusicology* (2006) and many other ethnomusicologists have written extensively about their participatory approach to learning about the music they study. Mantle Hood premises his "bi-musicality" on learning to play.

34. Barz and Cooley, "New Ethnomusicology."

Chapter 8

1. Ampem, 173.
2. See Dor, "Uses of Indigenous Music."
3. Ampem, 114.
4. I also learned that many positions in Asafo had not been filled because people ran away when they are approached for installation.
5. Ampem, 101.
6. Bendrups et al. (2013); Cooley (2019); Schippers and Bendrups (2015); Titon (2009a/b, 2015).

Nkekaho / Re-Invocation

1. Ampem, 157.
2. Ibid, 189.
3. Ampem, 98.
4. Ampem, 97.

REFERENCES

Abe, Marié. 2015. "Walking, Parading, and Footworking through the City: Urban Processional Music Practices and Embodied Histories." Paper presented at the Society for Ethnomusicology Annual Meeting, Austin, TX.

Abu-Lughod, Lila. 1993. *Writing Women's Worlds: Bedouin Stories*. Berkeley, Los Angeles, and Oxford: University of California Press.

Achebe, Chinua. 1958. *Things Fall Apart*. London: Heineman.

Acquah, Emmanuel Obed. 2013. "New Trends in Asafo Music Performance: Modernity Contrasting Traditions." *Journal of African Arts and Culture* 1: 21–32.

Adler, Peter. 1992. *Asafo: African Flags of the Fante*. London: Thames and Hudson.

Adjei, Godwin Kwafo. 2000. "Asafo Music of the Fantes: A Study of the History, Development, and Form of Asafo Music of Cape Coast and Elmina." Master's thesis, University of Ghana, Legon, Ghana.

Adu-Gyamfi, Yaw. 2002. "Orality in Writing: Its Cultural and Political Significance in Wole Soyinka's 'Ogun Abibiman.'" *Research in African Literatures* 33, no. 3: 104–124.

Aduonum, Ama Oforiwaa. 2014. "Walking with My Ancestors: Elmina Castle." Performance and talk back, Normal, IL.

———. 2015. "A Tapestry of Sweet Mother(hood): African Scholar, Mother, and Performer?" In Anna M. Young, ed., *Teacher, Scholar, Mother: Re-Envisioning Motherhood in the Academy*, 217–236. Lanham, MD, Boulder, CO, New York, London: Lexington Books.

———. 2019a. "Ethnomusicologists, Keep Walking." *SEM Newsletter* 54, no. 5: 19–21.

———. 2019b. "Walking with My Ancestors: Cape Coast Castle." Performance art piece, Normal, IL.

———. 2021a. "Ethnomusicology, *Ayɛ Kradow*?" *Ethnomusicology* 65, no. 2 (Summer): 203–220.

———. 2021b. "Walking as Fieldwork Method in Ethnomusicology." *Ethnomusicology* 65, no. 2 (Summer): 221–258.

Aduonum, Kwasi. 1980. "A Compilation, Analysis, and Adaptation of Selected Ghanaian Folktale Songs for Use in the Elementary General Music Class." PhD dissertation, University of Michigan, Ann Arbor, Michigan.

———. 1975. "Traditional Musical Ensemble of Ghana: 'Akosua Tuntum.'" Master's thesis, University of Michigan, Ann Arbor, Michigan.

Affrifah, Kofi. 2000. *The Akyem Factor in Ghana's History 1700–1875*. Accra: Ghana Universities Press.

Agawu, Kofi. 2016a. *The African Imagination in Music*. New York: Oxford University Press.

———. 2016b. "Tonality as a Colonizing Force in Africa." In Ronald Radano, and Tejumola Olaniyan, eds., *Audible Empire: Music, Global Politics, Critique*, 334-355. Durham, NC: Duke University Press.

———. 2003. *Representing African Music: Postcolonial Notes, Queries, Positions*. New York and London: Routledge.

Aggrey, J. E. K. 1978. *Asafo*. Accra: Ghana Publishing.

Agorsah, E. Kofi. 1993. "Archaeology and Resistance History in the Caribbean." *African Archaeological Review* 11, no. 1: 175–195.

———. 2014. "Spiritual Vibrations of Historic Kormantse and the Search for African Diaspora Identity and Freedom." In Akinwumi Ogundiran and Paula Sanders, eds., *Materialities of Ritual in the Black Atlantic*, 87–107. Bloomington and Indianapolis: Indiana University Press.

Agorsah, E. Kofi, and Thomas Butler. 2008. "Archaeological Investigation of Historic Kormantse, Ghana: Cultural Identities." *African Diaspora Archaeology Newsletter* 11, no. 3: 1–22.

Aidoo, Ama Ata. 1965. *The Dilemma of a Ghost*. New York: Longmans.

———. 1987. *Two Plays: The Dilemma of a Ghost and Anowa*. Harlow, UK: Longman African Classics.

Alcoff, Linda. 1991/92. "The Problem of Speaking for Others." *Cultural Critique* 20 (Winter): 5–32.

Amadiume, Ifi. 1997. *Reinventing Africa: Matriarchy, Religion and Culture*. London and New York: Zed Book Press.

Ampem, Agyewodin Adu Gyamfi. 1999. *Akan Mmbebusem Bi: Akan Proverbs in Akan and English*. Kumasi, Ghana: University Press.

Ampene, Kwasi. 2005. *Female Song Tradition and the Akan of Ghana: The Creative Process in Nnwonkoro*. New York: Taylor and Francis.

Amponsah, Paulina Ekua. 2004. "Seismic Activity in Ghana: Past, Present and Future." *Annals of Geophysics* 47, no. 2/3: 539–543.

Anderson, Jonathan Mark. 2004. "Talking Whilst Walking: A Geographical Archaeology of Knowledge." *AREA* 36, no. 3: 254–261.

Anyidoho, Akosua. 1994. "Tradition and Innovation in Nnwonkorɔ: An Akan Female Verbal Genre." *Research in African Literature* 23, no. 3 (Autumn): 141–159.

Anyidoho, Kofi. 1984. *A Harvest of Our Dreams, with Elegy for the Revolution: Poems*. London: Heinemann.

Appert, Catherine, and Sidra Lawrence. 2020. "Ethnomusicology beyond #MeToo: Listening for the Violences of the Field." *Ethnomusicology* 64, no. 2: 225–253.

Armah, Ayi Kwei. 1968. *The Beautyful Ones Are Not Yet Born*. Boston: Houghton Miffin.

Asante, Emmanuel K. A. 2002. *Akan Proverbs: Their Origins, Meanings and Symbolical Representations in Ghanaian Material Cultural Heritage*. Accra: Asempa Publishers.

Asiamah, A. E. A. 2000. *The Mass Factor in Rural Politics: The Case of the Asafo Revolution in Kwahu Political History*. Accra: Ghana Universities Press.

Augoyard, Jean-François. 2007. *Step by Step: Everyday Walks in a French Urban Housing Project*. London and Minneapolis: University of Minnesota Press.

Ba, Mariama. 1982. *So Long a Letter*. London: Virago.

Bakan, Michael. 1999. *Music of Death and New Creation: Experiences in the World of Balinese Gamelan Beleganjur*. Chicago and London: University of Chicago Press.

Barz, Gregory, and Timothy Cooley. 2008 (1997). *Shadows in the Field: New Perspectives for Fieldwork in Ethnomusicology*. New York and Oxford: Oxford University Press.

Bassett, Keith. 2004. "Walking as Aesthetic Practice and a Critical Tool: Some Psychogeographic Experiments." *Journal of Geography in Higher Education* 28, no. 3: 397–410.

Baumann, Richard. 1990. "Poetics and Performance as Critical Perspectives on Language and Social Life." *Annual Review of Anthropology* 19: 59–88.

Beaudry, Nicole. 2008. "The Challenge of Human Relations in Ethnographic Inquiry: Examples from Arctic and Subarctic Fieldwork." In Gregory F. Barz and Timothy J. Cooley, eds., *Shadows in the Field: New Perspectives for Fieldwork in Ethnomusicology*, 224–245. Oxford and New York: Oxford University Press.

Bebey, Francis. 1975. *African Music: A People's Art*. Chicago: Lawrence Hill.

Bendrups, Dan, and Huib Schippers, eds. 2015. "Sound Futures: Exploring Contexts for Music Sustainability." *World of Music*, Special Issue 4, no. 1.

Bentum, Samuel Adentwi. 2006. "Cultural Significance of Edina Asafo Military Company Posts." PhD dissertation, Kwame Nkrumah University of Science and Technology, Kumasi, Ghana.

Berliner, Paul. 1981. *The Soul of Mbira: Music and Traditions of the Shona People of Zimbabwe*. Chicago and London: University of Chicago Press.

Bhabha, Homi K. 2004. *The Location of Culture*. New York and London: Routledge.

Bilby, Kenneth. 1981. "The Kormanti Dance of the Windward Maroons of Jamaica." *New West Indian Guide* 1/2: 52–101.

Blake, Lady, and Edith Black. 1898. "The Maroons of Jamaica." *North American Review* 167, no. 504: 558–560.

Bodunde, Charles A. 1992. "Oral Traditions and Modern Poetry: Okot p'Bitek's Song of Lawino and Okigbo's Labyrinths." In Eldred Jones, Eustace Palmer, and Marjorie Jones, eds., *Orature in African Literature Today*, 9–23. Trenton, NJ: African World Press.

Bohlman, Philp V. 2008. "Returning to the Ethnomusicological Past." In Gregory F. Barz and Timothy J. Cooley, eds., *Shadows in the Field: New Perspectives for the Fieldwork in Ethnomusicology*, 2nd ed., 246–270. Oxford and New York: Oxford University Press.

Bonilla, Yarimar. 2011. "The Past Is Made by Walking: Labor Activism and Historical Production in Postcolonial Guadeloupe." *Cultural Anthropology* 26, no. 3: 313–339.

Brackenbury, Captain H., and Captain G. L. Huyshe. 1873. *Fanti and Ashanti Papers: Three Papers Aboard the S.S. Ambriz on the Voyage to the Gold Coast*. Edinburgh and London: William Blackwood and Sons.

Buah, F. K. 1998. *A History of Ghana: Revised and Updated*. London: Macmillan Education.

Bynoe, Yvonne. 2006. *Encyclopedia of Rap and Hip-Hop Culture*. Westport, CT: Greenwood.

Cadogan, Garnette. 2016. "Walking While Black." lithub.com.walking-while-black/, accessed March 18, 2022.

Careri, Francesco. 2002. *Walkscapes: Walking as an Aesthetic Practice*. Barcelona: Editorial Gustavo Gili.

———. 2017. *Walkscapes: Walking as an Aesthetic Practice*. Ames, IA: Culicidae Architectural Press.

Careri, Francesco, and Stephen Picolo. 2017. *Walkscapes: Walking as Aesthetic Practice*. Ames, IA: Culicidae Press.

Césaire, Aime. 1986. *Lost Boy*. New York: Braziller.

Chatwin, Bruce. 1987. *The Songlines*. New York: Elizabeth Sifton Books.

Chernoff, John. 1979. *African Rhythm and African Sensibility: Aesthetics and Social Action in African Musical Idioms*. Chicago and London: University of Chicago Press.

Chinweizu, Onsucheka Jemie, and Ihechukwu Madubuike. 1980. *Toward the Decolonization of African Literature*. Enugu, Nigeria: Fourth Dimension.

Christensen, James Boyd. 1954. *Double Descent among the Fanti*. New Haven, CT: Human Relations Area Files.

Chukwukere, I. 1980. "Perspectives on the Asafo Institution in Southern Ghana." *Journal of African Studies* 7, no. 1: 39–47.

Chukwuma, Helen. 1976. "The Oral Nature of Traditional Poetry and Language." *Journal of the Nigerian English Studies* 8, no. 1 (May): 12–22.

Connerton, Paul. 1989. *How Societies Remember*. New York and London: Cambridge University Press.

Collins, Peter, and Anselma Gallinat. 2010. *The Ethnographic Self as Resource: Writing Memory and Experience into Ethnography.* London and New York: Berghahn.

Cooley, Timothy J. 2019. *Cultural Sustainabilities: Music, Media, Language, Advocacy.* Urbana, Chicago, Springfield: University of Illinois Press.

Corringham, Viv. 2013. "Shadow-Walks: A Sound Art Project." In Pauline Minevich and Ellen Waterman, eds., *Art of Immersive Soundscapes*, 155–161. Regina, Canada: University of Regina Press.

———. 2016. *Shadow-Walks: New York.* HARVESTWORKS—Digital Media Arts Center. https://www.youtube.com/watch?v=1zL8dubRL5U, accessed March 18, 2022.

Cruickshank, Brodie. 1853. *Eighteen Years on the Gold Coast of Africa, Including an Account of the Native Tribes and Their Intercourse with Europeans.* Vol. 2. London: Hurst and Blackett.

Cultural Division of the Ministry of Education and Culture. 1975. "Cultural Policy in Ghana." Paris: UNESCO Press.

Datta, Ansu K., and Richard Porter. 1971. "The 'Asafo' System in Historical Perspective." *Journal of African History* 12, no. 2: 279–297.

Davis, John T. 1979. *Walking!* Kansas City, MO: Andrews and McMeel.

De Certeau, Michel. 1984. *The Practice of Everyday Life.* Los Angeles and Berkeley: University of California Press.

DeCorse, Christopher R. *An Archaeology of Elmina: Africans and Europeans on the Gold Coast, 1400–1900.* Washington, DC: Smithsonian Institution Press.

De Graft Johnson, J. C. 1932. "The Fanti Asafu." *Africa: Journal of the International African Institute* 5, no. 3 (July): 307–322.

Dei, George Sefa. 2015. "Indigenous Scholar." TED Talk. https:www.youtube.com/watch?v=DvQxDS7hEMg, accessed March 18, 2022.

Dei, George Sefa, and Alireza Asgharzadeh. 2001. "The Power of Social Theory: The Anti-Colonial Discursive Framework." *Journal of Educational Thought (JET)* 35, no. 3: 297–323.

Dei, George Sefa, and Mairi McDermott, eds. 2019. *Centering African Proverbs, Indigenous Folktales, and Cultural Stories in Curriculum: Units and Lesson Plans for Inclusive Education.* Toronto and Ontario: Canadian Scholars.

Deren, Maya. 1985. *Divine Horsemen: The Living Gods of Haiti.* New York: Mystic Fire Video.

Diabah, Grace, and Nana Aba Appiah Amfo. 2015. "Caring Supporters or Daring Usurpers? Representations of Women in Akan Proverbs." *Discourse in Society* 26, no. 1: 3–28.

Dirksen, Rebecca. 2019. "Haiti Drums and Trees: Facing Loss of the Sacred." *Ethnomusicology* 63, no. 1: 43–77.

Dokosi, Michael Eli. 2017. "The History of Kormantse and Abandze." https://blakkpepper.com/2017/08/the-history-of-kormantse-abandze/

Dor, George. 2005. "Uses of Indigenous Music Genres in Ghanaian Choral Art Music: Perspectives from the Works of Amu, Blege, and Dor." *Ethnomusicology* 49, no. 3, 441–475.

Doran, Corey Ross, and Silvia Forni. 2016. *Art, Honor, and Ridicule: Asafo Flags from Southern Ghana.* Toronto: ROM.

Drew, Allison. 1995. "ASAFO! Fante Asafo Flags of Ghana." *Critical Arts: South-North Cultural and Media Studies* 9, no. 1: 58–76.

Edensor, Tim. 2008. "Walking Through Ruins." In Tim Ingold and Jo Lee Vergunst, eds., *Ways of Walking: Ethnography and Practice on Foot*, 123–142. Farnham, UK: Ashgate.

———. 2010. "Walking in Rhythms: Place, Regulation, Style, and the Flow of Experience." *Journal of Visual Studies* 25, no. 1: 69–79.

Elimimian, Isaac I. 1992. "Kofi Awoonor as a Poet." *Orature in African Literature Today* 18: 35–48.

Ellerson, Beti. 2004. "Africa through a Woman's Eyes: Safi Faye's Cinema." In Françoise Pfaff, ed., *Focus on African Films*, 185–202. Bloomington and Indianapolis: Indiana University Press.

———. 2019. "Safe Faye's Mossane: A Song to Women, to Beauty, to Africa." *Black Camera: An International Film Journal* 10, no. 2 (Spring): 250–265.

Ellis, A. B. 1893. *A History of the Gold Coast of West Africa.* London: Chapman and Hall.

Evans, James. 2011. "The Walking Interview: Methodology, Mobility and Place." *Applied Geography* 31, no. 2: 849–858.

Fanon, Frantz. 1963. *The Wretched of the Earth.* New York: Grove Weidenfeld.

Feld, Steven. 1996. "Waterfalls of Song: An Acoustemology of Place Resounding in Bosavi, Papua New Guinea." In Keith H. Basso and Steven Feld, eds., *Senses of Place*, 91–135. Santa Fe, NM: School of American Research Press.

Feld, Steven, and Keith H. Basso. 1996. *Senses of Place.* Santa Fe, NM: School of American Research Press.

Fenn, John. 2013. "An Interview with Jeff Todd Titon." *Folklore Forum* 34, no. 1/2 (January): 119–132.

Finnegan, Ruth. 1972. *Oral Literature in Africa.* London: Oxford University Press.

Freeman, Richard Austin. 1898. *Travels and Life in Ashanti and Jaman.* Westminster, UK: A. Constable.

Fynn, John J. K. 1971a. *Asante and Its Neighbors, 1700–1807.* London: Longman Group.

———. 1971b. *Oral Traditions of the Fante States, 41: Edina (Elmina).* Legon, Ghana: Institute of African Studies.

Gallinat, Anselma. 2008. "Being 'East German' or Being 'at Home in Eastern Germany': Identity as Experience." *Identities: Global Studies in Culture and Power* 15, no. 6: 665–685.

Geertz, Clifford. 1973. *The Interpretation of Cultures: Selected Essays by Clifford Geertz.* New York: Basic Books.

Ghunney, Edwin Atta. 2015. "Gyamkaba: An Original Composition Derived from Asafo Songs of Aboakyir Festival of Winneba." MPhil thesis, University of Education, Winneba, Ghana.

Hartman, Saidiya. 2007. *Lose Your Mother: A Journey along the Atlantic Slave Route.* New York: Farrar, Straus, and Giroux.

Hayford, Casely. 1903. *Gold Coast Native Institutions. With Thoughts Upon a Healthy Imperial Policy for the Gold Coast and Ashanti.* London: Sweet and Maxwell.

Henige, David P. 1974. "Kingship in Elmina before 1869: A Study in 'Feedback' and the Traditional Idealization of the Past." *Cahiers d'Etudes Africaines* 14, no. 3: 499–520.

———. 1973. "The Problem of Feedback in Oral Tradition: Four Examples from the Fante Coastlands." *Journal of African History* 14, no. 2: 223–235.

Henry, Meredith. 1812 (1967). *An Account of the Gold Coast of Africa, with a Brief History of the African Company.* London: Cass.

Herd, Mirjam. 2019. "Decolonizing Research Paradigms in the Context of Colonialism: An Unsettling, Mutual, and Collaborative Effort." *International Journal of Qualitative Methods* 18: 1–6.

Hernaes, Per. 1998. "Asafo History: An Introduction." *Transactions of the Historical Society of Ghana* 2: 1–5.

Herzfeld, Michael. 2001. *Anthropology: Theoretical Practice in Culture and Society.* Hoboken, NJ: Wiley-Blackwell.

Hirsch, Marianne. 1997. *Family Frames: Photography, Narrative, and Postmemory.* Cambridge, MA: Harvard University Press.

Holsey, Bayo. 2008. *Routes of Remembrance: Refashioning the Slave Trade in Ghana.* Chicago and London: University of Chicago Press.

hooks, bell. 1989. *Talking Back: Thinking Feminist, Thinking Black.* Boston, MA: South End Press.

Impey, Angela. 2018. *Song Walking: Women, Music, and Environmental Justice in an African Borderland.* Chicago and London: University of Chicago Press.

Ingold, Tim. 2006. "Fieldwork on Foot: Perceiving, Routing, Socializing." In Simon Coleman and Peter Collins, eds., *Locating the Field: Space, Place, and Context in Anthropology,* 67–86. Oxford: Berg.

———. 2010. "Footprints through the Weather-World: Walking, Breathing, Knowing." *Journal of the Royal Anthropological Institute* 16, no. S1: S121–139.

Ingold, Tim, and Jo Lee Vergunst. 2008. *Ways of Walking: Ethnography and Practice on Foot.* Aldershot, UK, and Burlington, VT: Ashgate.

Jackson, Bruce. 1987. *Fieldwork.* Champaign: University of Illinois Press.

Kea, Ray A. 1982. *Settlements, Trade, and Polities in the Seventeenth-Century Gold Coast.* Baltimore: John Hopkins University Press.

Keinänen, Mia, and Eevi E. Beck. 2017. "Wandering Intellectuals: Establishing a Research Agenda on Gender, Walking, and Thinking." *Gender, Place, and Culture: A Journal of Feminist Geography* 24, no. 4: 515–533.

Kendi, Ibram. 2019. *How to Be an Antiracist*. London: One World.

Keyes, Cheryl. 1996. "At the Crossroads: Rap Music and Its African Nexus." *Ethnomusicology* 40 (2): 223–248.

Kidula, Jean Ngoya. 2006. "Ethnomusicology, the Music Canon, and African Music: Positions, Tensions, and Resolutions in African Academy." *Africa Today* 52, no. 3: 99–113.

———. 2013. *Music in Kenyan Christianity: Logooli Religious Song*. Bloomington and Indianapolis: Indiana University Press.

Kisliuk, Michelle. 1998. *Seize the Dance! BaAka Musical Life and the Ethnography of Performance*. New York and Oxford: Oxford University Press.

———. 2008. "Undoing Fieldwork: Sharing Stories, Sharing Lives." In Gregory F. Barz and Timothy J. Cooley, eds., *Shadows in the Field: New Perspectives for Fieldwork in Ethnomusicology*, 183–205. Oxford and New York: Oxford University Press.

Ki-Zerbo, Joseph. 1981. "General Introduction." In Joseph Ki-Zerbo, ed., *General History of Africa*, vol. 1: *Methodology and African Prehistory*, 1–9. Oakland: University of California Press.

Koskela, Hillie. 1997. "'Bold Walk and Breakings': Women's Spatial Confidence versus Fear of Violence." *Gender, Place, and Culture: A Journal of Feminist Geography* 4: 301–319.

Koskoff, Ellen, ed. 2014. *A Feminist Ethnomusicology Writings on Music and Gender*. Urbana, Chicago, and Springfield: University of Illinois Press.

———. 1987. *Women and Music in Cross-Cultural Perspective*. Urbana and Chicago: University of Illinois Press.

Krug, Jessica. 2014. "Social Dismemberment, (Re)Membering: Obeah Idioms, Kromanti Identities and Trans-Atlantic Politics of Memory ca. 1675–Present." *Slavery and Abolition* 35, no. 4: 537–558.

Kulick, Don, and Margaret Wilson, eds. 1995. *Taboo: Sex, Identity and Erotic Subjectivity in Anthropological Fieldwork*. London: Routledge.

Kusenbach, Magarethe. 2003. "Street Phenomenology. The Go-Along as Ethnographic Tool." *Ethnography* 4: 455–485.

Kwabon, Obadélé. 2018. "Afrikan—Black Combat Forms Hidden in Plain Sight: Engolo/Capoeira, Knocking-and-Kicking and Asafo Flag Dancing." *Journal of Pan African Studies* 12, no. 4: 327–363.

Labi, Kwame A. 2002. "Fante Asafo Flags of Abandze and Kormantse: A Discourse between Rivals." *African Arts* 35, no. 4: 28–37.

———. 1998. "Fights, Riots, and Disturbances with 'Objectionable and Provocative Art' among the Fante 'Asafo' Companies." *Transactions of the Historical Society of Ghana*, no. 2: 101–116.

Landsberg, Alison. 2004. *Prosthetic Memory: The Transformation of American Remembrance in the Age of Mass Culture*. New York: Columbia University Press.

Lawal, Babatunde. 1996. *The Gèlèdé Spectacle: Art, Gender, and Social Harmony in an African Culture*. Seattle and London: University of Washington Press.

Laye, Camara. 1954. *The Dark Child*. New York: Noonday Press.

Lee, Joe Vergunst, and Tim Ingold. 2006. "Fieldwork on Foot: Perceiving, Routing, Socializing." In Simon Coleman and Peter Collins, eds., *Locating the Field: Space, Place, and Context in Anthropology*, 67–85. Oxford, New York: Berg.

Legat, Allice. 2008. "Walking Stories: Leaving Footprints." In Tim Ingold and Lee Joe Vergunst, eds., *Ways of Walking: Ethnography and Practice on Foot*, 35–50. Farnham, UK: Ashgate.

Lorde, Audre. 2017. *The Master's Tools Will Never Dismantle the Master's House*. London: Penguin Random House.

Loukaitou-Sideris, Anastasia. 2008. "Is It Safe to Walk Here? Design and Policy Responses to Women's Fear of Victimization in Public Places." 103–112.

Mah, Mark. 2016. *Take Up Your Mat and Walk: Metaphor of Walking to the Spiritual Life*. Searcy, AZ: Resource.

Mbembe, Achille. 1992. "Provisional Notes on the Postcolony." *Journal of the International African Institute* 62, no. 1: 3–37.

McCartney, Andra. 2014. "Soundwalking: Creating Moving Environmental Sound Narratives." In Sumanth Gopinath and Jason Stanyek, eds., *The Oxford Handbook of Mobile Music Studies*, vol. 2, 212–237. Oxford and New York: Oxford University Press.

McCollum, Jonathan. 2014. *Theory and Method in Historical Ethnomusicology*. London and New York: Lexington.

Mensah, Daniel Darkwa. 2014. "A Study of Conflict and Politics in the Music of Dentsefo and the Tuafo Asafo Companies of Effutu, Winneba." Masters' thesis, University of Ghana, Legon, Ghana.

Meyerowitz, Eva, L. R. 1951. *Akan Traditions of Origin*. London: Faber and Faber.

———. 1952. *The Sacred State of the Akan*. London: Faber and Faber.

Miscots, Courtnay. 2010. "African Coastal Elite Architecture: Cultural Authentication during the Colonial Period in Anomabo, Ghana." PhD dissertation, University of Florida, Gainesville, FL.

———. 2012. "Performing Ferocity: Fancy Dress, Asafo, and Red Indians in Ghana." *African Arts* 45, no. 2: 24–35.

Morrison, Toni. 1990. "The Site of Memory." In Russell Ferguson et al., eds., *Out There: Marginalization and Contemporary Culture*, 299–305. New York: New Museum of Contemporary Art and Massachusetts Institute of Technology.

Muller, Carol. 2011. *Musical Echoes*. Durham, MD, and London: Duke University Press.

Nannyonga-Tamusuza, Sylvia. 2005. *Baakisimba: Gender in the Music and Dance of the Baganda People of Uganda*. London and New York: Routledge.

Nannyonga-Tamusuza, Sylvia, and Thomas Solomon. 2012. *Ethnomusicology of East Africa: Perspectives from East Africa and Beyond*. Kampala, Uganda: Fountain.

Nettl, Bruno. 2015. *Ethnomusicology: Thirty-Three Discussions*. Urbana-Champaign: University of Illinois Press.

———. 1992. *The Radif of Persian Music: Structures and Cultural Contexts in the Classical Music of Iran*. Champaign, IL: Elephant and Cat.

Nhat Hanh, Thich. 2016. *At Home in the World: Stories and Essential Teachings from a Monk's Life*. Berkeley, CA: Parallax.

Nketia, J. H. Kwabena. 1955. *Funeral Dirges of the Akan People*. Achimota, Ghana: James Townsend and Sons.

———. 1974a. *Ayan*. Accra: Ghana Publishing.

———. 1974b. *The Music of Africa*. New York and London: W. W. Norton.

Nkrumah, Kwame. 1970. *Consciencism: Philosophy and Ideology for De-Colonization*. New York: Monthly Review Press.

———. 1965. *Neocolonialism: The Last Stage of Imperialism*. London: Nelson.

Nnaemeka, Obioma. 1998. "Introduction: Reading the Rainbow." In Obioma Nnaemeka, ed., *Sisterhood, Feminisms, and Power: From Africa to the Diaspora*. Trenton, NJ: Africa World Press.

Nti, Kwaku. 2011. "Modes of Resistance: Colonialism, Maritime Culture, and Conflict in Southern Gold Coast, 1860–1932." Ann Arbor: University of Michigan.

Nzewi, Meki. 1997. *African Music: Theoretical Content and Creative Continuum: The Culture's Exponents' Definition*. Olderhausen, Germany: Institut fur Popularer Musik.

Oddey, Alison, and Christine Wright. 2009. *Modes of Spectating*. Bristol, UK: Intellect Books, and Chicago: University of Chicago Press.

Oduyoye, Mercy Amba. 1995. *Daughters of Anowa: African Women and Patriarchy*. Maryknoll, NY: Orbis.

Ogborn, David. 2013. "Listening to Venice: Remarks on the Late Nono." In Pauline Minevich and Ellen Waterman, eds., *Art of Immersive Soundscapes*, 37–49. Regina, Canada: University of Regina Press.

Ogede, Ode S. 1992. "Oral Echoes in Armah's Short Stories." In Eldred Durosimi Jones, Eustace Palmer, and Majorie Jones, eds., *Orature in African Literature Today*, 73–84. Trenton, NJ: Africa World Press.

Ogundiran, Akinwuli, and Paula Saunders, eds. 2014. *Materialities of Ritual in the Black Atlantic*. Bloomington and Indianapolis: Indiana University Press.

Okeke, Chika. 1998. *Fante*. New York: Rosen.

Olmstead, Gracie. 2018. "The Art of the Stroll: Traversing the Sidewalk Enables Us to Look and See." *American Conservative*. https://www.theamericanconservative.com/articles/the-art-of-the-stroll/, accessed March 20, 2022.

Opondo, Patricia Achieng. 2002. "Strategies for Survival by Luo Female Artists in the Rural Environment in Kenya." In Catherine Higgs, Barbara A. Moss, and Earline Rae Ferguson, eds., *Stepping Forward: Black Women in Africa and the Americas*, 205–226. Athens: Ohio University Press.

Oppezzo, Marily, and Daniel E. Schwartz. 2014. "Give Your Ideas Some Legs: The Positive Effect of Walking on Creative Thinking." *Journal of Experimental Psychology: Learning, Memory, and Cognition* 40, no. 4: 1142–1152.

Ousmare, Halifu. 2011. *The African Aesthetics in Global Hip-Hop: Power Moves*. London and New York: Palgrave Macmillan.

Ottenberg, Simon. 1968. *Double Descent in an African Society: The Afipko Village-Group*. Seattle: University of Washington Press.

Owusua-Annopong, Sussie. 1990. "A Case Study of Asafo Music in Winneba Aboakyer Festival." Diploma, University of Ghana, School of Performing Arts.

Oyěwùmí, Oyèrónké. 2003. *African Women and Feminism: Reflecting on the Politics of Sisterhood*. Trenton, NJ, and Asmara, Eritrea: African World Press.

Pain, R. 2001. "Gender, Race, Age, and Fear in the City." *Urban Studies* 38, no. 5/6: 899–914.

Pawson, E., and G. Banks. 1993. "Rape and Fear in a New Zealand City." *Area* 25, no. 1: 55–63.

p'Bitek, Okot. 1984. *Song of Lawino, Song of Ocol*. London: Heinemann.

Perbi, Akosua Adoma. 2004. *A History of Indigenous Slavery in Ghana: From the 15th to the 19th Century*. Accra, Ghana: Sub-Saharan.

Perkins, Brian, L. 1994. "Traditional Institution in Coastal Development: Asafo Companies in Cape Coast History." African Diaspora ISPs Paper 33.

Pierce, Joseph, and Mary Lawhon. 2015. "Walking as Method: Toward Methodological Forthrightness and Comparability in Urban Geographical Research." *Professional Geographer* 67, no. 4: 1–8.

Pink, Sarah. 2009. *Doing Sensory Ethnography*. Thousand Oaks, CA: SAGE.

Probyn, Elspeth. 1992. "Theorizing through the Body." In Lana F. Rakow, ed., *Women Making Meaning: New Feminist Directions in Communication*, 83–99. London and New York: Routledge.

Public Records and Archives Administration (PRAAD). Accra Branch, ADM 11/1/748.

———. Cape Coast Branch, ADM 23/1/1503.

Reindorf, Carl Christian. 1895. *History of the Gold Coast and Asante, Based on Traditions and Historical Facts: Comprising a Period of More than Three Centuries from about 1500 to 1860*. Basel, Switzerland: Missionbuchhandlung.

Rice, Timothy. 2014. *Ethnomusicology: A Very Short Introduction*. Oxford and New York: Oxford University Press.

Rogers-Brown, Jennifer B. 2011. "More than a War Story: A Feminist Analysis of Doing Dangerous Fieldwork." *At the Center: Feminism, Social Science and Knowledge* 20: 111–131.

Rosaldo, Renato. 1980. *Llongot Headhunters: 1883–1974*. Stanford, CA: Stanford University Press.

Sarbah, John Mensah. 1906. *Fanti National Constitution: A Short Treatise on the Constitution and Government of the Fanti, Ashanti, and Other Akan Tribes of West Africa*. 2nd ed. London: Frank Cass and Co.

Schafer, R. Murray. 1993. *The Soundscape: Our Sonic Environment and the Tuning of the World*. Rochester, VT: Dewey Books.

Schaffer, William C., and E. Kofi Agorsah. 2010. "Bioarchaeological Analysis of Historic Kormantse, Ghana." *African Diaspora Archaeology Newsletter*. 13, no. 1: 1–12.

Scheub, Harold. 1975. "Oral Narrative and the Uses of Models." *New Literary History* 6, no. 2: 353–377.

Schippers, Huib, and Dan Bendrups. 2015. "Ethnomusicology, Ecology and the Sustainability of Music Cultures." *World of Music* 4, no. 1: 9–19.

Schippers, Huib, and Catherine Grant, eds. 2016. *Sustainable Futures for Music Cultures: An Ecological Perspective*. New York: Oxford University Press.

Seamon, David. 1980. "Body-Subject, Time-Space Routines, and Place-Ballets." In Anne Buttimer and David Seamon, eds., *The Human Experience of Time and Space*, 149–165. Routledge: London.

Seeger, Anthony. 2004. *Why Suya Sing: A Musical Anthropology of an Amazonian People*. Urbana and Chicago: University of Illinois Press.

Shechner, Richard. 1985. *Between Theater and Anthropology*. Philadelphia,:University of Pennsylvania Press.

Shonekan, Stephanie. 2015. *Soul, Country, and the USA Race and Identity in American Music Culture*. New York: Palgrave Macmillan.

Showers, Paul. 1993. *The Listening Walk*. New York: Harper Collins.

Shumway, Rebecca. 2011. *The Fante and the Transatlantic Slave Trade*. Rochester, NY: University of Rochester Press.

Sklar, Deidre. 2001. *Dancing with the Virgin: Body and Faith in the Fiesta of Tortugas, Mexico*. Berkeley and London: University of California Press.

Small, Christopher. 1998. *Musicking: The Meanings of Performing and Listening*. Middletown, CT: Wesleyan University Press.

Solis, Ted. 2004. *Performing Ethnomusicology: Teaching and Representation in World Music Ensembles*. Berkeley, Los Angeles, and London: University of California Press.

Solnit, Rebecca. 2000. *Wanderlust: A History of Walking*. New York: Viking.

Soyinka, Wole. 1963. *A Dance of the Forests*. Oxford, New York: Oxford University Press.

St. Clair, William. 2006. *The Door of No Return: The History of Cape Coast Castle and the Atlantic Slave Trade*. New York: Bluebridge.
Stone, Ruth. 1982. *Let the Inside Be Sweet: The Interpretation of Music Event among the Kpelle of Liberia*. Bloomington: Indiana University Press.
Sutherland-Addy, Esi. 1998. "Discourse and Asafo: The Place of Oral Literature." *Transactions of the Historical Society of Ghana*, New Series no. 2: 87–100.
Tamale, Sylvia. 2020. *Decolonization and Afro-Feminism*. Ottawa: Daraja.
Tang, Patricia. 2007. *Masters of the Sabar: Wolof Griot Percussionists of Senegal*. Philadelphia: Temple University Press.
Thiong'o, Ngugi wa. 1986. *Decolonizing the Mind*. Portsmouth, NH: Heineman.
———. 1987. *Devil on the Cross*. London: Heineman.
Thornton, John. 1998. "The Coromantees: An African Cultural Group in Colonial North America and the Caribbean." *Journal of Caribbean History* 32, no. 1–2: 161–178.
Trouillot, Michel-Rolph. 1995. *Silencing the Past: Power and the Production of History*. Boston, MA: Beacon.
Truc, Gérôme. 2012. "Memory of Places and Places of Memory: For a Halbwachsian Socio-Ethnography of Collective Memory." *International Social Science Journal* 62, no. 1/2: 147–159.
Tsukada, Kenichi. 2008. "Asafo and Fontomfrom as Indices of Social Sentiments among the Fante (Ghana)." In Regine Allgayer-Kaufmann and Michael Weber, eds., *African Perspectives: Pre-Colonial History, Anthropology, and Ethnomusicology*, 252–272. Berlin and Frankfurt: Peter Lang.
Turkson, Adolphus Acquah Robertson. 1972. "Effutu Asafo Music: A Study of a Traditional Music in Ghana with Special Reference to the Role of Tonal Language in Choral Music Involving Structural and Harmonic Analysis." PhD dissertation, Northwestern University, Evanston, IL.
Turner, Victor. 1977. "Variations on a Theme of Liminality." In Sally Falk Moore and Barbara Myerhoff, eds., *Secular Ritual*, 36–52. Amsterdam: Van Gorcum.
Tutuola, Amos. 1953. *The Palm-Wine Drinkard (and His Dead Palm-Wine Tapster in the Dead's Town)*. New York: Grove.
Valentine, G. 1990. "Women's Fear and the Design of Public Spaces." *Built Environment* 16, no. 4: 288–303.
Various Artists. *Traditional Women's Music from Ghana*. 1981. Folkways Records. FE 4257, vinyl record.
Vansina, Jan. 1962. "'Ethnohistory in Africa.'" 126–136.
———. 1985. *Oral Traditions as History*. New York: James Currey.
Vergunst, Joe Lee. 2008. "Taking a Trip and Taking Care in Everyday Life." In Tim Ingold and Jo Lee Vergunst, eds., *Ways of Walking: Ethnography and Practice on Foot*, 105–122. Aldershot, UK, and Burlington, VT: Ashgate.

Visweswaran, Kamala. 1994. *Fictions of Feminist Ethnography:* Minneapolis: University of Minnesota Press.
Wagstaff, Greg. 2000. "Soundwalking: Follow Your Ears." https://naisa.ca/radio-art-companion/soundwalking-follow-your-ears/., accessed March 20, 2022.
Ward, W. E. F. 1948. *A History of Ghana.* London: George Allen and Unwin.
Weisser, Susan Ostrov. 1994. *Feminist Nightmares: Women at Odds, Feminism and the Problem of Sisterhood.* New York and London: New York University Press.
Wenjun, Li et al. 2014. "Utilitarian Walking, Neighborhood Environment, and Risk of Outdoor Falls among Older Adults." *American Journal of Public Health* 104, no. 9: 30–37.
Wenner, Barbara Britton. 2006. *Prospect and Refuge in the Landscape of Jane Austen.* London: Routledge.
Westbrook, Alonzo. 2002. *Hip Hoptionary TM: The Dictionary of Hip Hop Terminology.* New York: Broadway.
Westerkamp, Hildegard. 1974 (2000). "Soundwalking." *Sound Heritage* 3, no. 4: 18–27.
Wherton, Joseph et al. 2019. "Wandering as a Sociomaterial Practice: Extending the Theorization of GPS Tracking in Cognitive Impairment." *Qualitative Health Research* 29, no. 3: 328–344.
Wiederhold, Anna. 2015. "Conducting Fieldwork at and away from Home: Shifting Researcher Positionality with Mobile Interviewing Methods." *Qualitative Research* 15, no. 5: 600–615.
Wiredu, Kwasi. 1998. "Towards Decolonizing African Philosophy and Religion." *African Studies Quarterly* 1, no. 4: 17–46.
Wunderlich, F. 2008. "Walking and Rhythmicity: Sensing Urban Space." *Journal of Urban Design* 13: 125–139.
Zhao, Yawei. 2017. "Doing Fieldwork the Chinese Way: A Returning Researcher's Insider/Outsider Status in Her Home Town." *Area* 49, no. 2: 185–191.

INDEX

Page numbers in italics indicate illustrations.

Abakah, Ekow ɔdomankoma Kyerɛma (divine master drummer), 216, 221
abakɔsɛm, 72–79, 88–89, 93, 110, 188–90, 277
abakɔsɛm walk, 63–72
Aban Enyim (local parliament), 97–103
"Abanyi" (song), 273
Abbam, Kofi, 254, 259
Abé, Maria, 3
Achebe, Chinua, 27, 144
Acquah, Emmanuel Obed, 180
"Adende" (song), 253, 315–20, 323
Adjei, Akosua Pokua, 32
Adjei, Godwin Kwafo, 357n14
Adler, Peter, 242
Adom Communication Centre, 328–32
Aduonum, Ama Oforiwaa, 31, 234, 277; at egwuaradze parade, 205; family of, 11–13, 16–17, 32, 135–38, 356n3; at Methodist Junior High School, 324–26, 326; at Owumena pit, 140; singing lessons of, 315–18, 317, 327; walking trail maps of, 6–7; Walking with My Ancestors, xi, 176, 322–24
Aduonum, KoJo Kisseh, 16, 17, 135–38, 140, 349n32
Aduonum, Kwasi, 11, 13, 32
Aduonum, MaAdwoa, 16–17, 349n32
adzewa songs, 171, 181–84
Afahyɛ, 259, 350n48
Afɛdze, Egya, 285–89

Afful, Akɔdɛɛ, 42–48, 56
Aframba, Aba, 327, 328
African musicology, 23, 25, 190, 324
Afrifah, Kofi, 90
Agawu, Kofi, 210, 211, 281
agbeko rhythm, 171
Aggrey, J. E. K., 194, 218
Agorsah, E. Kofi, 18–20, 170, 179, 354n5
Ahɔr (priest), 94–100
Ahuba Kuma, 94–95
ahwenee beads, 12, 133, 311–13, 318
Aidoo, Ama Ata, xv, 149
Akɔfena walk, 5–8
Akosua Tuntum songs, 141
"Akyem Esuantse" (song), 267–68
Allotey, Gladys, 261
Amankwah, Kwaa, 49, 351n4
Amissah, Kwamena, 55–57
Amissah, Safohen Panyin, 93
amodaka, 64
Ampadu, Kwame, 254
Amu, Ephraim, 323–24
Ankoma, ɔdomankoma Kyerɛma, 26
Annan, Kwesi, 5, 13
Annan, Nana, 5
Anthony, Saint, 44–45
anticolonialism, 24–25. See also decolonization
Aprokuwa, Ama, 95–96, 98–99, 111, 120–34; on Asafo tradition, 321; funeral of, 229, 232
Arhin, Kweku, 206

Asafo, etymology of, 270
Asafo Akyerɛ, 267, 271, 334
Asafo *ndwom*, xvi, 61–77, 186, 266; Atta on, 165–69, 175–80; categories of, 180; funeral rites and, 194–96, *195*, 218; future of, 323–25; gender and, 29–30, 161, 165–67, 259–63; instrumental music for, 213–14, *214*; *kasa twii* in, 287–88; musicking walks and, 212–19; rousing calls and, 1, 279–80, 340n1; structures of, 251, *263*, 278, 290, *293*. See also individual song titles
Asafommba, 231, 256–60, 262–65, 280–82, 291–94
"*Asamankama Aba*" (song), 186
Asantewaa, Yaa, 267–68
Asebir (teacher), 149–53, *150*
asekambɔfo. See flag guardians
Asgharzadeh, Alireza, 28
Atta, Ekua, 93, 111, 154–60, 188–89; on *adzewa* songs, 181–84; on Asafo *ndwom*, 165–69, 175–80; on Bentsir-Nkum conflict, 163–65; on birth stories, 184–86; on Eminsa rites, 170–75; on "*Kormantse na Abandze*," 157–60; on "*ɔawar Eminsa*," 160–62; portrait of, *156*; on *samantaadze*, 167–68; speaking style of, 155–57
Atta, Kwame, 278–85
Australian Aborigines, 101
"*Awo nye*" (song), 158–59

Ba, Mariama, xv
BaAka people, 210–11
Badu, Kwasi, 50–51
Barnard, Nicholas, 242
Beaudry, Nicole, 3
Bebey, Francis, 46, 260, 261
Bedu, Kobena, 258, 262, 278–85, 312–13; on *kenkan*, 289–96,

307–9, 315–17; singing lesson with, 315–18, *317*
Berliner, Paul, 3
"*Beseadze Kyiremfo*" (song), 275
Bhabha, Homi, 50
bientehur tree, 138–39, *140*
birth stories, 184–86
Black Lives Matter Movement, xii, 34, 300–302, 323
Boadum, Safohen, 308
Bonilla, Yarimar, 29, 61, 101, 353n14
Bosom (Deities of trees, rivers, rocks), 58, 158
Bosompo (Sea Deity), 125
Budo III, Obaatan Nana, 119
Butler, Thomas, 18–20

call-and-response singing, 160, 181, 203, 251; embodied, 26, *241*, 250, 255; with kenkan, 287; musicking walks and, 215
Central African Republic, 210–11
Christensen, James Boyd, 94, 125–26, 146
Christianity, 172, 178–79, 236–37, 331; denominations of, 271–72, 355n7; Odum on, 271–72
colonization, 23–24
colorism. See "white-body supremacy"
Connerton, Paul, 74, 166–67
Coromantine Fort, 90
Corringham, Vi, 84–85
Crayner, J. B., 73–74, 94
Crentsil, A. B., 254
Cromanti communities, 20, 76, 170

"*Daano Wɔnye Hɛn Yɛ*" (song), 183–84
Dahomey, 67, 72, *74*
Datta, Ansu K. & Porter, Richard, 39
David (pastor), 331
dawur, 86, 99, 102, 216, 221, 275, 294

De Graft Johnson, J. C., 39, 259, 260, 261
decolonization, 23–25, 32, 314, 319
Dedu, Kofi, 97–98, 118, 266, 323
Dei, George Sefa, 23–24, 28, 30, 344
Deren, Maya, 197
diss tracks, 288–89
diviners, 310, 311
Drew, Allison, 242–43
"Dua no ebu" (song), 307
Dunkwa, Appia, 119

earthquakes, 185
ebusua lineage songs, 111, 115–16, 167–68. *See also* lineage houses
Edensor, Tim, 136, 138, 232
"Efua Krowa" (song), 182–83
"Efua Odondo" (song), 183
Ego (Eguapon, Ebien, Anan, Enum), 92, 94, 102–3
egwuaradze, 196–209, 205, 229, 340–41, 355n2
"Egya yɛma hom akɔaba o" (song), 315
Egypt, 155
Eku (priestess), 146
"Ekua Oguanyi na ɔreba n" (song), 102
Ellerson, Beti, 108
Elliot, E. C., 76, 289
Ellis, A. B., 75, 89–90, 353n6
Elmina, xi, xv, 28, 55
"Eminsa Osuom" (song), 66, 97, 326–27. *See also* Nana Eminsa
Eshun, Ato, 39–40
Essel, Fiifi, 48
Esuon, Ama, 95, 111, 120, 142
Euba, Akin, 324
ewu-akɔ (ancestral spirits), 58

Fanon, Frantz, 314, 319
Faye, Safi, 29
Feld, Steven, 101

Fenn, John, 337
"fetishism," 2, 21, 31, 50, 256–58, 337
flag bearers, 50, 201, 242–43
flag dancers, 200–202, 222, 224, *227*, 244–45, 341; funeral of, 233–35, 239–49, *241*, *244*
flag guardians, 200–201, 224, 225, 234, 246, 248
funerals, 52–53, 194–209, *205*, 296; *adzewa* groups at, 183; Christian, 236–37; *egwuaradze* for, 196–209, *205*, 229, 340–41; of flag dancer, 233–35, 239–49, *241*, *244*; kɔtɔkorba L-shaped sticks and, 197–99, 209, 216, 222, 227; at lineage houses, 215–16, 221, 229–32; lineage songs at, 111; musicking walks at, 212–19, 228–33, 237–49; at *posuban*, 221; schedule of events for, 195; soundwalks at, 210
Fynn, John K., 90, 352n3, 353n7

"galamsey" (illegal gold mining), 138
Geertz, Clifford, 356n9
gender, 14, 46, 329; Asafo traditions and, 29–30, 161, 165–67, 259–63; conflicting versions of stories and, 88; of deities, 46; equal rights movement and, 109–12; of marketplace, 294–95; Odum on, 273
Ghana Cultural Policy (1975), 336, 343
"going native," 41–42
gold mining, 103, 138
gospel music, 220, 255, 356n7, 357n16
Grant, Charles, 50
grant money, 41–42
Gyaahyewaa, Yaa, 119
Gyegyentwi (Deity), 5–8
"Gyesi Mbo" (song), 169, 276, 308–9
gyina ho hwɛ (Kormantse talking drum), 132, *133*, 254, 274, 296, 334–36

Hammond. *See* Odum III, Safohen Nana
haptic knowledge, 204–9
herbalists, 240, 308, 310
Herzfeld, Michael, 39, 88, 309
Hi-Life music, 62, 157, 220, 229, 253–54, 295
hip-hop music. *See* rap music
hiplife music, 94, 203, 289, 295
Hoefnagel, Anna, 38–39
Hood, Mantle, 358n33
hooks, bell, 33–34

Impey, Angela, 3, 66, 96, 100, 212–13, 348n10
Ingold, Tim, 100, 212, 295–96
"intangible cultural heritage," 218, 297

Jamaicans, 18, 42, 313, 357n18
jeliya tradition, 291
Jones, A. M., 281
juju woman, 311

Kaluli "song paths," 101
Kambon, Obádélé, 245
kasa twii, 287–88
kenkan, 169, 190–91, 319–20; Bedu on, 289–96, 307–9, 316–17; as rapping, 285–89, 293; as recitative, 291
kente cloth, 27
Keyes, Cheryl, 287
Ki-Zerbo, Joseph, 23, 101, 176
Kidula, Jean Ngoya, 3
Kisliuk, Michelle, 3, 210–11
Kom, Kwesi, 278–85
Kome Kuma, 73–74
Komer Kakra, 72–74
kɔna (ebusua), 85, 114, 131, 147–48, 162
Kormantine, xii–xiv, 18, 72–73
Kormantse, 4, 18–22; Caribbean communities of, 170; Gods of, 66, 170–75, 277–78; King of, xiv, 80–81; maps of, *19, 74, 91*; migratory history of, 67–68, 72–73, *74*; name of, 74; population of, 20, 350n40; slaves from, 76
Kormantse Bentsir, 18, 66, 112–15; Aprokuwa on, 120; Asafo divisions of, *262*, 270–71, *271*; flag of, 243, –244, *244*; name of, 239–40; Nkum conflict with, 163–65
Kormantse Communication Centre, 323–35
"*Kormantse na Abandze*" (song), 62, 157–58
Koromantse, 72–73
kɔtɔkorba L-shaped sticks, 197–99, 209, 216, 222, 227, 230, 334–35
"*Kweku Anankor ei*" (song), 71

Labi, Kwame A., 39
Lawhon, Mary, 17
Legat, Alice, 321
lineage houses (*ebusua fie*), 145–54, *147, 148, 150*, 179; funerals at, 215–16, 221, 229–32; totems of, *147, 148*
lineage songs, 111, 115–16, 144–45, 153, 167–68
listening walk, 210
Lorde, Audre, 32

Mahama, John, 119–20, 354n5
Maison, Joseph, 251, 323–24
Mamon, Egyir, 73
Mann, C. K., 62, 157, 323
Mansa, Ekua, 185
Maputaland, 100, 213, 348n10
matrilineal societies, 145–47
"*Mayɛ Kwansin M'abɛ*" (song), 194
McCartney, Andra, 209
memory walks, 4, 80–105, 311; Bedu on, 308–9; Bonilla on, 101; Impey on, 96, 100; multisensory, 166–67; shadow walking and, 84–88

Menakem, Resmaa, 358n28
Methodist Church, 272, 324, 355n7
Meyerowitz, Eva L. R., 72, 76
Mfantsiman Girls' Secondary School, 251, 323
minstrel choir, 52
mmotia (dwarfs), 58
Mohanty, Chandra Talpade, 25
Mprah, Kwesi. *See* Odum, Safohen Nana
musicking walks, 212–19, 228–33, 237–49

Nako, Kwame, 256–57, 278–85
Nana Abosee, 67–68, 75
Nana Bosompo (Sea Spirit), 296, 297, 302
Nana Dzerma (Lagoon Deity), 71, 277–78
Nana Eminsa (Mother/Principal Goddess), 93–95, 325; appellations of, 97, 170–72, 327; Christian syncretism and, 172, 178–79; shrine of, 66, 121, 158–59, 172–74; song to, 66, 97, 326–27, 355n8
Nana Gyaahyewa (warrior), 148, 267
Nana Komer, 67, 72–75, 87, 96–97, 266
Nana Sesá (Guardian Deity), 95, 124, 354n5
"Nana Sesa Kwesi" (song), 160
Nannyonga-Tamusuza, Sylvia, 260, 261
Nettl, Bruno, 3
Nketia, J. H. Kwabena, 281
"Nkowa no wɔkɔ" (song), 292
Nkrumah, Kwame, 251, 347n6
Nkum, Gifty, 21
"Nkum na Abandze" (song), 93, 162–63, 253, 265, 281, 307–8
Nlesi Adowa, 181
Nnaemeka, Obioma, 261

Nnuroh, Kwadwo, 253, 256–60, 262–63
nsu-mba (water spirits), 58
Nunsin, Ekow, *133*
nwomtonyi (lead singer), 171, 183, 303–5
Nyame, E. K., 254
Nyame, Me, 285–89
"Nyew Nana Nyame" (song), 57
"Nyew o Odum ee" (song), 272–73
"Nyew o Sogya" (song), 108
"Nyimpa atɔ nsu mu" (song), 307, 320

"ɔawar Eminsa" (song), 160–61, 189
"ɔbra Nye Woara Abɔ" (song), 252
Oburmankoma (Eagle quality), 146, 251
oburonyi, 309–10, 319
ɔdapagyan (Whale quality), 146, 251
"ɔdɔm Kyirem" (song), 272
Odum III, Safohen Nana, 20, 64, 80, 84–87, 92–93; Aban Enyim and, 101–2; full name of, 268; interview with, 267–78, *269, 277*; on *kenkan*, 289–96, 307–8, 316–17; Kona lineage house of, 85; at Methodist Junior High School, 325–26, *326*; Nyame on, 285; singing lesson of, 327; on teen pregnancy, 325; training of, 290–91
"Odum na Eminsa" (song), 160
Oduyoye, Mercy, 146
"Odziamon" (song), 144–45, 153
"ɔkɔtɔfo Gyesi" (song), 272
"Okura akɛkyer egyinambowa ne Ba" (song), 253
ɔkyerɛma (master drummer), 1, 9, 21, 103, 259
"ɔman yi abɔ" (song), 321–22
opera, 252, 255–56, 291
Opondo, Patricia, 281
Oppong, Christine, 146–47

"ɔroko e ɔanyɛ yie" (song), 323
oson (Elephant quality), 146, 251
Owumena (death pit), 69–71, 79–81, 119, 135–42; Odum ond, 270, 274; photos of, *81, 140*
Owusuma, Ama, 111, 145, 278–79; on *adzewa* songs, 181–84; on Bentsir-Nkum conflict, 163–65; on birth stories, 184–86; on Eminsa rites, 170–75; on "ɔawar Eminsa," 160–62; portrait of, *155*; on *samantaadze*, 167–68; speaking style of, 155–57; on "Ye fi Abo m'ee," 153–54
"Oye, Oye Kofi Dedu mba e" (song), 253, 266, 323
Oyéwumi, Oyeronke, 144, 161

Panyin, Komer, 350n41
Papua New Guinea, 101
Pax Britannica, 21, 350n42
Pierce, Joseph, 17
"place-ballet," 295
plague, 94
Poli, Ama, 83, 87–88, 111, 115
posuban (military post), 40–48, 59–66, 96–97, 221, 243
Pra, Kwamena, 242–43
Pra, ɔdomankoma Kyerɛma Kwamena, 57–58, 196; drums of, *215*; on *egwaradze*'s origins, 199–200; on Owumena death pit, 69–70

rap music, 286–89, 293, 357n18. See also Hi-Life music
Reindorf, Carl, 89, 352n4
rousing call, 1, 279–80, 340n1

Sackey, Aba, 95, 111, 134–42, *140*, 167–68, 193
Sackey, Egya, 135, 163, 167–68
Sackey, Safohen Kwame, 163–65

samanta (elves), 58
samantaadze, 135, 167–68
"*Santrofi Anoma*" (song), 120
Sarbah, Mensah, 94, 243
Schaffer, William C., 20
Schippers, Huib, 31, 297–98, 342
Seamon, David, 295
Seeger, Anthony, 3, 87
Sekyi, Ekow ɔdomankoma Kyerɛma (divine master drummer), 201, 203, 240
Senegal, 108, 111, 261, 289, 291
shadow walks, 84–88. See also memory walks
Shayak, Efik, 311
Shindoya music, 3
Shumway, Rebecca, xiv–xv
Sisi, Kɔmfo (priest), 134
slavery, 322–23; Kormantse and, 76; protest songs about, 49; as taboo topic, xiv, 331, 347n4
Small, Christopher, 212
Smith, Venture, 199
Solnit, Rebecca, 137
"song paths," 101
sound walking, 209–11
spiritual entities, 58
Stone, Ruth, 221
Suapim, Kweku, 328–30
Sudan, 67, 72–73
suman (protective spirits), 58
sustainability advocates, 335–37
Sutherland-Addy, Esi, 180

Teacher Hammond. See Odum III, Safohen Nana
teen pregnancy, 325
Tekyiwa, Ekua, 111, 115–20
Thich Nhat Hanh, 80, 87
Thompson, Awotwi, 291
Titon, Jeff Todd, 31, 297–98, 337, 342
totems of Fante lineages, *147, 148*

"trauma ghosted," 300, 358n27
Trouillot, Michel-Rolph, 75
Truth, Sojourner, 109
Tsukada, Kenichi, 355n9
Tutu I, Osei, Asante Hene, 89–92, 119, 352n3
Twerammpɔn Traditionals (folklore group), 323
Twidan (ebusua), 147, 149–52, 154

Uncle Ebo (radio host), 48–50
UNESCO: Convention on Cultural Diversity, 31, 343; Sustainability Development Initiatives, 31, 297–98

Vergunst, Jo Lee, 100, 212

"Wadweoo waadwe" (song), 80, 85, 86
Wagstaff, Greg, 209–10
Walking with My Ancestors (Aduonum), xi, 176, 322–24
walks, 3–5, 136–38, *277*, 294–96, 340; abakɔsɛm, 63–72; *Akɔfena*, 5–8; Bonilla on, 353n14; Legat on, 321; musicking, 212–19, 228–33, 237–49; scholarship on, 348n11; sound, 209–11; trail maps of, *6–7. See also* memory walks
Ward, W. E. F., 90, 352n3
Westerkamp, Hildegard, 210
"white-body supremacy," 300, 310–11, 313–14, 339, 358n28
Wobir, Kobena, 328–29
"Wɔmfa nyɛ hɔn Nanom" (song), 61, 175–76
"Wontsei Asɛm a ɔaba" (song), 250
"Wɔse menkyerɛ m'" (song), 153
Wunderlich, F., 40, 219

"Ya ara nkyɛ" (song), 98, 265, 281, 332
Yaa Asantewaa War, 267–68
Yaaba, Ekua, 266
"Yaanom Abibirimma é" (song), 323
Yamoah (Hi-Life musician), 254
"Ye fi Abo m'ee" (song), 153–54
"Yɛkɔr Akyemfo nyimpa nnyi hɔ" (song), 253, 288–89
"Yɛyɛ Kɔnafo" (song), 95
Yiiyii, Agya, 278–85

www.ingramcontent.com/pod-product-compliance
Lightning Source LLC
Chambersburg PA
CBHW050526300426
44113CB00012B/1968